MAMMALS
OF
MADAGASCAR

A Complete Guide

Nick Garbutt

A&C BLACK
LONDON

Published in 2007 by A&C Black Publishers Ltd, 38 Soho Square, London W1D 3HB

Copyright © 2007 Nick Garbutt
Copyright in the photographs remains with the individual photographers (see credits on page 8)

The right of Nick Garbutt to be identified as the author of this work has been asserted by him in accordance with the Copyright, Designs and Patents Act 1988.

ISBN: 978-0-7136-7043-1

A CIP catalogue record for this book is available from the British Library.

This book is produced using paper that is made from wood grown in managed sustainable forests. It is natural, renewable and recyclable. The logging and manufacturing processes conform to the environmental regulations of the country of origin.

Commissioning Editor: Nigel Redman
Project Editor: Julie Bailey
Designer: Julie Dando, Fluke Art, Cornwall

Printed in China by C&C Offset Printing Co., Ltd.

10 9 8 7 6 5 4 3 2 1

www.acblack.com

Front Cover: Golden-crowned Sifaka
Back Cover: male Fosa, Eastern Sucker-footed Bat, Petter's Sportive Lemurs
Title page: Eastern Ring-tailed Mongoose

CONTENTS

ACKNOWLEDGEMENTS

The original text for *Mammals of Madagascar* (Pica Press, 1999) took four years to research and write. I assumed that updating and refining it into this volume would be relatively simple and less time consuming. How wrong I was. The task of collating all the necessary information has been a considerable one, but has been made easier by the thoughtfulness and generosity of numerous friends and colleagues who work in the field and have provided assistance and the latest information. Many have also taken time to comment on my manuscript, which has subsequently been refined, updated and improved more times than I care to remember. I am indebted to:

Benjamin Andriamihaja, Summer J. Arrigo-Nelson, Matthew Banks, Karla Biebouw, Adam Britt, Helen Crowley, Reiner Dolch, Luke Dollar, Joanna Durbin, Manfred Eberle, Shannon Engberg, Anna Feistner, Joanna Fietz, John Flynn, Jörg Ganzhorn, Thomas Geissman, Chris Golden, Steven M. Goodman, Colin Groves, Andreas Hapke, Hilton Hastings, Clare Hawkins, Frank Hawkins, Mike Hoffman, Tony Hutson, Mitchell Irwin, Paulina Jenkins, Richard Jenkins, Alison Jolly, Peter Kappeler, Andrea Katz, Frances Kerridge, Bill Konstant, Olivier Langrand, Emma Long, Ed Louis, David Meyers, Russell Mittermeier, Thomas Mutschler, Stephen Nash, Martin Nicoll, Gillian Olivieri, Eric Patel, Sharon Pochron, Joyce Powzyk, Paul Racey, Serge Rajaobelina, Johah Ratsimbazafy, Yves Rumpler, Jutta Schmid, Christophe Schwitzer, Elwyn Simons, Ian Tattersall, Urs Thalmann, Astrid Vargas, Natalie Vasey, Charlie Welch, Patricia Wright and Anne Yoder.

The following have generously allowed the inclusion of personal comments and, in some instances, unpublished data that is not mentioned in the listed references. I am extremely grateful to; M. Banks, K. Biebouw, A. Britt, L. Dollar, J. Durbin, J. Flynn, A. Feistner, J.U. Ganzhorn, S. Goodman, A.F.A. Hawkins, M. Irwin, R. Jenkins, A. Jolly, P. Kappeler, E. Louis, G. Olivieri, J. Pastorini, E. Patel, J. Powzyk, J. Ralison, F. Ratrimomanarivo, Y. Rumpler, C. Schwitzer, U. Thalmann, P. Wright, A. Yoder and J. Zaonarivelo.

The map showing remaining forest cover on page 15 is based on an original provided by Marc Steininger (G20a) at Conservation International. I am very grateful for their permission to use this.

For the past eight years my tours and travels in Madagascar have, for the most part, been organised through Za Tours in Antananarivo. I am very grateful to Nivo Ravelojaona and her staff for all the assistance they have given me: their efficiency of operation has helped make my endeavours so much simpler.

Since 1999, I have escorted over 20 tours to Madagascar. On the majority of these I have been helped by my good friend Hery Andrianiantefana. Further we have travelled widely together, exploring new forest areas all over the island. His enthusiasm for the natural history of his native land knows no bounds and is infectious. From the heat of Andavadoaka, to the humid depths of Masoala and the peak of Marojejy, I have enjoyed his friendship and company and benefited enormously from his knowledge.

Many of my photographs have been supplied via my agents, Natural History Photographic Agency and Nature Picture Library. I am grateful to Tim Harris at NHPA and Helen Gilkes at NPL, who have been particularly supportive and given swift and straightforward access to these images and spent time retrieving them from files.

The staff at Fixation in London, especially Barry Edmonds, have efficiently serviced and repaired my Nikon camera equipment after the rigours of Madagascar and air travel have taken their toll. Sometimes this has been at very short notice and their help and friendliness are much appreciated.

Nigel Redman at A&C Black commissioned the first edition *Mammals of Madagascar* and has been equally supportive and enthusiastic about this project, while my editor, Julie Bailey, has been patient and thorough at all times, even when deadlines came and went.

This time around, the Alabama 3, R. L. Burnside, Tom Waits, Dixie Chicks and Lucinda Williams provided much of the soothing background inspiration long into the night.

Nick Garbutt
Cumbria, UK, 2007

PHOTOGRAPHIC CREDITS

Front cover: Nick Garbutt/Indri Images

Back cover: Left & right: Nick Garbutt/Indri Images. Centre: Jon Russ

By page number

Adam Britt: 220

Stephen Dalton/NHPA/Photoshot (www.nhpa.co.uk): 243, 244, 245

Manfred Eberle: 109

Nick Garbutt/Indri Images (www.nickgarbutt.com): 3, 12, 13, 14, 16 top, 17 bottom, 18, 20 top, 22, 23 top & bottom, 36, 57, 63, 85, 86, 90, 92, 94, 97 bottom, 100, 104, 106, 110, 117, 121, 124, 129, 131, 134, 135, 136, 138, 139, 148 bottom, 151, 153, 154, 155, 156, 157, 158, 159, 160, 161 bottom, 164, 170, 178, 182, 183, 184, 187, 188, 190, 193 top, 196, 197, 202 bottom, 203, 206 bottom, 212, 215 top & bottom, 216, 222, 226, 227, 231, 233, 240, 241, 259, 271, 275

Nick Garbutt/NHPA/Photoshot (www.nhpa.co.uk): 19 bottom, 20, 21 bottom, 33, 35, 37, 38 top, 60, 67, 69, 87, 89, 93 top & bottom, 95 top, 103, 107, 115, 128, 133, 143, 145 top & bottom, 148 top, 150, 161 top, 162 top & bottom, 165, 175, 176, 177, 179, 193 bottom, 195, 199, 200, 202 top, 204, 206 top, 209, 213, 221, 248, 254, 256, 257, 258, 260, 261, 262, 263, 264, 265, 266, 267, 272

Nick Garbutt/Nature Picture Library (NPL) (www.naturepl.com): 10, 16 bottom, 17 top, 19 top, 27, 61 top, 62, 125, 126, 147, 149, 152, 166, 167, 169 top, 170, 171, 174, 185, 186, 191, 192, 198, 207, 225, 249 top & bottom, 250, 255, 268

Nick Garbutt/Getty Images (www.gettyimages.com): 29

Dominique Halleux/BIOS/Still Pictures (www.biosphoto.com): 236

David Haring: 169 bottom

Daniel Heuclin/NHPA/Photoshot (www.nhpa.co.uk): 58

Olivier Langrand/BIOS/Still Pictures (www.biosphoto.com): 45, 238

Ed Louis: 95 bottom, 96, 97 top, 116, 118, 119, 120, 122, 123

Bernhard Meier: 101

Pete Morris: 91

Thomas Mutschler: 141, 142

Madagasikara Voakajy (Bat Conservation Madagascar): 65, 70, 71, 74, 77, 79, 81, 84

Martin Nicoll/BIOS/Still Pictures (www.biosphoto.com): 38 bottom, 39, 40, 44, 232, 234

Gillian Olivieri: 98, 99

Pete Oxford/Nature Picture Library (NPL) (www.naturepl.com): 64

Yves Rumpler: 163 top & bottom

Jon Russ: 73, 76

Peter Schachenmann: 218

Roland Seitre: 46, 47, 51 bottom, 54, 113, 211

Simone Sommer: 223

Peter J. Stephenson: 42, 50, 51 top, 53

Colin Taylor: 34

Urs Thalmann: 130, 132, 181

Roger Tidman/NHPA/Photoshot (www.nhpa.co.uk): 78

Hellio van Ingen/NHPA/Photoshot (www.nhpa.co.uk): 61 bottom

Chris Wozencraft: 219

INTRODUCTION

When I first visited Madagascar in May 1991, the country had just three national parks – Montagne d'Ambre, Isalo and the then recently created one at Ranomafana. Today the island boasts no fewer than 18 national parks plus more than 25 other major protected areas. This is testimony to the increased level of commitment to conserving the island's unique biodiversity in the face of ever escalating threats: a commitment underlined in 2003 by President Marc Ravalomanana, at the 5th World Parks Congress when he announced his government's intention to triple the area of Madagascar's forests under protection. In what is now known as 'The Durban Vision' he said: 'We can no longer afford to watch our forests go up in flames, nor let our many lakes, marshes and wetlands dry up, nor can we inconsiderately exhaust our marine resources. This is not just Madagascar's biodiversity, it is the world's biodiversity. We have the firm political will to stop this degradation.'

Further, the past 16 years has seen a corresponding surge in the volume of research being carried out within the island's forests, wetlands and other natural habitats. Even by the early 1990s there were still only a relatively small number of species that had been studied in any detail and for which anything other than scant information was available. Most research concentrated on the higher profile (and relatively accessible) lemurs that were without question the island's flagship species. Since then, gaps have been filled at an ever-increasing rate. Lemurs undoubtedly remain the island's best studied group, and there has now been field research looking at members of every genus – many of these have turned into long-term investigations.

Research into Madagascar's carnivores, insectivores, rodents and bats has also gathered considerable momentum. In particular, a programme of detailed biological inventories covering forests primarily in the east e.g. Marojejy, Anjanahasibe-Sud, Masoala, Andringitra and Andohahela, but also latterly in the south and west e.g. Zombitse and Mitea, have added greatly to our knowledge of the distributions and ranges of these smaller mammals.

This increased knowledge has led to the recent publication of some landmark volumes perhaps most notably *The Natural History of Madagascar*, Goodman, S.M. and Benstead, J.P. (eds), The University of Chicago Press, Chicago, USA., a collection of essays and reviews covering a huge range of subjects and aspects of the island's biodiversity from soils and geology to botany, invertebrate zoology, vertebrate zoology, conservation and land management. The chapter covering the mammal fauna is particularly comprehensive and informative.

However, even a volume of this magnitude serves to highlight how many gaps in our knowledge still exist. For instance, since its publication in 2003 no fewer than 35 new mammal species have been described (two rodents, two insectivores, five bats and 26 lemurs) and a number of micro-mammals (bats, rodents, shrew tenrecs) that have already been collected still await formal description. What is more, this is a trend that seems certain to continue as scientists begin to investigate isolated patches of forest for the first time in some of Madagascar's remotest regions.

In this volume I have tried to incorporate all the latest information and make each species account as up to date as possible. Comparison with the original *Mammals of Madagascar* (Pica Press, 1999) will highlight how far knowledge has moved on. Yet, what is presented here remains far from complete and in some cases will become outdated relatively quickly. Nonetheless this concise synopsis should prove a useful and informative guide for those wishing to discover more about one of the most fascinating and unusual mammalian assemblages on Earth.

Female Ring-tailed Lemur carrying two-week-old infant.

HOW TO USE THE GUIDE

This book aims to provide a concise and up-to-date review of Madagascar's mammals and a practical guide for visitors to the island. As can be seen from the extensive list of references, information has been drawn from a wide variety of disparate sources, many of which are accessible only to specialists and the scientific community.

Despite the vast amount of research that has taken place since the first *Mammals of Madagascar* was published (Pica Press, 1999), little remains known about a substantial number of Madagascar's less glamorous mammal species. Hence, depth and detail in the species profiles vary considerably. Information given here is meant as a first step for those wishing to learn about the species concerned; the reference list provides access to more detailed information.

Introductory Chapters

These discuss the creation of the island of Madagascar and the effect its long isolation has had on the evolution of its fauna and flora in general, and its mammal communities in particular. This is followed by a review of the major habitat types.

Species Accounts

Species accounts for each of the five mammalian orders that naturally occur on Madagascar comprise the majority of the book. Accounts are subdivided into the following categories: Measurements, Description & Identification, Habitat & Distribution, Behaviour and Where to See.

Measurements

Basic body measurements that aid field recognition. Where applicable, differences between the sexes or significant seasonal variations are outlined. Where information is not available, estimates have been made using museum specimens or knowledge from closely related forms. Estimated measurements are indicated by an asterisk (*).

Description & Identification

Descriptions concentrate on external features that help field identification, including pelage characteristics and coloration and notable morphological traits. Differences between the sexes or between adult and immature individuals are highlighted. Variations between populations, some of which may be regarded as subspecific, are outlined where appropriate.

A concise summary of the main features used in identifying a species, for instance, approximate size and body posture, is followed by comparisons with taxa that may potentially cause confusion or misidentification.

Habitat & Distribution

Madagascar's terrestrial mammals are essentially native forest dwellers. There are a number of distinct forest types on the island and the preferred habitat type of each species is given: in some instances, species with extensive distributions have wider tolerances and may be found in more than one forest type and perhaps also in some human-altered habitats and cultivated areas.

Distributions outline in as much detail as is feasible a species' known range and also suggest altitudinal preferences and limits where they are known.

Maps illustrate a species' range and attempt to outline the approximate actual range by relating distributional information to remaining native forest cover. This approach has its pitfalls and will be erroneous in places. Even within the shaded areas, forests are not continuous and neither are the species' populations. Further, there may also be isolated fragments of forest lying outside the shaded areas in which small remnant populations survive. However, as perhaps only 10% of original forest remains intact, this approach should provide a far more realistic impression of present distributions. A number of species are known from only a single locality or a handful at most. In these instances the localities are pinpointed and the probable range that extends between them suggested. Again, this is to be treated only as an approximate guide.

Behaviour

Includes information on daily and seasonal activity patterns, social interaction, group composition and structure, range size, foraging preferences, diet, breeding habits, development and predation.

Where to See

The best localities to see a species, including any seasonal variations. Alternative localities in different parts of a species' range are also suggested to offer variety.

Conservation and Protected Areas

Outlines the conservation concerns facing Madagascar and its fauna and flora, and discusses some of the solutions currently being pursued.

Top Mammal-watching Sites

Selected on the basis of quality of potential viewing and accessibility. Aims to provide a complete cross-section of habitat types and, therefore, to cover an extensive array of mammal species. Lists key species at each location. A species highlighted in bold type indicates that observations can be particularly rewarding and corresponds to the recommended sites suggested in the 'Where to See' section of the species accounts.

Black-and-white Ruffed Lemur (probably Varecia variegata *'variegata'), Ranomafana National Park.*

Greater Bamboo Lemur in giant bamboo, Ranomafana National Park.

BIOGEOGRAPHY AND REGIONS OF MADAGASCAR

How Did Mammals Get to Madagascar?

Madagascar is home to one of the most unusual mammalian assemblages on Earth. Why this should be is an intriguing question that has yet to be fully resolved. To state that Madagascar is an island, and that its biota is different because it has evolved in isolation, is a dramatic oversimplification that reveals little of the many complexities relating to the composition and historic development of the island's wildlife.

It is widely accepted that many animals reach isolated islands by rafting on clumps of floating vegetation, washed out to sea from large rivers on continental mainlands. This might seem a highly improbable method for any land-based animal to reach distant shores. However, if the immensity of geological time is appreciated it becomes highly plausible – after all, any event that is not impossible becomes probable if enough time elapses.

Certainly, crossing the Mozambique Channel by rafting (sweepstake dispersal) is a prime candidate for explaining the arrival of Madagascar's first mammals. However, this explanation alone is not detailed enough to answer all the questions. For instance, if the forebears of Madagascar's mammal communities could make the crossing, why have other groups that proliferate in Africa not done so subsequently? After all, we know Madagascar has been in its current position for approximately 120 million years, so reaching it on floating vegetation ought to be as easy today as it was when the early colonists made the journey many millions of years ago.

Consequently, we need to consider possible reasons that may have made the pioneer mammals better mariners (in terms of their ability to survive a long accidental sea-crossing) than mainland species that came along later in evolutionary history. It is obvious that a small body size would be an advantage in being able to stay afloat on a makeshift raft. And although relatively large species have existed, and continue to exist, on Madagascar, evidence suggests these evolved at a later date and that original colonising stock consisted only of small species. Why then are there many small mammals in Africa which are absent from Madagascar? Further, small body size usually correlates to a high metabolism and the need to eat regularly. Clearly this trait would place small mammals at a severe disadvantage in the sea-crossing stakes. The results of recent research may provide clues to the missing elements.

Many of Madagascar's smaller mammals have the capacity to lower their metabolism and become dormant during periods of low food availability (G30). In conjunction, they can also build up fat reserves during times of plenty to sustain themselves through lean periods. This ability has been demonstrated both in mouse and dwarf lemurs (family Cheirogaleidae), which are probably very similar to Madagascar's early primate colonists, and in tenrecs (family Tenrecidae). It is also known that some of the island's endemic carnivores (family Eupleridae) are able to lay down fat reserves in their tails.

Here then may be the answer. Madagascar was colonised from Africa by small mammal species rafting on natural debris, and the only species to survive the journey were those with the ability to lower their metabolism, become dormant and/or live without food for long periods

Lesser Galago (Galago senegalensis), *a prosimian from East Africa. Obvious external similarities betray a common ancestry with Mouse and Dwarf Lemurs. The ancestors of both evolved in Africa. Some then inadvertently crossed the Mozambique Channel to Madagascar on floating debris and then evolved and diversified spectacularly into the lemurs.*

on reserves built-up previously. As it turned out, the successful species represented only four mammal groups: lemurs, herpestine-like carnivores, tenrecs and rodents. Further weight is added to this argument by recent molecular research that has demonstrated that each of these four mammalian lineages on Madagascar is derived from a single colonising ancestral stock (G31; G32; G26; G21). To complete the picture, it is assumed that the remaining mammalian group present on Madagascar, the bats, reached the island by flying.

Regions and Habitats

Madagascar has a remarkable diversity of habitats and associated flora. Covering an area of about 587,000km², it is the world's fourth largest island (after Greenland, New Guinea and Borneo), yet its environmental diversity rivals that of an entire continent. There are rainforests in the east, deciduous forests in the north and west, dense xerophytic forests in the south and high mountain forests in the island's interior. Not surprisingly such variety has fostered the evolution of a faunal assemblage so unusual as to rival that of any comparable area on Earth.

Habitat variety is the result of dramatic climatic variability, which in turn is a consequence of Madagascar's position and topography. The island lies virtually entirely within the tropics and has a corresponding climate. From north to south it spans some 1,650km, between 12° and 25° S and there is notable variation in basic sea-level temperatures: in the far north the annual mean is 81°C, while at the southern extremity the mean drops to 71°C.

The island consists of a backbone of Precambrian crys-

Remaining primary forest areas (after G20a).

humid forest

deciduous forest

dry (spiny) forest

talline rocks running from north to south down the island. This forms the high plateau. To the east there is an abrupt escarpment, while in the west the highlands slope gently down to the Mozambique Channel. The highest mountains are in the north and rise to 2,876m (Maromokotro, the island's highest peak in the Tsaratanana Massif), and there are other scattered massifs and peaks, some of which reach over 2,000m. The eastern coastal plain between the escarpment and the Indian Ocean is generally narrow, while the coastal plain to the west is far broader.

The prevailing weather comes from the Indian Ocean brought by the trade winds, which rise over the escarpment. Consequently, the majority of rain falls in the east. The western regions lie in a permanent rain shadow. Hence, conditions gradually become hotter and drier towards the west coast.

During the austral summer western regions are subject to a monsoon regime which originates in the north and whose influence dwindles towards the south. Hence, there is a double rainfall gradient over the island: declining from east to west on the one hand, and north to south on the other. As a result the north-east is the wettest part of the island and the south-west is the driest (G22).

The combined effect is a profusion of climatic conditions, which consequently result in the variety of habitat types. Attempts to classify the island's vegetation are principally according to region and altitude (G9; G10; G12). Difficulties occur in many eastern rainforest regions where steep slopes result in quick changes of altitude over short distances. Here, the underlying substrate may vary as do exposure to wind and sun. Thus, there are numerous localised micro-climates that contradict general rules. For instance, in some sheltered valleys at higher elevations in Marojejy, forest characteristic of the 'mid-altitude type' grows above 1,400m, whereas on exposed ridge tops in Mantadia, the forest resembles 'high-altitude montane' even though the elevation is only around 1,100m to 1,200m. Nonetheless, some general rules can be applied and a 'broad' classification produced.

Lowland rainforest flourishes in valley bottoms of Marojejy National Park.

Eastern Lowland Rainforest

Sea-level to around 800m asl, extending along east coast from south of Vohemar in north to Tolagnaro region in south. Corresponds to areas of highest rainfall – at least 2,500mm per year and in north-east, up to 5,900mm per annum, e.g. Masoala Peninsula (G23). No clearly defined dry season, although December to March consistently wetter than other times.

Enormous species richness and diversity coupled with very high levels of endemism. Largest trees have huge buttress roots and canopy averages 30–35m. Understorey dominated by small trees, with little herbaceous growth beneath. Epiphytic plants such as orchids are abundant.

Mammal diversity very high; all major taxonomic groups are represented. Examples include Masoala National Park and lower elevations of Marojejy National Park.

Mid-altitude Montane Rainforest

Occurs between 800m and 1,400m asl, with localised patches at higher elevations. Occurs to west of lowland rainforest belt, extending parallel to east coast from north of Sambava in north to vicinity of Tolagnaro in south. Annual rainfall exceeds 1,500mm with no discernible dry season; wettest period corresponds to austral summer.

Diverse and species-rich, with levels of endemism equivalent to lowland rainforest. Canopy averages 20–25m, occasionally reaching 30m. Understorey and herbaceous

Understory dominated by Draceana *species in lowland rainforest, Masoala National Park.*

Pandanus species flourish by streams in mid-altitude montane forest, Andasibe-Mantadia National Park.

layers better developed than in lowland forests. Epiphytes like tree-ferns abound, many trees are festooned with mosses and lichens.

Mammal diversity very high, all the major taxonomic groups represented. Both Tenrecidae and Nesomyinae reach their highest levels of species richness. Island's more familiar rainforest locations correspond to this habitat, including; Andasibe-Mantadia National Park and Ranomafana National Park.

High-altitude Montane Forest

Restricted to elevations between 1,400m and 1,800m asl. Occurs in broken belt inland from montane rainforest zone; northerly limit is Sambava area (Marojejy Massif) and southern extreme is Andohahela Massif (north of Tolagnaro). Annual precipitation high, much occurring as dense mists and low cloud, hence often referred to as 'cloud forest'.

Species diversity lower than montane or lowland rain-forests; levels of endemism remain high. Canopy height between 10m and 15m at lower elevations, declining gradually with altitude. Canopy layers and understorey often difficult to differentiate: forest appears a dense single stratum. Leaves on most trees smaller than in lower-altitude rainforests and have leathery cuticle to counter desiccation. Trees encrusted with mosses and lichens. Mosses form a dense carpet on the forest floor.

Mammal diversity moderately high, most major taxonomic groups represented, but species diversity reduced in comparison with rainforest at lower elevations, e.g. bat diversity drops dramatically above 1,500m. Examples are higher elevations of Ranomafana National Park (Vohiparara) and areas above Camp Simpona (Camp 3) in Marojejy National Park.

High-altitude montane forest at around 1600m, Andringitra National Park.

The spectacular view from the summit of Marojejy. Sclerophyllous forest clings to the steep exposed slopes.

Sclerophyllous Forest and High Mountain Thicket

Found above 1,800m asl with highest areas (generally above 2,000m) above tree-line. Between 1,800m and 2,000m stunted trees and bushes 2m to 5m high, and above this vegetation consists of dwarf open-bush thicket less than 2m in height dominated by Ericaceae and Asteraceae formations. Ferns a significant element (G12). Daily and seasonal temperature variations; during austral winter night-time temperatures can fall below freezing (G29).

Mammal diversity low, only groups regularly present being Tenrecidae and Nesomyinae, although some lemurs have been recorded, e.g. Ring-tailed Lemurs on Andringitra Massif (G17) and Red-bellied Lemurs in Marojejy. Only a few examples: Tsaratanana (summit 2,876m), Anjanaharibe-Sud (summit 2,064m), Ankaratra (summit 2,643m), Marojejy (summit 2,133m) and Andringitra (summit 2,658m); the latter two are the only ones that can be visited relatively easily.

Seasonal Humid Forest (Sambirano)

An enclave of humid rainforest restricted to north-west. Lies approximately between Nosy Faly Peninsula to north and Andranomalaza River to south and represents an extension of north-eastern rainforest zone. Annual rainfall above 2,000mm; at lower elevations there is a drier season between July and September.

Represents a transition between floral communities of east and west, sharing many features with both eastern and western regions. High species diversity and high levels of endemism. Canopy reaches 30m, at lower elevations some trees emerge to around 35m. Understorey and shrub layers substantial, with epiphytes, vines and creepers abundant (G12).

Mammal diversity moderate, most major taxonomic groups represented, with some notable exceptions, e.g. *Propithecus* spp. Example is Manongarivo Special Reserve.

Eastern Anthropogenic Grasslands

Where forest has been removed, it is replaced by a mosaic of secondary vegetation, dominated by grassland created and maintained by humans. At lower elevations, coastal savanna interspersed with stands of *Ravenala madagascariensis*. Grassland dominates higher elevations including western slopes of high plateau. Highland savanna also found on some mountain ridges.

The deforested central highlands; barren grassland and rice cultivation now dominate.

Species diversity and endemism very low. Maintained and extended by deliberate fires and overgrazing resulting in large-scale erosion.

Mammal diversity very low. Largely devoid of native terrestrial mammal species; in some marginal areas tenrec and rodent species occur and some indigenous bats live where trees are present.

Western Dry Deciduous Forest

Extends at altitudes from sea-level to 800m from area of Antsiranana in north to vicinity of Morombe in south-west, excluding Montagne d'Ambre Massif and Sambirano domain (which are distinct, see above). Annual rainfall ranges from 2,000mm in north to only 500mm in south: majority falls between December and March, rest of year mainly dry (G9).

Western deciduous forest around Lac Ravelobe, Ankarafantsika National Park.

Grandidier's Baobab (Adansonia grandidieri) in deciduous forest, north of Morondava.

Rugged limestone karst surrounds and protects deciduous forest. Ankarana Special Reserve.

Species diversity very high, although lower than in eastern region. Levels of species endemism are higher – often around 90%. Canopy averages 12m to 15m but in some areas reaches 20m-25m. Understorey and shrub layers well developed; herbaceous and epiphytic growth rare. Most trees lose their leaves during dry season (May to October).

In some areas forests may be dominated by baobabs (*Adansonia* spp.). Excellent examples of Grandidier's Baobab *A. grandidieri* can be seen near Morondava.

Most dry deciduous forests have already been cleared, and the few remaining areas are under severe threat from slash-and-burn agriculture, timber extraction and uncontrolled pasture fires (G8). Mammal diversity high, most major taxonomic groups represented, but species diversity is reduced in comparison with rainforest areas. Best examples are Ankarafantsika National Park and Kirindy Forest, together with limestone karst areas such as Namoroka, Ankarana and Bemaraha.

Subarid Thorn Scrub or Spiny Forest

Subarid thorn scrub is often referred to as spiny forest. Extends southwards along coastal plain from Morombe on west coast; includes whole of southern area to a point approximately 40km west of Tolagnaro (western flank of the Anosyennes Mountains). Restricted to elevations below 400m. In Morombe region annual rainfall reaches around 500mm; this declines further south, driest areas

A bizarre shaped baobab (Adansonia za) in spiny forest north of Toliara.

Spiny forest dominated by the family Didiereaceae.

receiving only 300mm per year. Dry season marked and long, extending up to ten months (March to December). This is highly variable and 18-month dry periods have been recorded (G11).

Species diversity high; levels of endemism extremely high. Height and density of vegetation varies with climatic and soil conditions: in some areas trees reach 8m to 12m, but in other areas only around 2m. All plant species adapted for harsh conditions, with abundant thorns and small waxy leaves. Region is dominated and characterised by endemic family Didiereaceae and members of the Euphorbiaceae.

Along major watercourses, spiny forest replaced by narrow bands of riparian habitat called gallery forest, showing vague resemblance to western deciduous forests. Canopy of similar height (up to 15m), with extensive understorey and herbaceous layer. Tamarind trees *Tamarindus indica* often dominate.

Forest clearing for firewood and charcoal is major threat. In marginal areas browsing by goats is also detrimental.

Mammal diversity moderate. Several major taxonomic groups are notable absentees, e.g. *Eulemur* spp. Small mammal diversity also reduced. Examples are Tsimanampetsotsa National Park, Andohahela National Park (Parcel 2) and unprotected forests near Ifaty, north of Toliara.

At marginal localities, where western and southern formations meet, there are areas of 'transition forest' exhibiting characteristics from both areas. These include forests north of Morombe and south of Mangoky River and Zombitse and Vohibasia well inland. In the south-east there is also a transition zone between southern and eastern formations on western slopes of Anosyennes Mountains (G11).

Western Anthropogenic Grasslands and Palm Savanna

Majority of original forest in western region has been replaced by grassland and palm savannas, covering around 90% of the area. Very low levels of species diversity and endemism. Coarse grasses dominate but in some areas are broken by stands of fire-resistant palms such as *Bismarckia nobilis*, *Hyphaene coriacea* and *Borassus madagascariensis*. Further impoverished by deliberate fires started several times per year, to encourage new shoots for cattle grazing. Overgrazing also commonplace and locally severe.

*Fire-resistant palms (*Borassus madagascariensis*) near Isalo National Park.*

Mammal diversity extremely low. In majority of areas, native terrestrial mammal species totally absent; one exception appears to be Western Big-footed Mouse *Macrotarsomys bastardi*, which is known to occur locally. Some bats are able to utilise these habitats in areas where palms are present. As with regions in east, the commensals, *Rattus rattus*, *Mus musculus* and *Suncus murinus* are common.

Bismarkia *and* Hyphaene *species dominate many deforested areas in the west.*

THE MAMMALS OF MADAGASCAR

Overview

The mammal fauna of Madagascar is perhaps as remarkable for the major taxonomic groupings that are absent as it is for the collection of unusual species that are present. Given the island's proximity to mainland Africa, it would be easy to assume Madagascar contains simply an impoverished version of the diversity of mammals living on the continent. This could not be further from the truth. For instance, there are none of the large herbivores that dominate the plains of Africa; carnivores, such as wild cats and wild dogs are conspicuous by their absence, as are monkeys and apes and a host of other smaller forms like lagomorphs (rabbits and hares).

In fact, only five major mammal groups are found on Madagascar (six if a probable introduced species, Bush Pig, is included): bats (order Chiroptera), tenrecs (order Lypotyphla: family Tenrecidae), rats and mice (order Rodentia: family Muridae), civet-like carnivores and mongooses (order Carnivora: family Eupleridae) and the lemurs (order Primates: infraorder Lemuriformes).

This mammal fauna is exceptional for two major reasons. Firstly, every native terrestrial species (a total of approximately 148) is endemic, i.e. they occur naturally nowhere else. No other island or place on Earth boasts such a combination of species richness and endemism. And secondly, these mammals have evolved an extraordinary diversity of body forms and lifestyles often displaying significant convergence with continental forms but also at times evolving utterly unique features (G15). The reason for this is simple: Madagascar has been an island for a very long time, which has allowed its mammals to evolve along totally different lines from anywhere else.

The ancestors of all Madagascar's terrestrial mammals reached the island by rafting on natural debris across the Mozambique Channel, although it is difficult to pinpoint when the first colonists arrived. The lottery and rigours of such a crossing severely restricted mammalian invasions and only a handful of forms proved capable. In fact recent and ongoing research suggests that each of the four major terrestrial groups (rodents, tenrecs, lemurs and carnivores) is derived from a common ancestor and, by implication, therefore, a single colonisation event (G21; G26; G31; G32).

Once on Madagascar, these early colonists largely had the island to themselves (as the dinosaurs had long since died out) and were able to diversify spectacularly, evolving into species exploiting niches occupied elsewhere by other groups of mammals and even birds. Ring-tailed Lemurs live in a similar manner to some baboons; Giant Jumping Rats show remarkable similarities in body form and lifestyle to rabbits and hares; the Long-tailed Shrew Tenrec looks and behaves like a small arboreal mouse; the Fosa, in aspects of appearance and behaviour, resembles a cat; while the bizarre Aye-aye extracts insect grubs from tree bark much as woodpeckers would do (birds that are absent from the island).

There are some anomalies in the mammal fauna that warrant explanation. Subfossil evidence shows in the recent past three species of dwarf hippopotamus (*Hexaprotodon madagascariensis*, *Hippopotamus lemerlei* and *H. laloumena*) and two 'false' aardvarks (*Plesiorycteropus madagascariensis* and *P. germainepetterae*) were present on Madagascar (G19). The dwarf hippos may have been later arrivals (late Quaternary) on the island than any of the original mammalian founder species. It is likely they made the crossing from Africa during the mid to late Cenozoic (38 to 7 million years before present), but how is not known. Being semi-aquatic the hippos could have made their own way across the Mozambique Channel in freak circumstances. It is suspected they became extinct around 1,000 years ago as a consequence of human persecution, although some recent evidence suggests they might have survived as recently as 200 years ago (G13; G2). Further, an ungulate, the Bush Pig *Potamochoerus larvatus*, still survives on the island today. It is suspected this animal is either a comparatively recent natural arrival or, more likely, was introduced by early human colonists (G1).

Classification

There is currently no single reference that offers an up-to-date and complete classification of Madagascar's mammals. Recent research has shed further light on evolutionary relationships which has prompted various revisions within each of the mammalian orders that naturally occur on the island. Given that much of this research is ongoing and that new genetic techniques are constantly being refined to elucidate taxonomic relationships, it seems reasonable to presume that further revisions will be proposed in the future; this applies particularly to the small mammal communities (tenrecs, rodents and micro-bats), where the current inventories are almost certainly incomplete.

Therefore, the classification followed here is a synthesis based on a number of previous publications. The classification of the Lemuriformes follows Groves (2001) and Mayor *et al.* (2004), with the addition of several newly described species (L152; L360; L7; L165; L166; L11; L259a; L208a).

The arrangement of the carnivores is based on Yoder and Flynn (2003) confirming that the group is monophyletic. Though precise relationships within the group are still to be clarified, it is now accepted that all belong in the endemic family Eupleridae.

Within the Tenrecidae, two subfamilies are recognised from Madagascar: Tenrecinae and Oryzorictinae. The taxonomy of the latter remains confused, particularly with respect to the shrew tenrecs (genus *Microgale*). New species are regularly being described and existing forms often amalgamated as synonyms. Here the sequence follows that of Goodman (2003) with the addition of species later described or lifted from synonymy (G18; G27).

Madagascar's native rodents all belong in the endemic subfamily Nesomyinae, which is placed within the broad Old World family Muridae. There have been several recent additions to the inventory including two new genera, *Monticolomys* and *Voalavo* (R3; R4), and new species (R11; R23).

Bats, particularly within the suborder Microchiroptera, present the greatest challenge to the mammalian taxonomist in Madagascar. Such is their diversity and number of species that several classifications have been proposed, often radically differing from one another. That new species will be described in the future seems without doubt. However, for present purposes, the latest reviews relating to the taxonomy of the Malagasy bat fauna (G15; B16; B50) have been followed, with the subsequent additions of three new species (B22; B25; B26a).

The following sequence should provide a sound basis for the classification of Madagascar's mammals within the context of this book. However, it is clear that many taxonomic questions still need to be addressed and answered; hence this list can only be treated as provisional.

Order Lypotyphla
Family Tenrecidae (Tenrecs and Otter-Shrews)
Subfamily Tenrecinae (Spiny Tenrecs)
Common Tenrec *Tenrec ecaudatus*
Greater Hedgehog Tenrec *Setifer setosus*
Lesser Hedgehog Tenrec *Echinops telfairi*
Lowland Streaked Tenrec *Hemicentetes semispinosus*
Highland Streaked Tenrec *Hemicentetes nigriceps*
Subfamily Geogalinae (Large-eared Tenrecs)
Large-eared Tenrec *Geogale aurita*
Subfamily Oryzorictinae (Furred Tenrecs)
Aquatic Tenrec *Limnogale mergulus*
Hova Mole Tenrec *Oryzorictes hova*
Four-toed Mole Tenrec *Oryzorictes tetradactylus*
Lesser Long-tailed Shrew Tenrec *Microgale longicaudata*
Greater Long-tailed Shrew Tenrec *Microgale principula*
Major's Long-tailed Shrew Tenrec *Microgale majori*
Talazac's Shrew Tenrec *Microgale talazaci*
Thomas's Shrew Tenrec *Microgale thomasi*
Gracile Shrew Tenrec *Microgale gracilis*
Dobson's Shrew Tenrec *Microgale dobsoni*
Cowan's Shrew Tenrec *Microgale cowani*
Pygmy Shrew Tenrec *Microgale parvula*
Short-tailed Shrew Tenrec *Microgale brevicaudata*
Lesser Shrew Tenrec *Microgale pusilla*
Taiva Shrew Tenrec *Microgale taiva*
Striped Shrew Tenrec *Microgale drouhardi*
Naked-nosed Shrew Tenrec *Microgale gymnorhyncha*
Pale-footed Shrew Tenrec *Microgale fotsifotsy*
Mountain Shrew Tenrec *Microgale monticola*
Tree Shrew Tenrec *Microgale dryas*
Shrew Tenrec *Microgale soricoides*
Nasolo's Shrew Tenrec *Microgale nasoloi*
Jenkins' Shrew Tenrec *Microgale jenkinsae*

Introduced Species
Family Soricidae (Shrews)
Asian Musk Shrew *Suncus murinus*
Pygmy (Madagascar) Musk Shrew *Suncus etruscus madagascariensis*

Order Chiroptera
Suborder Megachiroptera
Family Pteropodidae (Old World Fruit Bats)
Madagascar Flying Fox *Pteropus rufus*
Madagascar Straw-coloured Fruit Bat *Eidolon dupreanum*
Madagascar Rousette *Rousettus madagascariensis*

Suborder Microchiroptera
Family Emballonuridae (Sheath-tailed Bats)
Peters's Sheath-tailed Bat *Emballonura atrata*
Emballonura tiavato
African Sheath-tailed Bat *Coleura afra*
Mauritian Tomb Bat *Taphozous mauritianus*
Family Nycteridae (Slit-faced Bats)
Madagascar Slit-faced Bat *Nycteris madagascariensis*
Family Hipposideridae (Old World Leaf-nosed Bats)
Commerson's Leaf-nosed Bat *Hipposideros commersoni*
Trouessart's Trident Bat *Triaenops furculus*
Rufous Trident Bat *Triaenops rufus*
Triaenops auritus
Family Myzopodidae (Sucker-footed Bats)
Eastern Sucker-footed Bat *Myzopoda aurita*
Western Sucker-footed Bat *Myzopoda schliemanni*
Family Vespertilionidae (Vespertilionid Bats)
Subfamily Vespertilioninae
Malagasy Mouse-eared Bat *Myotis goudoti*
Pipistrellus nanus
Pipistrellus kuhlii
Pipistrellus sp.
Madagascar Serotine *Eptesicus matroka*
Neoromicia malagasyensis
Scotophilus robustus
Scotophilus borbonicus
Scotophilus tandrefana
Scotophilus marovaza

Subfamily Miniopterinae
Miniopterus majori
Miniopterus manavi
Lesser Long-fingered Bat *Miniopterus fraterculus*
Miniopterus gleni
Family Molossidae (Free-tailed Bats)
Peters's Goblin Bat *Mormopterus jugularis*
Large Free-tailed Bat *Tadarida fulminans*
Chaerephon leucogaster
Little Free-tailed Bat *Chaerephon pumilus*
Chaerephon jobimena
Midas Mastiff Bat *Mops midas*
Mops leucostigma
Madagascar Free-tailed Bat *Otomops madagascariensis*

Indri coloration is very variable. This animal is from near Zahamena National Park.

Order Primates
Infraorder Lemuriformes

Family Cheirogaleidae (Mouse and Dwarf Lemurs)

    Subfamily Cheirogaleinae

Grey Mouse Lemur *Microcebus murinus*

Brown Mouse Lemur *Microcebus rufus*

Western Rufous Mouse Lemur *Microcebus myoxinus*

Golden-brown Mouse Lemur *Microcebus ravelobensis*

Sambirano Mouse Lemur *Microcebus sambiranensis*

Northern Rufous Mouse Lemur *Microcebus tavaratra*

Madame Berthe's Mouse Lemur *Microcebus berthae*

Grey-brown Mouse Lemur *Microcebus griseorufus*

Goodman's Mouse Lemur *Microcebus lehilahytsara*

Jolly's Mouse Lemur *Microcebus jollyae*

Simmon's Mouse Lemur *Microcebus simmonsi*

Mittermeier's Mouse Lemur *Microcebus mittermeieri*

Claire's Mouse Lemur *Microcebus mamiratra*

Lokobe Mouse Lemur *Microcebus lokobensis*

Bongolava Mouse Lemur *Microcebus bongolavensis*

Danfoss Mouse Lemur *Microcebus danfossi*

Hairy-eared Dwarf Lemur *Allocebus trichotis*

Greater Dwarf Lemur *Cheirogaleus major*

Furry-eared Dwarf Lemur *Cheirogaleus crossleyi*

Sibree's Dwarf Lemur *Cheirogaleus sibreei*

Greater Iron Grey Dwarf Lemur *Cheirogaleus ravus*

Lesser Iron Grey Dwarf Lemur *Cheirogaleus minusculus*

Fat-tailed Dwarf Lemur *Cheirogaleus medius*

Spiny Forest Dwarf Lemur *Cheirogaleus adipicaudatus*

Coquerel's Giant Dwarf Lemur *Mirza coquereli*

Northern Giant Dwarf Lemur *Mirza zaza*

    Subfamily Phanerinae

Eastern Fork-marked Lemur *Phaner furcifer*

Pariente's Fork-marked Lemur *Phaner parienti*

Pale Fork-marked Lemur *Phaner pallescens*

Amber Mountain Fork-marked Lemur *Phaner electromontis*

Family Lepilemuridae (Sportive Lemurs)

Weasel Sportive Lemur *Lepilemur mustelinus*

Betsileo Sportive Lemur *Lepilemur betsileo*

Small-toothed Sportive Lemur *Lepilemur microdon*

James' Sportive Lemur *Lepilemur jamesi* (*jamesorum*)

Wright's Sportive Lemur *Lepilemur wrighti* (*wrightae*)

Fleurete's Sportive Lemur *Lepilemur fleuretae*

Seal's Sportive Lemur *Lepilemur seali*

Daraina Sportive Lemur *Lepilemur milanoii*

Northern Sportive Lemur *Lepilemur septentrionalis*

Ankarana Sportive Lemur *Lepilemur ankaranensis*

Grey-backed Sportive Lemur *Lepilemur dorsalis*

Hawk's Sportive Lemur *Lepilemur tymerlachsoni*

Mittermeier's Sportive Lemur *Lepilemur mittermeieri*

Sahamalaza Sportive Lemur *Lepilemur sahamalazensis*

Grewcocks' Sportive Lemur *Lepilemur grewcocki* (*grewcockorum*)

Verreaux's Sifaka skipping across a forest clearing, Berenty Reserve.

Milne-Edwards's Sportive Lemur *Lepilemur edwardsi*
Red-shouldered Sportive Lemur *Lepilemur aeeclis*
Ahmanson's Sportive Lemur *Lepilemur ahmansoni*
Randrianasolo's Sportive Lemur *Lepilemur randrianasoli*
Red-tailed Sportive Lemur *Lepilemur ruficaudatus*
Hubbard's Sportive Lemur *Lepilemur hubbardi*
Petter's Sportive Lemur *Lepilemur petteri*
White-footed Sportive Lemur *Lepilemur leucopus*

Family Lemuridae ('True'. Lemurs)

Subfamily Hapalemurinae (Bamboo or Gentle Lemurs)
Eastern Grey Bamboo Lemur *Hapalemur griseus*
Western Grey Bamboo Lemur *Hapalemur occidentalis*
Southern Grey Bamboo Lemur *Hapalemur meridionalis*
Alaotra Reed Lemur *Hapalemur alaotrensis*
Golden Bamboo Lemur *Hapalemur aureus*
Greater Bamboo Lemur *Prolemur simus*

Subfamily Lemurinae ('True' Lemurs)
Ring-tailed Lemur *Lemur catta*
Mongoose Lemur *Eulemur mongoz*
Crowned Lemur *Eulemur coronatus*
Red-bellied Lemur *Eulemur rubriventer*
Common Brown Lemur *Eulemur fulvus*
Sanford's Brown Lemur *Eulemur sanfordi*
White-fronted Brown Lemur *Eulemur albifrons*
Red-fronted Brown Lemur *Eulemur rufus*
White-collared Brown Lemur *Eulemur albocollaris*
Collared Brown Lemur *Eulemur collaris*
Black Lemur *Eulemur macaco*
Black Lemur *Eulemur macaco macaco*
Blue-eyed Black Lemur *Eulemur macaco flavifrons*
Black-and-white Ruffed Lemur *Varecia variegata*
Varecia variegata 'subcincta'
Varecia variegata 'editorum'
Varecia variegata 'variegata'
Red Ruffed Lemur *Varecia rubra*

Family Indriidae (Avahis, Sifakas and Indri)
Eastern Avahi *Avahi laniger*
Western Avahi *Avahi occidentalis*
Sambirano Avahi *Avahi unicolor*
Cleese's Avahi *Avahi cleesei*
Diademed Sifaka *Propithecus diadema*
Milne-Edwards's Sifaka *Propithecus edwardsi*
Silky Sifaka *Propithecus candidus*
Perrier's Sifaka *Propithecus perrieri*
Verreaux's Sifaka *Propithecus verreauxi*
Coquerel's Sifaka *Propithecus coquereli*
Decken's Sifaka *Propithecus deckeni*
Crowned Sifaka *Propithecus coronatus*
Golden-crowned Sifaka *Propithecus tattersalli*
Indri *Indri indri*

Family Daubentoniidae (Aye-aye)
Aye-aye *Daubentonia madagascariensis*

Order Carnivora

Family Eupleridae (Malagasy Carnivores)
Fanaloka *Fossa fossana*
Falanouc *Eupleres goudotii*
Fosa *Cryptoprocta ferox*
Subfamily Galidiinae (Mongooses)
Ring-tailed Mongoose *Galidia elegans*
Narrow-striped Mongoose *Mungotictis decemlineata*
Broad-striped Mongoose *Galidictis fasciata*
Giant Striped Mongoose *Galidictis grandidieri*
Brown-tailed Mongoose *Salanoia concolor*
Introduced Species
Family Viverridae (Civets and their allies)
Subfamily Viverrinae (Civets)
Small Indian Civet *Viverricula indica*

Order Rodentia

Family Muridae (Old World Rats and Mice)
Subfamily Nesomyinae (Malagasy Rodents)
Giant Jumping Rat *Hypogeomys antimena*
Eastern Red Forest Rat *Nesomys rufus*
Lowland Red Forest Rat *Nesomys audeberti*
Western Red Forest Rat *Nesomys lambertoni*
Grandidier's Tuft-tailed Rat *Eliurus grandidieri*
Major's Tuft-tailed Rat *Eliurus majori*
White-tipped Tuft-tailed Rat *Eliurus penicillatus*
Tanala Tuft-tailed Rat *Eliurus tanala*
Ellerman's Tuft-tailed Rat *Eliurus ellermani*
Lesser Tuft-tailed Rat *Eliurus minor*
Webb's Tuft-tailed Rat *Eliurus webbi*
Petter's Tuft-tailed Rat *Eliurus petteri*
Western Tuft-tailed Rat *Eliurus myoxinus*
Tsingy Tuft-tailed Rat *Eliurus antsingy*
Voalavo *Voalavo gymnocaudus*
Voalavoanala *Gymnuromys roberti*
White-tailed Tree Rat *Brachytarsomys albicauda*
Hairy-tailed Tree Rat *Brachytarsomys villosa*
Gregarious Short-tailed Rat *Brachyuromys ramirohitra*
Betsileo Short-tailed Rat *Brachyuromys betsileoensis*
Malagasy Mountain Mouse *Monticolomys koopmani*
Western Big-footed Mouse *Macrotarsomys bastardi*
Long-tailed Big-footed Mouse *Macrotarsomys ingens*
Petter's Big-footed Mouse *Macrotarsomys petteri*
Introduced Species
Subfamily Murinae (Old World Rats and Mice)
Black Rat *Rattus rattus*
Brown Rat *Rattus norvegicus*
House Mouse *Mus musculus*

Order Artiodactyla

Introduced Species
Family Suidae (Old World Pigs)
Bush Pig *Potamochoerus larvatus*

INSECTIVORES
Order Lypotyphla

TENRECS Family Tenrecidae

The Tenrecidae comprise ten genera, divided between four subfamilies: the otter-shrews (Potamogalinae) from West and Central Africa, and the spiny tenrecs (Tenrecinae), large-eared tenrecs (Geogalinae) and furred tenrecs (Oryzorictinae) that are endemic to Madagascar.

Tenrecs are early offshoots from the lineage that gave rise to the Insectivores and are the oldest surviving mammalian lineage on the island. They are derived from a single common ancestor (IN66) and since initial colonisation, have undergone a remarkable and extensive radiation, diversifying to fill numerous small mammal niches occupied elsewhere by several families. Morphological adaptations include parallels with hedgehogs (*Tenrec, Setifer* and *Echinops*), fossorial moles (*Oryzorictes*), desmans and otter-shrews (*Limnogale*), true-shrews (*Microgale*) and even small arboreal mice (*Microgale longicaudata*) (IN71).

Equally remarkable is the diversity within habitats. At some sites up to 17 species of tenrecs occur in the same area of forest, including 11 species of shrew tenrecs (*Microgale* spp.) (IN32). Tenrec diversity varies with altitude, different species having different elevational preferences: mid-elevations (1,200–1,500m) in rainforests support the greatest diversity.

SPINY TENRECS Subfamily Tenrecinae

Spiny tenrecs are all more or less hedgehog-like in appearance, but have considerably shorter tails than true hedgehogs (Erinaceidae). Five species are arranged in four genera, ranging in size from around 80g to 2kg. They are widely distributed through the various forest types of the island. They are primarily terrestrial, although one species – the Lesser Hedgehog Tenrec *Echinops telfairi* does show semi-arboreal characteristics. Except for *Hemicentetes* they are mainly solitary although they do sometimes aestivate in small groups.

COMMON TENREC genus *Tenrec*

This genus, which gave its name to the entire family, contains just a single endemic species. The genus *Centetes* is synonymous with *Tenrec*.

Lowland Streaked Tenrec

Adult Common Tenrec, Andasibe-Mantadia National Park.

COMMON TENREC

Tenrec ecaudatus

MEASUREMENTS

Total length: 285–400mm. Head/body length: 265–390mm. Tail length: 10–15mm. Weight: 1–2kg. Males larger than females (IN60; IN59).

DESCRIPTION & IDENTIFICATION

Adults rotund with shortish limbs, hindlimbs longer than forelimbs. Basic colour grey-brown, with reddish-brown areas. Males appear paler. Face and venter light tan (IN60). Snout long and pointed with conspic-uous long dark vibrissae. The gape is huge (span up to 10cm) and canines long (up to 15mm); a snapping defen-sive bite inflicts deep wounds (IN60). Tail is very short.

Pelage is sparse and is a mixture of coarse hairs and spine-like hairs, the latter more apparent on crown and nape (IN55). Young are much darker, sometimes almost black, with paler cream spines arranged in longitudinal rows, giving a streaked appearance.

The largest tenrec and one of the largest extant insectivores (IN589).

HABITAT & DISTRIBUTION

Endemic. Common in all native forest areas (except arid south-west), from sea level to montane regions (although probably absent from highest peaks) (IN60). Also found in range of altered habitats, agricultural fields, secondary woodland, grassland and urban environments (IN36; IN8; IN12). Prefers environs with brush/undergrowth and free-standing water. Introduced to the Comoros, Seychelles, Reunion and Mascarene Islands (during nineteenth century), as food for plantation workers (IN60).

BEHAVIOUR

Mainly nocturnal, activity peaking at 18:00–21:00 and 01:00–05:00 hours (IN55; IN56). Spends day in burrow under tree roots or in hollow log. Forages in leaf-litter and top soil, vigorously 'rooting' with long, powerful snout to break up soil fragments. Omnivorous, feeding on insects, especially beetle larvae and termites (IN1; IN71), also other invertebrates, fruits and even small vertebrates (IN55). Prey detected by combination of smell, sound and touch, the last from long, sensitive vibrissae that are swept from side to side (IN60). Has better eyesight than other tenrecs but relies on well-developed tactile and olfactory

Common Tenrec

Female Common Tenrec with young brood.

senses. When alarmed erects a mane on upper back (longer, coarser hair than the rest of the body); simultaneously may emit a low hissing sound in conjunction with squeaks and squeals.

Aestivates during austral winter (May to October) due to unfavourable climate and decreased food availability (IN57); in rainforest areas period of torpor is reduced. Aestivation takes place in long (1–2m) narrow burrow, plugged with soil (IN60). Breathing rate drops to 30 breaths per minute, body temperature fluctuates with ambient, known to fall to 11°C. Sleep is continuous and animal is reliant on fat reserves (IN58).

Solitary for most of year: associations between sexes are brief and occur during the austral spring (October–November). Births occur in wet season (December–January) when invertebrate food base is at peak (IN59). Gestation period is 56 to 64 days (IN8).

Reproduction is remarkable and prolific. Maximum litter size is 32; in captivity 31 young have been reared (IN9). Wild litters are smaller (IN8; IN56; IN61). Also evidence that litter size varies with age and habitat: in the west 25 is average, in the east it drops to 20 (IN60).

Mothers feed young from 17 pairs of nipples (most in any mammal) (IN34). Young are altricial and do not open their eyes until nine to 14 days. Emerge from nest at 18–20 days and forage in a group with the mother (IN60).

The demand for milk is high; females draw on all their fat reserves during lactation (IN60). Mothers and young regularly extend foraging beyond darkness, when striped coloration of young increases camouflage and reduces predation. Adult females with young are darker than males for same reason. Infant mortality is still high, rarely do more than ten offspring survive.

At 35 days young begin foraging independently, initially in small groups; later they become solitary (IN60). Moult to adult coloration begins around 36 days and there is a shift to nocturnal activity. The juvenile streaks disappear by 60 days; fully grown by three to four months.

Predators include the Fosa *Cryptoprocta ferox* (IN39) and large boas (*Sanzinia* and *Acrantophis*). Hunted extensively for food (IN60).

WHERE TO SEE
Potentially visible in most reserves in west or east, during warmer, wetter months (November to April), particularly Andasibe-Mantadia, Montagne d'Ambre and Ankarafantsika (Ampijoroa) National Parks.

GREATER HEDGEHOG TENREC

Setifer setosus

MEASUREMENTS

Total length: 160–225mm. Head/body length: 105–210mm. Tail length: 15mm. Weight: 175–300g, average 280g. (IN8; IN3; IN34)

DESCRIPTION & IDENTIFICATION

Body rounded with short legs. Completely covered in stiff non-detachable spines, except face and underparts, that are covered in sparse hair. Appears grey-brown in colour. Spines are creamy-white, dark grey-brown towards tip, with a white point. Darker melanistic forms have been reported. Snout moderately long and pointed with many vibrissae (IN8).

Appearance is of a small long-bodied hedgehog.

HABITAT & DISTRIBUTION

Found throughout the eastern rainforests, and recorded at numerous locations, from Montagne d'Ambre in the north to Andohahela in the south. Prefers lower elevations (below 900m) (IN70: IN27, IN31; IN17; IN19). Also found in deciduous forests of the west (IN11) and spiny forest in south-west (IN61). More common in rainforest regions. Colonised some urban areas, including Antananarivo, occasionally encountered around rubbish (IN8).

BEHAVIOUR

Nocturnal and omnivorous, diet includes insects, grubs, other invertebrates and fruit (IN71). Will also scavenge (IN8). Foraging occurs at ground level, but known to climb. Anti-predator response is to curl into

Greater Hedgehog Tenrec

Greater Hedgehog Tenrec.

tight ball with spines outermost (IN9).

Excavates short tunnels underneath logs or tree roots ending in leaf-lined nest chamber where it sleeps curled with head tucked under body. There is a latrine site close to burrow entrance. Active throughout the year, but individuals in more seasonal areas (west and higher elevations in east) do reduce levels of activity and become torpid for short periods (IN65).

Probably solitary, with temporary male/female associations occurring during the breeding season: communicates through a series of grunts, squeaks and chirps. Mating occurs between late September and mid-October (IN8). Nest-building activity increases the week prior to birth. Litters are one to four (average three) (IN6). Gestation varies with ambient conditions from 51 to 69 days; higher temperatures result in a shorter gestation (IN6; IN52). Young closely tended for first two weeks; eyes begin to open at nine days and are fully open at 14 days. Then begin to take solid food and accompany mother outside burrow on short foraging excursions.

Predated by large snakes e.g. *Sanzinia* and *Acrantophis* and the Fosa *Cryptoprocta ferox* (IN39).

WHERE TO SEE
May be seen on night walks in many of the popular reserves e.g. Montagne d'Ambre, Andasibe-Mantadia, Ranomafana and Ankarafantsika (Ampijoroa) National Parks, Nosy Mangabe, Ankarana and Kirindy Forest.

LESSER HEDGEHOG TENREC genus *Echinops*

A monotypic genus, morphologically similar to *Setifer* (IN13). Internally there are dental differences, *Echinops* has the most reduced dentition within the Tenrecidae (IN8).

Lesser Hedgehog Tenrecs are capable climbers. Ifaty Spiny Forest.

LESSER HEDGEHOG TENREC

Echinops telfairi

MEASUREMENTS
Total length: 140–180mm. Head/body length: 130–170mm. Tail length: around 10mm. Weight: 110–230g, average 140g. (IN8; IN34)

DESCRIPTION & IDENTIFICATION
Coloration variable, ranging from very pale grey to deep slate-grey. Face and underparts paler, sometimes almost white. Similar to *Setifer*, but smaller, with less pointed snout.

HABITAT & DISTRIBUTION
Confined to dry deciduous forests of west and xerophytic spiny forest and gallery forest in south-west (IN59). Also records from Andohahela region in south-east (IN31).

BEHAVIOUR
Nocturnal and semi-arboreal (IN59); surprisingly agile and capable of climbing along thin branches, when short tail is used as a brace. Forages alone in dense shrubbery, both on ground and in branches. Feeds on insects and fruits (IN8).

During very dry seasons, when food is scarce, may become torpid for three to five months (May to September) (IN14; IN64). Aestivates in hollow log or tree hole, several metres above the ground; nest is lined with grasses and leaves that are carried in the mouth and arranged to form a neat

Lesser Hedgehog Tenrec

cup. Sleeps in a tightly curled ball, alone or in twos or threes. Anti-predator response is to roll into a tight ball and emit hisses and grind its teeth (IN9).

Males may be very aggressive towards one another, but males and females are more tolerant when together. Mating begins in October, shortly after emergence from torpor (IN68). Females build the natal nest a week before birth and continue to add to nest even after the young have been born (IN8). Gestation period is 60 to 68 days; litter size is one to ten, seven being average. Young weigh less than 10g at birth and are naked. They open their eyes between seven and nine days and at ten days will follow mother to nest entrance. Female will retrieve offspring that fall from nest. Young take solid food from 14 days, are weaned at 18 days and become

Lesser Hedgehog Tenrec, Anjampolo.

independent in just over a month. Sexual maturity is reached after the first period of aestivation (IN14).

WHERE TO SEE
Berenty Private Reserve,

Anjhampolo Spiny Forest, Parcels 2 and 3 of Andohahela National Park and the spiny forests around Ifaty, north of Toliara, are the best places to see this species.

STREAKED TENRECS genus *Hemicentetes*

A genus containing two small, distinctive tenrecs broadly similar in appearance. They are recognisable by their charac-teristic coloration and markings: blackish-brown with either yellowish or creamy-white longitudinal stripes.

If threatened, they produce an audible rattling sound from a specialised patch of quills on the middle of the back behind the neck. Called the stridulating organ, this is capable of producing sounds varying widely in frequency.

Although day-time activity does sometimes occur, these species are principally nocturnal. Predated by the Fosa *Cryptoprocta ferox* (IN30; IN39) and possibly smaller carnivores like the Fanaloka *Fossa fossana* and Ring-tailed Mongoose *Galidia elegans* and large snakes such as *Sanzinia* and *Acrantophis*.

LOWLAND STREAKED TENREC

Hemicentetes semispinosus

MEASUREMENTS
Total length: 130–190mm. Head/body length: 130–190mm. Tail length: none. Weight: 90–220g, average 130g. (IN72, IN81; IN34)

DESCRIPTION & IDENTIFICATION
A medium-small, fairly slender tenrec

with pronounced pointed snout. Blackish-brown, with longitudinal yellowish stripes and yellowish crown. A narrowing yellowish band runs from crown down forehead and nose to near the tip of snout. Quills are barbed and detachable and prominent around the crown (nuchal crest). Underparts are chestnut-brown. Similar in appearance to juvenile Common Tenrecs *Tenrec ecaudatus*, but more spiny.

HABITAT & DISTRIBUTION
Endemic. Restricted to lowland and

mid-altitude rainforests of eastern region. Recorded to elevations of 1,550m (IN33). Also survives on periphery and outside native forests and recorded in agricultural land and gardens (IN8).

BEHAVIOUR
The resemblance to immature Common Tenrecs is not coincidental, as *H. semispinosus* is partially active during daylight hours, when its color-ation and pattern provides a degree of crypsis (IN81). Forages amongst leaf-litter, actively seeking earthworms

Lowland Streaked Tenrec, Maroantsetra.

Lowland
Streaked Tenrec

(IN81); litter size varies between two and eleven in the wild (average six). Young weigh around 8g at birth (IN87) and develop with speed, reaching sexual maturity after 35 to 40 days. They are able to reproduce in the same season as their birth. Family groups may produce several litters per season and number more than 20 individuals from three related generations. Such multi-generational

family groups form the most complex social systems of any insectivore (IN8).

They forage together in subgroups or singly. When together, they communicate by vibrating quills in the stridulating organ that produces low-frequency ultrasonic sounds (similar to dry grass being rubbed together) (IN35; IN92). This is important in keeping mother and offspring in contact in the undergrowth.

and other soft-bodied invertebrates: this more specialised diet correlates with a substantially reduced dentition.

Excavates a burrow, often near stream or body of water, up to 150cm in length. This descends to a depth of 15cm and contains a nest chamber. The entrance is plugged with leaves and there is a latrine site close by (IN8).

Young born during wet season after gestation of 55 to 63 days

Lowland Streaked Tenrec with young.

During winter months (May–October) animals are able to reduce body temperature to within 2°C of ambient to conserve energy, yet remain active (IN85). Also may become torpid if prevailing conditions (temperature and food supply) are unsuitable. If temperatures remain higher and conditions are favourable they are able to breed year round (IN85). Therefore, there is considerable variation in this behaviour across this species' north–south range.

They have an effective deterrent when threatened, erecting a crest of spines (nuchal crest) and bucking their heads violently, attempting to embed detachable barbed quills into the snout of a would-be predator (IN81).

WHERE TO SEE
More readily seen during warmer wetter months (November to April). Often encountered in Ranomafana and Andasibe-Mantadia National Parks. Also common in gardens around Maroantsetra in the north-east.

HIGHLAND STREAKED TENREC
Hemicentetes nigriceps

MEASUREMENTS
Total length: 120–160mm. Head/body length: 120–160mm. Tail length: none. Weight: 70–160g, average 100g. (IN72; IN81; IN34)

DESCRIPTION & IDENTIFICATION
Very similar in size, shape and coloration to *H. semispinosus*, but less spiny and its streaks are more whitish than yellowish. No median stripe on crown. Underparts creamy-white, forehead and crown black. Under fur more developed than in

Highland Streaked Tenrec, Andringitra National Park.

H. semispinosus, giving a more woolly appearance (IN81).

HABITAT & DISTRIBUTION
Restricted to montane and schlerophyllous forests and adjacent habitats at higher altitudes on eastern escarpment and parts of central plateau. Generally, *H. semispinosus* and *H. nigriceps* do not occur sympatrically. Where ranges

Highland Streaked Tenrec

do overlap, e.g. the Andringitra and Ivohibe Massifs, they occur at different elevations (IN81). There are records of both species living side by side in Tsinjoarivo Forest (Mahatsinjo) at 1,550m (IN33).

BEHAVIOUR
Strictly nocturnal with peak activity three or four hours after darkness (IN81). Aestivation more marked than congener, occurs between May and October (IN85). Torpor is stimulated by reductions in ambient temperature, day length and food supply, but also influenced by endogenous rhythms.

Females become sexually mature after 35 to 40 days. Litter size is two to eight (IN81; IN34). Other aspects of behaviour and ecology are similar to Lowland Streaked Tenrec.

WHERE TO SEE
Common in the Andringitra Massif, south-west of Fianarantsoa. Night walks around Antanifotsy and Camp Belambo can be very productive.

LARGE-EARED TENRECS Subfamily Geogalinae

A recently elevated subfamily containing a single genus.

LARGE-EARED TENREC genus *Geogale*

Currently regarded as monotypic, however, a second species awaits description. *Geogale* may have been amongst the first tenrecs to evolve. In common with other tenrecs, demonstrates a number of characteristics probably typical of the earliest eutherian mammals (IN80).

LARGE-EARED TENREC

Geogale aurita

MEASUREMENTS

Total length: 90–107mm. Head/body length: 61–76mm. Tail length: 34–41mm. Weight: 5–8.5g, average 7g. (IN72, IN74; IN31; IN34)

DESCRIPTION & IDENTIFICATION

Small with large ears, a triangular head and a pointed snout. Pelage soft and dense. Upperparts pale grey, underparts creamy-white, sometimes with orange flecks on flanks. Tail scaly and covered in fine hairs. Ears large, rounded and clearly visible (IN74).

One of the smallest tenrecs; general appearance is intermediate between that of a shrew and a field mouse.

HABITAT & DISTRIBUTION

Widely distributed in deciduous forests of north-west and west and spiny forests of south and south-west, together with gallery forests within this region (IN63; IN16). Eastern limits appear to be spiny forests (Parcel 2) of Andohahela National Park in the extreme south-east (IN31).

BEHAVIOUR

Strictly nocturnal and able to enter daily torpor at all times of the year, but more frequently during dry season (austral winter). Often sleep inside fallen logs (IN72; IN80).

Large-eared Tenrec.

Large-eared Tenrec

with a preference for ants and termites (IN87).

Mating is between late September and March. Gestation ranges from 54 to 69 days, in some instances females become temporarily torpid during pregnancy and embryonic development is arrested (IN74; IN87). Births occur between November and February. Litter size is one to five (average three or four). Young are highly altricial, weigh less than 1g and are born naked with eyes closed. Eyes open between 21 and 33 days. Weaning and independence are after around 35 days (IN74).

During foraging the large ears are extended and help detect prey. A variety of invertebrates are eaten,

This species is unique within the Tenrecidae: females are able to conceive a second litter while still suckling their first (called post-partum oestrous) (IN74). They can produce up to ten offspring per year (average six to seven). This strategy allows reproductive output to be maximised when favourable breeding conditions prevail (IN74).

Predated by Barn Owls *Tyto alba* and Madagascar Long-eared Owls *Asio madagascariensis* (IN24; IN25) and also by snakes and small carnivores (IN80).

WHERE TO SEE
Best looked for at Beza Mahafaly Special Reserve, where it appears to be particularly abundant, Kirindy Forest and Zombitse National Park.

FURRED TENRECS Subfamily Oryzorictinae

A subfamily comprising three highly diversified endemic genera, some of which have radiated spectacularly, most notably the shrew tenrecs (genus *Microgale*). A number of species provide good examples of convergent evolution as they demonstrate similar morphological and ecological traits to those found in other insectivore groups. Different Oryzorictinae species exploit niches filled elsewhere by shrews (*Microgale*), moles (*Oryzorictes*) and desmans (*Limnogale*).

AQUATIC TENREC genus *Limnogale*

A genus containing a single, highly specialised species, whose morphology, ecology and behaviour relates to a semi-aquatic lifestyle. It is the only Malagasy mammal exploiting such a niche and demonstrates close parallels to the otter-shrews (Potamogalinae) of West and Central Africa and the desmans (Talpidae) of Europe.

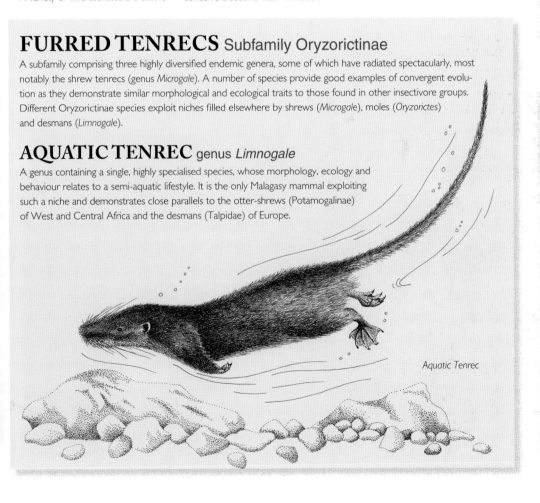

Aquatic Tenrec

AQUATIC TENREC

Limnogale mergulus

Other name: Web-footed Tenrec

MEASUREMENTS

Total length: 250–325mm. Head/body length: 121–170mm. Tail length: 128–161mm. Weight: 60–107g, average 80g. (IN77; IN4; IN34)

DESCRIPTION & IDENTIFICATION

Largest Oryzorictinae species (IN4). Pelage is dense and soft. Head and upperparts greyish-brown with subtle reddish and blackish guard hairs. Underparts paler yellowish-grey. Eyes and ears small and all but hidden beneath dense fur. Muzzle appears swollen with long, conspicuous vibrissae. Forefeet are fringed and toes webbed to base of claws. Tail covered in dense hairs, which form a distinct keel on the underside (IN4). All features are adaptations to aquatic mode of life.

HABITAT & DISTRIBUTION

Associated with faster flowing streams of the eastern central highlands. Range limits are poorly understood. Confirmed from just ten sites, from Sihanaka Forest in north (south of Lac Alaotra) to region of upper Iantara River to east of Andringitra Massif in south, at altitudes between 600m and 2,000m (IN5). Most of these rivers flow east to the Indian Ocean; however, one site on the eastern edge of the central highlands (headwaters of Mania River) is on western side of the island divide (IN4). In the Ranomafana area, found in streams no longer bordered by native forest (IN5).

BEHAVIOUR

Nocturnal and carnivorous. Day is spent in burrows, excavated in a bank close to the water's edge. Burrows around 10cm in diameter and lined with grass (IN53). Emerges shortly after sunset, but activity period appears to be variable. On occasion, remains active all night, but at other

probable range

Aquatic Tenrec

times may return to burrow for prolonged rest periods lasting up to four hours. Always returns to burrows 1–1.5 hours before sunrise (IN5).

During activity, appears to remain within same stream channel and spends majority of time in water. Nightly distance travelled within stream varies widely from day to day and between individuals but can be up to 1,550m. Tenrecs inhabiting

Aquatic Tenrec.

narrow streams appear to travel longer distances than those living in broader streams (IN5).

Unusual amongst tenrecs in using specific latrine sites; repeatedly defecates on favoured prominent boulders in streams or around fallen trees. Piles of faeces at latrines can become visible and are an obvious sign of *Limnogale* activity. Not known if latrines demarcate territorial boundaries or whether they are communal (IN4).

In Ranomafana area, feeds heavily on aquatic insect larvae and to a lesser extent crayfish (IN5). In other areas, frogs and freshwater shrimps are important dietary components (IN53 IN8). When swimming, uses hindfeet for propulsion and tail as a rudder. Sweeping motions of head help cover large areas, and prey is located with the sensitive vibrissae (IN5). Prey is caught in mouth and brought to water's edge, held in forefeet and consumed (IN53). Foraging bouts are successive short-duration dives to the stream bed, lasting no longer than 15 seconds (IN4).

Young are born between December and January; with a probable average litter size of three (IN8).

Does not appear to become dormant: studies around Ranomafana National Park found active animals in October, November, May, July and August (IN77; IN5).

WHERE TO SEE
Apparently rare and secretive and very difficult to see. Ranomafana National Park offers a possibility, although considerable effort and luck is required. Has been seen in the stream by village of Ambatolahy, one kilometre from the park entrance.

The most conspicuous feature of *Limnogale* presence is prominent latrine sites. When walking along watercourses in eastern montane rainforest areas always keep an eye out for faeces on boulders in streams.

MOLE TENRECS OR RICE TENRECS genus *Oryzorictes*

A specialised and distinctive genus containing two species that outwardly resemble moles (Talpidae). The name, *Oryzorictes*, is derived from Greek and means 'rice burrower'. Formerly, three species were recognised, but *O. talpoides* is now regarded as synonymous with *O. hova*.

Mole Tenrecs are adapted to a fossorial lifestyle; they have extremely strong forelimbs and broad spade-like forefeet as well as reduced eyes and ears, all clear adaptations for burrowing. They are good examples of convergent evolution with golden moles (Chrysochloridae) and true moles (Talpidae) (IN15).

Characteristically rotund, they are easily distinguished from other furred tenrecs by their stockiness, robust limbs, broad feet, long claws, broad naked snout, small ears and eyes. The pelage is very soft, dense and velvety but coloration is highly variable, even within species (IN15).

They are principally associated with humid forests and marshy areas in the east and are also found in areas converted to rice paddies (IN15). They forage underground or in leaf-litter and humus. Their diet probably consists of insects and other invertebrates, particularly worms. They appear to be mainly nocturnal but may be active at all times of the day in their extensive burrow systems.

Known predators include the Madagascar Red Owl (IN18) and some snakes, for example, the fossorial colubrid *Pseudoxyrhopus* (IN31).

Because of their lifestyle they are rarely encountered. Most known specimens have been caught in forest floor pitfall traps at night and often after heavy rain when they appear more active (IN15).

HOVA MOLE TENREC
Oryzorictes hova

MEASUREMENTS
Total length: 137–186mm. Head/body length: 99–124mm. Tail length: 38–62mm. Weight: 28–40g, average 34g. (IN15; IN34)

DESCRIPTION & IDENTIFICATION
The fur is soft, dense and velvety and highly variable in colour. Upperparts dark grey-brown and blackish brown to light-tan brown, underparts dark brown to buffy-white. On Nosy Mangabe albino individuals are known (IN15). Tail naked and short (50% head/body length). Forefeet have five digits. *O. talpoides* is no longer valid and is synonymous with *O. hova*.

HABITAT & DISTRIBUTION
Inhabits a variety of environs from lowland rainforest to sclerophyllous forest approaching the tree line, from sea level to around 2,000m. Also recorded at high densities in rice paddies (IN15).

Range extends over the eastern humid forest region, from Andohahela in south to Masoala in north, including the island of Nosy Mangabe and into the Sambirano region (Manongarivo) (IN78; IN22; IN15). Also recorded in forest fragments in central highlands

Hova Mole Tenrec

(Réserve Spéciale d'Ambohitantely) (IN20).

BEHAVIOUR

Observed foraging at ground level using muzzle to probe beneath leaf-

Hova
Mole Tenrec

litter and humus (IN8). In captivity observed dragging earthworms underneath soil surface before consumption (IN76).

Widely recognised by villagers tilling rice paddies, when disturbed from burrows. Burrow networks thought to damage crops by uprooting seedlings (IN15).

Based on embryo counts the maximum litter size is four (IN15).

FOUR-TOED MOLE TENREC
Oryzorictes tetradactylus

MEASUREMENTS

Total length: 148–172mm. Head/body length: 105–115mm. Tail length: 43–57mm. Weight: 36g*. (IN15). *Based on single specimen

DESCRIPTION & IDENTIFICATION

Mainly dark brown, with mottled areas of lighter brown on upperparts. Has four digits on forelimbs and tail is shorter than *O. hova* (IN15).

probable range
• confirmed locality

Four-toed
Mole Tenrec

HABITAT & DISTRIBUTION

Known from few locations; appears limited to high mountain areas on eastern edge of central highlands. Most are outside forest and above tree line, e.g. ericoid scrub at 2,050m in Andringitra and in marshy areas at 2,450m near the foot of Pic Boby (IN21).

BEHAVIOUR

Unknown.

Four-toed Mole Tenrec. Strong fore-limbs, broad front feet and reduced eyes and ears are clear indications of a burrowing lifestyle. Often associated with wet and marshy areas and are even found around rice paddies.

SHREW TENRECS genus *Microgale*

This genus contains more species than any other in the family Tenrecidae. The taxonomy has been reviewed and refined several times (IN49; IN79; IN67) and no fewer than seven new species have been described recently (IN42; IN43; IN44; IN47; IN48; IN17; IN46; IN23). Currently 20 species are recognised, varying from the tiny insectivorous Pygmy Shrew Tenrec *M. parvula* (less than 3g) to the relatively large carnivorous Talazac's Shrew Tenrec *M. talazaci* (nearly 40g). This inventory remains incomplete and further new species await description and discovery, particularly from western and southern regions that have been neglected in small mammal surveys to date.

Morphological variation within *Microgale* is remarkable: extreme examples are the partially arboreal species *M. longicaudata* and *M. principula*, which have exceptionally long prehensile tails to help grip twigs and branches (IN34).

These are the most problematic Malagasy mammals to identify. Size, relative tail length and pelage colour are the only external characters which are of use, and considerable overlap exists between species. Accurate identification is possible only after detailed morphological examination.

GENERAL DESCRIPTION & IDENTIFICATION Pelage soft and velvety. Head and upperparts buffy to olive-brown, dark russet-brown or slate grey-black. Ears prominent and project well above the fur. Generally, tail length is longer than the head/body length, except for *M. brevicaudata* that has a relatively short tail, and *M. longicaudata* and *M. principula* that have exceptionally long tails.

Forelimbs not well developed, all limbs have five digits. All are very shrew-like in appearance and occupy similar habitats and niches to true shrews (Soricidae).

HABITAT & DISTRIBUTION Prefer primary forests and generally associated with dense vegetation, some species have been found in disturbed, non-forested and agricultural areas and marshes (IN45). Species richness is greatest within the eastern humid forests, where the majority of species (16) occur exclusively. Two species, *M. brevicaudata* and *M. majori*, have been recorded in both eastern regions and drier western regions and two further species, *M. nasoloi* and *M. jenkinsae*, appear exclusive to dry regions in the south-west.

Some species – *M. parvula, M. longicaudata* and *M. fotsifotsy* – occur the length of the eastern rainforest belt from Montagne d'Ambre in the north to Andohahela in the south (IN70; IN48; IN31), and many other species cover the majority of this range from Marojejy and Anjanaharibe-Sud in the north to Andohahela in the south (IN45).

Shrew tenrecs occur in a variety of habitats – lowland and mid-altitude rainforest, high-altitude mossy schlerophyllous forest and montane ericoid scrub – that correspond to a very wide elevational range, from sea level to over 2,450m (IN45).

Microgale diversity is considerable. This new species from Marojejy awaits formal description.

Some species occur through a broad elevational range, e.g. *M. parvula, M. talazaci* and *M. cowani* all occur from lowland forests to high mountain habitats (IN45). Other species are more specialized, e.g. *M. monticola* prefers montane habitats between 1,550m and 1,950m (IN17; IN19). Throughout the eastern rainforests, middle elevations between 1,200m and 1,500m support the greatest diversity of *Microgale* species (IN78; IN45) and this may correspond to maximum invertebrate diversity at similar altitudes (IN26; IN27).

In humid forest areas, nine or more shrew tenrecs may occur together and these generally include *M. cowani, M. gymnorhyncha, M. longicaudata, M. parvula* and *M. soricoides* (IN45); in the forests of Tsinjoarivo, eleven species have been recorded in sympatry (IN32). Each species occupies a slightly different niche, but how such fine ecological separation is achieved is not fully understood.

Where communities are very diverse, the medium-sized species, like *M. cowani, M. drouhardi* and *M. taiva*, are the most common. Large species like *M. dobsoni* and *M. talazaci* appear relatively rare (IN45).

BEHAVIOUR Assumed to be primarily solitary and both diurnal and nocturnal (i.e. cathemeral). Terrestrial activity is common, foraging occurs amongst leaf-litter, root tangles and fallen branches, but most species are also scansorial and climb lianas and low under bush (IN45).

Births coincide with the onset of the rainy season (November–December), so that juveniles can take advantage of the seasonal increase in invertebrate populations (IN46).

DIET Varied and includes invertebrates, especially insects and their larvae (crickets and grasshoppers, ants and termites and beetles, in particular) (IN71), but also small vertebrates such as frogs and reptiles for the larger carnivorous species like *M. talazaci, M. soricoides* and *M. dobsoni.*

WHERE TO SEE May be found in any humid forest area. However, because of their small size and secretive lifestyle, they are rarely observed.

LESSER LONG-TAILED SHREW TENREC

Microgale longicaudata

MEASUREMENTS

Total length: 182–225mm. Head/body length: 62–74mm. Tail length: 115–151mm. Weight: 5.6–9.5g. (IN47; IN17; IN19; IN31)

DESCRIPTION & IDENTIFICATION

Dorsal pelage dark brown with reddish-brown wash, underparts grey with reddish-buff wash. Tail grey-brown above, reddish-buff underneath and naked at tip. Hindlimbs are proportionally long (IN45).

Extreme body proportions make this the most easily recognisable *Microgale* (together with *M. principula*). Actual body size is small, but tail is extremely long (more than twice the head/body length). Tail tip is prehensile indicating an arboreal lifestyle.

HABITAT & DISTRIBUTION

Occurs in lowland, mid-altitude and high altitude rainforest from Montagne d'Ambre in the north to Andohahela in the south (IN70; IN47; IN17; IN19; IN31). Appears equally common on ridge tops, slopes or valley bottoms and this may be a reflection of its arboreal lifestyle.

Has an extreme altitudinal

Lesser Long-tailed Shrew Tenrec

tolerances, e.g. at Montagne d'Ambre occurs between 650m and 1,350m, in Anjanaharibe-Sud between 1,260m and 1,950m, in Marojejy at 1,225m, in Andringitra recorded from 720m to 1,990m, while in Andohahela it extends from 440m to 1,875m (IN34). It is more common at higher elevations.

There are records from forests in dry western regions (IN2; IN67). Some of these may correspond to new taxa currently awaiting description.

BEHAVIOUR

Several morphological features (prehensile tail, elongate limbs and digits) indicate this species is largely arboreal. It actively climbs and forages in vegetation and is able to jump amongst branches (IN45).

Lesser Long-tailed Shrew Tenrec. The tail is prehensile.

GREATER LONG-TAILED SHREW TENREC

Microgale principula

MEASUREMENTS

Total length: 216–251mm. Head/body length: 70–80mm. Tail length: 146–171mm. Weight: 8.5–12.5g. (IN17; IN19; IN31)

DESCRIPTION & IDENTIFICATION

Medium-sized with tail up to twice head/body length. Upperparts reddish-brown, underparts grey with buff wash. The distal portion of tail is naked. Fifth digit on hindfoot is elongate.

HABITAT & DISTRIBUTION

Prefers lowland and mid-altitude rainforest. Recorded from sites stretching the length of the eastern rainforest belt, from Marojejy and Anjanaharibe-Sud in the north, to Andohahela in the south (IN17; IN19; IN31).

At several localities, e.g. Marojejy, Anjanaharibe-Sud and Andohahela, occurs sympatrically with *M. longi-caudata*. While habitat overlap does occur at middle elevations, *M. princi-pula* prefers lower altitudes, while *M. longicaudata* prefers upper elevations (IN17; IN19; IN31).

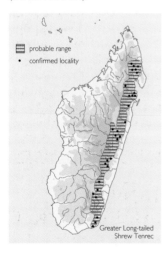

probable range
confirmed locality

Greater Long-tailed Shrew Tenrec

BEHAVIOUR

Several morphological features, including long prehensile tail and elongate hind digit, indicate a partially arboreal way of life. It is an agile climber and forages in vegetation above ground level. Tail is used as a counter-balance and can coil around twigs. Also able to jump short distances between branches (IN45).

MAJOR'S LONG-TAILED SHREW TENREC
Microgale majori

MEASUREMENTS

No figures available.

DESCRIPTION & IDENTIFICATION

Originally described in 1918 (IN91), later thought synonymous with *M. longicaudata* (IN54; IN49). Recent research confirms *M. majori* a good species (IN67). Appearance is a smaller version of *M. longicaudata*.

probable range
confirmed locality

Major's Long-tailed Shrew Tenrec

HABITAT & DISTRIBUTION

Museum specimens and field studies suggest this is most widespread *Microgale*, covering most of central eastern and south-eastern rainforest areas, plus sites in far north, central west and south-west at elevations between 785m and 2000m (IN67; IN93).

BEHAVIOUR

Possibly semi-arboreal or scansorial. Otherwise behaviour unknown.

TALAZAC'S SHREW TENREC
Microgale talazaci

MEASUREMENTS

Total length: 225–288mm. Head/body length: 105–138mm. Tail length: 120–150mm. Weight: 31.5–47g, average 36g. (IN45; IN34)

DESCRIPTION & IDENTIFICATION

The largest *Microgale*, with tail slightly longer than head/body length. Head large and robust. Dorsal pelage mid-brown, venter grey with reddish-buff wash (IN17; IN19). Similar to *M. dobsoni*, but on average larger, although size overlap does occur. *M. talazaci* is darker brown than *M. dobsoni* and lacks rufous tinges.

HABITAT & DISTRIBUTION

One of the most widely distributed *Microgale*. Recorded throughout the eastern rainforest region from Vondrozo in the south to Montagne d'Ambre in the north, including humid forests of the Sambirano (IN49; IN17; IN27). Prefers primary forests and has a broad altitudinal tolerance: recorded at elevations from 100 to over 2,000m (IN34). In areas of sympatry with *M. dobsoni*, it appears to favour higher altitudes.

probable range

Talazac's Shrew Tenrec

BEHAVIOUR

Carnivorous, with small vertebrates like frogs part of the diet, as well as insects (IN87; IN89). Forages on ground and in lower undergrowth (IN73), and it may dig burrow systems. Shows no seasonal inactivity and does not lay down fat reserves, a reflection of its more stable rainforest habitat. Males and females may be together throughout the year and breed in the austral spring/summer. Gestation is 58 to 63 days; litter size varies from one to three (average two) (IN87).

THOMAS'S SHREW TENREC

Microgale thomasi

MEASUREMENTS

Total length: 149–176mm. Head/body length: 86–96mm. Tail length: 63–80mm. Weight: 19.5–25g, average 22g. (IN31; IN34)

DESCRIPTION & IDENTIFICATION

Moderately large with tail shorter than head/body length and moderately prominent ears. Upperparts speckled dark rufous brown, underparts paler. Tail is bicoloured and covered in dense hair (IN31). *M.*

Thomas's
Shrew Tenrec

thomasi is similar to Cowan's Shrew Tenrec, but slightly larger in size.

HABITAT & DISTRIBUTION

Has a restricted range and is rather rare. Known only from localities in the southern part of eastern rainforests, from the Andasibe area south to Andohahela (IN49; IN31) at altitudes up to 2,000m. In Andohahela it is relatively common at low and middle elevations (440–1,200m) (IN31).

BEHAVIOUR

Known to forage on the ground. The maximum litter size is two (IN34).

GRACILE SHREW TENREC

Microgale gracilis

MEASUREMENTS

Total length: 160–198mm. Head/body length: 85–105mm. Tail length: 75–93mm. Weight: 19.5–25g. (IN47; IN19; IN31)

DESCRIPTION & IDENTIFICATION

This is a largish *Microgale* species, with a tail shorter than the head/body length. The head is elongate and gracile and the muzzle is very long. The eyes and ears are very small and partially obscured by the pelage. The fur is soft and velvety and the upperparts are dark brown with buff speckles, while the underparts are dark grey with a buff wash. The tail is bicoloured, dark brown dorsally and light brown ventrally (IN47; IN31; IN19). Juveniles appear to be less speckled than adults, particularly around the rump. The dentition is much reduced; both incisors and canines are very slender.

HABITAT & DISTRIBUTION

This is a poorly known species that has been captured at a small number of localities across the extent of

probable range
confirmed locality

Gracile
Shrew Tenrec

the eastern rainforests. The type of locality is the Ambohinitombo Forest, 40km south-east of Ambositra, and specimens have also been caught in Andohahela (IN31), the Andringitra Massif (IN47), Ranomafana (IN63), the Ankaratra Massif (IN28) and the Marojejy Massif (IN19). From these localities *M. gracilis* has an elevational range between 1,210m and 2,100m, and appears more common at higher altitudes (IN47).

BEHAVIOUR

A number of morphological features, for example, elongate muzzle, reduced eyes and ears and broadened feet with large claws, suggest this species' habits are semi-fossorial.

DOBSON'S SHREW TENREC

Microgale dobsoni

MEASUREMENTS

Total length: 195–250mm. Head/body length: 95–130mm. Tail length: 102–128mm. Weight: 20.5–39g, average 25g. (IN47; IN17; IN19; IN31; IN34)

DESCRIPTION & IDENTIFICATION

Large, tail roughly equal or slightly

longer than head/body length. Pelage quite long, upperparts brown, underparts grey with buff wash. Tail grey, buff below (IN19).

HABITAT & DISTRIBUTION
Widespread. Recorded in eastern rainforests and eastern central highlands including disturbed and deforested areas (IN45), from Marojejy and Anjanaharibe-Sud in north (IN17; IN19) to Andohahela in south (IN31). Has wide elevational tolerance: in Andohahela, between 440m and 1,875m (IN31); in Andringitra, above tree line up to 2,050m (IN19). Where sympatric with close relative *M. talazaci*, e.g. Anjanaharibe-Sud and Marojejy in north-east, *M. dobsoni* prefers slightly lower elevations, but at times both species have overlapping home ranges (IN17; IN19). *M. dobsoni* also recorded from non-forested areas and agricultural zones in the central highlands.

BEHAVIOUR
Forages on ground amongst leaf-litter, detecting prey by sound. Some evidence for a basic echolocation

probable range

Dobson's
Shrew Tenrec

system to help foraging in dark undergrowth (IN8). Also trapped on branches over 1m above the ground, suggesting it is also scansorial (IN45). Solitary and shows some territorial behaviour – individuals normally spread out, evenly distributed and highly antagonistic towards one another. Males and females may establish stable relationship during breeding season, in austral spring/summer. Gestation 58–64 days, litter

size one to six (IN87; IN34).

Only *Microgale* known to accumulate fat reserves in body and tail prior to austral winter: body weight may increase to over 80g (IN8). Does not enter full torpor in winter, but does become inactive, constructing nest and sleeping, eating less and lowering body temperature (IN89): an adaptation to higher elevations with marked seasonal climatic variation.

COWAN'S SHREW TENREC
Microgale cowani

MEASUREMENTS
Total length: 130–170mm. Head/body length: 66–95mm. Tail length: 60–75mm. Weight: 10.5–16.5g. (IN47; IN17; IN19; IN31)

DESCRIPTION & IDENTIFICATION
Medium-sized, with moderately short tail – shorter than or equal to head/body length. Dorsal pelage dark brown to rufous-brown with

Dobson's Shrew Tenrec.

Cowan's Shrew Tenrec.

some paler russet flecking that is reduced on rump. Upperparts appear speckled brown. May be faint darker dorsal stripe. Underparts grey with reddish-brown wash. Tail bicoloured: dark brown dorsally, reddish-buff ventrally (IN47).

HABITAT & DISTRIBUTION

Prefers mid-altitude rainforest and high altitude mossy schlerophyl-lous forest, also found above tree line in ericoid scrub. Recorded in non-forested areas, grassland and agricultural areas (IN45). Range extends length of eastern rainforest belt, including the eastern escarp-

- ▦ probable range
- • confirmed locality

Cowan's
Shrew Tenrec

ment of central highlands from Andohahela in south to Marojejy in north (IN47; IN32). Recorded from 800m to over 2,400m, most common between 1,200m and 1,800m.

In several locations, e.g. Marojejy, Anjanaharibe-Sud and Andohahela, where numerous *Microgale* species occur sympatrically, *M. cowani* often the most common, comprising between 25% and 50% of the shrew tenrec communities (IN45).

BEHAVIOUR

Forages in leaf-litter, moving in cryptic fashion. Females may become sexually mature while still dentally immature. Litter size up to five (IN34).

PYGMY SHREW TENREC

Microgale parvula

MEASUREMENTS

Total length: 95–130mm. Head/body length: 50–64mm. Tail length: 46–66mm. Weight: 2–4g. (IN45)

DESCRIPTION & IDENTIFICATION

Very small. Tail less than or equal to head/body length. Head very small, delicate and elongate. Dorsal pelage dark brown, almost black in places, ventrally dark grey-brown. Tail and feet uniform dark grey-brown (IN17; IN19; IN31).

Can only be confused with *M. pusilla*: *M. parvula* dark grey-brown

Pygmy Shrew Tenrec.

Pygmy
Shrew Tenrec

HABITAT & DISTRIBUTION

Unusual as found in both humid eastern and dry western biomes. Recorded in variety of habitats from lowland rainforests to dry deciduous forests and even degraded forests and agricultural areas (IN45). Range extends from around Marojejy north to Montagne d'Ambre and then down the coastal areas of north-west and west as far south as Onilahy River (IN23). All localities at relatively low elevations: 340m to 650m in Montagne d'Ambre (IN70); 450m in Marojejy; around 50m in Kirindy Forest (IN2); and 160m to 200m in Ankarafantsika (IN19).

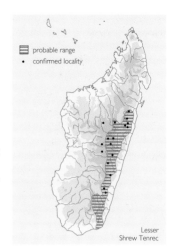

probable range
confirmed locality

Lesser
Shrew Tenrec

above and only slightly paler below, while *M. pusilla* is reddish buffy-brown dorsally with abrupt transition to grey-brown venter.

HABITAT & DISTRIBUTION

Found in all intact native eastern forests from Montagne d'Ambre in north to Andohahela in the south at elevations from 100m to over 2,000m (IN70; IN47; IN48; IN17; IN19; IN31). Also found in degraded habitats and forest fragments (IN28).

BEHAVIOUR

Mainly terrestrial. Litter size up to four (IN34).

SHORT-TAILED SHREW TENREC

Microgale brevicaudata

MEASUREMENTS

Total length: 107–129mm. Head/body length: 63–74mm. Tail length: 35–41mm. Weight: 6.3–12g. (IN23)

DESCRIPTION & IDENTIFICATION

Small to medium-sized with relatively short tail. Pelage short and coarse. Upperparts grizzled, brown with buffy-brown speckles, underparts pale grey-brown (IN19). Very short tail is distinctive.

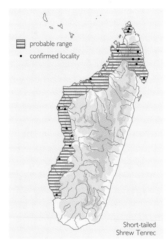

probable range
confirmed locality

Short-tailed
Shrew Tenrec

BEHAVIOUR

Probably semi-fossorial.

LESSER SHREW TENREC

Microgale pusilla

MEASUREMENTS

Total length: 119–136mm. Head/body length: 47–56mm. Tail length: 65–77mm. Weight: 3.1–4.2g. (IN23)

DESCRIPTION & IDENTIFICATION

Recognisable by very small size and relatively long tail. Upperparts

reddish buffy-brown and grizzled, underparts grey-brown; transition between the two abrupt and notice-able. Tail dark grey-brown with underside slightly paler. Similar in size to *M. parvula*, but paler.

HABITAT & DISTRIBUTION

Known from scattered localities in eastern rainforest belt, in central highland and in littoral forests near Tolagnaro in south-east (IN49; IN29; IN31). Found in wide variety of habitats including non-forested areas, agricultural zones and sedge marshes (IN45).

Predated by Barn Owls *Tyto alba* near Antananarivo, where presumed to live in marshlands, grasslands and rice paddies (IN29).

BEHAVIOUR

Forages on ground and in lower branches of undergrowth.

TAIVA SHREW TENREC

Microgale taiva

MEASUREMENTS

Total length: 160–177mm. Head/body length: 71–89mm. Tail length: 80–95mm. Weight: 10.5–14.5g, average 12.4g. (IN47; IN34)

DESCRIPTION & IDENTIFICATION

Medium-sized, with moderately long tail – equal to or slightly longer than head/body length. Dorsal pelage dark russet-brown with buffy-brown speckling, ventrally grey-brown. Tail dark grey above and slightly paler grey below (IN47).

HABITAT & DISTRIBUTION

Scattered records from extreme northern and southern portion of rainforest belt. Recorded from near Ambositra (type specimen) and in Andringitra in both lowland and montane rainforests between 645m and 1,990m (IN21).

Striped Shrew Tenrec.

Taiva Shrew Tenrec

BEHAVIOUR

Males may become sexually mature before they attain other adult characteristics.

STRIPED SHREW TENREC

Microgale drouhardi

MEASUREMENTS

Total length: 114.5–166mm. Head/body length: 62.5–83mm. Tail length: 53–83mm. Weight: c. 10–15g. (IN48)

DESCRIPTION & IDENTIFICATION

Medium-sized with tail slightly shorter than head/body length. Variable colour; upperparts range from dark grey-brown to light rufous-brown with some yellowish speckles, underparts silver-grey with buff or reddish-buff wash. Transition moderately distinct. So named because of dark brown mid-dorsal stripe, extending from head to base of tail. Tail is bicoloured: dark grey dorsally and buff ventrally (IN48).

Considerable size variation between populations; those from central-eastern regions (Ambatovaky and Zahamena) appreciably smaller than elsewhere. Similar to *M. cowani* and *M. taiva*, but paler with distinctive dorsal stripe.

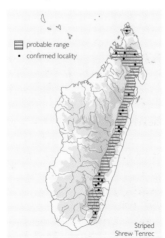

Striped Shrew Tenrec

HABITAT & DISTRIBUTION

Found in lowland and mid-altitude rainforests of north, north-west (include Manongarivo and Tsarantanana) and east, from Montagne d'Ambre in north to Andohahela in south-east. Elevational range from around 350m (Ambatovaky) to over 2,300m (Tsaratanana). Many specimens collected in valley bottoms (IN48).

In Montagne d'Ambre, six species of *Microgale* occur and *M. drouhardi* is by far the most common, comprising up to 70% of the *Microgale* community (IN45).

BEHAVIOUR

Terrestrial and fossorial. Conceals itself under leaves and vegetation on the forest floor. Active and can move rapidly beneath this layer.

NAKED-NOSED SHREW TENREC

Microgale gymnorhyncha

MEASUREMENTS

Total length: 138–176mm. Head/body length: 79–101mm. Tail length: 59–75mm. Weight: 13.5–26g, average 16g. (IN47; IN17; IN19; IN31; IN34)

DESCRIPTION & IDENTIFICATION

Moderately large with tail shorter than head/body length. Dorsal pelage dense, soft and velvety, dark grey-brown, with dark brown guard hairs. Ventral pelage dark grey. Tail dark grey above, light grey below. Head long, gracile and muzzle very long, forming proboscis which extends well beyond mouth. Eyes and ears very small and virtually concealed in pelage. Forefeet broad with claws (IN47).

Differs from all congeners, except *M. gracilis*, in having elongate head, long muzzle, small concealed ears, broad forefeet with large claws. *M. gymnorhyncha* slightly smaller and less gracile than *M. gracilis*, with shorter tail.

HABITAT & DISTRIBUTION

A broad distribution from Anjanaharibe-Sud and Marojejy in the north to Andohahela in extreme south (IN19). Also found on eastern side of central highlands and along eastern escarpment (IN47; IN19). Prefers mid-altitude rainforest and higher elevation mossy cloud forest at elevations from around 1,000m to nearly 2,000m (IN21).

Widespread but relatively rare; no more than 5−6% of the *Microgale* communities at any location (IN45).

probable range
confirmed locality

Naked-nosed
Shrew Tenrec

BEHAVIOUR

Shares significant adaptive features with *M. gracilis* − an elongate proboscis-like muzzle, small eyes, reduced ears and broadened forefeet with large claws − suggesting it is semi-fossorial (IN45).

PALE-FOOTED SHREW TENREC
Microgale fotsifotsy

MEASUREMENTS

Total length: 135−175mm. Head/body length: 64−85mm. Tail length: 71.5−94mm. Weight: c. 6−15g. (IN48; IN31; IN19; IN23)

DESCRIPTION & IDENTIFICATION

Small to medium-sized, with tail slightly longer than head/body length. Pelage soft and silky; upperparts grizzled yellowish grey-brown with dark guard hairs, underparts pale grey with buff or reddish wash. Ears prominent and pale. Tail bicoloured; grey-brown above, light grey-buff below, ending in thin pencil of fine white hairs. Fore- and hindfeet are light brown with very pale digits: *fotsifotsy* is Malagasy for pale or whitish (IN48).

Closely related to *M. soricoides*, but light body coloration, large ears, conspicuous pale feet and tail tip differentiate it from all other *Microgale* species.

Variation is apparent; Montagne d'Ambre individuals generally paler than from other sites to the south. Animals from Zahamena and Andringitra are slightly larger (IN48).

HABITAT & DISTRIBUTION

Prefers lowland and lower eleva-tion mid-altitude rainforest (400m to 1,500m)(IN34), although in Andringitra, also occurs in high alti-tude forests (1,990m)(IN21). Range extends from Montagne d'Ambre in north to Andohahela in south (IN70; IN48; IN31).

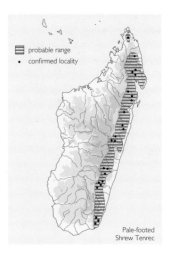

probable range
confirmed locality

Pale-footed
Shrew Tenrec

BEHAVIOUR

Probably mainly terrestrial, has some scansorial adaptations (IN45), but not as extreme as *M. longicaudata*.

MOUNTAIN SHREW TENREC
Microgale monticola

MEASUREMENTS

Total length: 170−209mm. Head/body length: 72−92mm. Tail length: 98−117mm. Weight: 12−17.5g. (IN17; IN19)

DESCRIPTION & IDENTIFICATION

Medium-sized, with tail longer than head/body length. Upperparts dark brown and slightly grizzled with dark guard hairs. Underparts dark brown with grey-buff under fur. Tail dark brown above, slightly paler below. Feet dark brown: forefeet slightly broadened and hindfeet elongate with lengthened digits (IN17).

HABITAT & DISTRIBUTION

Prefers mountain habitats − higher altitude rain and cloud forests − currently known from mountains in Andapa region; Anjanaharibe-Sud recorded between 1,550m and 1,950m, Marojejy between 1,625m and 1,875m (IN17; IN19). Appears

Mountain Shrew Tenrec.

Mountain Shrew Tenrec

to be one of commonest *Microgale* at these localities (IN19).

Close resemblance to *M. thomasi*, but does not occur sympatrically. *M. thomasi* known from higher elevations in south-eastern humid forests. *M. monticola* is the ecological equivalent in the north (IN45).

BEHAVIOUR
Unknown.

TREE SHREW TENREC
Microgale dryas

MEASUREMENTS
Total length: 170–180mm. Head/ body length: 105–110mm. Tail length: 65–70mm. Weight: c. 40g.

DESCRIPTION & IDENTIFICATION
Upperparts grizzled, dark reddish-brown or grey-brown with long dark guard hairs. Merges to grey underparts. Tail uniformly grey. Intermediate between smaller *M. thomasi* and *M. gracilis* and larger *M. dobsoni* and *M. talazaci*. Distinguished from other *Microgale* by unusual dorsal pelage. Also has shorter tail than other larger *Microgale*.

HABITAT & DISTRIBUTION
Known only from few sites in north-east, including Ambatovaky Special Reserve, at elevations between 500m

Tree Shrew Tenrec

and 950m. Occurs sympatrically with *M. cowani*, *M. principula* and *M. talazaci*.

BEHAVIOUR
Unknown.

SHREW TENREC
Microgale soricoides

MEASUREMENTS
Total length: 169–207mm. Head/ body length: 79–103mm. Tail length: 84–104mm. Weight: 14–22g. (IN44; IN47; IN17; IN19; IN31)

DESCRIPTION & IDENTIFICATION
Medium-large with tail equal to or longer than head/body length. Upperparts light buff-brown, slightly grizzled, fades to paler grey-brown underparts with reddish-buff wash. Tail grey-brown above and paler buffy-brown below, tip may be white (IN44; IN19).

Resembles *M. dobsoni* and *M. taiva*; differentiated by unusual dental traits, including distinct incisor morphology.

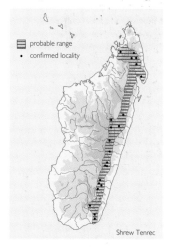

Shrew Tenrec

HABITAT & DISTRIBUTION
Widely distributed and common. Range extends from Anjanaharibe-Sud and Marojejy in north to Andohahela in south, including eastern edge of central plateau. May also occur in Manongarivo and Tsaratanana in

north-west (IN19). Found at elevations from around 750m to nearly 2,000m, but prefers higher altitudes (IN34).

BEHAVIOUR
Probably semi-scansorial: collected on branches and tangles of vines around 2m above ground (IN45). Massive incisors indicate predatory tendencies: in pitfall traps, *M. soricoides* has often partially eaten the other *Microgale* (IN19).

NASOLO'S SHREW TENREC
Microgale nasoloi

MEASUREMENTS*
Total length: 132-134mm. Head/body length: 70-81mm. Tail length: 53-62mm. Weight: 5.9-14g. (IN46)
* based on two specimens

DESCRIPTION & IDENTIFICATION
Pelage soft and uniform slate-grey, which distinguishes it from other *Microgale*. Head flattened, tail short and thin (IN46).

HABITAT & DISTRIBUTION
Only known from deciduous and slightly transitional humid forests of Vohibasia and Analavelona Massif in south-west, between 780m and 1,050m asl (IN46).

probable range
• confirmed locality

Nasolo's
Shrew Tenrec

BEHAVIOUR
Probably scansorial. Other behaviour unknown.

JENKINS' SHREW TENREC
Microgale jenkinsae

MEASUREMENTS*
Total length: 143−147mm. Head/body length: 59−62mm. Tail length: 79−81mm. Weight: 4.9−5.3g. (IN23)
* based on two specimens

DESCRIPTION & IDENTIFICATION
Small with tail length exceeding

head/body length. Fur dense and soft. Upperparts tannish-brown with darker flecks (agouti). Underparts paler grizzled slate-grey (IN23). Ears relatively long (up to 18mm) and prominent. Tail dark brown, paler on under side.

HABITAT & DISTRIBUTION
Known only from transitional dry deciduous forests and spiny bush of Mikea region between Morombe and Manombo River in south-west at elevations up to 80m asl (IN23).

BEHAVIOUR
Probably primarily terrestrial.

probable range
• confirmed locality

Jenkins'
Shrew Tenrec

INTRODUCED SPECIES
Two species of shrew (Soricidae) from the genus *Suncus* – musk or pygmy shrews – occur on Madagascar and are assumed to be introductions, although in one case this is by no means certain.

The Asian Musk Shrew *Suncus murinus* is introduced and might have arrived initially with the early human colonists. More recently this species has been accidentally introduced to other parts of the world via freight in ships, etc., so several subsequent waves of introduction to Madagascar may have also occurred (IN41).

The second *Suncus* species is more problematic and contentious. The Pygmy Musk Shrew *Suncus etruscus* is widespread throughout the Old World and some authorities regard populations on Madagascar as an endemic subspecies, *S. e. madagascariensis*. More recently, some have elevated this to a full species, *Suncus madagascariensis* (IN40). For convenience, it is treated here as a race of *S. etruscus*.

SHREWS Family Soricidae
One of the largest insectivore families, containing around 312 species divided between 23 genera (IN40). Soricidae includes the world's smallest terrestrial mammal species – the Pygmy Musk Shrew *Suncus etruscus*. Their distribution

is extensive, being found on all major landmasses with the exception of Arctic islands, Greenland, Iceland, the West Indies, New Guinea, Australia, New Zealand and some other Pacific islands. In the New World, they have spread as far as northern South America.

In Africa the family Soricidae is extremely diverse; well over 100 species fill a huge variety of niches. The Tenrecidae and Soricidae show obvious similarities in body form, lifestyle, behaviour and ecology and provide excellent examples of parallel evolution (IN34).

Shrews are all small, short-legged insectivores, with elongate pointed snouts. Their pelage is short and dense. Upperparts are generally grey to grey-brown, becoming paler underneath. Eyes are very small and often almost hidden, while the vibrissae (whiskers) are long and prominent and the ears small.

MUSK SHREWS genus *Suncus*

The resemblance of *Suncus* to members of the native genus *Microgale* (shrew tenrecs) is striking, and confusion may occur if only brief views of an animal are gained in the field. On closer examination the differences are significant. The dentition of true shrews is reduced (not more than 32 teeth) in comparison with the shrew tenrecs. Also, *Suncus* does not possess a cloaca, which *Microgale* does.

ASIAN MUSK SHREW

Suncus murinus

MEASUREMENTS

Total length: 170–200mm. Head/body length: 120–135mm. Tail length: 50–65mm. Weight: across entire range: 30–100g (IN65). In Madagascar: females 30–35g; males 45–50g.

DESCRIPTION & IDENTIFICATION

One of the largest shrews with very strong and distinct odour. Pelage short, soft and velvety. Two colour morphs: one has pale grey upperparts, slightly paler underparts and a whitish tail; the other, dark greyish-brown upperparts, paler grey underparts and dark grey tail. Both occur on Madagascar. Pale form more common. Males are larger than females.

Many introduced populations on different islands around the world, and these subpopulations have now diverged considerably in morphology, physiology and size, hence subspecific differentiation may apply. In Madagascar individuals are relatively small.

probable range

Asian Musk Shrew

Asian Musk Shrew.

HABITAT & DISTRIBUTION

Originates in Asia where widespread: natural distribution extends from Japan to Pakistan. All records further west are probably introductions by humans (IN41). Now widely distributed in Arabia, East Africa, the Comoros, the Mascarene Islands and Madagascar.

Malagasy population derived from several separate colonisations involving different founder stock localities: some probably came from Arabian Peninsula via East Africa, others arrived directly from Southeast Asia. First record on Madagascar was in 1858 (IN41). Has now spread over entire island but does not appear to penetrate primary forest (R13).

BEHAVIOUR

Lives as human commensal throughout range (IN41) and found in man-made habitats, cultivated areas and around habitation. Nocturnal and solitary. Vocal repertoire of high-pitched chirrups, clicks and buzzes is associated with aggressive behaviour. Day spent in burrow or inside buildings.

Voracious hunters that eat a variety of insects, other invertebrates, small vertebrates and edible human refuse.

May breed throughout year in Madagascar, with peak between October and December. Gestation 30 days, litter size two to six, three is average. Weaning between 17 and 20 days and apparent sexual maturity is reached after 36 days.

There appears to be no correlation between high densities of S. murinus and reduced diversity in Microgale and other tenrecs (IN20).

WHERE TO SEE

May be encountered at night in most areas around human settlements.

PYGMY (MADAGASCAR) MUSK SHREW

Suncus etruscus (madagascariensis)

MEASUREMENTS

Total length: 70–86mm. Head/body length: 39–51mm. Tail length: 31–35mm. Weight: 1.8–3.2g, average 1.7g. (IN31; IN34)

DESCRIPTION & IDENTIFICATION

Pelage short, soft and greyish-brown. Ears rounded and prominent. Smallest shrew and smallest of terrestrial mammals. In Madagascar sometimes treated as an endemic species, S. madagascariensis (IN40).

HABITAT & DISTRIBUTION

Widely distributed including eastern, western and southern regions, from sea level to 1,500m asl. Forest dwelling, more common in drier regions although full range is uncertain (IN34). In Andohahela National Park, not recorded in rainforest areas (Parcel 1), but commonly encountered in disturbed spiny forest areas (Parcel 2) (IN31).

BEHAVIOUR

Probably solitary and nocturnal. Diet primarily small insects. Litter size up to five (IN34).

probable range

Pygmy (Madagascar) Musk Shrew

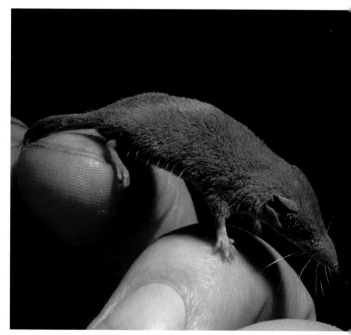

Pygmy (Madagascar) Musk Shrew.

BATS
Order Chiroptera

Bats are amongst the most diverse and geographically dispersed of mammalian orders. They form the largest mammal aggregations and may also be the most abundant: within the mammals, only the order Rodentia contains a greater number of species.

The order Chiroptera is divided into two suborders: the Megachiroptera, which constitutes a single family Pteropodidae, and the Microchiroptera (microbats), which contains the other 16 families. The terms can be misleading; some Megachiroptera are smaller than the larger microbats (Megachiroptera approximately 15–1,600g; Microchiroptera approximately 2–200g) (B32; B34).

Bats are the only mammals capable of powered flight (other 'flying' mammals, e.g. flying squirrels, can only glide). This has obviously been a major factor in their wide distribution. Their ability to migrate has resulted in reduced levels of endemism in the bats of Madagascar as compared with the other mammalian orders on the island. Approximately 60% of Madagascar's bats are endemic (cf. 100% endemism for other mammal species). Nonetheless, bat endemism is very high when compared to chiropteran assemblages on similar-sized islands elsewhere (e.g. New Guinea 16% and Borneo 6.5%) and is testament to Madagascar's relative isolation.

The majority of bats on Madagascar owe their origins to founder populations from Africa, however, the closest affinities of three genera lie in Asia (*Pteropus, Emballonura* and *Mormopterus*) (B15).

There are currently at least 36 species of bats on Madagascar: 24 of these are endemic, the others are shared with Africa and are Afrotropical in origin. At higher taxonomic levels only one of the seven families is endemic, Myzopodidae (B41; B16).

Bats are found in all areas on the island and some species are able to survive in the central highlands well away from native forests. However, their presence and activity decline dramatically in high mountain areas above 1,500m.

Suborder Megachiroptera

OLD WORLD FRUIT BATS Family Pteropodidae

The suborder Megachiroptera consists of a single family, Pteropodidae, restricted to the Old World. This family of exclusively fruit and nectar-feeding bats contains around 170 species. There is considerable size variation within the family: total lengths range from around 50mm to over 400mm and weights from 15g to 1,600g. In most species the tail is short or rudimentary.

In general they lack ultrasonic echolocation and have large eyes, with a reflective tapetum, and good vision together with well-developed olfactory senses. Three species, in three genera, are known from Madagascar; *Pteropus rufus, Eidolon dupreanum* and *Rousettus madagascariensis*. All three are important pollination agents; in deforested areas where trees like large baobabs (*Adansonia* spp.) are marooned, fruit bats may be the only pollinators (B37).

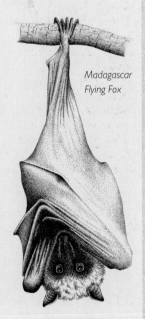

Madagascar Flying Fox

FLYING FOXES genus *Pteropus*

The genus *Pteropus* are often known as flying foxes and include the largest bats: some attain wingspreads up to 1.7m. They originate in South-east Asia, Australasia and islands in the western Pacific and have spread across to western Indian Ocean islands, but have not reached the African mainland.

Islands in the western Indian Ocean are remarkable for the radiation of *Pteropus*. Several species occur (or did so until recently) on islands within the region: Madagascar, *P. rufus*; Mauritius, *P. niger, P. subniger, P. rodricensis*; Réunion, *P. niger, P. subniger*; Rodrigues, *P. rodricensis*; Aldabra, *P. aldabrensis*; Seychelles, *P. seychellensis seychellensis*;

Comoros, *P. seychellensis comorensis*; Anjouan and Moheli islands (Comoros), *P. livingstonii*; Mafia Island (off Tanzania), *P. seychellenis comorensis*; and Pemba Island (off Tanzania), *P. voeltzkowi* (B9; B39).

They roost in trees, often in large colonies and may use the same sites year after year, resulting in defoliation of the trees. During the day colonies are generally noisy as individuals jostle for prime spaces. They are easily disturbed and will take to the air if threatened.

At dusk they leave the roost in search of fruit trees in which to feed. They are strong flyers and can cover large distances, sometimes flying for more than two hours in one direction (20–30km or more). They are almost entirely frugivorous, feeding on fruit pulp and fruit juices, although some also feed on flowers and occasionally leaves. They eat, rest and digest their food at the feeding site before returning to the roost site by dawn (B5).

MADAGASCAR FLYING FOX

Pteropus rufus

MEASUREMENTS
Total length: 235–270mm. Forearm: 155–175mm. Wingspan: 1,000–1,250mm. Weight: 500–750g. (B37)

DESCRIPTION & IDENTIFICATION
Basic colour is dark brown; upper chest, shoulders and head are lighter, varying between rufous-brown and yellow-golden brown. Pronounced muzzle gives face a 'fox-like' appearance. Eyes large and ears pointed, prominent and widely separated. Wings slate-grey to black. There is a claw on the second digit in addition to the thumb. This is the largest bat in Madagascar and one of the world's largest species.

HABITAT & DISTRIBUTION
Found in all regions where substantial tracts of native forest remain, including eastern rainforest, western dry forest and southern spiny forest. Many major roosts are within 100km of the coast, near the coast or on offshore islands. A few roost sites remain in the central highlands, these are increasingly being deserted (B37).

BEHAVIOUR
During the day, rests in colonies, up to several thousand (range 10 to 5,000, 400 to 500 average), in canopy of roost trees in primary and secondary forests, mangroves and occasionally plantations (B37).

Activity at roost sites is constant: colonies are very noisy and generally heard before seen. Chatter intensifies when disturbed. Potential predators, like the Fosa *Cryptoprocta ferox*, may cause whole colony to take flight (B37). Large raptors circling above roosts cause distress. Bats often fly to different localities within the roost; when landing, there are noisy and agonistic exchanges between the incoming individual and the bats already at the site.

During the early hours, they often hang with wings outstretched to absorb heat. Later, when temperatures are higher, they will lick the inner and outer wing membranes and hang with them outstretched, to reduce body temperature by evapo-

When roosting Madagascar Flying Foxes are extremely susceptible to disturbance.

probable range

Madagascar Flying Fox

ration. May also 'fan' wings to keep cool: this is common in mothers with suckling or roosting young (B56).

At dusk they fly to foraging sites, up to several kilometres away (over 30km recorded). Several 'scouts' may fly ahead of main group to locate suitable fruiting trees (B36). Bats on offshore islands fly to neighbouring islands or back to the mainland to feed. They have excellent vision and do not navigate by echolocation.

Fruit juices dominate the diet: obtained by squeezing pieces of fruit in the mouth, then swallowing the juice and rejecting remaining pulp fibres. Very soft fruit pulps may be swallowed, along with some seeds. Wide variety of native fruits are taken (over 35 species recorded); *Ficus*

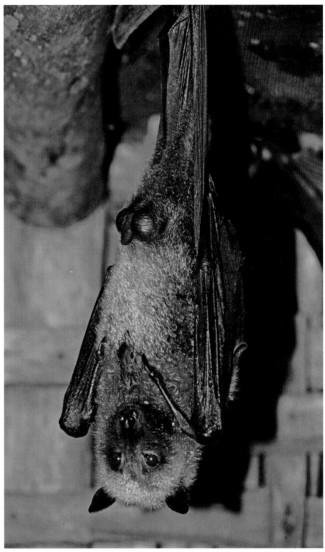

Madagascar Flying Fox.

Madagascar Flying Fox.

spp. are particularly relished, also crops like papayas, lychees and guava. Pollen also an important component (over 25 species recorded). When fruit is scarce, leaves, containing proteins that a fruit-based diet lacks, are eaten. Some flowers, e.g. *Ceiba* spp., are chewed to obtain juices, nectar and pollen. Flying foxes are important agents of both seed dispersal and pollination in forests (B35; B36).

Normally inverts body to defecate and urinate to avoid soiling itself. When sexually active (April to May), males urinate onto chest and neck and rub it into the fur with their feet and forearms. Males pursue females by crawling along branches with thumbs and feet. Young are born in October and November; singletons the norm, and twins very occasional (B37).

Hunted for food throughout the

island. Continued disturbance a major factor in roost desertion. Overall population on Madagascar is declining (B37).

WHERE TO SEE
Most accessible colony is at Berenty Reserve, west of Tolagnaro, where 800 to 1,800 bats roost in gallery forest (numbers vary seasonally). Also colonies on Nosy Ravina to the south of Nosy Mangabe; Nosy Tanikely off Nosy Be; and in the mangroves near Anjajavy. Colonies should never be approached too closely (less than 100m), as this causes distress and can be particularly detrimental when females are pregnant or lactating.

STRAW-COLOURED FRUIT BATS genus *Eidolon*

There are two species: *Eidolon helvum*, Africa's most widely distributed fruit bat, found on the Arabian Peninsula and throughout sub-Saharan Africa; and *E. dupreanum*, restricted to Madagascar (B41).

Both are gregarious and roost by day in colonies in large trees and also buildings and caves. On mainland Africa some colonies attain huge proportions and may contain several million bats (B43).

Eidolon has a more pointed head than other fruit bats and very long, narrow wings adapted for flying long distances during seasonal migrations. These are also used for climbing in branches at roost sites (B12).

MADAGASCAR STRAW-COLOURED FRUIT BAT

Eidolon dupreanum

MEASUREMENTS
Total length: 190–215mm.
Forearm: 115–130mm. Wingspan: 750–950mm. Weight: 250–340g.
Males are around 10% larger than females. (B37)

DESCRIPTION & IDENTIFICATION
Pelage short, covering head, dorsum and venter. Neck fur is longer and woollier. Face in front of and below the eyes is bare. Overall colour of head and body is medium grey-brown, upperparts may be dull yellow, underparts often tawny-olive. Reddish-cinnamon patches form a collar around neck; more conspicuous in males, but otherwise sexes are alike. Wings are dark blackish-brown.

E. dupreanum is larger than *E. helvum* and is the second largest bat on Madagascar. Dull coloration, long narrow wings and small tail help distinguish this species from *P. rufus*.

HABITAT & DISTRIBUTION
Patchily distributed, but recorded in all regions of Madagascar. Numerous roosts in the central highlands where surrounding areas have been deforested. These tend to be much smaller (fewer than 100 bats) compared to roosts from forested areas.

BEHAVIOUR
Spends day at roost sites around rocky crags, river cliffs, caves and the canopy of dense stands of trees.

Madagascar Straw-coloured Fruit Bat.

On Madagascar, colonies typically between 10 and 500 individuals (average 200), although three roosts up to 1,400 are known from Ankarana (B37). Roosting bats are restless and noisy and regularly move from place to place. They leave at dusk to search for fruiting trees. Roost size varies seasonally, particularly in south-west, when smallest during the dry months when food is limited. This suggests some inter-island migration.

Ranges widely in search for food. Large roosts rarely close to one another, often more than 60km apart; suggests bats forage up to 30km away from roost site. Diet primarily fruit juice, squeezed out of fruit pulp, also nectar, blossoms and young shoots. Tip of long tongue is 'brush-like' (papillaceous) to extract nectar and pollen from deep flowers. Pulp of *Borassus* palm fruit is important and soft wood is occasionally chewed for moisture. The diet is varied; faecal samples reveal pollen from 40 plant species and fruits of more than 30 species. Also an important pollinator, including key species like baobabs (*Adansonia* spp.) (B14; B37).

Delayed implantation is possible; mating to birth (i.e. apparent gestation period) is about nine

Madagascar Straw-coloured Fruit Bats.

probable range

Madagascar
Straw-coloured Fruit Bat

months, but period of embryonic development is only four months (B40; B17). Births occur in December and January; single infant weighs approximately 50g. Large numbers of females may gather to form 'nursery' colonies. *E. dupreanum* is thought to live for over 20 years.

Widely hunted, especially in the central highlands; a common technique is to smoke them out of their roosts.

WHERE TO SEE
Roosts in *Raphia* palms in the Parc Botanique et Zoologique de Tsimbazaza in Antananarivo. Another well-known roost is at Lac Tritriva, near Antsirabe. The largest roosts in forested areas are in Ankarana Special Reserve (B37), the most visible in *Grotte des Chauve-souris*.

ROUSETTE FRUIT BATS genus *Rousettus*

A genus containing nine species, widely distributed from the Middle East to South-east Asia as far as New Guinea, Sulawesi and Solomon Islands. In Africa the genus extends to South Africa including the Comoros and Madagascar where a single species is present (B4; B6).

Rousettus produce very high-pitched sounds by clicking their tongues (with an audible 'buzz'); this forms the basis of a rudimentary echolocation system (B28; B47). Unlike microbats, this is only used for orientation; vision and olfaction remain the primary senses for food detection.

MADAGASCAR ROUSETTE

Rousettus madagascariensis

MEASUREMENTS
Total length: 115–145mm. Forearm: 65–75mm. Wingspan: 425–520mm. Weight: 50–80g. (B37)

DESCRIPTION & IDENTIFICATION
Pelage longish and dense, less so on neck, throat and shoulders. Upperparts greyish-brown with some reddish-brown hues, underparts paler grey-brown. Muzzle rather pointed, ears relatively short. Wings are proportionately broad.

A small-sized, delicate fruit bat; the smallest fruit bat on Madagascar and the smallest *Rousettus* in the African region. In flight could be mistaken for a large microbat, but

Madagascar Rousette roost in dense colonies in caves in Ankarana Special Reserve.

eye-shine and direct darting flight distinguish it from the back and forth flight of microbats.

HABITAT & DISTRIBUTION
Endemic to Madagascar. Known in both the east and the west in association with forested areas, forest edge and caves (B42; B20). Majority of records from lower elevations. Appears to be absent from arid south and south-west, although specimens have been caught in the semi-arid transition zone (Parcel 3) in Andohahela National Park (B21). No records from deforested central highlands.

BEHAVIOUR
Known to roost in large trees and tree holes, but prefers deep caves

well beyond the twilight zone. May be restricted to areas where caves are present. Larger colonies contain

probable range

Madagascar Rousette

several thousand individuals (B37).

Feeds on fruit juices, soft fruit pulp and nectar. Able to grasp fruit in the mouth and fly off before consuming it (B21). Flies considerable distances each night to find sufficient food. Single young are most common, twins are born occasionally. Gestation period around four months. In Ankarana females have been seen with young in June.

WHERE TO SEE
Caves in Ankarana in the north are the best places to see this species especially *Grotte des Chauve-souris*. Other roosts include caves in Bemaraha National Park and Anjohibe near Mahajanga.

Suborder Microchiroptera

The suborder Microchiroptera (microbats) is more ecologically diverse than Megachiroptera. It contains 16 families, around 135 genera and over 760 species, distributed worldwide. Their greatest diversity occurs in tropical regions – species richness decreases with increasing latitude (B32, B34). Seven families occur on Madagascar and one, Myzopodidae, is endemic.

All microbats possess echolocation that is used for orientation and prey capture. Most calls are ultrasonic and beyond the range of 'normal' human hearing. Sounds are produced by contractions of the muscles in the larynx and are emitted from the mouth. Calls are characterised by their frequency or pitch, duration and intensity.

SHEATH-TAILED BATS Family Emballonuridae

Around 50 species widely distributed in tropical and subtropical regions, with four in Madagascar. Characterised by a shortish tail, which extends freely beyond the interfemoral membrane, but is retracted into a sheath in the membrane during flight.

OLD WORLD SHEATH-TAILED BATS genus *Emballonura*

A genus of South-east Asian origin containing 11 species, including two on Madagascar.

PETERS'S SHEATH-TAILED BAT

Emballonura atrata

MEASUREMENTS
Total length: c. 55–60mm. Forearm: c. 37–40mm. Wingspan: 268mm*. Weight: 3.5–5g. (B16) *Based on a single specimen.

DESCRIPTION
Small, uniformly dark slate-grey to black, generally slightly paler underneath. Nasal appendages poorly developed, snout quite pointed. Ears prominent, broad and rounded, with a distinct 'notch' near tip.

DISTRIBUTION
Endemic to Madagascar. Recorded the length of rainforest belt and parts of the eastern central highlands, from localities near Maroantsetra in the north to Tolagnaro in the south (B25a).

Peters's Sheath-tailed Bat.

probable range

• confirmed range

Peters's
Sheath-tailed Bat

BEHAVIOUR

Known to roost in caves or rock crevices, invariably within the twilight zone, and also below exposed tree roots. In roosts often associated with *Triaenops* and *Miniopterus*. Also found in houses in the central highlands (Antsirabe) (B41). Roosts in forested areas contain between ten and 30 bats (B3).

Recorded foraging at 2–8m at the forest edge and over rivers (B47). Diet consists of insects.

Emballonura tiavato

MEASUREMENTS*

Total length: 55–64mm. Forearm: 35–41mm. Wingspan: unknown. Weight: 2.7–3.8g. (B26A) *Based on 13 specimens.

DESCRIPTION

Pelage long, slightly shaggy and silky. Upperparts medium greysh-brown, slightly paler on lower

body. Underparts paler buff-brown. Noticeably paler than *E. atrata* (B26A). Ears long (11-15mm) and slightly pointed.

DISTRIBUTION

Endemic to Madagascar. Recorded in drier regions of north and north-west (Daraina and Ankarana) and in western areas south to at least Bemaraha (B26A).

probable range

• confirmed range

Emballonura tiavato

BEHAVIOUR

A delicate flyer. One of first species to emerge at dusk and begins foraging in forest under-storey before complete darkness falls (B26A). Specific name *tiavato* comes from Malagasy meaning 'likes rocks': seems to prefer areas with rock outcrops and caves. Stomach contents suggest moths are impor-tant in diet (B45A).

AFRICAN SHEATH-TAILED BAT

Coleura afra

MEASUREMENTS

Total length: 55–65mm. Forearm: 45-55mm. Wingspan: 220mm. Weight: 10–12g (B52; B53).

DESCRIPTION

Upperparts mid-brown, underparts paler. Muzzle pointed, naked and black. Ears large and rounded, eyes large. Wings very pale brown and translucent. Females slightly larger than males (B53).

DISTRIBUTION

Found from West Africa, to south-west Arabia, through East Africa and south to Mozambique. In Madagascar known only from Ankarana and Namoroka. May occur locally in other northern regions (B24).

BEHAVIOUR

In Kenya females give birth to single offspring. Gestation period 15–16 weeks (B53).

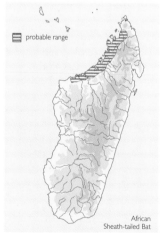

probable range

African
Sheath-tailed Bat

TOMB BATS genus *Taphozous*

A wide distribution across Africa, Asia and Australasia: 13 species currently recognised, including one from Madagascar. Found in a variety of habitats from rainforest to open country. Known to roost in tombs, other buildings, rocky crevices and shallow caverns. Amongst the largest insectivorous microbats.

MAURITIAN TOMB BAT

Taphozous mauritianus

MEASUREMENTS

Total length: 100–110mm.
Forearm: 58–64mm. Wingspan: not
measured. Weight: 25–36g. (B52;
B16)

DESCRIPTION

Medium-sized with grizzled grey
upperparts and head and creamy-
white underparts. Juveniles generally
darker than the adults. Head is flattish
and triangular, face bare below and
in front of the eyes. Ears broad and
moderately rounded.

Mauritian Tomb Bat, Ampijoroa.

probable range

Mauritian Tomb Bat

DISTRIBUTION

Occurs throughout sub-Saharan
Africa, as well as the islands of
Mauritius, Réunion, Assumption,
Aldabra and Madagascar (B41). On
Madagascar, found throughout most
regions and habitats below 900m,
except central highlands (B13; B16).

BEHAVIOUR

Day roosts include tree trunks
(particularly palms), rock faces and
walls of buildings (B51). Preferred
sites give overhead shelter. When
disturbed moves quickly sideways in
a crab-like manner or will fly off to a
neighbouring site.

Hunts mainly after dark. An
aerial feeder in open spaces and
over water, moths are primary prey
(B53; B51). Generally encountered
in small groups between six and 12
individuals.

WHERE TO SEE

Regularly found roosting on the
trunks of large trees in the camp-
site at Ampijoroa Forest Station.
Also seen in rock crevices along
Manambolo River Gorge near
Bekopaka (Tsingy de Bemaraha
National Park).

SLIT-FACED BATS Family Nycteridae

A monogeneric family, found throughout Africa, the eastern Mediterranean and across Asia to Indonesia. Characterised by folds of skin flanking a groove containing the nostrils and a deep pit between the eyes (sometimes called hollow-faced bats). Ears are typically large. Unique amongst mammals in having a T-shaped tail (B54).

SLIT-FACED BATS genus Nycteris

The genus contains 14 species including one endemic to Madagascar. All are insectivorous/carnivorous. Larger taxa can take arthropods like spiders and scorpions. Roost singly or in small groups.

MADAGASCAR SLIT-FACED BAT

Nycteris madagascariensis

MEASUREMENTS

Total length: around 115mm. Forearm: 50–52mm. Wingspan: not measured. Weight: 15–20g*. *Estimated measurement.

DESCRIPTION

Medium-sized with longish pelage. Upperparts reddish-brown, underparts predominantly grey. Recognisable by very large ears and distinctive slit in the muzzle with folds of skin either side.

DISTRIBUTION

Distribution appears very localised; may be restricted to the northern part of the island. Type specimen probably collected from Irodo region ('Valley of Rodo') north of Analamera. Also record from nearby Ankarana Massif (B41), although

probable range

Madagascar Slit-faced Bat

recent surveys failed to confirm this (B24).

BEHAVIOUR

Very little known. Preferred roost sites include caves and hollow trees.

OLD WORLD LEAF-NOSED BATS

Family Hipposideridae

A family occuring throughout the Old World tropics from Africa, through Asia, South-east Asia and into Australasia; contains nine genera and at least 77 species. Easily recognisable by a well-defined and elaborate nose-leaf and large pointed ears. Closely related to horseshoe bats (family Rhinolophidae) but lack lancet on nose-leaf and have a different ear and foot structure. Both families emit ultrasounds from their nostrils, where the nose-leaf acts like a megaphone.

OLD WORLD LEAF-NOSED BATS

genus *Hipposideros*

The largest genus in the family, containing 55 species including one in Madagascar. Large insects and other arthropods dominate the diet; very large individuals are capable of tackling vertebrate prey. Roost mainly in caves, will also use other similar shelters including buildings. Most species are colonial, a few roost singly.

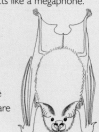

COMMERSON'S LEAF-NOSED BAT

Hipposideros commersoni

MEASUREMENTS

Total length: 110–145mm. Forearm: 83–97mm. Wingspan: 475–560mm. Weight: 40–80g. Males around 5–10% larger than females. (B41)

DESCRIPTION

Upperparts and head pale grey-brown to reddish-brown, underparts pale tawny. Ears very large, falcate and rounded at tips. Nose-leaf large and elaborate.

H. commersoni is the largest microbat on Madagascar (B16). Large size, large ears and prominent leaf-nose are distinctive.

Commerson's Leaf-nosed Bat, Nosy Mangabe Reserve.

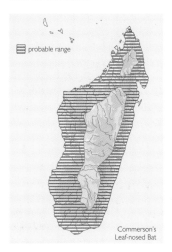

probable range

Commerson's Leaf-nosed Bat

DISTRIBUTION

H. commersoni is endemic to Madagascar. Formerly treated as one of four subspecies: *H. c. commersoni* (Madagascar); *H. c. marungensis* (East and Southern Africa); *H. c. gigas* (West Africa); *H. c. tomensis* (São Tomé) (B41), but now considered a full species (B50).

H. commersoni is widespread in Madagascar. Recorded in most major habitats, including southern spiny forest, western deciduous forest and eastern humid forest. Most records between sea level and 850m, but known up to 1,210m in Andringitra (B19; B16).

BEHAVIOUR

Preferred roosts include caves and hollow trees, although will also utilise the open roofs of rural buildings. In Africa, *Hipposideros* regularly forms colonies numbering several hundred; similar aggregations are known from caves in Ankarana (B38) but most colonies in Madagascar contain fewer than 20 individuals. Each bat roosts slightly apart – at wing-tip distance – from it neighbour, rather than in a tight cluster.

Generally hunts in lower levels of forest, often hawking along trails and similar open areas for large insects. Individuals use tree trunks or horizontal branches as roosts from which they hunt. When suspended, they move their head from side to side searching for prey (typical of large predatory bats) (B47). Individuals often return to a roost to consume larger prey items. Most prey are large insects, including moths and beetles. In rainforest regions also suspected of predating small vocalising frogs along narrow streams (B16).

Not considered threatened, but suffers considerable hunting pressure in certain areas (B24).

WHERE TO SEE
May be encountered along forest trails and around campsites at many locations: Ankarana, Kirindy, Ampijoroa and Nosy Mangabe are the more reliable sites.

TRIDENT OR TRIPLE LEAF-NOSED BATS genus *Triaenops*

Resembles *Hipposideros*, but differs by having a trident-shaped nose leaf. Distributed throughout East Africa, north into Ethiopia, Somalia, around the coast of the Arabian Peninsula and into Iran and southern Pakistan. Three species known from Madagascar, all absent from eastern and central regions.

TROUESSART'S TRIDENT BAT

Triaenops furculus

MEASUREMENTS
Total length: 60–75mm. Forearm: 42–47mm. Wingspan: 268–281mm. Weight: 4–7g. (B41)

Trouessart's Trident Bat.

DESCRIPTION
Relatively small, with drab grey-brown upperparts (some individuals have russet tinges) and light grey underparts. Ears moderately large, broad at their bases, slightly falcate and pointed at tips. *T. auritus* sometimes regarded as synonymous with *T. furculus*.

DISTRIBUTION
Endemic to Madagascar; restricted to western regions, from Anjohibe in north to the south-west (B57). The type specimen comes from Namoroka in the west.

BEHAVIOUR
Roost in caves, often in large mixed-species colonies that include *Miniopterus*, *Myotis* and *Otomops*. Often emerges before total darkness and may hunt close to ground. Diet mainly insects and other small arthropods.

Trouessart's
Trident Bat

DESCRIPTION
Variable in colour, from rufous all over, to pale grey with rufous patches. Has a very complex nose leaf and is slightly larger than *T. furculus*.

Rufous
Trident Bat

RUFOUS TRIDENT BAT

Triaenops rufus

MEASUREMENTS
Total length: 85–90mm. Forearm: 50–56mm. Wingspan: 270–305mm. Weight: 9–12g. (B41)

DISTRIBUTION
Broadly sympatric with the ranges of *T. furculus* and *T. auritus*; found throughout the west, south-west and south to Tolagnaro region (B57). Also known from northern and north-eastern areas (Marojejy). Not common in central highlands.

BEHAVIOUR
Little is known. Has been found on the edge of marshes and forests (B10), known to roost in caves or similar sites, often in mixed colonies numbering several hundred. Diet is insect-based.

Triaenops auritus

MEASUREMENTS
Total length: approx 60–65mm*. Forearm: approx 45.5mm. Wingspan: approx 20mm*. Weight: approx 5g*. *Estimated measurements.

Triaenops auritus

Rufous Trident Bat.

DESCRIPTION

Upperparts greyish-black, underparts are grey. Ears large and tail short. Previously many regarded *T. auritus* as synonymous with *T. furculus*. Recent research confirms separate species with non-overlapping ranges (B57).

DISTRIBUTION

Type specimen collected near Antsiranana in 1910. All recent records are from the north, Ankarana and Analamera (B24). The southern limit is between Andavokoera and Anjohibe. One of the major northern rivers is probably a barrier separating *T. auritus* from *T. furculus* (B57).

BEHAVIOUR

Probably forest dependent and roosts in caves or similar. Roosts may contain over 1,000, and exceptionally up to 2,000, animals.

SUCKER-FOOTED BATS Family Myzopodidae

A family consisting of two species. The name is derived from suction discs on the hands and feet. Unlike convergent adaptations on Disc-winged Bats (family Thyropteridae) from South America, suckers of this bat are not on stalks.

SUCKER-FOOTED BATS genus *Myzopoda*

Formerly regarded as monotypic, recent research indicates populations from eastern and western regions are different and each warrant species status (B25B). Genus now contains two species both endemic to Madagascar. Two unique morphological features distinguish *Myzopoda*: a mushroom-shaped process partly enclosing the ear opening and the conspicuous horseshoe-like adhesive discs on the thumb and sole of hindfoot.

EASTERN SUCKER-FOOTED BAT

Myzopoda aurita

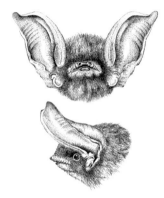

MEASUREMENTS

Total length: 101–118mm. Forearm: 46–49mm. Wingspan: not measured. Weight: 9-9.5g. (B25B)

DESCRIPTION

Pelage moderately dense, mid-brown to dark-brown and even blackish in some individuals. Occasional specimens have weak russet tinges. Ears large (30–35mm in length) and separate with a tragus. Upper lip protrudes over lower. Tail long and extends beyond membrane between the hindlegs. Thumb also has a small vestigial claw. Conspicuous suction discs on thumbs and hindfeet.

DISTRIBUTION

Endemic to Madagascar. Probably restricted to eastern regions from around Marojejy in north to Tolagnaro in south (B42; B27). Majority of records from lowland and coastal areas: highest elevational record is 970m near Andasibe (B25B). May be locally common, but appears rare throughout range (B48).

BEHAVIOUR

The suction pads allow it to cling to smooth vertical surfaces, such as large leaves. These organs also contain glands that secrete directly onto the surface of the suction pads and help adhesion, so entire body weight can be supported (B27).

Majority of records from forest margins and marshland dominated by *Ravenala madagascariensis* and *Typhonodorum* sp. (Araceae). *Ravenala* and similar broad-leaved species like *Pandanus* and some palms are the principal roost sites (B25B). Roosts with head uppermost using its stiff projecting tail as a prop.

Also records from within forest, e.g. Tampolo Forest Reserve and Saint Luce littoral forest. Extent to which roosting and foraging requirements differ is unknown.

Ravenala and similar species have proliferated where deforestation is acute; it is possible this is one of the few endemic mammals to have benefited from habitat modification by humans (B16).

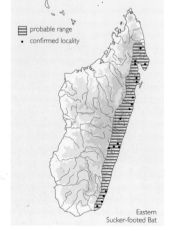

probable range
• confirmed locality

Eastern Sucker-footed Bat

Eastern Sucker-footed Bat.

Possesses a complex and distinctive echolocation system that is identifiable. Hunts insects, like small moths in open areas, including rice paddies (B47).

WESTERN SUCKER-FOOTED BAT

Myzopoda schliemanni

MEASUREMENTS
Total length: 92-107mm. Forearm: 45-49mm. Wingspan: not measured. Weight: 7.8-10.3g. (B25B)

DESCRIPTION
Smaller and paler than its congener, *M. aurita*. Upperparts buff-brown, underparts paler mouse-grey. Prominent funnel-like ears with a peculiar mushroom-shaped process (tragus) at base of each. Also distinct suckers on thumbs and hindfeet.

DISTRIBUTION
Sparsely distributed and currently known from three specific lowland localities in the west: Ankaboka in the north-west, Ankarafantsika and Namoroka National Parks (B25B). May also occur in similar dry habitats to the north and south of this range. Generally associated with marshy areas, rivers and transitional humid-dry forests (B25B).

BEHAVIOUR
Presumed to be similar to *M. aurita*. Sites of capture associated with broad-leaved species like *Ravenala*, *Pandanus* and *Raphia* palms. In Namoroka has also been seen roosting deep inside caves within dry deciduous forest (B31A).

VESPERTILIONID BATS Family Vespertilionidae

The most abundant and widespread bat family, contains 42 genera and at least 355 species. Found throughout the world except for polar regions and some very remote islands. Colonised all habitats from arid deserts to rainforests and to elevations at the limits of tree growth. Characterised by tail completely, or almost completely, contained within the tail membrane (interfemoral).

On Madagascar represented by six genera arranged between two subfamilies. *Myotis*, *Pipistrellus*, *Eptesicus*, *Neoromicia* and *Scotophilus* in subfamily Vespertilioninae; *Miniopterus* in its own subfamily Miniopterinae.

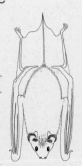

MOUSE-EARED BATS genus *Myotis*

Divided among four subgenera containing some 83 known species; probably the most widely distributed mammalian genus. Most are insectivorous, but at least one (*M. vivesi*) and possibly two others feed on fish. In Madagascar represented by a single endemic species.

Malagasy Mouse-eared Bat.

MALAGASY MOUSE-EARED BAT

Myotis goudoti

MEASUREMENTS
Total length: 90–100mm. Forearm: 32–41mm. Wingspan: not measured. Weight: 5–9g. (B20; B16)

DESCRIPTION
Upperparts sombre brown, underparts paler. Head somewhat flattened, large rounded ears and short muzzle.

DISTRIBUTION
Widely distributed in the east, west and south-west. Also recorded at sites in central highlands. Reported from sea level to 800m in lowland and mid-altitude montane forest, and a record in higher montane forest at 1,600m (B41; B19, B21; B16).

BEHAVIOUR
Generally roosts in small colonies, often with other species, particularly *Miniopterus*. Roosts up to 1,000 found in Namoroka (B24). One of the first bats to emerge at dusk. Often hunts along stream lines in forest (B16). Reported breeding in October and November (B42; B41).

probable range

Malagasy
Mouse-eared Bat

PIPISTRELLE BATS genus *Pipistrellus*
A large genus divided into seven subgenera containing at least 60 species. *Pipistrellus* on Madagascar have yet to be determined but it is thought two or three different species occur.

One species is closely related to the Banana Bat *P. nanus* from sub-Saharan Africa. A second species exhibits close morphological links to *P. kuhlii* from South Africa. A third taxon probably represents an undescribed species.

SEROTINES OR BROWN BATS genera *Eptesicus* and *Neoromicia*
Genera similar to *Pipistrellus*. After taxonomic review, two genera are now recognised in Madagascar (B55; B31).

MADAGASCAR SEROTINE

Eptesicus matroka

MEASUREMENTS

Total length: 75–90mm. Forearm: 29–35mm. Wingspan: 220–257mm. Weight: 4–9g. (B16)

DESCRIPTION

Shows variation in size and colour, females generally larger than males. Upperparts shades of brown, underparts paler yellowish-white. Name *matroka* refers to colour of dorsal fur and means 'dark' in Malagasy.

DISTRIBUTION

Endemic to Madagascar. Known from eastern regions from lowland rainforest to humid forest areas in the eastern central highlands. Upper elevational range appears to be 1,300m (B16, B23).

BEHAVIOUR

Roosts in small numbers under bark of trees or eaves of buildings; one roost of 30 females found between

probable range

Madagascar Serotine

floorboards of an old building near Andasibe (B41). This could be a nursery colony. Females give birth to one or two and exceptionally three young.

Flies at a height of 10–15m, often follows the same route around canopy, also been caught over water.

Neoromicia malagasyensis

MEASUREMENTS

Total length: 82-84mm. Forearm: 30-32mm. Wingspan: unknown. Weight: 4-9g. (B23)

DESCRIPTION

Originally described as endemic subspecies of Somali Serotine *N. s. somalicus* from Africa (B41).

Because of different pelage coloration, external measurements (it is larger) and cranial and dental features, now regarded as a distinct species (B23).

Dorsal pelage dark brown, underparts similarly dark but more buff to dark grey, with the grey becoming paler towards the tail (B23).

DISTRIBUTION

Known only from the Sakaraha and Isalo National Park area in the central south (B41; B23). Elevational range is 450m to 700m.

BEHAVIOUR

Type specimen collected in palm savanna; specimens from Isalo caught around the perimeter of the massif (Canyon des Singes). Assumed to be associated with dry open habitats. Feeds on insects.

Neoromicia malagasyensis

MADAGASCAR HOUSE BATS genus *Scotophilus*

Contains around 12 species, widely distributed throughout Africa, Middle East, portions of Asia and South-east Asia (B50). The name comes from habit (in Africa particularly) of roosting in buildings, although natural cavities in trees and palms are also used. Most species roost in small colonies of 20 or less.

Taxonomy of the genus is contentious, especially as to how several mainland African taxa relate to those on Indian Ocean islands (B33; B46). Recent work has clarified the situation (B50). At least four species are known to occur on Madagascar, including two newly described species (B25; B26).

Scotophilus robustus.

Scotophilus robustus

MEASUREMENTS

Total length: 135-170mm. Forearm: 62-65mm. Wingspan: not measured. Weight: 40.5-49g. (B16; B25)

DESCRIPTION

Largish, heavy-bodied with robust head. Upperparts and underparts mid-brown. Jaws and teeth are powerful.

DISTRIBUTION

Endemic to Madagascar and wide-spread; recorded at sites in the northeast (Marojejy and Masoala), central east (Tsinjoarivo and Anjozorobe), west (Bemaraha) and south

(Zombitse) (B42; B44; B3; B24; B25). Found up to 1,400m, appears rare throughout range (B16).

BEHAVIOUR

Roosts around human habitation and also natural sites (B45). A strong flyer, leaves its roosting sites around dusk. Hunting occurs between three and 12 metres above the ground. Diet is insects, including beetles, moths and termites.

Scotophilus borbonicus

MEASUREMENTS

Total length: not measured. Forearm: 51-52mm. Wingspan: not measured. Weight: not measured.

DESCRIPTION

Upperparts reddish, underparts and throat paler and often appear whitish.

DISTRIBUTION

Originally described from two specimens collected on Réunion in the early 19th century, not recorded on Madagascar since 1868 (B25). Original specimen probably a vagrant (B24).

BEHAVIOUR

Behaviour and ecology are unknown.

Scotophilus tandrefana

MEASUREMENTS

Total length 111mm; Forearm: 44-47mm. Wingspan: unknown. Weight: 14.2g. (B25)

DESCRIPTION

Relatively small, upper body fur rich, dark chocolate-brown, underparts, chest and throat paler medium brown. Muzzle relatively short and rounded; black ears are also short (B25).

DISTRIBUTION

New species known only from Tsingy de Bemaraha National Park; captured in open areas adjacent to deciduous forest, close to limestone outcrops and sites at Mahabo and Sarodrano

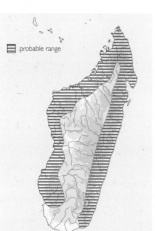

probable range

Scotophilus robustus

Scotophilus tandrefana

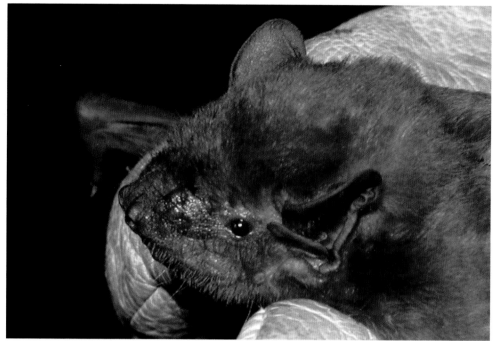

Scotophilus tandrefana.

all of which are below 100m in elevation (B25). An individual from Kirindy
Forest may also be this species (B25);
tandrefana is from the Malagasy
meaning 'from the west'.

BEHAVIOUR
Currently unknown.

Scotophilus marovaza

MEASUREMENTS
Total length: unknown. Forearm:
unknown. Wingspan: unknown.
Weight: unknown.

DESCRIPTION
Shortly to be published (B26).

DISTRIBUTION
Known only from the central west,
the vicinity of Marovaza.

BEHAVIOUR
Found roosting in dense layers of
dry palm leaves of a roof; known to
roost in small groups (B45).

LONG-FINGERED AND BENT-WINGED BATS
genus *Miniopterus*

A genus with a broad distribution in the Old World, occuring widely across Europe, Africa, Asia, South-east Asia and
Australasia. Second finger bone of the longest finger (third finger) is around three times the length of the first finger
bone. At rest hangs by hindfeet with third finger folded back.

All species are superficially similar, only differences often being in size. Taxonomy is confused. Four species known
from Madagascar, three are endemic (B41). All are insectivorous and prefer moths and beetles.

Miniopterus majori

MEASUREMENTS
Total length: 89–100mm*.
Forearm: 42–47mm. Wingspan:
310mm*. Weight: 8g. (B41)
*Single specimen.

DESCRIPTION
Pelage greyish-brown, generally
slightly paler on ventral side. Head
is rounded and muzzle short.
Ears moderately large, squarish in
shape; tragus kidney-shaped and
prominent.

DISTRIBUTION
Endemic to Madagascar; found
mainly in eastern regions, including
the high plateau from sea level to
around 1,200m. Also records
south of Toliara in south-west
(B16).

Miniopterus majori

Miniopterus sp.

BEHAVIOUR

A cave-dwelling species, gregarious, often roosting in mixed colonies with congeners, *M. fraterculus* and *M. manavi* (B41). Caves are essential, *M. majori* preferring to hang from the ceiling in tightly packed groups. Occasionally also recorded in tree holes. A very rapid flyer; tends to fly high and swoops in the air when hunting. Small beetles and moths are main prey.

Miniopterus manavi

MEASUREMENTS

Total length: 90–110mm. Forearm: 34–41mm. Wingspan: 258–287mm. Weight: 3–7g. (B16)

DESCRIPTION

Pelage variously greyish-brown to reddish-brown. Ears angular and tragus prominent. Smallest *Miniopterus* in Madagascar.

DISTRIBUTION

Endemic to Madagascar, widely distributed including the high plateau.

Miniopterus manavi

Miniopterus manavi.

Found at elevations from sea level to 1,500m, records at high elevations are rare (B21; B16).

BEHAVIOUR
Roosts in caves and similar environs, often in mixed-species colonies. Reported as most common and widespread bat in caves of Ankarana; a roost on Mikira Plateau contained approximately 4,000 bats (B3). This may be a maternity colony. Feeds on small insects like moths and beetles; known to hunt within forests, along forest edges and by streams and rivers.

LESSER LONG-FINGERED BAT
Miniopterus fraterculus

MEASUREMENTS
Total length: 100–115mm. Forearm: 40–44mm. Wingspan: 319–328mm. Weight: 7–11g. (B20; B16)

DESCRIPTION
Pelage is greyish to greyish-brown.

DISTRIBUTION
Principally distributed on the African mainland, from South Africa north to Malawi and Zambia and possibly as

probable range

Lesser
Long-fingered Bat

far as Kenya. In Madagascar appears to be restricted to eastern areas in secondary forest and outside forest near river margins (B42). Recorded from 500m to 2,000m (B41).

BEHAVIOUR
Only species of *Miniopterus* in Madagascar known to hibernate (B16).

Miniopterus gleni

MEASUREMENTS
Total length: 95–100mm. Forearm: 47–50mm. Wingspan: 342–369. Weight: 11–17g. (B16)

DESCRIPTION
Pelage is long, soft and sombre grey-brown. The largest Bent-winged Bat on Madagascar.

DISTRIBUTION
A recently described species thought to be endemic to Madagascar. Recorded in all regions, except the Sambirano in the north-west. Larger populations found in areas with extensive cave systems, such as the north and south-west.

BEHAVIOUR
Roosts of up to 90 recorded,

probable range

Miniopterus gleni

often communal: in sea caves at St Augustin found together with *Miniopterus majori, M. manavi, Myotis goudoti, Triaenops furculus* and *Otomops madagascariensis* (B24).

FREE-TAILED BATS Family Molossidae

Widely distributed in warm and tropical areas around the world with at least 80 species recognised. Robust and small to medium-sized. A large proportion of their thick tail projects beyond the tail (interfemoral) membrane. Membranes are leathery, the wings long and narrow for fast flying. Ears have a tragus, usually joined across the forehead and directed forward (B18).

After recent revisions, a family represented on Madagascar by eight species divided between five genera: *Mormopterus, Tadarida, Chaerephon, Mops* and *Otomops*.

GOBLIN OR FLAT-HEADED BATS

genus *Mormopterus*

A genus containing ten species: most occur in Australasia, but there are other representatives in South America, the Caribbean and on south-west Indian Ocean islands, including one on Madagascar. Divided into two subgenera, *Mormopterus* and *Micronomus*: the former on Madagascar.

PETERS'S GOBLIN BAT

Mormopterus jugularis

MEASUREMENTS
Total length: 90–95mm. Forearm: 37–40mm. Wingspan: 262–288mm. Weight: 8–14g. (B16)

DESCRIPTION
Pelage soft and dense. Upperparts greyish-brown to charcoal, underparts paler. Muzzle blunt and slightly upturned. Ears large, rounded and not joined together, tragus well developed.

DISTRIBUTION
Endemic to Madagascar. Widespread; recorded in central, western and southern regions: one record from Ankarana in the north. From sea level up to around 1,200m (B16).

BEHAVIOUR
Roosts in caves, also associated with buildings. Detected by distinctive

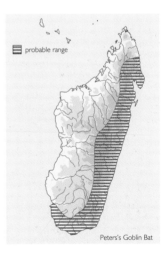

probable range

Peters's Goblin Bat

odour. Probably a crevice roosting species adapted to commensal living. Bats leave roosts simultaneously each evening.

LESSER MASTIFF OR FREE-TAILED BATS genus *Tadarida*

Characterised by wrinkled lips, relatively thin jaws and large ears joined by a band of skin across the crown. May form the largest colonies of any warm-blooded vertebrate – large nursery colonies of some species are estimated to contain several million bats.

LARGE FREE-TAILED BAT

Tadarida fulminans

MEASUREMENTS

Total length: 120–130mm. Forearm: 57–60mm. Wingspan: 421–438mm. Weight: 23–43g. (B16)

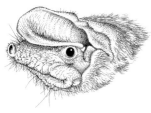

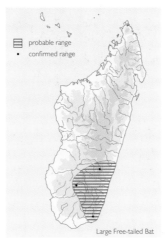

Large Free-tailed Bat

DESCRIPTION

Body dark chestnut-brown dorsally, pale grey to whitish on chest and belly. Wings noticeably paler than body. Head small and relatively narrow. Tail up to 50mm in length.

DISTRIBUTION

Originally described from a specimen collected near Fianarantsoa in 1903. There are recent records from Isalo National Park (B24) and the Tolagnaro area. Elsewhere, found in Central and East Africa as far south as the Transvaal.

BEHAVIOUR

In Africa a gregarious species seldom seen in colonies of more than 20. Rock crevices and small caves are the usual daytime roost sites. A fast and agile flyer (B11).

Chaerephon leucogaster

MEASUREMENTS

Total length: 80–95mm. Forearm: 33–38mm. Wingspan: 262–280mm. Weight: 6–11g. (B16; B22)

DESCRIPTION

Dorsal region, throat and chest dark to mid-brown, abdominal regions generally pale greyish-white. Wings

Chaerephon leucogaster.

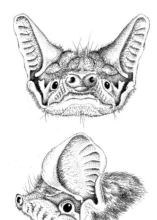

medium brown with whitish edges. The smallest Malagasy representative of this group.

DISTRIBUTION

Recorded in south-western and western regions but not north of Mahajanga (B16; B24). Often associated with more open habitat.

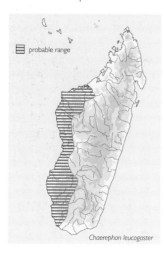

probable range

Chaerephon leucogaster

BEHAVIOUR

Collected from roosts in old buildings (B16), either in single species colonies or with *Mops leucostigma* and *Mormopterus jugularis* (B22).

LITTLE FREE-TAILED BAT

Chaerephon pumilus

MEASUREMENTS

Total length: 90–99mm. Forearm: 38–41mm. Wingspan: 287–298mm. Weight: 9.5–15. (B16; B22)

DESCRIPTION

Pelage variable in colour. In Madagascar, upperparts dark brown, underparts lighter and throat brown. In southern Africa, ranges from deep blackish-brown upperparts with a paler under-side to more brownish upperparts with a broad whitish band extending from the chest down to the anus.

probable range

Little Free-tailed Bat

DISTRIBUTION

Occurs from south-west Arabian Peninsula, through most of sub-Saharan Africa and also on Madagascar and the island of Aldabra. On Madagascar found only in northern half of eastern rainforest region and eastern band of the high plateau at elevations between 500m and 1,100m (B41).

BEHAVIOUR

Found roosting singly or in small colonies in the roofs of buildings, also uses crevices in rocks and trees. In Africa, clusters of over 20 females and their single offspring have been found, these 'harems' being attended by a single male.

Generally flies at heights up to 12m; often swoops down suddenly to three or four metres above ground level. The flight is fast and erratic.

Chaerephon jobimena

MEASUREMENTS

Total length: 107-117mm. Forearm: 45-48mm. Wingspan: around 300mm*. Weight: 12.5-16g. (B22)
* estimated

DESCRIPTION

Dorsal pelage dense and velvety. Two colour phases known; in one, upperparts rich chocolate-brown, in other, distinctly rufous. Throat similar colour to dorsal regions, rest of underparts are brownish-grey. Transition is diffused. Muzzle covered in hair and relatively blunt, upper lips have five to six wrinkles each side. Ears longer than in congeners on Madagascar (B22).

DISTRIBUTION

Recently described species collected at widely separated sites in deciduous forest up to 800m asl, including caves in Ankarana in north, Namoroka in west and Isalo and Zombitse National Parks in central south (B22).

BEHAVIOUR

Apparently prefers drier areas.

Chaerephon jobimena

MIDAS MASTIFF BAT

Mops midas

MEASUREMENTS
Total length: 150–170mm. Forearm: 62–63mm. Wingspan: 448mm*. Weight: 40–50g. (B16) *Based on African specimens.

probable range

Midas Mastiff Bat

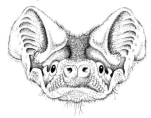

DESCRIPTION
Upperparts brown to greyish-brown, underparts paler and more tawny. Overall appearance is of uniform coloration. Reddish and orange-red colour phases have also been described. Characterised by band of skin joining the ears across the crown, very wrinkled lips, a robust skull and heavy jaw.

DISTRIBUTION
Occurs from south-west Arabian Peninsula south through savanna regions of sub-Saharan Africa. In Madagascar widespread but discontinuous; recorded in western and south-western regions; Zombitse National Park (B44), Toliara (B41), Ranobe, north of Toliara (B22), Mikea Forest (B24).

BEHAVIOUR
Habits remain largely unknown in Madagascar, but probably similar to African populations, where it prefers open woodland and savanna habitats. Small colonies have been found roosting in hollow trees, larger colonies (up to 600 in Madagascar) are found in old buildings.

Mops leucostigma

MEASUREMENTS
Total length: 110–120mm. Forearm: 42–45mm. Wingspan: 315–347mm. Weight: 13–22g. (B16)

DESCRIPTION
Upperparts brown to greyish-brown, underparts paler with variable amounts of white.

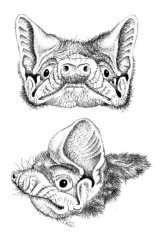

DISTRIBUTION
Endemic to Madagascar. Widespread; recorded in eastern, western and central regions up to 1,300m but appears absent from the extreme south (B16).

BEHAVIOUR
Roosts in large colonies, sometimes in buildings (B41). Hawks over rivers, open areas and even beaches (B47).

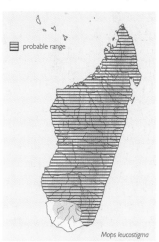

probable range

Mops leucostigma

LARGE-EARED FREE-TAILED BATS genus *Otomops*

A genus containing seven widely distributed species: two from Papua New Guinea, one in the Lesser Sunda Islands, one from Java, one from southern India, one from mainland Africa and one from Madagascar. All medium-large bats with very large forward-facing ears and a series of small dermal projections along their leading edge. Little is known of the genus as a whole.

MADAGASCAR FREE-TAILED BAT

Otomops madagascariensis

MEASUREMENTS

Total length: 130–140mm. Forearm: 59–65mm. Wingspan: 415–454mm. Weight: 20–29g. (B16)

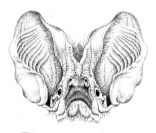

DESCRIPTION

A largish bat (males are slightly larger than females) notable for its flattened head and large ears. Upperparts vary from dark brown to reddish-brown,

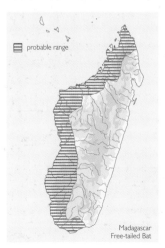

probable range

Madagascar Free-tailed Bat

Madagascar Free-tailed Bat.

underparts a slightly paler brown. There may also be a greyish area on nape and upper dorsal region. Ears are 30–35mm in length and directed forward at a very oblique angle. The wings are long and narrow.

DISTRIBUTION

Endemic to Madagascar. Appears to be restricted to far north, north-west, west and south-west (B16; B24).

BEHAVIOUR

A fast-flying, high-aerial feeder, preying almost exclusively on moths (B53). Both solitary and gregarious, can occur in large colonies. Roosts

in caves and hollow trees; roosts up to 100 recorded in caves in limestone karst formations (B24). In marine caves to the south of Toliara has been recorded roosting together with *Triaenops furculus*, *Myotis goudoti*, *Miniopterus manavi*, *Miniopterus majori* and *Miniopterus gleni* (B41).

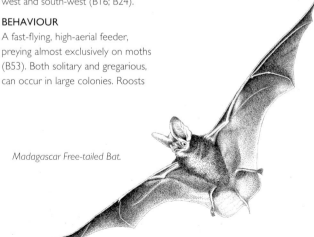

Madagascar Free-tailed Bat.

LEMURS
Order Primates
Infraorder Lemuriformes

Early biologists coined the term 'lemur' as the calls of some species (probably from the family Lemuridae) were reminiscent of the cries of Roman *lemures*, or 'spirits of the dead'. Subsequently, this has become widely accepted as an encompassing vernacular for all of Madagascar's primates.

Lemurs, together with galagos and pottos from Africa, and lorises from Asia, form the suborder Strepsirhini. This group is collectively and commonly known as prosimians (literally 'before the monkeys') and is restricted to the Old World, where all species are largely confined to tropical arboreal habitats, the sole exception being the Ring-tailed Lemur *Lemur catta* that is partially terrestrial.

The earliest primates perhaps evolved around 60 million years ago and may have been similar in a number of ways to some present-day small nocturnal lemurs. Later more advanced forms evolved that were better able to exploit their environment. This lineage eventually became monkeys and apes, and was able to outcompete and oust the more primitive forms. Critically, some of the early lemur-like primates became isolated on Madagascar prior to this. Their cousins elsewhere were driven to extinction by the new arrivals, but on Madagascar they found refuge. Once in residence, the early lemurs evolved to exploit their new home to best advantage. This resulted in spectacular diversification and speciation. Contemporary lemurs display an extraordinary array of morphologies, different types of behaviour and lifestyles, which rival those of monkeys and apes combined.

Even within some genera there has been considerable speciation, for instance ten species of Typical Lemur (genus *Eulemur*) and 23 species of sportive lemur (genus *Lepilemur*) are currently recognised. Many of these have very specific ranges, and boundaries between species are often major rivers or similar geographical barriers. Indeed, there is no location on the island where more than two *Eulemur* species and one *Lepilemur* species naturally occur together. The boundaries between some taxa are less distinct and there are narrow bands of hybridisation.

There has been a recent major taxonomic revision of lemur groups (L115; L170), together with the discovery and description of several new species (e.g. L274; L152; L360; L7; L165; L166; L11; L259a; L208a). Currently 86 extant species are recognised, divided between 15 genera and five families (Cheirogaleidae, Lepilemuridae, Lemuridae, Indriidae and Daubentoniidae), all of which are endemic to Madagascar.

Because of their diversity, the evolutionary affinity of the lemurs has been the subject of considerable debate. Much of this has revolved around whether or not they are derived from a single ancestor, the implication being, that if they do not form a natural group, then there must have been several colonisation events between Madagascar and the African mainland. However, recent molecular analysis suggests the contrary. From this, it would appear that all lemurs, including the bizarre Aye-aye *Daubentonia madagascariensis*, are derived from a single ancestor that may have arrived from Africa on floating mats of vegetation between 47 and 54 million years ago (L401).

Spectacular as the present-day assemblage of lemurs is, it is only a shadow of the array that once existed on pristine Madagascar. The original lemur fauna included at least 17 other species that are now all sadly extinct (L95). Without exception these species were larger than extant forms and some, like the Giant Sloth Lemurs (*Archaeoindris*), attained body weights up to 200kg. What is more, many of these species probably survived until after humans arrived on Madagascar, and their demise was almost certainly a consequence of overhunting and habitat destruction (L39; L40).

Lemurs are by far the most intensively studied of Madagascar's mammals. Detailed behavioural and ecological investigation began in the 1960s, although it

Subfossil skull of giant extinct lemur possibly Megaladapis *species.*

was not until the mid-1980s that interest in Madagascar really blossomed. Since then there has been a huge advancement of knowledge and the discovery of numerous new species. Encouragingly, this trend shows no sign of abating; as remote forests are explored exciting discoveries are still being made.

All lemurs are threatened by habitat loss and hunting; the latter threat is particularly acute in some areas and has largely been overlooked in the past. Larger species like sifakas (*Propithecus* spp.) are obvious targets, but so too are many of the smaller species (L90; L103). In many areas lemurs are hunted in remote localities to provide bushmeat both locally and for more distant larger villages and towns (L98).

MOUSE AND DWARF LEMURS Family Cheirogaleidae

With recent taxonomic revisions and the discovery of new taxa, this family now consists of at least 30 species of small to small-medium nocturnal lemurs, divided between five genera. Four of these genera – *Microcebus, Allocebus, Cheirogaleus* and *Mirza* – comprise the subfamily Cheirogaleinae; while the genus *Phaner* is placed in its own subfamily Phanerinae (L114; L115; L274). They are characterised by medium to medium-long bodies, long tails, short legs and a horizontal body posture. All run and jump quadrupedally. They may be both solitary and gregarious when active and sleep alone or in small groups. The family is represented throughout the various forest types in Madagascar, and in most areas two or more species live sympatrically.

MOUSE LEMURS genus *Microcebus*

Mouse lemurs are the smallest primates in the world, ranging from around 30 grams to 75 grams. They have colonised all suitable forest types in southern, western and eastern regions and are without question the most abundant group of primates on Madagascar (L151). All are broadly similar in appearance and habits and prefer the lower forest layers with tangles of fine branches and lianas. As their vernacular name implies, they are all 'mouse-like' in appearance. In light of field studies over the past ten years, the taxonomy of *Microcebus* has recently been revised.

At one time this genus was thought to contain just two species with non-overlapping ranges: the Grey Mouse Lemur *M. murinus* found in the drier regions of the north, west and south, and the Brown Mouse Lemur *M. rufus* of the humid rainforest regions of the east (L120).

However, the situation is now known to be far more complex. Surveys over the past decade in southern and western forests have revealed a number of distinctive populations resulting in the description of eight new species, *M. tavaratra, M. sambiranensis, M. berthae, M. ravelobensis, M. mamiratra, M. lokobensis, M. bongolarensis* and *M. danfossi* along with the re-evaluation of previously described species, *M. myoxinus* and *M. griseorufus* (L406; L274; L403; L11).

The situation in the eastern rainforests is similar. Recent studies have found four new species, *M. lehilahytsara* (L152), *M. mittermeieri, M. jollyae* and *M. simmonsi* (L165) and further discoveries may follow. The distributions and precise range limits of all these species are currently uncertain and this situation will only become clear after further fieldwork. At present the genus *Microcebus* contains 16 species.

GREY MOUSE LEMUR

Microcebus murinus

MEASUREMENTS

Total length: 245–290mm. Head/body length: 120–140mm. Tail length: 125–150mm. Weight: average 60g, known range 40–70g. (L69; L307; L274; L403)

DESCRIPTION & IDENTIFICATION

Largest mouse lemur. Upperparts and tail variable greyish-brown to

Grey Mouse Lemur, Ankarafantsika National Park.

Grey Mouse Lemur

Frequents secondary vegetation and may even be found in degraded roadside and scrub-type vegetation and gardens on edge of villages (L81; L84), prefers lower levels and under-storey, where branches and vegetation are dense (L151).

BEHAVIOUR

Nocturnal and omnivorous, largely solitary when foraging (L148) and occupies small home range of 1–2 hectares. Male home ranges may overlap with one another and always overlap with home range of at least one female (L26; L70). Male home range size increases up to three times during breeding season (L151).

Can be extremely abundant, reaching apparent densities of several hundred individuals/km^2 (L260; L60). However, abundance not uniform and even in apparently similar habitat it may occur in localised concentrations or 'population nuclei' (L167; L307).

By day sleeps in tree holes lined with leaf-litter or purpose-built

brownish-grey, sometimes slightly browner towards tip. Underparts and throat dull beige to cream/off-white. Nose-bridge and between eyes are creamy-white. Ears relatively long, protruding noticeably. Face rounded, eyes relatively large.

Distinguished from sympatric mouse lemurs by larger size and long, highly visible ears. Smaller and more active than other nocturnal species like *Cheirogaleus* and *Mirza*.

HABITAT & DISTRIBUTION

Dry deciduous, semi-humid deciduous, moist lowland forest, transitional forest, littoral forest, spiny forest and some degraded forests including plantations.

Limits of distribution poorly understood. Occurs throughout forests of west from Onilahy River, north to region of Ankarafantsika. South of Onilahy River there are populations in Beza Mahafaly, although very rare (L273), and also an apparently isolated and disjointed population in south-east, either side of Mandrare River and in moist coast, transitional and gallery forests around Andohahela (L274; L151).

The identity of *Microcebus* sp. from Zombitse, Vohibasia and Isalo has yet to be confirmed and may be *M. murinus* or *M. griseorufus*.

Grey Mouse Lemur, Kirindy Forest.

spherical nests constructed from dead leaves and moss amongst twigs of dense undergrowth (L149). May use between three and nine different tree holes that are shared – with up to 15 other individuals – and used for up to five consecutive days. Composition of sleeping groups changes seasonally. During breeding season (September–October) males and females may sleep together. At other times females sleep in groups with dependent offspring, while males sleep alone or in pairs (L308; L261).

During daytime period of inactivity may enter temporary torpor and able to reduce metabolic rate and body temperature to ambient (body temperatures as low as 7°C recorded) (L209). During cooler winter months (May–August) choose tree holes very close to ground level, where ambient temperatures remain lower and more stable, which allows them to remain torpid for longer. This helps conserve body resources (L305).

In dry season (April/May to September/October) females become totally inactive and remain dormant in tree holes for several weeks and up to five months to conserve energy and reduce predation. Males rarely remain inactive for more than a few days and are fully active before females; allows them to establish hierarchies for access to breeding females. Both sexes lay down large reserves of fat in hindlegs and tail – up to 35% of body weight – which sustains them through the dry season and periods of aestivation (L69; L304).

Females advertise oestrus by distinctive high-frequency calls and scent-marking (L38). Mating from mid-September until end of October, gestation about 60 days, twins the norm. Birth occurs in tree hole or leaf nest and timed to coincide with onset of rainy season (L70). Offspring inde-

pendent within two months, females able to breed themselves within first year. Reproductive lifespan no more than five years (L151). Closely related females remain loosely associated after maturation, while males tend to move away from natal area (L389). Diet mainly fruit, flowers, nectar (so act as pollinators), insects and secretions produced by insects (L48). Also eats sap and gum from *Euphorbia* and *Terminalia* trees and even small vertebrates like treefrogs, geckos and chameleons.

Predators include raptors and owls, carnivores like Ring-tailed Mongoose, Narrow-striped Mongoose and Fosa and large snakes (L107; L108; L109; L99).

WHERE TO SEE
Easy to see at a variety of locations; Ampijoroa (Ankarafantsika NP), Kirindy Forest and Berenty Private Reserve probably best.

BROWN MOUSE LEMUR
Microcebus rufus

MEASUREMENTS
Total length: 170–250mm. Head/body length: 70–90mm. Tail length: 100–160mm. Weight: average 40–45g, seasonal variation 30–55g. (L21)

DESCRIPTION & IDENTIFICATION
Head, upperparts and tail characteristic brown to rufous-brown, with greyish tinges showing through. Face rounded, often more rufous than body. Underparts and throat creamy grey-white. Ears relatively small and do not protrude.

A very small active lemur with long tail. Moves quickly through branches and foliage; much smaller than sympatric dwarf lemurs *Cheirogaleus* spp.

HABITAT & DISTRIBUTION
Lowland and montane rainforests and similar habitat, including secondary vegetation and some adjacent plantations. Observed from ground level to canopy. Also seen in marshes and reed beds around Lac Aloatra.

Based on current information, found throughout eastern rainforest belt, from Tolagnaro in south to Tsaratanana Massif in north. North of Tsaratanana picture is unclear. Isolated populations also occur in Ambohitantely and Tampoketsa Analsmaitso, remnant patches of forest in central highlands.

Microcebus in eastern regions now known to be diverse, and several new species have recently been described (L152; L165). Ranges of new species – *M. lehilahytsara*, *M. jollyae*, *M. mittermeieri* and *M. simmonsi* – not yet determined, so distributions of eastern *Microcebus* species must be treated as tentative at present.

BEHAVIOUR
Nocturnal and omnivorous. Both solitary and gregarious, and common; population densities range from around 110 animals/km^2 (L81) to over 330 individuals/km^2 (L20). Can be more abundant in secondary vegetation than primary forest (L84).

Forages in understorey and low trees. When resources are concentrated, individuals may gather in small numbers. Diet mainly fruit (over 40 species eaten), flowers and nectar, young shoots, gum, insects and other arthropods (L80). Composition highly variable and reflects seasonal changes in food availability (L18).

By day sleeps in groups of one to four in tree holes, leaf nests and sometimes disused birds' nests, often close to ground (L396). Composition of sleep groups unknown, but females sleep with small infants. Regularly scent-marks territorial boundaries with urine and faeces but

still considerable overlap of home ranges. Males have larger territories and move over greater distances (L20).

Both sexes lay down fat reserves in tail and other areas of body during wet season and become inactive during part of winter, during which time they may lose 30% of pre-aestivation body weight (L19).

Males prepare for breeding in mid-August when testes enlarge. Mating occurs between September and November, births from November to January. Females construct nest of leaves 1–3m off ground, producing one to three young; gestation around 60 days. Young around 5g at birth.

Widely predated: carnivores like Ring-tailed Mongoose and Fosa are able to excavate them from sleep sites; raptors and other birds, e.g. Hook-billed Vanga *Vanga curvirostris* also eat them (L109); some owls and large snake are significant nocturnal predators (L99; L154).

WHERE TO SEE

Easily seen throughout its range. Best places are Nosy Mangabe and Ranomafana National Park. At last site several individuals visit a feeding station, where exceptionally close views are common.

Brown Mouse Lemur, Ranomafana National Park.

WESTERN RUFOUS MOUSE LEMUR
Microcebus myoxinus

MEASUREMENTS
Total length: 260–280mm. Head/
body length: 120–130mm. Tail
length: 140–150mm. Weight:
40–55g. (L274; L403)

DESCRIPTION & IDENTIFICATION
Upperparts and tail rufous-brown
with distinctive reddish-brown mid-
dorsal stripe. Tip of tail darker. Head
more rufous. Underparts pale grey.
Ears relatively short. Cinnamon patch
between eyes darkens to tawny
crown (L274).

HABITAT & DISTRIBUTION
Dry deciduous forest and degraded
forests adjacent to savanna up to
900m asl. Also records from coastal

Western Rufous
Mouse Lemur

mangrove forests at Besalamy well
removed from deciduous forest
(L123).
   Range now thought to extend in
apparently discontinuous popula-
tions from the northern banks of
Tsiribihina River north to at least
Soalala Peninsula (L274).

BEHAVIOUR
Yet to be studied. Probably similar to
other mouse lemurs from western
regions.

WHERE TO SEE
Only locality with relatively easy
access is Bemaraha National Park.
Best to search forested areas near
park entrance and close to village
of Bekopaka on northern banks of
Manambolo River.

GOLDEN-BROWN MOUSE LEMUR
Microcebus ravelobensis

MEASUREMENTS
Total length: 260–313 mm. Head/
body length: 120–139mm. Tail
length: 144–172mm. Weight: average
72g, known range 59–110g. (L406;
L274; L403)

DESCRIPTION & IDENTIFICATION
Head and upperparts rufous to
golden-brown and distinctly mottled,
mid-dorsal stripe indistinct. Underparts
paler, yellowish-white and slightly
mottled. Tail long, thin, darker brown
than body and darkens at tip. Head
relatively small; faint white stripe
extends from lower forehead to tip

Western Rufous Mouse Lemur.

Golden-brown
Mouse Lemur

Sambirano
Mouse Lemur

Golden-brown Mouse Lemur, Ankarafantsika National Park.

of muzzle. Dark brown rings around eyes. Ears long and sparsely furred.

Rufous pelage and long tail help distinguish from Grey Mouse Lemur.

HABITAT & DISTRIBUTION
Dry deciduous forest up to around 450m asl. Prefers forest with lower canopy and higher density of lianas than *M. murinus*. Also uses tree holes less frequently.

Known from Ankarafantsika region, 120km south-east of Mahajanga in north-west Madagascar. First collected adjacent to Lac Ravelobe at Ampijoroa, hence specific name, *ravelobensis*. Also thought to occur in Bongolava Classified Forest, north of Ankarafantsika and Bora Special Reserve. *Microcebus* in Mariarano Forest on coast north of Mahajanga may be this species.

BEHAVIOUR
Nocturnal and more active than sympatric Grey Mouse Lemur. Moves from branch to branch by leaping, rather than quadrupedally like *M. murinus*. May remain more active during dry season as does not have capacity to store fat in same way as *M. murinus*.

Sleeps in nests in tangles of branches, lianas, vines and dead leaves, whereas *M. murinus* prefers tree holes. Males and females sleep together in mixed groups (L261).

Breeding begins in August, before Grey Mouse Lemur. Gestation not known, but probably around 60 days.

WHERE TO SEE
Forest around Lac Ravelobe at Ampijoroa Forestry Station (Jardin Botanique B) is most accessible locality.

SAMBIRANO MOUSE LEMUR
Microcebus sambiranensis

MEASUREMENTS*
Total length: 247–271mm. Head/body length: 113–123mm. Tail length: 134–148mm. Weight: average 44g, known range 38–51.5g. (L274; L403) *Based on six specimens

DESCRIPTION & IDENTIFICATION
Second smallest mouse lemur species. Dorsal pelage rufous with indistinct amber mid-dorsal stripe beginning at shoulder, extending to tip of tail. Ears short. Underparts dull whitish-beige with dark grey under fur. Tail densely furred especially towards darker tip. Head more orange-amber with distinct dark eye-rings (L274).

HABITAT & DISTRIBUTION
Humid lowland and mid-altitude forests of Sambirano region. Also seen in secondary and degraded habitats adjacent to intact forest.

Recently described, currently known only from Manongarivo Reserve in north-west and probably adjacent Ampasindava Peninsula. Collected on both western and eastern side of Manongarivo Massif (L105).

BEHAVIOUR
Yet to be studied.

WHERE TO SEE
Vicinity of Manongarivo and Ampasindava.

Sambirano Mouse Lemur.

NORTHERN RUFOUS MOUSE LEMUR

Microcebus tavaratra

MEASUREMENTS*
Total length: 276–296mm. Head/body length: 113–139mm. Tail length: 145–167mm. Weight: average 61g, known range 48–83.5g. (L274; L403) *Based on six specimens

DESCRIPTION & IDENTIFICATION
Medium-large *Microcebus* with dark brown-cinnamon back, slightly paler flanks, rufous coloration around head and distinct mid-dorsal stripe continuous from crown to base of tail. Underparts whitish/beige, under fur dark grey. Superficially similar to *M. ravelobensis*, but their ranges do not overlap.

HABITAT & DISTRIBUTION
Dry deciduous and gallery forests

Northern Rufous
Mouse Lemur

of Ankarana Massif, including forests within limestone canyons up to around 250m asl (L274).

Recently described, currently confirmed only from Ankarana Reserve in far north. Probable that *Microcebus* from Analamera to east are also this species. Identity of *Microcebus* in nearby Montagne d'Ambre to north remains undetermined.

Also rufous-coloured *Microcebus* in forests around Daraina whose taxonomic status has yet to be established.

BEHAVIOUR
Yet to be studied.

WHERE TO SEE
Ankarana Special Reserve, 100km south of Antsiranana is best place to see this lemur, especially close to both Campement Anilotra (formerly Camp des Anglais) and Campement d'Andrafiabe (formerly Camp des American).

MADAME BERTHE'S MOUSE LEMUR

Microcebus berthae

MEASUREMENTS
Total length: 223–230mm. Head/body length: 90–95mm. Tail length: 134–138mm. Weight: average 30.5g, known range 24.5–38g. (L307; L274)

DESCRIPTION & IDENTIFICATION
Smallest *Microcebus* species and smallest primate in world. Pelage short and dense. Upperparts and tail rufous to cinnamon-brown with distinct orange tinge, underparts creamy-white. Well-defined tawny dorsal stripe down back to end of tail. Head more orange and brighter than body. Dull whitish patch above nose to forehead (L274). Tail relatively long and more densely furred than other *Microcebus*.

Can be confused only with *M. murinus*, but is noticeably smaller, brown/orange, with small ears and relatively long tail.

HABITAT & DISTRIBUTION
Dry deciduous forest up to 50m

Northern Rufous Mouse Lemur.

Madame Berthe's
Mouse Lemur

Predated by Barn Owl and
Madagascar Long-eared Owl (L275).

WHERE TO SEE
Best looked for in Kirindy Forest,
north-east of Morondava. Can be
seen in forest close to research
camp.

*The world's smallest primate, Madame Berthe's Mouse Lemur (left), with Grey
Mouse Lemur (right).*

asl. Recently described, currently
confirmed only from Kirindy Forest
and surrounding areas of Central
Menabe. Range may extend north
to Ambadira (region of Analabe)
and south to Andranomena
Reserve. Patchily distributed within
range and possibly occurs in 'population nuclei'.

BEHAVIOUR
Little known. Nocturnal and solitary.
Probably omnivorous.

Both males and females enter
daily, but not prolonged, torpor to
conserve body resources (L309).
Home ranges around 1.2ha, although
male ranges larger than females.
These differences increase during
breeding season (L313). Prefer to
sleep in nests in dense liana tangles,
not tree holes, because they cannot
compete with larger sympatric
nocturnal lemurs (L314).

Madame Berthe's Mouse Lemur.

Grey-brown Mouse Lemur.

GREY-BROWN MOUSE LEMUR

Microcebus griseorufus

MEASUREMENTS*

Total length: 253–280mm. Head/body length: 113–132mm. Tail length: 136–153mm. Weight: average 62.5g, known range 46–85g. (L274; L403) *Based on six specimens

DESCRIPTION & IDENTIFICATION

Distinctively coloured and diminutive. Dorsal areas grey contrasting noticeably with cinnamon-brown dorsal stripe and tail and rufous-washed markings on head. Underparts creamy-white, with distinct change in colour between dorsal and ventral regions.

Sympatric with Grey Mouse Lemur in some locations, e.g. Beza Mahafaly where both species occur in both spiny forest and gallery forest and in Mikea Forest where both occur in transitional forest (transition between deciduous forest and spiny forest). In Berenty both species occur but are apparently separated by habitat preference, *M. griseorufus* in spiny forest, *M. murinus* in gallery forest.

HABITAT & DISTRIBUTION

Found in variety of southern habitats: spiny forest, dry thorn scrub, gallery forest and dry deciduous forest up

Grey-brown Mouse Lemur

to 250m asl. More common in spiny forests (L273).

Limits of range unclear. Occurs from south of Morombe in south-west to Andohahela region in south-east. Known from Beza Mahafaly Reserve with historical records from Lamboharana, north of Onilahy River 200km north-west of Beza Mahafaly. In Beza Mahafaly sympatric with *M. murinus* but much more common (L273).

Microcebus also occur in forests of Zombitse, Vohibasia and Isalo but identities have yet to be confirmed and may be *M. griseorufus* or *M. murinus*.

BEHAVIOUR

Diet varied; fruit and insects, but in Beza Mahafaly shows a preference for gum, especially in spiny forest habitats (L273).

Regularly predated by Barn Owl and Madagascar Long-eared Owl (L274).

WHERE TO SEE

Most easily seen in spiny forest areas of Berenty Reserve. Also readily seen, even during day in its sleep-sites, at Arboretum d'Antsokay near Toliara. Other suitable habitats within range worth exploring, e.g. coastal spiny forests around Ifaty, north of Toliara.

GOODMAN'S MOUSE LEMUR

Microcebus lehilahytsara

MEASUREMENTS

Total length: 200–210mm**. Head/body length: 90–92mm*. Tail length: 110–120mm**. Weight: average 45–48g, known range 30–64g*. (L152) *Based on nine specimens **Estimates

DESCRIPTION & IDENTIFICATION

Small rainforest *Microcebus* species. Pelage short and dense. Upperparts

Goodman's Mouse Lemur, Andasibe.

reddish-brown, rust to orange tinges on back, head and tail, with darker brown mid-dorsal stripe. Underparts creamy-white. Distinct off-white stripe from forehead, between eyes and down nose. Tail similar to body colour and uniform. Ears short and round (L152).

Similar to Brown Mouse Lemur, but smaller, more gracile and paler in colour.

HABITAT & DISTRIBUTION
Currently known only from the mid-altitude rainforests of Andasibe-Mantadia National Park.

BEHAVIOUR
Discovered in 2005 and yet to be studied.

WHERE TO SEE
Readily seen in Andasibe-Mantadia

National Park. Night walks along the road or around the Orchid Garden can be very productive.

JOLLY'S MOUSE LEMUR
Microcebus jollyae

MEASUREMENTS
Total length: 211-219mm. Head/body length: 90-96mm. Tail length: 121-123mm. Weight: average 61g, known range 56.8-65.8g. (L165) *Based on three specimens

DESCRIPTION & IDENTIFICATION
Upperparts, including head uniform reddish-brown. Pale whitish area under chin that grades with grey underparts (L165).

HABITAT & DISTRIBUTION
Known from coastal, lowland and mid-latitude rainforest. Based on current data, occurs in south-eastern portion of eastern rainforest belt. Recorded in Manombo Special Reserve and forests of Kianjavato to east of Ranomafana, Vevembe, Mananjary and Karianga (L165).

BEHAVIOUR
Discovered in 2003 and recently

Goodman's Mouse Lemur

Jolly's Mouse Lemur.

SIMMONS'S MOUSE LEMUR

Microcebus simmonsi

Jolly's Mouse Lemur

MEASUREMENTS*

Total length: 231-235mm. Head/body length: 90-92mm. Tail length: 141-143mm. Weight: average 65g, known range 47.3-82.3g. (L165). *Based on six specimens

DESCRIPTION & IDENTIFICATION

Largest and most robust *Microcebus* from eastern rainforests. Upperparts and head dark reddish-brown to orange-brown, underparts pale grey to off-white. Distinctive black streak in middle of crown, white patch on rostrum.

Differs from Brown Mouse Lemur in having dark reddish-brown head with black streak; head of *M. rufus* is more rufous and without stripe.

Simmons's Mouse Lemur

HABITAT & DISTRIBUTION

Lowland and mid-altitude rainforest in the central east. Currently known only from Betampona Special Reserve and Zahamena National Park (L165).

BEHAVIOUR

Recently discovered and yet to be studied.

WHERE TO SEE

Betampona Special Reserve, approximately 50km north-west of Toliara, is the easier of two known sites to reach, but still requires a long strenuous walk.

described. Behaviour and ecology not yet studied.

WHERE TO SEE

No current sites are readily accessible. Best looked for in Manombo Special Reserve south of Farafangana on south-east coast.

Simmons's Mouse Lemur.

MITTERMEIER'S MOUSE LEMUR

Microcebus mittermeieri

MEASUREMENTS*

Total length: 196-204mm. Head/body length: 85-89mm. Tail length: 111-115mm. Weight: average 44g, known range 33.7-51.5g. (L165) *Based on five specimens

DESCRIPTION & IDENTIFICATION

Most diminutive of rainforest *Microcebus*. Dorsal pelage reddish-brown to rust with darker brown

Mittermeier's Mouse Lemur.

CLAIRE'S MOUSE LEMUR
Microcebus mamiratra

MEASUREMENTS*
Total length: 264-308mm. Head/body length: 117-139mm. Tail length: 147-169mm. Weight: average 61g, known range 52.5-69.2g. (L11) *Based on four specimens

DESCRIPTION & IDENTIFICATION
Meduim-sized *Microcebus*. Dorsal fur and tail light reddish-brown, more reddish on crown, nape and upper dorsum. Clear whitish stripe on muzzle and between eyes. Underparts white to cream. Some individuals have light greyish-brown mid-dorsal stripe (L11). Larger than *M. sambiranensis* and *M. tavaratra*, smaller than *M. ravelobensis*.

HABITAT & DISTRIBUTION
Currently known only from humid Sambirano type forests on Nosy Be. Type locality Lokobe Reserve.

Mittermeier's Mouse Lemur

BEHAVIOUR
Discovered in 2003, this species has yet to be studied.

WHERE TO SEE
Anjanaharibe-Sud Special Reserve to west of Andapa is only site this species is currently known to occur. This is a difficult reserve to reach.

mid-dorsal stripe. Ventral fur whitish-brown. Tail similar in colour to body. Yellowish areas under chin and around neck (L165).

Similar to Brown Mouse Lemur, but paler, slightly smaller and more gracile.

HABITAT & DISTRIBUTION
Currently known only from mid-altitude forests in vicinity of Anjanaharibe-Sud Special Reserve (L165). Surveys in neighbouring areas, for instance the Mikira Plateau, may extend range.

Claire's Mouse Lemur, Lokobe.

Claire's
Mouse Lemur

BEHAVIOUR
Yet to be studied.

WHERE TO SEE
The only locality this species is currently known from is Lokobe Special Reserve on Nosy Be.

LOKOBE MOUSE LEMUR
Microcebus lokobensis

MEASUREMENTS*
Total length: 260-280mm**. Head/body length: 105-120mm**. Tail length: 156-164mm. Weight: average 58g, known range 42-73g. (L208a) *Based on 17 specimens ** Estimates

DESCRIPTION & IDENTIFICATION
Small-bodied, reddish *Microcebus*. Head uniformly rufous, distinct white stripe between eyes. Dorsal fur and tail light reddish-brown. Tail tip darker. Underparts creamy-white (L208a). Probably synonymous with recently described *M. mamiratra*, which takes priority.

HABITAT & DISTRIBUTION
Currently known only from humid forests on Nosy Be and mainland

close to village of Manehoka. Confines on the mainland may be the Mahavavy and Sambirano Rivers (L208a). Type locality Lokobe Reserve: same type location as *M. mamiratra* (L11).

BEHAVIOUR
Probably similar to other *Microcebus* in western regions.

Lokobe
Mouse Lemur

WHERE TO SEE
Lokobe Special Reserve on Nosy Be is the most accessible place to see this lemur.

BONGOLAVA MOUSE LEMUR
Microcebus bongolavensis

MEASUREMENTS*
Total length: 265-290mm. Head/body length: 116-132mm**. Tail length: 149-165mm. Weight: average 54g, known range 45-63g. (L208a) *Based on 37 specimens **Estimates

DESCRIPTION & IDENTIFICATION
Relatively large rufous Mouse Lemur. Fur dense and short. Head uniformly rufous in some individuals; others have rufous areas over the eyes, with crown pale grey. Distinct white stripe between eyes. Upperparts and tail

Bongolava Mouse Lemur.

Danfoss Mouse Lemur.

rich brownish-maroon, sometimes with faint dorsal line. Underparts creamy-white (L208a).

HABITAT & DISTRIBUTION
Western deciduous forest. Known from three forest fragments, including Bongolava and Ambodimahabibo Forests, between Sofia and Mahajamba Rivers in north-west Madagascar. These rivers may be barriers confining species' range.

BEHAVIOUR
Probably similar to other *Microcebus* in western regions.

WHERE TO SEE
Bongolava Forest and adjacent fragments. This is an extremely difficult area to reach.

DANFOSS MOUSE LEMUR
Microcebus danfossi

MEASUREMENTS*
Total length: 250-290mm**. Head/body length: 100-130mm**. Tail length: 152-170mm. Weight: average 63g, known range 51-75g. (L208a) *Based on 72 specimens **Estimates

DESCRIPTION & IDENTIFICATION
Larger-bodied, reddish *Microcebus*. Dorsal fur and tail maroon with orange tinge. Head rufous in some individuals; others have grey crown with traingular rufous area above eyes. White stripe between eyes is distinct. Underparts creamy-white (L208A).

HABITAT & DISTRIBUTION
Deciduous forest. Known from forest fragments between Sofia and Maevarano Rivers (probable limits of range) in north-west Madagascar.

BEHAVIOUR
Probably similar to other *Microcebus* in western regions.

WHERE TO SEE
A range that is difficult to reach. Bora and Anjiamangirana Forests are possible locations (L208a).

HAIRY-EARED DWARF LEMUR genus *Allocebus*

Initially included in the genus *Cheirogaleus*, the Hairy-eared Dwarf Lemur was later found to have its closest affinities within the genus *Microcebus*, although a number of morphological features – aspects of dentition and cranium structure – were considered sufficiently distinct to warrant elevation to the monotypic genus *Allocebus*. *Allocebus* was originally known from just five museum specimens, four of which were collected in the late 19th century and the fifth was collected in 1965. It was not located again until 1989 (L171; L172).

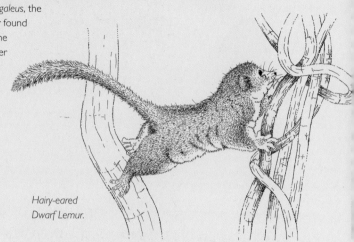

Hairy-eared Dwarf Lemur.

HAIRY-EARED DWARF LEMUR

Allocebus trichotis

MEASUREMENTS

Total length: 265–355mm. Head/body length: 125–160mm. Tail length: 140–195mm. Weight: 65–90g. (L172; L102)

DESCRIPTION & IDENTIFICATION

Head and upperparts darkish-grey, with slight rosy tinge. Tail often darker grey-brown, darkening further towards tip and becoming slightly bushy. A faint dark dorsal stripe apparent on some individuals. Underparts paler, varying from light grey to almost white. Narrow dark rings around eyes and sometimes a pale whitish stripe from between eyes to tip of nose. Ears small and largely concealed beneath long wavy ear-tufts that extend around cheeks.

A small, active lemur with long tail. Smaller than *Cheirogaleus*, but larger than *Microcebus*. Distinguishing *A. trichotis* from *Microcebus* in field is problematic requiring close observation. Larger size and ear-tufts

are obvious features to look for. *A. trichotis* also greyer in colour and tends to move in more sporadic, stop-start fashion than *Microcebus* (L102).

HABITAT & DISTRIBUTION

Occurs in lowland and mid-altitude rainforests up to around 1,600m asl

(L102). Lower elevations (below 1,000m) probably preferred. Also recorded in partially degraded habitat (L310).

Far more widespread than previously thought and now recorded at variety of locations. From north to south: Marojejy National

Hairy-eared Dwarf Lemur, Andasibe-Mantadia National Park. This rarely seen species has previously been overlooked in some popular areas.

Park (810m–1,175m)(L102);
Anjanaharibe-Sud Special Reserve
(865m–1,250m) (L310; L312);
Masoala Peninsula National Park
(L337); Mananara-Nord (L171;
L177; L400); Marotandrano
Reserve (around 850m) (L269);
Zahamena National Park (L263);
Mantadia National Park (around
950m); Forêt de Vohimana, east
of Andasibe (around 780m);
Forêt de Vohidrazana, east of
Andasibe (680m–1,235m) (L265);
Analamazaotra Special Reserve
adjacent to Andasibe (around 900m)
(L89); and Maromizaha Forest.

Appears restricted to northern
half of eastern rainforests, from
vicinity of Andasibe in south to
Marojejy in north, including the
Masoala Peninsula.

Throughout range encounters
are sporadic and rare with perhaps
fewer than 20 confirmed sightings,
suggesting it occurs either at very
low densities and/or is overlooked as
easily confused with *Microcebus*.

Hairy-eared Dwarf Lemur.

BEHAVIOUR

Nocturnal and active from around
dusk until dawn. Observed both
singly and in pairs (probably male/
female). Foraging concentrated in
dense tangles of vegetation at lower
levels in forest. Sleeps in tree holes, in

Hairy-eared
Dwarf Lemur

groups of two to six; holes in larger
trees are preferred (L3; L171; L172).

Diet yet to be accurately determined. Initial observations suggest
insects, including ones in flight, are
important. *Allocebus* is a swift and
adept predator. May move its ears
when searching for insect prey
(L102). Dentition and nails suggest
gum eating is important. Also has
very long tongue presumably for
nectar feeding.

Little known about vocalisations.
Heard to emit series of short whistles
and alternating squeals similar to
those of *Microcebus*. When alarmed
stands erect on hindlimbs to spot
danger (L3; L172).

May become torpid and
aestivates during austral winter
(May–September/October). Prior
to onset of drier, cooler period, it

deposits reserves of fat over entire
body, and body weight reaches
annual maximum in May and June
(L265). Testes size in males regresses
dramatically during same period, only
increasing again in September and
early October, when they emerge to
breed.

Births reported in January and
February (L3; L172).

WHERE TO SEE

The most accessible known localities
are Analamazaotra Special Reserve
and Forest Station and Mantadia
National Park where it has now
been seen numerous times. Nearby
Forêt de Vohimana is an alternative.
Anyone going on night walks in the
Andasibe-Mantadia National Park
area should look closely at any small
nocturnal lemur they see.

DWARF LEMURS genus *Cheirogaleus*

The taxonomy of the genus *Cheirogaleus* (which means hand-weasel) has been revised significantly (L114). Previously, two species were recognised: The Fat-tailed Dwarf Lemur (*Cheirogaleus medius*) from the west and the south, and the Greater Dwarf Lemur (*Cheirogaleus major*) from eastern Madagascar. Analysis of museum specimens, combined with recent fieldwork, has led to the recognition of seven species; the *C. medius* group has been split into two, *C. medius* and *C. adipicaudatus*, while the *C. major* group now contains five distinct species: *C. major*, *C. crossleyi*, *C. sibreei*, *C. ravus* and *C. minusculus*. Original descriptions of some species were based on sub-adults from imprecise localities and considerable field work is required to verify these revisions. Therefore, the ranges of new taxa and how they relate to one another has yet to be accurately established (L118), and the taxonomy of this group is likely to change further. Distributions given here are by no means definitive and should be treated with caution.

Cheirogaleus are strictly nocturnal, squirrel-sized lemurs with horizontal body posture that move quadrupedally. They are the only primates that automatically enter a prolonged period of seasonal torpor during the austral winter and accumulate reserves of fat prior to this (L396; L73).

All wild studies to date have involved either *C. major* or *C. medius* as defined before the revision of the genus and information given here is based on these.

GREATER DWARF LEMUR

Cheirogaleus major

MEASUREMENTS

Total length: 500–550mm. Head/body length: 230–250mm. Tail length: 250–280mm. Weight: seasonal variation 250–600g. (L73)

DESCRIPTION & IDENTIFICATION

Pelage short and dense. Head, upperparts and broad tail brown to rufous-brown, head may be slightly more rufous. Underparts paler grey to off-white. Dark rings around eyes with lighter whitish-grey areas outside, joining between eyes and extending down muzzle. Snout dark and slightly pointed with relatively large fleshy nose.

Largest *Cheirogaleus*, a squirrel-sized lemur with horizontal posture. Distinguishable from similar-sized *Avahi* and *Lepilemur* by horizontal rather than vertical posture. Also runs quadrupedally, whereas other genera are leapers. Should not be confused with Fork-marked Lemur *Phaner* whose face is more elongate and distinctively marked.

HABITAT & DISTRIBUTION

Primary rainforest, well-established secondary forest and more degraded forests, including coffee and lychee plantations and deciduous forest in west.

With recent taxonomic revisions, range is now poorly understood (L118). Extends from Andohahela in south to region of Sambava in north (possibly further north). Principally found in lowland areas but recorded up to 1800m asl.

C. major also recorded in the west to south and north of Manambolo River in region of Bemaraha, and in

Greater Dwarf Lemur

Bongolava Massif (L354). Here it is potentially sympatric with *C. medius*; the specific status of these populations requires clarification.

BEHAVIOUR

Strictly nocturnal, foraging alone or in small groups of two or three. Adult females have home ranges around 4ha, males and juveniles also occupy these areas. Foraging occurs at all levels in forest from understorey to canopy. Also descends to ground to search for insects in leaf-litter. By day sleeps in small groups in tree holes or dense clumps of tangled vegetation (L396).

Becomes dormant during austral winter (normally July to September); in Ranomafana, it is not seen from mid-April until September. Activity levels drastically reduced at this time. Prior to torpor, fat reserves are laid down in tail, which swells and constitutes up to 30% of body weight. In July, after prolonged feeding body weight can be 600g, in September after torpor can be down to 250g. Aestivating animals probably conceal themselves in leaf-litter at base of large trees or in tree holes (L396).

Feeds on nectar, ripe fruit, and to lesser extent young leaves and buds. Insects also taken but form small

Greater Dwarf Lemur.

part of diet (L80; L396). May be primarily responsible for pollinating species of liana, e.g. *Strongylodon craveniae* (Leguminosae) – it is only lemur not to destroy inflorescence while feeding and so triggers flower's pollen removal/receipt mechanism. Pollen is deposited on lemur's forehead and transferred to another flower when feeds elsewhere (L206). During November and December pollen is a particularly important energy source.

Mating in late October/early November, when larger aggregations of up to 14 individuals occur. Such groups are very noisy, highly active and agitated; may be groups of males competing for females. Female constructs nest of leaves and vines 6–12m above ground level. Litter of two or three born in January, gestation around 70 days (L237). Initially mother carries young in her mouth, but later they cling to her back. At one month infants able to follow mother and begin eating soft fruit,

but lactation lasts up to six weeks (L238).

Predated by Ring-tailed Mongoose and Fosa – both are able to remove lemurs from sleep-sites – and large snakes like Tree Boas *Sanzinia madagascariensis* (L109, L111; L99; L154).

WHERE TO SEE

During austral summer/wet season (November to April) can potentially be seen in most forests within range. Often seen in Masoala, Marojejy and Ranomafana National Parks. *Cheirogaleus* also easily seen in Andasibe-Mantadia National Park, but detailed study is required to confirm whether this is *C. major* or *C. crossleyi*.

FURRY-EARED DWARF LEMUR
Cheirogaleus crossleyi
Other name: Crossley's Dwarf Lemur

MEASUREMENTS
Total length: 430–530mm. Head/body length: 220–260mm. Tail length: 210–270mm. Weight: probably seasonal range 250–500g*.
*Estimate

DESCRIPTION & IDENTIFICATION
Upperparts reddish-brown, underparts pale grey becoming creamy

sites museum specimens were collected

Furry-eared Dwarf Lemur

in Mantadia. They can also been seen at close quarters in trees outside the Hotel Feon'ny ala.

SIBREE'S DWARF LEMUR
Cheirogaleus sibreei

MEASUREMENTS
No information available.

DESCRIPTION & IDENTIFICATION
Known only from museum specimens. Dorsal pelage grey-fawn, with white flecking and defined darker mid-dorsal stripe. Ventral fur pale cream extending up flanks and down outside of thighs. Ears dark and lightly furred, eye-rings are not well defined (L114).

sites museum
• specimens were collected

Sibree's Dwarf Lemur

Dwarf Lemur, possibly Cheirogaleus crossleyi, *Andasibe-Mantadia National Park.*

around mid-line. Mid-face and forehead more yellowish-rufous with clear dark eye-rings. Ears covered inside and out in dark fur.

Distinguished from *C. major* by more reddish-rufous colour, darker more pronounced eye-rings and distinctive flattened nose-bridge.

HABITAT & DISTRIBUTION
Occurs in middle and higher elevation rainforest. Range has yet to be determined, but may extend from Andohahela in south (L118) to vicinity of Vohimar in north and possibly further north to Montagne d'Ambre (L114).

In Analamazaotra (now Andasibe-

Mantadia National Park) *Cheirogaleus*, now thought to be *C. crossleyi* (but regarded as *C. major* during study), was recorded at densities of 70 to 110 individuals/km^2 (L250).

BEHAVIOUR
No specific studies. Behaviour and ecology assumed to be similar to *C. major.*

WHERE TO SEE
Only seen during summer/wet season (October to April), when most active. *Cheirogaleus* at Andasibe-Mantadia National Park probably correspond to this species and are easily seen on night walks along road near park entrance or along the road

HABITAT & DISTRIBUTION
Described from three museum specimens collected at different localities in the Central Domain. Type locality is described as Ankeramadinika, a day's journey east of Antananarivo (L114).

BEHAVIOUR
No information is available.

WHERE TO SEE
No known sites.

GREATER IRON-GREY DWARF LEMUR

Cheirogaleus ravus

MEASUREMENTS*

Total length: 480mm. Head/body length: 240mm. Tail length: 240mm. Weight: not known. *Based on single specimen (L114)

sites museum
• specimens were
collected

Greater Iron-grey
Dwarf Lemur

DESCRIPTION & IDENTIFICATION

Described from museum specimens. Head, upperparts and tail iron-grey with brownish tones and a vague mid-dorsal line. Underparts also grey. Ears dark and lack fur. Tail tip and feet are white (L114). Presumed to be sympatric with *C. major*, but smaller and predominantly grey rather than brown. Also has distinctive white feet and tail tip.

HABITAT & DISTRIBUTION

Described from museum specimens from coastal localities to north of Toamasina between sea level and 800m (L114).

BEHAVIOUR

Unknown.

WHERE TO SEE

No known localities.

LESSER IRON-GREY DWARF LEMUR

Cheirogaleus minusculus

MEASUREMENTS

No information is available.

DESCRIPTION & IDENTIFICATION

Described from museum specimens. A small species, similar in size to *C. medius*. Head, dorsal region and tail iron-grey with brownish tones and indistinct mid-dorsal line. Underparts also grey. Ears furred and feet white (L114).

HABITAT & DISTRIBUTION

Type locality is Ambositra north of Fianarantsoa. No other information is available.

BEHAVIOUR

Unknown.

WHERE TO SEE

No known sites.

FAT-TAILED DWARF LEMUR

Cheirogaleus medius

MEASUREMENTS

Total length: 400–500mm. Head/body length: 200–230mm. Tail length: 200–270mm. Weight: seasonal variation 120–275g. (L198; L73)

DESCRIPTION & IDENTIFICATION

Pelage short and dense. Head, dorsal region and broad tail pale fawn-grey, with rufous tints and darker hair bases showing through. There is a brown dorsal stripe. Underparts creamy-white with yellowish tinges and a distinct partial white collar around throat extending up sides of neck. Face and cheeks pale grey-white with obvious dark rings around eyes and nose is pinkish.

Snout and short ears also slightly darker.

A small squirrel-sized lemur with horizontal body posture. Confusion with *Mirza* is possible as size and colour are broadly similar; *Mirza* is larger, more reddish in colour, has bigger, highly conspicuous ears and lacks obviously fattened tail. Movements of *Mirza* are more continuous and rapid than those of *C. medius*.

Distinctive facial markings and more rapid movements of Fork-marked Lemur *Phaner* serve to differentiate with *C. medius*. Larger size and slower movements should prevent confusion with *Microcebus*. See also Greater Dwarf Lemur *C. major*.

HABITAT & DISTRIBUTION

Dry deciduous forest and well-established secondary forest in the west. Also evergreen humid forest in south-east. With recent revisions of this genus more fieldwork is needed before accurate ranges can be established. Current suggested range extends from region of Mangoky River north to Sambirano, and perhaps further north to Ankarana and Analamera and similar forests in vicinity of Daraina near Vohemar. Also found near Saint Luce, north-east of Tolagnaro in south-east (L118).

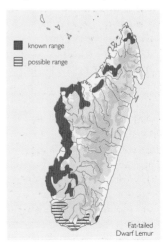

known range

possible range

Fat-tailed
Dwarf Lemur

Fat-tailed Dwarf Lemur.

Fat-tailed Dwarf Lemur.

BEHAVIOUR

Nocturnal and omnivorous. Lives in small family groups – an adult pair and offspring from one or more breeding seasons. Males and females form lifelong pair bonds, broken only if one individual dies (L198; L199; L71; L72). Families occupy territories of 1–2.5ha. By day they sleep communally in tree holes. Territory and sleep-sites are defended by scent-marking (L71; L72).

Agile climbers that forage at all levels within forest (L200). Diet varied consisting of fruit, flowers, nectar, pollen, leaf buds, gum, insects and other invertebrates, but proportion of animal prey varies seasonally and can comprise up to 20% of diet (L73). Prior to dormancy, high calorie fruits preferred to maximise accumulation of fat (L74).

An important agent of small seed dispersal: during rainy season (November to April) smears faeces into branches of trees – a unique behaviour. Particularly beneficial to germination of parasitic plants like mistletoes (e.g. *Viscum*), thus fills a role usually played by birds (L85; L73).

During wet season builds reserves of fat (up to 75g) in tail resulting in increase in body weight up to 40% (L74; L199; L200). At beginning of dry season (usually April, although juveniles remain active longer) gradually begin reducing their levels of activity, eventually becoming inactive for several months. Aestivation occurs in a tree hole, sometimes in small groups (L237), although individuals may change tree holes periodically during dormant phase (L200).

Majority of individuals emerge by October/November, although considerable regional variation is linked with climate – towards north they become fully active sooner.

Mating occurs in December (L72); gestation around 62 days; litters one to five (average two to three) (L200; L73). Both parents raise young. For first two weeks remain within nest hole, parents taking turns babysitting so offspring are never alone. Seen successfully fending off a snake (*Madagascarophis* sp.) from close to nest (L73). When young initially explore outside nest, they

are accompanied by one of parents and guided back to sanctuary of nest (L72). Offspring from previous season that may still be part of family group do not appear to assist. Juveniles become dormant later into the dry season (May/June) than adults and so benefit from a period of reduced competition for food. Sexual maturity reached after two years, but only after leaving natal group. Individuals are not 'socially mature' until three years (L200; L73).

Predated by Fosa *Cryptoprocta ferox*, which excavates victims from tree holes. Other predators include large boas and the Barn Owl *Tyto alba* and Madagascar Long-eared Owl *Asio madagascariensis*. Madagascar Harrier-Hawk *Polyboroides radiatus* is known to remove sleeping dwarf lemurs from holes, using its long legs (L99).

WHERE TO SEE

The best sites are Ampijoroa Forestry Station (part of Ankarafantsika National Park), south-east of Mahajanga and Kirindy Forest, north-east of Morondava. Here *C. medius* is regularly encountered on nocturnal walks during the austral summer.

SPINY FOREST DWARF LEMUR

Cheirogaleus adipicaudatus

Other name: Southern Fat-tailed Dwarf Lemur

MEASUREMENTS*

Total length: approx 360mm. Head/body length: 165–180mm. Tail length: 180–190mm. Weight: not available, probably less than *C. medius*. (L114) *Estimates

DESCRIPTION & IDENTIFICATION

Darker fawn-grey pelage is short and dense and, unlike *C. medius*,

sites museum
• specimens were
collected

Spiny Forest
Dwarf Lemur

the dorsal stripe less apparent. Underparts pale grey with creamy-yellow towards midline. Whitish collar much less distinct than *C. medius*. Thick black eye-rings are continuous with dark coloration around nose. Ears long and more prominent than *C. medius* and tail is appreciably longer than head/body length (L114).

HABITAT & DISTRIBUTION

Extent of range is unclear, but is probably centred on arid spiny forest regions of south-west (L181). Range may mirror extent of preferred spiny forest habitat and continue further north to Mangoky River.

Some original specimens were apparently collected in spiny forest west of Tolagnaro (L114), however, recent studies failed to record *C. adipicaudatus* in this region (L118).

BEHAVIOUR

Assumed to be similar to *C. medius*.

WHERE TO SEE

Cheirogaleus in spiny forests dominated by *Allaudia* at Beza Mahafaly Special Reserve and transition forest in Zombitse National Park are thought to be this species.

GIANT DWARF LEMURS genus *Mirza*

When first described *M. coquereli* was included in the genus *Microcebus*. On the basis of larger size, morphological differences, dental characteristics and some aspects of behaviour the genus *Mirza* is now regarded as distinct. Two species, including one recently described, are recognised.

COQUEREL'S GIANT DWARF LEMUR

Mirza coquereli

MEASUREMENTS

Total length: 550–585mm. Head/body length: 235–265mm. Tail length: 315–320mm. Weight: average 310g, range 285–335g. (L150; L152)

DESCRIPTION & IDENTIFICATION

Fur short and dense. Upperparts and head primarily grey-brown, with some reddish, pinkish or yellowish tinges, underparts lighter creamy-grey. Most conspicuous features are relatively long, bushy tail that darkens towards tip and large, hairless very distinctive ears.

Larger than newly described *M. zaza* (L152). A squirrel-sized lemur with long bushy tail and horizontal body posture. Moves quadrupedally, with short leaps and bounds

(L150). Movements tend to be rapid, helping distinguish it from similar-sized *Cheirogaleus*. Ears also very prominent, but in *Cheirogaleus* are concealed. Might be confused with similar sized Fork-marked Lemur *Phaner*, but characteristic facial markings, small ears and loud vocalisations of *Phaner* should distinguish the two.

HABITAT & DISTRIBUTION

Inhabits dry deciduous forests, coastal moist forest and some secondary forests. In dry forests seems to prefer slightly taller and thicker vegetation found along riverbanks and by semi-permanent still water.

Range in west apparently discontinuous but exact limits remain unclear. Probably occurs from north bank of Onilahy River 40km inland from Toliara, east to Zombitse Forest near Sakaraha (L80; L107) and north to vicinity of Antsalova. Further population occurs along west coast possibly from region of Bemarivo to Mahavavy River, including Tsingy

de Namoroka National Park (L148). In dry deciduous forests population density estimates are 120 animals/km² (L144).

BEHAVIOUR

Strictly nocturnal; day spent in spherical nest constructed from interwoven lianas, twigs and leaves. These are chewed off by animal from nearby trees. Nests up to half a

Coquerel's Giant
Dwarf Lemur

metre in diameter and located high in canopy, surrounded by tangles of lianas, so difficult for predators to reach (L289; L144; L146). Up to 12 different nests are used in rotation. Generally occupied by solitary adults – very occasionally shared by adults and juveniles. Unlike *M. zaza*, adult males and females never share. Also utilised by other species like Fork-marked Lemur and introduced Black Rat (L150).

Emerge at dusk to groom and stretch before beginning foraging. Particularly vocal at this time. Active throughout the night, returning to nests just prior to dawn. Remain active all year and do not enter seasonal or daily torpor, but activity is reduced in winter (L150).

Omnivorous; diet varied and includes fruit and flowers, insects and other invertebrates. Unusual amongst Cheirogaleidae as small vertebrates (baby birds, frogs, lizards and snakes)

are eaten periodically (L128; L219). Circumstantial evidence that they may occasionally prey on small lemurs like *Microcebus* (L150). During dry season (June–August), when resources are scarce, sugary secretions from homopteran nymphs and tree gum are important elements (L128).

Excellent climbers, using all levels of canopy; typically travel and forage between 5m and 10m. Occasionally and briefly, they descend head first down tree trunks to ground level to hunt insects in leaf-litter (L150).

Generally solitary. Males and females occupy overlapping home ranges of 1–4ha; these remain constant throughout year. Male home ranges vary in size between non-breeding and breeding seasons. Most of year they are similar in size to those of females and non-over-lapping, but overlap with ranges of two or three females. When males and females meet, they interact and

remain together for short periods. During October mating season, male ranges quadruple in size (L148). Smell important: saliva, urine and anogenital secretions are used to mark branches within range (L14650). *Mirza* has pungent distinctive odour that can be used to detect it presence.

During breeding season males have dramatically enlarged testes. This, coupled with considerable vari-ance in male home ranges between breeding and non-breeding season, suggests competition between males for receptive females is intense and that *M. coquereli* is promiscuous (L148).

In Kirindy mating is restricted to brief period in November (L219; L148). One or two young are born after 90-day gestation. Young poorly developed weighing 12–15g and spend first three weeks in nest (L219; L324; L149). Infants leave nest after three to four weeks and initially

Coquerel's Giant Dwarf Lemur, Kirindy Forest.

carried by mother in her mouth. They are vocal and remain in contact with each other during first stages of independence. Sexual maturity reached quickly; females can reproduce at ten months (L150).

Occasionally predated by Fosa *Cryptoprocta ferox* and Narrow-striped Mongoose *Mungotictis decemlineata* and birds such as Madagascar Long-eared Owl *Asio madagascariensis* and Madagascar Buzzard *Buteo brachypterus* (L99).

WHERE TO SEE

Kirindy Forest, 60km north-east of Morondava, is best locality: nocturnal walks along most of major forest trails should give reasonable chance of success. Alternatively, Zombitse National Park can also be rewarding. Encounter rates are probably higher during the breeding season when males, in particular, are more active.

NORTHERN GIANT DWARF LEMUR

Mirza zaza

MEASUREMENTS

Total length: 490–540mm. Head/body length: 230–250mm. Tail length: 260–290mm. Weight: average 290g, range 265–320g. (L152)

DESCRIPTION & IDENTIFICATION

Pelage is short; upperparts and head greyish-brown with reddish tinges, underparts more grey. Tail long, bushy and darkens at tip. Ears rounded and short relative to *M. coquereli*.

A horizontal squirrel-sized lemur with a bushy tail, that moves quadrupedally. Smaller than *M. coquereli* with a relatively short tail (L152). See *M. coquereli* for differences between *Mirza* and *Cheirogaleus* and *Phaner*.

Northern Giant Dwarf Lemur, from near Ambanja.

HABITAT & DISTRIBUTION

Dry forests, some humid forests and secondary forests dominated by cashew and mango trees and coffee plantations.

A newly described species with an unclear range centred on Sambirano region; probably occurs from northern Mahavavy River south to region of Analalava, including Ampasindava and Sahamalaza Peninsulas.

In Sambirano densities of 385/km² have been recorded in humid secondary forests dominated by mango and cashew trees (L9) and at

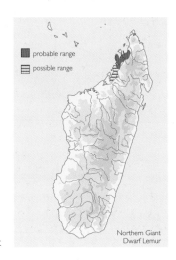

probable range
possible range

Northern Giant Dwarf Lemur

Ambato densities reach 1086/km², probably because the forest is fragmented with many introduced fruit trees (e.g. mangos) and little competition from other lemurs (L152).

BEHAVIOUR
Strictly nocturnal; day spent in large nests. Apparently gregarious (unlike *M. coquereli*) and sleeps in groups of two to eight (average four) containing males, females and juveniles (L152).

Omnivorous; varied diet assumed to be similar to *M. coquereli*. Feeds heavily in cashew and mango plantations.

Time of mating very different to *M. coquereli*; at Ambato takes place in July and August. Also evidence that it is more promiscuous than *M. coquereli* (L152). Other aspects of behaviour probably similar to *M. coquereli*.

WHERE TO SEE
Often easily seen in secondary forests and abandoned cashew nut groves near Ambanja.

FORK-MARKED LEMURS genus *Phaner*

When first described, the Fork-marked Lemur was placed in the genus *Lemur* (as *Lemur furcifer*). Later studies prompted taxonomic separation and it is now placed in its own subfamily, Phanerinae, within the broad family Cheirogaleidae (L117).

Recent revisions have elevated taxa previously described as subspecies to full species (L115). These occupy apparently discontinuous ranges, the limits of which are poorly understood in some cases. All *Phaner* are broadly similar in size, habits and general markings, although some differences in coloration exist between them. A general overview of *Phaner* is followed by more detailed accounts of each species.

MEASUREMENTS
Total length: 500–650mm. Head/body length: 225–285mm. Tail length: 285–370mm. Weight: 350–500g.

DESCRIPTION & IDENTIFICATION
Pelage quite dense. Upperparts various shades of brown to brownish-grey, underparts lighter shades of brown and grey. Tail similar in colour to upperparts, but darkens towards tip: extreme tip may be white. Obvious characteristic is broad dark stripe beginning at base of tail and running along dorsal ridge and up back of neck to crown, where it divides, two stripes continuing down face, around eyes and sometimes down muzzle. Hence species' vernacular name.

Largest member of family Cheirogaleidae. Adopts horizontal posture and moves quadrupedally in characteristic manner, running at speed along branches and leaping from one branch to next without pause, therefore difficult to follow. At rest bobs head in distinctive manner. Viewed from below male's throat gland quite visible.

Eastern Fork-marked Lemur.

DISTRIBUTION
Current information suggests five major discontinuous populations which broadly correspond to specific divisions. Hence location remains the most reliable guide for identifying each species. Several recently discovered populations have yet to be specifically identified. These undetermined populations occur at the following localities: spiny forest region (Parcel 2) of Andohahela National Park; region to north and east of Bombetoka Bay near Mahajanga; Tsaratanana Massif in far north-west; and dry deciduous and semi-evergreen forests in vicinity of Vohemar in north-east.

EASTERN FORK-MARKED LEMUR

Phaner furcifer

Other Name: Masoala Fork-marked Lemur

DESCRIPTION & IDENTIFICATION

Largest-bodied and darkest *Phaner* with longer, denser pelage. Facial fork and dorsal stripe very pronounced; stripe does not reach base of tail. Tip of tail dark but extreme tip sometimes pale grey.

Distinctive markings and rapid movements should prevent confusion with *Cheirogaleus* that is similar size, colour and posture.

Eastern
Fork-marked Lemur

HABITAT & DISTRIBUTION

Lowland and mid-altitude rainforest up to around 1,000m asl. Extent of range uncertain. *Phaner* recorded in Zahamena, Betampona, Ambatovaky, Mikira Forest, Masoala Peninsula and Marojejy (L102). Currently, these populations described as *P. furcifer*. Implied range from around Toamasina area, north to Marojejy Massif, including Masoala Peninsula.

BEHAVIOUR

Nocturnal. Not yet studied in wild.

See *P. pallescens* for details of *Phaner* behaviour and ecology.

WHERE TO SEE

Can be seen at number of localities on Masoala Peninsula, but access is often problematic. It is worth looking in forests inland from Lohatrozona and Tampolo.

PARIENTE'S FORK-MARKED LEMUR

Phaner parienti

DESCRIPTION & IDENTIFICATION

Upperparts light brown to grey. Darker than *P. electromontis* found to its north, and lighter than *P. pallescens* that occurs to south. Facial fork prominent, dorsal stripe reaches base of tail. Distinct darkening of tail towards tip, but extreme tip is white.

Two sympatric lemurs, *Cheirogaleus* and *Mirza,* are similar size, colour and posture – the distinctive facial markings and rapid movements of *P. parienti* should prevent misidentification.

HABITAT & DISTRIBUTION

Found in lowland moist forest and secondary forest, e.g. shade-grown coffee plantations around villages, up

Pariente's
Fork-marked Lemur

to 800m asl. Typical of genus, there is strong preference for areas with tall trees.

Apparently restricted to Sambirano in north-west, south of Ambanja between Andranomalaza River to south and Sambirano River to north, including Ampasindava Peninsula to west and Tsaratanana Massif at eastern extreme of Sambirano region.

BEHAVIOUR

Nocturnal and probably omnivorous. Not yet studied in wild. See *P. pallescens* for details of Fork-marked Lemur behaviour and ecology.

WHERE TO SEE

Well-preserved forest on Ampasindava Peninsula. Also forests around village of Beraty on western edge of Manongarivo Special Reserve, some 45km south of Ambanja, can be productive (L181).

PALE FORK-MARKED LEMUR

Phaner pallescens

MEASUREMENTS

Total length: 500–650mm. Head/body length: 255–275mm. Tail length: 315–330mm. Weight: 305–350g. (L311)

DESCRIPTION & IDENTIFICATION

Upperparts light grey to grey-fawn with silvery tints. Distal two-thirds of tail is slightly darker than main body, but unlike other *Phaner* tail does not end in a dark tip. Dorsal stripe and facial fork less distinct than in other *Phaner* species. Palest and smallest member of genus.

Occurs sympatrically with several other nocturnal lemurs, including Fat-tailed Dwarf Lemur *Cheirogaleus medius* and Coquerel's Giant Dwarf Lemur *Mirza coquereli*, which are

Pale Fork-marked Lemur, Kirindy Forest.

broadly similar in size, colour and posture. Distinctive markings and rapid movements of *P. pallescens* should prevent confusion.

HABITAT & DISTRIBUTION
Utilises variety of habitats, including dry deciduous forest, transitional forest (between deciduous forest and spiny forest) and secondary forest. Confined to western Madagascar but has largest range of the *Phaner* species. Main population occurs in a strip, northward from Fiherenana River, including Mikea Forest and Zombitse, to around Antsalova, north of Tsiribihina River.

A second population is centred on Namoroka National Park and the Baly Bay area; this is tentatively ascribed to *P. pallescens* (L364).

Further north, to north and west of Bombetoka Bay is a third population. Both northerly populations appear isolated and they may constitute distinct species.

In Kirindy densities are 60–70 individuals/km² (L311); in other areas estimates are 50–60 individuals/km² (L43).

BEHAVIOUR
Most information on behaviour and ecology in Fork-marked Lemurs is based on studies of this species in dry deciduous forests north of Morondava.

Nocturnal, although activity begins at dusk before complete darkness. Can be extremely vocal, frequently answering calls of neighbours; bouts of calling are a distinctive twilight

characteristic in forests they inhabit. Further bouts of calling occur as individuals return to sleep sites prior to dawn (L311).

Pale Fork-marked Lemur

Appears to be monogamous (L367) and pairs remain together for several breeding seasons (L311). Territories of 3–10ha are defended and remain constant in size throughout year. When active, males and females spend time together grooming one another, but tend to separate and forage alone while maintaining vocal contact (L311).

Little territorial overlap; interactions between pairs at boundaries are frequent, although not necessarily antagonistic as neighbouring females and juveniles often groom one another. Males are aggressive towards other males and females but females are invariably dominant (L311).

By day, sleeps alone or in pairs in hollows and holes towards tops of large trees (L311), including baobabs *Adansonia* spp. (L59) and occasionally in abandoned nests of Coquerel's Giant Dwarf Lemur (L150). Sleep sites lined with leaves. Individuals can use over 30 different sites per year. *P. pallescens* is sympatric with several other nocturnal lemurs, its preference for sleep sites towards to the canopy top may reduce competition (L311).

Mating occurs in early November, births in February and March. Single young are born in tree hole and remain within nest for first couple of weeks. Offspring stay with parents in family unit for up to three years (L311).

Dentition and diet specialised; lower incisors modified into inclined 'dental comb', used to scrape and gouge tree bark to stimulate flow of sap and gums (L43). These rich sources of sugar are primary dietary constituents throughout year. Gum from *Terminalia* trees especially favoured (L311). Other foods include flowers, nectar (responsible for pollinating some baobabs (L27)), insects (adults, larvae and pupae) and insect secretions. *Phaner*

has long extensible tongue, which helps exploit its diet (L311). Two species of Needle-clawed Bush Baby (*Euoticus* spp., Galagonidae) from rainforests of West Africa have very similar adaptations, and also feed on tree gums and sap.

As a specialist gum feeder, *P. pallescens* is able to remain active throughout year, without physiological adaptations to low temperatures and low food availability (L128), however, during austral winter experiences weight loss up to 20% (L311).

Predated by Fosa *Cryptoprocta ferox* and several raptors, e.g. Madagascar Buzzard *Buteo brachypterus*, Madagascar Harrier-Hawk *Polyboroides radiatus* and Madagascar Cuckoo-Hawk *Aviceda madagascariensis* (L99).

WHERE TO SEE
Kirindy Forest, north of Morondava, is the best locality. Also Zombitse National Park east of Sakaraha offers good opportunities. The animals' loud vocalisations at dusk are unmistakable, as is their habit of head-bobbing.

AMBER MOUNTAIN FORK-MARKED LEMUR
Phaner electromontis

DESCRIPTION & IDENTIFICATION
Second largest *Phaner*. Upperparts light grey to silver with dark and well-defined broad dorsal stripe extending to base of tail. Tip of tail also very dark. Facial fork highly prominent.

Distinctive markings and rapid movements should prevent confusion with *Cheirogaleus*, the only

Amber Mountain
Fork-marked Lemur

sympatric species of similar size and posture.

HABITAT & DISTRIBUTION
Found in rainforest, moist tropical forest, dry deciduous forest and secondary forest between 50m and 1,500m asl.

Restricted to areas centred on Montagne d'Ambre complex of protected areas in far north, including drier forests of Ankarana and Analamera. Also seen in Sahafayi Classified Forest east of Montagne d'Ambre and north of Analamera. *Phaner* recorded in vicinity of Daraina might correspond to this species but taxonomy of this population remains undetermined.

BEHAVIOUR
Nocturnal and omnivorous, but not yet studied in wild. See *P. pallescens* for details of Fork-marked Lemur behaviour and ecology.

WHERE TO SEE
Montagne d'Ambre National Park is most accessible place – the botanical garden and areas around the campsite and Petite Cascade are good places to concentrate efforts. As trees are tall views are often distant. Other possible locations include Forêt d'Ambre Special Reserve and Analamera Special Reserve.

SPORTIVE LEMURS Family Lepilemuridae

The evolutionary affinity of the sportive lemurs is contentious. Previously, dental features were used to show links with extinct forms in the family Megaladapidae (L341; L115). However, recent genetic research suggests otherwise and implies the group forms their own family Lepilemuridae (L402).

SPORTIVE LEMURS genus *Lepilemur*

Sportive lemurs belong to a single genus, *Lepilemur*, but considerable debate surrounds the taxonomy. Some authorities have regarded all forms as subspecies of *Lepilemur mustelinus* (L348). However, genetic and morphological differences suggest they are good species (L132; L7; L166).

Virtually all native forests contain *Lepilemur* species, but many populations show considerable external morphological similarity, so the number of species within the genus is uncertain. Genetic techniques have highlighted species differences and revealed numerous previously unrecognised 'cryptic' species.

With recent descriptions of 15 species (L7; L166; L259a), the genus now contains 23 species, each apparently occupying a distinct range, where major rivers appear to be boundaries between species (L166), although the boundaries between some ranges remain unclear (L223). Future research will prompt further revisions, including the probable description of new species.

Lepilemur are medium-small to medium-sized lemurs with long tails. They cling vertically to tree trunks and have powerful hindlegs enabling them to leap considerable distances. They are strictly nocturnal and are found throughout the varied native forest types. Overall morphology, appearance and coloration are broadly similar across species, and geographic location is often the most reliable factor for identification in the field. The generic name *Lepilemur* is often used as the vernacular.

Weasel Sportive Lemur, Mantadia National Park.

WEASEL SPORTIVE LEMUR

Lepilemur mustelinus

MEASUREMENTS
Total length: 550–640mm*.
Head/body length: 300–350mm*.
Tail length: 250–290mm*.
Weight: 800–1,200g*. *Estimated measurements

DESCRIPTION & IDENTIFICATION
Pelage long and dense. Upperparts and head grey-brown to chestnut-brown with slightly darker dorsal stripe sometimes apparent. Tail similar colour but darkens towards tip. Face, throat and underparts paler grey-brown, muzzle is darker. Together with *L. wrightae*, the largest *Lepilemur* species.

A medium-sized, vertically clinging lemur with tail equivalent to head/body length. Can be confused with Eastern Avahi *Avahi laniger* of similar size, coloration and posture. *L. mustelinus* has prominent ears, more pointed muzzle and uniform coloration, whereas *Avahi* has distinctive white thigh patches and eyebrow patches and distinctive 'facial mask'.

Weasel Sportive Lemur

HABITAT & DISTRIBUTION

Primary and secondary rainforest. *L. mustelinus* found over central northern portion of eastern rainforest belt, approximately from line formed by Onive and Mangoro Rivers in south (L7) to at least Onibe River in north (L166). Populations further north between Onibe and Antainambalana Rivers have yet to be determined. Also situation on Masoala Peninsula remains unclear, but these populations have previously been described as *L. mustelinus* (L337; L335).

At southern extreme of range, the boundary with range of *L. betsileo* is also unclear.

BEHAVIOUR

Nocturnal and totally arboreal. By day in wet season (November–March) sleeps in nests of leaves, constructed in hanging lianas. In dry season prefers tree holes 6–12m above ground (L277).

At dusk emerges and rests at edge of tree hole becoming active at onset of darkness. Very vocal around dusk, and high-pitched calls

from several individuals can be heard in rapid succession. Calling soon subsides and stops within an hour of nightfall. Solitary while foraging and feeds on leaves, but also some fruit and flowers (L80). Grooming is seen between mother and young, but never between adults.

Predated by Fosa *Cryptoprocta ferox* and raptors like Madagascar Long-eared Owl *Asio madagascariensis* and Madagascar Harrier-Hawk *Polyboroides radiatus* (L99). Also reports of Madagascar Tree Boa *Sanzinia madagascariensis* taking animals from nests or tree holes.

WHERE TO SEE

Regularly seen in Andasibe-Mantadia National Park, particularly along road in Mantadia or less frequently along the road or main ridge in Analamazaotra Reserve.

BETSILEO SPORTIVE LEMUR

Lepilemur betsileo

MEASUREMENTS*

Total length: 585–620mm. Head/body length: 323–331mm. Tail length: 264–290mm. Weight: average 1150g, known range 1020–1280g. *Based on three specimens (L166)

DESCRIPTION & IDENTIFICATION

Relatively large *Lepilemur*. Pelage predominantly reddish-brown to grey, darker on back with paler underparts. Head more grey, while body mainly reddish-brown. Face mainly grey, with lower jaw/muzzle creamy-white. Tail is dark grey to black and contrasts sharply with body (L166).

Betsileo Sportive Lemur.

Betsileo
Sportive Lemur

SMALL-TOOTHED SPORTIVE LEMUR

Lepilemur microdon

MEASUREMENTS

Total length: 550–640mm. Head/body length: 300–350mm. Tail length: 250–290mm. Weight: 800–1,000g.

DESCRIPTION & IDENTIFICATION

Pelage dense and red-brown on head and dorsal region with darkish dorsal stripe. Forelimbs and shoulders particularly rich chestnut. Tail similar colour to body and darker towards tip. Underparts, face and throat pale grey-brown. Sometimes yellowish-buff wash on belly.

A medium-sized vertically clinging lemur with longish tail. Most likely to be confused with Eastern Avahi

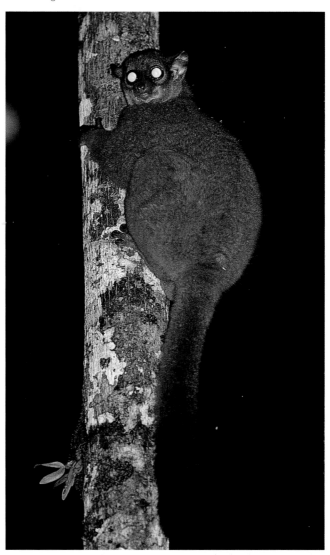

Medium-sized, vertically clinging lemur with long tail. Eastern Avahi *Avahi laniger* is similar size and posture, but *L. betsileo* has prominent ears, more pointed muzzle and reddish coloration. Avahi has distinctive white thigh patches and eyebrow patches.

HABITAT & DISTRIBUTION

Primary and secondary rainforest. Type locality is Fandriana Classified Forest. Range may extend between Namorona River in south to a line formed by Mangoro and Onive Rivers in north. Boundary with *L. mustelinus* to north and *L. microdon* to south require clarification (L166).

BEHAVIOUR

Nocturnal. Yet to be studied in wild.

WHERE TO SEE

No accessible sites are yet known. Any *Lepilemurs* occurring in forests between the Namorona and Mangoro Rivers may be this species. The Forêt Lalatsara (Lemur Forest Camp), north of Ambohimahasoa on Route National 7, may warrant investigation.

Small-toothed Sportive Lemur, Ranomatana National Park.

Small-toothed
Sportive Lemur

Avahi laniger, of similar size, coloration and posture. More obvious
ears, russet forelimbs and shoulders,
and absence of white thighs distinguishing features.

HABITAT & DISTRIBUTION

Occurs in primary and secondary
rainforest. With recent species
descriptions, range has become
unclear. Probably found south of
Namorona River to Andohahela
region. The boundary with range
of *L. betsileo* has yet to be
determined.

BEHAVIOUR

Nocturnal and totally arboreal.
Solitary and feeds on leaves, fruit
and flowers. Like other eastern
Lepilemur species may suffer direct
competition for food with Eastern
Avahi: *Avahi* feeds primarily on
better quality vegetation restricting
Lepilemur to leaves of lower nutritional value.

WHERE TO SEE

Ranomafana National Park is the
only accessible site. *Lepilemur* lemurs
are encountered very rarely in main
tourist area of Talatakely. Seen with
greater frequency in higher altitude
forests of Vohiparara.

James' Sportive Lemur.

JAMES' SPORTIVE LEMUR

Lepilemur jamesi (jamesorum)

MEASUREMENTS*

Total length: 600–670mm. Head/
body length: 319–355mm. Tail length:
279–315mm. Weight: average 780g.
*Based on two specimens (L166)

DESCRIPTION & IDENTIFICATION

A large sportive lemur. Dorsal pelage,
short and smooth; mainly brown
with distinctive black midline from
head down spinal ridge to base of
tail. Ears grey and edged with black,
some cream patches beneath ears.
Distinctive whitish-grey mask on face.
Underparts paler shade of brown
than upperparts. Brown tail gradually
darkens to black tip (L166).

HABITAT & DISTRIBUTION

Primary and secondary lowland
rainforest. Type locality is Manombo
Special Reserve (L166). Range
limits are unclear; may occur
from Manampatra River north of

James'
Sportive Lemur

Farafangana south to Mananara River near Vangaindrano.

BEHAVIOUR
Nocturnal. Yet to be studied in wild.

WHERE TO SEE
Manombo Special Reserve is currently the only known site to see this species. Access is difficult in wet season when local rivers swell and cut off portions of forest.

WRIGHT'S SPORTIVE LEMUR

Lepilemur wrighti (wrightae)

MEASUREMENTS*
Total length: 525–640mm. Head/body length: 288–376mm. Tail length: 239–271mm. Weight: average 950g. *Based on five specimens (L166)

DESCRIPTION & IDENTIFICATION
A large *Lepilemur* with distinctive appearance. Upperparts reddish-brown to greyish-brown, underparts paler greyish-brown. Some sexual dimorphism apparent (only *Lepilemur* to show this): females have uniform grey head which contrasts with body; male heads are reddish-brown to

Wright's Sportive Lemur.

grey with little contrast to body. Some females also have a facial mask.

HABITAT & DISTRIBUTION
Primary and secondary mid-altitude rainforest. Type locality is Kalambatritra Special Reserve, currently the only known site. Range is presumed to extend from north of Mandrare River and west of Mananara River (L166).

BEHAVIOUR
Nocturnal. Not yet studied in detail. Evidence suggests individuals regularly use specific latrine sites and scent-mark in the immediate vicinity; latrines

Wright's
Sportive Lemur

may serve a role in territorial demarcation and resource defence (L130). Population densities of *L. wrightae* in Kalambatritra are the highest yet recorded for the genus in rainforests. This is thought to be linked to the apparent absence of other folivorous lemurs, like *Avahi* spp. and *Propithecus* spp., from these forests (L130).

WHERE TO SEE

Kalambatritra Special Reserve in south-east Madagascar is very difficult to reach and there are no facilities.

Fleurete's Sportive Lemur.

FLEURETE'S SPORTIVE LEMUR

Lepilemur fleuretae

MEASUREMENTS*

Total length: 585–670mm. Head/body length: 304–354mm. Tail length: 281–323mm. Weight: average 980g, known range 820–1140g.
*Based on three specimens (L166)

DESCRIPTION & IDENTIFICATION

Medium-sized *Lepilemur*. Upperparts mainly grey with greyish-brown near extremities. Diffuse midline runs from crown to partially down spine. Underparts brownish-grey. Tail reddish-grey becoming darker at tip (L166).

HABITAT & DISTRIBUTION

Primary and secondary rainforest. Type locality is Manangotry, Andohahela National Park. Range probably covers rainforest areas between Mandrare River in west and Mananara River to north. Further work is required to determine northern range limits.

BEHAVIOUR

Nocturnal. Yet to be studied in wild.

WHERE TO SEE

Best looked for at Malio, the rainforest area of Andohahela National Park (Parcel I). This area should become more accessible as ecotourism is developed.

Fleurete's
Sportive Lemur

SEAL'S SPORTIVE LEMUR

Lepilemur seali

MEASUREMENTS*

Total length: 570–640mm. Head/body length: 324–370mm. Tail length: 249–277mm. Weight: average 950g, known range 870-1030g.
*Based on six specimens (L166)

DESCRIPTION & IDENTIFICATION

A large *Lepilemur*. Pelage long and luxuriant. Upperparts uniform light chocolate-brown to reddish-brown. Underparts pale brownish-grey. Face uniform light brownish-grey, hands and feet paler. Tail also brownish-grey but contrasts with main body.

Seal's
Sportive Lemur

HABITAT & DISTRIBUTION

Primary and secondary mid-altitude rainforest. Currently known only from type locality, Anjanaharibe-Sud Special Reserve (L166). Extent of range is unclear, but may also occur in Marojejy National Park to north-east and south to perhaps Antainambalana River. Populations on Masoala Peninsula also require specific determination. They have previously been described as *L. mustelinus* (L335; L337), but may now correspond to *L. seali* or even another unrecognised species. Similarly, identity of populations on Tsaranantanana Massif require clarification.

BEHAVIOUR

Nocturnal. Yet to be specifically studied in wild.

WHERE TO SEE

Currently Anjanaharibe-Sud near Andapa is the only known site to see this species. Sportive lemurs are easily seen in Marojejy National Park in forests around Camp Marojejia (Camp 2) and may correspond to this species.

Seal's Sportive Lemur, Anjanaharibe-Sud Special Reserve.

DARAINA SPORTIVE LEMUR

Lepilemur milanoii

MEASUREMENTS
Total length: 490–560mm. Head/body length: 248–292mm. Tail length: 246–274mm. Weight: average 720g, known range 620-820g. based on 14 specimens (L166)

DESCRIPTION & IDENTIFICATION
A relatively small *Lepilemur*. Upperparts reddish-brown, with diffuse dark midline stripe from crown, continuingly partially down back. Face is grey-brown. Underparts greyish-white. Limbs mainly grey, front of thighs reddish-brown. Tail uniformly reddish-brown (L166).

HABITAT & DISTRIBUTION
Found in dry deciduous, gallery and semi-evergreen forests. Type locality Andranotsimaty, near Daraina. Full range uncertain and needs further research to clarify, known from Lokia River south perhaps to Fanambana River.

BEHAVIOUR
Nocturnal. Yet to be studied in wild.

Daraina
Sportive Lemur

WHERE TO SEE
Daraina and surrounding area; various patches of forest can be easily reached. Best are those close to Andranotsimaty, 5km north-east of town. Sportive lemurs are easy to find. Before visiting, contact FANAMBY, who have an office in Daraina and can offer advice.

NORTHERN SPORTIVE LEMUR

Lepilemur septentrionalis

MEASUREMENTS*
Total length: 530mm. Head/body length: 280mm. Tail length: 250mm. Weight: 750g. *Estimated measurements (L181)

DESCRIPTION & IDENTIFICATION
Previous descriptions of '*L. septentrionalis*' relate to animals now reclassified as *L. ankaranensis* (L294). A relatively small sportive lemur: head and upperparts greyish-brown, underparts grey. Dark medial stripe often extends from crown down spine. Tail pale brown, darker at tip. Ears not as prominent as other *Lepilemur* species (L181).

Northern
Sportive Lemur

Daraina Sportive Lemur.

Northern Sportive Lemur.

ANKARANA SPORTIVE LEMUR

Lepilemur ankaranensis

MEASUREMENTS

Total length: *c.* 530mm. Head/body length: *c.* 280mm. Tail length: *c.* 250mm. Weight: *c.* 700–800g.

DESCRIPTION & IDENTIFICATION

A recently redefined species previously aligned with *L. septentrionalis.* Upperparts pale grey-brown, becoming darker towards and on tail, especially towards tip. Brown tinges apparent on crown and around shoulders. There is a darkish dorsal stripe running from the head. Underparts grey. Ears less prominent than other *Lepilemur* species.

A medium-small vertically clinging lemur; one of smallest *Lepilemur* species. Confusion unlikely with similar-sized Dwarf Lemur *Cheirogaleus* spp. and Fork-marked Lemur *Phaner* spp. as they have horizontal not vertical posture and quadrupedal not leaping locomotion.

Ankarana Sportive Lemur

HABITAT & DISTRIBUTION

Found in dry deciduous forest up to no more than 300m asl. Currently known only from a tiny patch of forest north of Irodo River. Type specimen was collected in forest of Sahafary. Recent studies recorded it in neighbouring forest fragments of Madirobe, Ankarongana and Andrahona (L294). The first two localities are maintained as community reserves, because of presence of village tombs it is *fady* (forbidden) to enter Andrahona Forest.

As currently understood, range covers no more than 350km². There may be no more than 250 mature individuals.

BEHAVIOUR

Wild studies of this species as recently redefined have yet to take place. Many aspects of behaviour and ecology are likely to be similar to *L. ankaranensis.*

WHERE TO SEE

The Sahafary Forest and neighbouring forest fragments north of Irodo River are the only localities where this species might be seen.

HABITAT & DISTRIBUTION

Occurs in dry deciduous forests and some humid evergreen forests. As currently defined, its range covers

Ankarana Sportive Lemur.

forest areas of Montagne d'Ambre, Ankarana and Analamera, but does not extend north of Irodo River. Lepilemurs north of Irodo now regarded as being distinct (*L. septentrionalis*).

Population density estimates vary between habitats from 150 to 550 animals/km^2, the higher densities associated with humid forests (L277; L122).

BEHAVIOUR
Nocturnal, with leaves forming bulk of diet. Solitary foragers with home ranges covering around one hectare (L277). Adults rarely associate, but mothers and infants have been observed together. Spends day in tree holes or dense tangles of vines. Most sleep sites are 6–8m above ground, but some as low as 1m.

Boas (*Sanzinia* and *Acrantophis*) have been reported to wait in ambush outside sleep sites. These snakes also take lemurs from within tree holes.

WHERE TO SEE
Common in Ankarana Special Reserve and readily seen in Canyon Forestière and forests around Campement Anilotra (Camp des Anglais). Also common in Montagne d'Ambre National Park, which is more accessible, although taller trees and denser foliage make good views less likely.

GREY-BACKED SPORTIVE LEMUR
Lepilemur dorsalis

MEASUREMENTS
Total length: 480–620mm. Head/body length: 250–355mm. Tail length: 230–270mm. Weight: 660-1110g. (L7)

DESCRIPTION & IDENTIFICATION
Upperparts and tail medium-brown

Grey-backed Sportive Lemur.

Grey-backed Sportive Lemur

to grey-brown with dark brown dorsal stripe, underparts paler grey-brown. Throat appears paler. Head more grey than brown, face tends to dark grey-brown with bluntish muzzle. Ears relatively small and rounded.

A medium-small vertically clinging lemur; one of smallest *Lepilemurs*. In Manongarivo region may be confused with Avahi *Avahi unicolor*, that has similar posture but is noticeably larger with smaller concealed ears, a rounded 'owl-like' face and distinctive white thigh patches.

HABITAT & DISTRIBUTION
Occurs in humid rainforest, sub-humid forest and some secondary and degraded forests. Restricted to Sambirano region in north-west, including Manongarivo Massif (L104). Previously recorded on off-shore islands of Nosy Be and Nosy Komba but these populations now described as *L. tymerlachsoni*. Southern range limit and boundary with recently described *L. sahamalazensis* remains unclear.

BEHAVIOUR
Nocturnal and feeds principally on leaves, some fruits, flowers and occasionally tree bark (L15).

In primary rainforests spends day in tree holes; in secondary forests,

with fewer or no large trees, spends day resting curled up on branches or in dense tangles of vegetation (L237). There is strong affinity for favoured sleep sites: individuals may return to same site for at least 14 consecutive nights.

WHERE TO SEE
Most forests within vicinity of Manongarivo Massif in Sambirano region in the north-west are likely to contain populations of this species.

HAWK'S SPORTIVE LEMUR
Lepilemur tymerlachsoni

MEASUREMENTS*
Total length: 500–580mm. Head/body length: 279–313mm. Tail length: 224–270mm. Weight: average 880g, known range 780-980g. *Based on ten specimens (L166)

DESCRIPTION & IDENTIFICATION
Moderately large sportive lemur. Upperparts mainly light brownish-grey, with more paler reddish-brown on upper half of back. Underparts light greyish-white. Fronts of thighs and edges of limbs are diffuse reddish-brown. Dark brown midline stripe runs from top of head down to lower half of back. Facial mask is grey. Tail uniform reddish-grey to brown (L166).

HABITAT & DISTRIBUTION
Humid Sambirano type forests, some modified secondary habitats, including coffee, vanilla and cashew nut plantations. Currently known only from type locality, Lokobe National Park on the island of Nosy Be off the north-west coast. May also occur on Nosy Komba. Further research is required to clarify extent of range relative to those of *L. dorsalis* and *L. sahamalazensis*.

Hawk's Sportive Lemur, Lokobe, Nosy Be.

Hawk's
Sportive Lemur

BEHAVIOUR
Nocturnal. Past annecdotal studies of *Lepilemur* on Nosy Be referred to *L. dorsalis* (L15). The behaviour of *L. tymerlachsoni* and *L. dorsalis* are assumed to be very similar.

In marginal areas at forest edges on Nosy Be, utilises purpose-built nest boxes fixed into trees (L15).

Little is known about breeding: single infant born between September and November. In secondary habitat on Nosy Be, predated by feral dogs and also Madagascar Buzzard *Buteo brachypterus* (L15).

WHERE TO SEE
Easy to see in buffer zone on north-east edge of Lokobe, inland from Ampasipohy on Nosy Be.

MITTERMEIER'S SPORTIVE LEMUR
Lepilemur mittermeieri

MEASUREMENTS
No data available

DESCRIPTION & IDENTIFICATION
Described on the basis of cytogenetic and molecular study, which differenti-

ates this species from *L. dorsalis* and *L. sahamalazenis* (L259A). No physical descriptions are currently available.

HABITAT & DISTRIBUTION
Sub-humid forest and some secondary forests. Type specimen collected on Ampasindava Peninsula in north-west, the site of all current records (L259A).

• confirmed locality

Mittermeier's
Sportive Lemur

BEHAVIOUR
Nocturnal. Yet to be studied in wild.

WHERE TO SEE
Ampasindava Peninsula is currently only known location.

SAHAMALAZA SPORTIVE LEMUR
Lepilemur sahamalazensis

MEASUREMENTS*
Total length: 510–540mm. Head/body length: 252–266mm. Tail length: 260-274mm. Weight: 687–892g. *Based on six specimens (L7)

DESCRIPTION & IDENTIFICATION
Pelage variable. Upperparts, including shoulders and arms, red-brown. Thighs and lower limbs less reddish, more greyish. Underparts pale grey to

Sahamalaza Sportive Lemur.

creamy. Face grey, forehead and ear bases red-brown. Diffuse mid-dorsal line runs from crown to mid/lower back, but no further; this is most distinct on middle back. Tail red-brown to deep brown (L7). Within known range, might be mistaken for *Cheirogaleus* or *Phaner*; these species are smaller and adopt horizontal rather than vertical posture.

HABITAT & DISTRIBUTION
Sub-humid forest and some secondary forests. Type specimen collected on Sahamalaza Peninsula in north-west, the site of all current records. Range probably

Sahamalaza
Sportive Lemur

encompasses Sahamalaza Peninsula
and perhaps north to Sambirano
River and south to Analalava (L7).
Range limits and boundary with *L.
dorsalis* and *L. mittermeieri* remain
unclear.

BEHAVIOUR
Nocturnal. Yet to be studied in wild.

WHERE TO SEE
Forests on Sahamalaza Peninsula.
Sites difficult to reach.

GREWCOCKS' SPORTIVE LEMUR

Lepilemur grewcocki
(*grewcockorum*)

MEASUREMENTS*
Total length: 550–630mm. Head/
body length: 288–332mm. Tail
length: 267–303mm. Weight: average
780g, known range 760–800g.
*Based on three specimens (L166)

**DESCRIPTION &
IDENTIFICATION**
Medium-sized sportive lemur. Pelage
grey dorsally becoming light grey to
white ventrally. Dark stripe on head
which may extend down dorsal ridge.
Tail all grey and lacks white tip often
seen in *L. edwardsi*.

Grewcocks' Sportive Lemur.

HABITAT & DISTRIBUTION
Found in dry deciduous forest. Type
locality is Anjiamangirana Classified
Forest. Occurs in region south of
Mahajamba River and north of
Maevarana and Sofia Rivers in north-
west Madagascar (L166). At southern
extreme, research is required to
determine boundary with range of *L.
edwardsi*. Similarly northern limits and
relation to *L. sahamalazensis* require
investigation.

Grewcock's
Sportive Lemur

BEHAVIOUR
Nocturnal. Yet to be studied in wild.

WHERE TO SEE
No sites within this species' range are
accessible.

MILNE-EDWARDS'S SPORTIVE LEMUR

Lepilemur edwardsi

MEASUREMENTS
Total length: 535–645mm. Head/
body length: 270–345mm. Tail
length: 265–300mm. Weight:
745–1,010g. (L382; L383; L355)

**DESCRIPTION &
IDENTIFICATION**
Upperparts and tail grey-brown,
with noticeable chestnut-brown
areas around shoulders, forelimbs
and upper thighs. Tail tip is white.
Underparts paler grey, with creamy
patches. A darker dorsal stripe is not
always distinct. Head grey and muzzle

grey-brown. Ears quite prominent.

A medium-sized, vertically clinging lemur, one of larger members of genus. Potentially confused with *Avahi* of similar size and posture. *Avahi* has smaller concealed ears, a rounded face with larger eyes and distinctive white patches on thighs. Also more likely to be seen in small groups, whereas *L. edwardsi* is generally solitary.

HABITAT & DISTRIBUTION

Restricted to dry deciduous forests up to 450m asl (Ankarafantsika). Southern limit of range is Betsiboka River, extending north to beyond Baie de Mahajamba, possibly to Maevarano River. Populations further north now regarded as *L. grewcocki*. *L. edwardsi* is common where it occurs. Densities up to 60 animals/km^2 recorded in typical dry deciduous forest areas (Ampijoroa).

BEHAVIOUR

Nocturnal; feeding on leaves, some fruits, seeds and flowers (L358). During dry season, when foliage is reduced, several individuals may feed in same tree, without apparent aggression.

Tree holes preferred sleep sites: most individuals sleep singly, but between two and four individuals of both sexes may share larger

Milne-Edwards's Sportive Lemur

Milne-Edwards's Sportive Lemur, Ankarafantsika National Park.

holes. Majority of sleep holes are 4–5m off the ground, some are as low as 1m: individuals utilise several different holes in their territory, but often return to same hole for several consecutive nights (L382; L383; L384; L385).

Activity begins around dusk and ends just before daybreak. After emerging, individuals sit at hole entrance for a short while before moving into forest. Most active for first two hours, thereafter, foraging bouts punctuated by extended periods of rest and grooming on favoured branches (L383). Nightly distance travelled varies seasonally; during austral winter (May–September) may move between 280m and 680m per night. In summer months (December–March) distances increase to between 400m and 1,200m (L358).

May share sleep sites, but individuals rarely remain together when active after dark. Effectively solitary but social, meaning it forages alone but regularly meets with other individuals throughout night (L356; L358). Encounters often include sessions of allo-grooming.

Males and females share home ranges of around one hectare (L358), spending majority of time in a core area around half this size (L382). Considerable overlap between adjacent ranges which are defended with loud calls. Vocalisations may be coordinated, with males and females contributing different elements to a duet. Most vocal towards end of dry season and beginning of rainy season (L358).

In Ankarafantsika is sympatric with Western Avahi, where there is apparent competition for food. To avoid this, *Avahi* is more active and feeds on leaves of high nutritional value, while *L. edwardsi* minimises its movements and is able to subsist on vegetation of poorer quality (L82). Predated by Fosa *Cryptoprocta ferox*, which is capable of excavating lemurs from sleep sites (L99).

WHERE TO SEE

Ampijoroa Forestry Station, part of Ankarafantsika National Park, is the best place to see this lemur. Forests around campsite provide good opportunities, but better views are often in Jardin Botanique B behind the campsite and Jardin Botanique A, on northern side of Lac Ravelobe.

RED-SHOULDERED SPORTIVE LEMUR

Lepilemur aeeclis

MEASUREMENTS*

Total length: 525–585mm. Head/body length: 285–315mm. Tail length: around 240–260mm. Weight: 765–970g. *Based on five specimens (L7)

DESCRIPTION & IDENTIFICATION

Recently described. Dorsal area greyish-brown, head, shoulders and arms more reddish-brown, thighs and lower limbs less reddish. Underparts pale grey with darker areas. Face grey, ears rounded and protruding. Above eyes darker diffuse stripes join on top of head and continue down neck and dorsal ridge, becoming darker and distinct on back (L7). Tail variable from deep rusty red to grey; when grey becomes more reddish towards tip.

Similar in size to *L. ruficaudatus* but larger than *L. randrianasoli*. Within known range, might be mistaken for *Cheirogaleus* or *Phaner*; these species are smaller and adopt horizontal rather than vertical posture.

HABITAT & DISTRIBUTION

Confined to dry deciduous forest in west. Type locality Antafia on north bank of Mahavavy River. Range poorly understood; probably extends from Betsiboka River south to at least Mahavavy River (L7). South of

Red-shouldered Sportive Lemur.

Red-shouldered
Sportive Lemur

Mahavavy River populations now described as *L. ahmansoni* (L166).

BEHAVIOUR
Nocturnal. Yet to be studied in wild.

WHERE TO SEE
Forests close to Anjamena on north bank of Mahavavy River and potentially any reasonable patches of forest within range.

AHMANSON'S SPORTIVE LEMUR

Lepilemur ahmansoni

MEASUREMENTS*
Total length: 470–540mm. Head/body length: 240–296mm. Tail length: 231–245mm. Weight: average 610g, known range 460–760g.
*Based on four specimens (L166)

DESCRIPTION & IDENTIFICATION
Relatively small *Lepilemur*. Upperparts primarily dark grey, with reddish-brown tinges around dorsal extremities. Lacks prominent dorsal midline of *L. aeeclis* (L166). Faint black stripe on crown. Underparts dark grey near midline becoming light grey underneath. Tail reddish-brown, darker dorsally and paler ventrally.

Ahmanson's Sportive Lemur.

HABITAT & DISTRIBUTION
Occurs in dry western forest. Type locality is Tsiombikibo Forest, north west of Mahavavy River, near Mitsinjo. Mahavavy River may form boundary with *L. aeeclis*. Further south, boundary may be Maningoza or Mananbaho River but this and relation to distribution of *L. randrianasoli* need further investigation (L166).

BEHAVIOUR
Nocturnal. Yet to be studied in wild.

WHERE TO SEE
Tsiombikibo Forest close to Mitsinjo in western Madagascar.

Ahmanson's
Sportive Lemur

RANDRIANASOLO'S SPORTIVE LEMUR

Lepilemur randrianasoli

MEASUREMENTS

Total length: 490–555mm**.
Head/body length: 280–300mm**.
Tail length: 210–255mm*. Weight:
660–880g*. *Based on nine specimens (L7) **Estimates

DESCRIPTION & IDENTIFICATION

Smaller with narrower and longer
head than *L. ruficaudatus* and *L.
aeeclis*. Unlike *Cheirogaleus* or *Phaner*
has vertical not horizontal posture.
Differs from Cleese's Woolly
Lemur *Avahi cleesei* in not having an
obvious 'facial disk' or white thigh
patches.

HABITAT & DISTRIBUTION

Known from type locality
Andramasay, Bemaraha and forests
on southern shore of Manambolo
River. Range probably extends from
Tsiribihina River in south to at least
Manambaho River and possibly
Maningoza River to north (L7). At
northern limits, boundary with range
of *L. ahmansoni* yet to be determined
(L166).

Randrianasolo's Sportive Lemur.

BEHAVIOUR

Nocturnal. Yet to be studied in wild.

WHERE TO SEE

Bemaraha National Park, near
Bekopaka on northern banks of
Manambolo River or similar forests
on southern bank of Manambolo.

RED-TAILED SPORTIVE LEMUR

Lepilemur ruficaudatus

MEASUREMENTS

Total length: 500–560mm. Head/body
length: 260–300mm. Tail length:
240–280mm. Weight: 500–800g.

DESCRIPTION & IDENTIFICATION

Upperparts grey-brown with
chestnut-rufous tinges on shoulders
and forelimbs, underparts paler grey,
throat creamy-white. Tail has distinct
reddish hue. Head grey with darker
grey around muzzle. Ears large,
rounded and prominent.

A medium-sized, vertically clinging
lemur. Within parts of range (only
Bemaraha) sympatric with the similar-
sized and postured Cleese's Avahi
Avahi cleesei.

HABITAT & DISTRIBUTION

Found in dry deciduous forest.
Accounting for new species, range
probably extends from Mangoky
River and north to Tsiribihina River

Randrianasolo's
Sportive Lemur

Red-tailed
Sportive Lemur

(L7). Previously recorded from Zombitse (L83) and Isalo National Parks (L121); these populations probably correspond to recently described *L. hubbardi* (L166).

In dry deciduous forests is known to reach very high densities: estimates vary between 180 and 350 individuals/km².

BEHAVIOUR

Nocturnal. Males and females have overlapping home ranges of around one hectare and live as a pair (L85; L240; L408). Foraging bouts usually solitary, but night-time resting periods may be synchronised; the pair often meet to share same tree hole. Foraging is punctuated by a single long period of inactivity. When aggressive, individuals bang their hindfeet on branches and shake the tree (L82).

Primarily folivorous, although fruits of some trees (*Diospyros* spp.) also eaten. Can tolerate leaves with high toxin concentrations and during dry season (May–November) is able to subsist on dry leaves (L128).

During daytime resting periods has one of the lowest metabolic rates of any mammal. This is raised substantially (doubled) prior to night-time activity; probably an adaptation to help survival at relatively high densities on a poor quality diet (L306).

Red-tailed Sportive Lemur, Kirindy Forest.

Mating between May and July; single young born after gestation of approximately 130 days. Infant initially carried by mother in her mouth; later it clings to fur on her back. When older, mother may leave or 'park' infant in tree hole or similar 'safe' site while she forages. Offspring continue suckling for at least four months, becoming independent around one year (L238).

In Kirindy Forest, predated by Madagascar Long-eared Owl *Asio madagascariensis*, Madagascar Harrier-Hawk *Polyboroides radiatus* and Fosa *Cryptoprocta ferox*: latter two species capable of excavating the lemurs from their tree holes (L99).

WHERE TO SEE

Most large areas of native forest within range provide an opportunity to see this lemur. The best locality is Kirindy Forest north-east of Morondava – indeed this is perhaps the best place in Madagascar to see a number of nocturnal species.

Hubbard's Sportive Lemur, Zombitse National Park.

HUBBARD'S SPORTIVE LEMUR

Lepilemur hubbardi

MEASUREMENTS*

Total length: 510–585mm. Head/body length: 283–335mm. Tail length: 229–251mm. Weight: average 990g, known range 840–1140g. *Based on ten specimens (L166)

DESCRIPTION & IDENTIFICATION

A largish *Lepilemur* species. Upperparts dark reddish-brown on shoulders and upper back, becoming paler reddish grey towards lower body and tail. Face greyish-brown, crown and nape reddish-brown. Underparts entirely white. Tail uniformly reddish blonde (L166).

HABITAT & DISTRIBUTION

Found in dry transitional forest. Type locality is Zombitse National Park. Currently known only from type locality; may range from Onilahy River in south to Mangoky River in north (L166) and include populations in Isalo National Park, previously assumed to be *L. ruficaudatus* (L121).

Hubbard's Sportive Lemur

BEHAVIOUR

Nocturnal. Yet to be studied in wild.

WHERE TO SEE

This species is easily seen in Zombitse National Park, both resting in sleep sites during the day and when active at night.

PETTER'S SPORTIVE LEMUR

Lepilemur petteri

MEASUREMENTS*

Total length: 490–540mm. Head/body length: 270–296mm. Tail length: 223–251mm. Weight: average 630g, known range 625-635g. *Based on five specimens (L166)

DESCRIPTION & IDENTIFICATION

A small *Lepilemur*, but larger than *L. leucopus*. Upperparts grey to greyish-brown, underparts pale grey to white. Face grey with pale patches under chin and around eyes. Front of thighs more brownish-grey. Faint brownish-grey dorsal midline (L166).

Small to medium-sized verti-cally clinging lemur. Confusion with *Cheirogaleus* spp. is unlikely as they adopt a horizontal posture and move quadrupedally.

HABITAT & DISTRIBUTION

Confined to dry habitats, principally spiny forest and some gallery forest. Type locality is Beza Mahafaly Special Reserve. Currently known only from areas south of Onilahy River and west of Linta and Menarandra Rivers (L166). Further research is required to clarify how distribution of this species relates to that of *L. leucopus*.

Petter's
Sportive Lemur

BEHAVIOUR

Nocturnal. *Lepilemur* studies have taken place in Beza Mahafaly when the species present was thought to be *L. leucopus* (L203; L296). The behaviour of *L. petteri* and *L. leucopus* are assumed to be very similar.

WHERE TO SEE

Beza Mahafaly south-east of Toliara is the best place to see this species.

WHITE-FOOTED SPORTIVE LEMUR

Lepilemur leucopus

MEASUREMENTS

Total length: 460–520mm. Head/body length: 245–260mm. Tail length: 215–260mm. Weight: 450–600g.

DESCRIPTION & IDENTIFICATION

Head and upperparts principally pale grey with brownish tinges around shoulders, upper forelimbs and upper thighs. Tail more brownish-grey. Underparts and throat very pale grey to off-white, this coloration extending part way up the flanks. Face grey-brown with whitish 'spec-tacles' around eyes. Ears relatively large and rounded with whitish tufts at bases.

A small to medium-sized lemur, probably the smallest in genus *Lepilemur*. Confusion with Spiny Forest Dwarf Lemur *Cheirogaleus adipicaudatus* is unlikely as *C. adipicau-datus* adopts horizontal posture and moves quadrupedally.

White-footed
Sportive Lemur

HABITAT & DISTRIBUTION

Confined to dry habitats of southern Madagascar, principally spiny forest and gallery forest. Range extends from western side of Andohahela Massif in south-east to at least Menarandra River in south-west. West and north of this populations are now thought to belong to *L. hubbardi*, although respective boundaries of these species' distributions require clarification.

BEHAVIOUR

Nocturnal. In spiny forest diet consists

Petter's Sportive Lemurs, Beza Mahafaly Special Reserve.

of leaves, primarily Didiereaceae, *Alluaudia procera* and *A. ascendens* (L296); in gallery forests leaves from *Tamarindus* and *Euphorbia*, together with those of various vines dominate (L203). During dry season (May–October), flowers from Didiereaceae also eaten. Copes with poor quality diet by remaining inactive for long periods.

By day either tree holes or tangles of lianas used as sleep sites; males and females can share sites as well as sleep separately. Considerable vocalisation just after dusk when they emerge. At night about 40% of time is spent foraging, bouts interspersed with prolonged periods of rest and/or self-grooming (L296). During cooler dry season periods of rest increase and shorter distances are travelled when foraging (as little as 200m to 300m per night), although total time spent foraging per night remains constant throughout year (L203).

Occupies small territories, 0.2ha to 0.4ha being average for both sexes (L296). Little overlap between territories of females, but male ranges overlap with those of up to three females. Females share territories with dependent offspring, and adult daughters sometimes remain within natal range. Territories defended by calls and displays rather than by scent-marking.

Mating occurs from May to July, gestation is around 130 days. Single infant born between October and November and attains sexual maturity by 18 months (L237).

Predated by Barn Owl *Tyto alba* and Madagascar Buzzard *Buteo brachypterus* (L99).

WHERE TO SEE

Easily seen in gallery forest and spiny forest areas at Berenty Reserve, east of Tolagnaro or spiny forest areas in Andohahela National Park (Mangatsiaka and Ihazofotsy).

White-footed Sportive Lemur, Berenty Reserve.

TRUE LEMURS Family Lemuridae

Subfamily Hapalemurinae

Bamboo lemurs are the smallest diurnal lemurs and are best known for their dietary preference for various species of bamboo. Although other primates opportunistically or seasonally eat bamboo in small quantities, bamboo lemurs are unique amongst primates in specialising in this diet (L193).

In evolutionary terms, bamboo lemurs are close enough relatives of 'True' Lemurs (Lemurinae) to belong in the same family, Lemuridae, but are sufficiently different to warrant their own subfamily, Hapalemurinae. Phylogenetic relationships within the genus remain contentious (L222), and there have been several recent taxonomic changes. Previously, three subspecies of Grey Bamboo Lemur were recognised; each has now been elevated to full species, *Hapalemur griseus*, *H. occidentalis* and *H. alaotrensis*. Additionally, Grey Bamboo Lemurs at the southern extremity of the rainforest belt are now considered a distinct species: Southern Grey Bamboo Lemur *Hapalemur meridionalis* (L65). Also, Greater Bamboo Lemur has now been removed from *Hapalemur* and assigned its own monotypic genus *Prolemur* (L115).

BAMBOO OR GENTLE LEMUR

genus *Hapalemur*

Hapalemur are characterised by medium-small to medium-sized bodies, long tails and moderately long back legs designed for leaping. Their muzzles are shorter than other members of the family Lemuridae (*Lemur*, *Eulemur* and *Varecia*), which gives their faces a rather blunt, rounded appearance. In general *Hapalemur* prefer to adopt a vertical posture and are capable of quick bounding leaps between close upright stems of bamboo and similar vegetation. One exception is Alaotra Reed Lemur *H. alaotrensis* which has evolved a specialised form of locomotion associated with its unique habitat.

Golden Bamboo Lemur.

EASTERN GREY BAMBOO LEMUR

Hapalemur griseus

Other names: Eastern Grey Gentle Lemur, Eastern Lesser Bamboo Lemur

MEASUREMENTS

Total length: 560–700mm. Head/body length: 240–300mm. Tail length: 320–400mm. Weight: 750–1,050g. (L345; L346)

DESCRIPTION & IDENTIFICATION

Upperparts medium-grey to olive-grey with chestnut-russet tinges over head, around shoulders and sometimes extending down dorsum; these areas more noticeable on individuals from south of species' range. Tail darker grey. Face and underparts slightly paler grey, gradually becoming creamy-grey on belly. Ears small and rounded, muzzle much shorter than other diurnal lemurs.

A medium-sized active lemur and amongst smallest diurnal lemur species. Most often seen in vertical clinging posture. Small size, blunt muzzle and rounded face should prevent confusion with other species.

In areas of sympatry, confusion with Golden Bamboo Lemur *H. aureus* or Greater Bamboo Lemur *P. simus* is possible. Distinguished from *H. aureus* by smaller size and grey, rather than golden-brown, coloration. *P. simus* is broadly similar in colour, but significantly larger with distinctive ear-tufts.

HABITAT & DISTRIBUTION

Found in primary and secondary lowland and montane humid forests with bamboo and bamboo vines:

Eastern Grey Bamboo Lemur

recorded from sea level to over 1,600m asl (Andringitra) (L336).

Range covers eastern rainforest belt, from Maroantsetra region in north, to vicinity of Mananara River in south. The Mananara River is the probable boundary with recently described *H. meridionalis*. Previously bamboo lemurs to north of Maroantsetra and Masoala Peninsula have been described as *H. griseus*. Recent research suggests these populations belong to *H. occidentalis* (L294).

BEHAVIOUR

Regarded as principally diurnal (L218; L346) but sometimes more active around dawn and dusk (crepuscular); bouts of nocturnal activity also observed (L237). Vocalisations begin around two hours before dawn and occasionally during the night. Around half a day spent foraging at all levels in forest (L390; L393).

Diet dominated by bamboo – around 80% – with a marked preference for bases of young leaves, branch shoots, some ground shoots and stem pith. Remainder of diet comprises non-bamboo foliage, fruit, flowers, grass stems and some fungi (L218; L345; L346). Demonstrates considerable dexterity, especially when feeding on bamboo.

Group size between two and seven, although larger groups up to 11 are seen occasionally (L252; L218; L345; L346). Smaller groups contain breeding pairs with offspring, larger groups include more than one breeding female plus two or more adult males. Territorial, uses scent-marking, vocalisations and direct chasing to defend home ranges of 15–20ha (L218; L345; L346; L113). Other species of bamboo lemur appear to be tolerated (L346). Size of home range correlated to amount of bamboo within occupied area. During a day's foraging, groups move up to 500m (L390). Prefers to sleep in taller trees.

Eastern Grey Bamboo Lemur.

Mating occurs in June and July, gestation 137 days, females give birth to single young between late October and November (L346). Infant carried by mother in her mouth for first two weeks, later clings to fur and rides on her back. When foraging, infant sometimes 'parked' by mother for brief periods. Young take solid food at three weeks, eating bamboo readily by six weeks and fully weaned at four months (L346). Both sexes disperse from natal area.

Predated by Fosa *Cryptoprocta ferox*, large raptors e.g. Madagascar Harrier-Hawk *Polyboroides radiatus* and Henst's Goshawk *Accipiter henstii* and large snakes such as Madagascar Tree Boa *Sanzinia madagascariensis* (L99, L154).

WHERE TO SEE
Both Andasibe-Mantadia and Ranomafana National Parks are very good places to seeing this species. At Andasibe, look in areas either side of road around the Orchid Garden. In Ranomafana, the main trail at Talatakely and areas around Belle Vue can be good.

Western Grey Bamboo Lemur.

WESTERN GREY BAMBOO LEMUR

Hapalemur occidentalis

Other names: Western Grey Gentle Lemur, Western Lesser Bamboo Lemur

MEASUREMENTS
Total length: 550–670mm. Head/body length: 270–280mm. Tail length: 360–390mm. Weight: 700–1,000g.

DESCRIPTION & IDENTIFICATION
Upperparts medium to pale grey-brown, face and underparts slightly lighter. Overall, more uniform coloration than *H. griseus*. Ears small and snout short.

A medium-sized active species; probably smallest diurnal lemur. Sympatric with several *Eulemur* species; small size, uniform colour, short muzzle and round face should prevent confusion.

HABITAT & DISTRIBUTION
Has a wide habitat tolerance; found in dry to subhumid deciduous, secondary and degraded forests and cacao plantations with stands of bamboo (L193). May also occur in some eastern humid forests (see right).

Range poorly understood and confusing: known from isolated and apparently discontinuous localities in west and north-west; in central west, recorded in Soalala, Baly Bay and Tsiombikibo Forest regions to west of Mahavavy River (L123; L53) south to Namoroka and Bongolava

and continuing south to Tsingy de Bemaraha region (L264). Between Mahavavy and Manambolo Rivers populations highly fragmented.

Also occurs in Sambirano region in north-west, from Andranomalaza

Western Grey Bamboo Lemur

River in south to Mahavavy du Nord River in north, including Ampasindava Peninsula, Ambato Massif and Sambirano River valley (L278; L104; L191). Records further to north in Ankarana may be attributable to this species (L122).

Recent research suggests *Hapalemur* in rain forests north of Maroantsetra and on Masoala Peninsula are *H. occidentalis*, not *H. griseus* as previously described (L294). This raises possibility that other bamboo lemurs between Masoala and Tsaratanana, including those in Anjanaharibe-Sud and Marojejy, are also *H. occidentalis*. Further investigation required.

BEHAVIOUR

In Sambirano region, group size between one and four (L278; L104); in Bemaraha groups up to six have been seen (L193).

Activity patterns vary seasonally; during wet season in Bemaraha active during day; during dry season (July–September) observations in both Bemaraha and the Sambirano suggest more after-dark activity, beginning around 16.30 with vocalisations (not heard by day) and continuing into the night (L191).

Forages on ground or in understorey vegetation. Diet probably contains high proportion of bamboo; in Bemaraha also seen feeding on liana flowers (L193).

WHERE TO SEE

Known haunts are remote. Perhaps best looked for in Tsingy de Bemaraha National Park. Groups of up to four animals have been seen in stands of bamboo and associated vines in forests close to village of Bekopaka, but animals are shy. May be encountered in Tsiombikibo Forest near Mitsinjo and forests along Sambirano River valley, south-east of Ambanja. Also known from Ambato Massif, on Nosy Faly Peninsula, north of Ambanja.

SOUTHERN GREY BAMBOO LEMUR

Hapalemur meridionalis

Other names: Southern Grey Gentle Lemur, Southern Lesser Bamboo Lemur

MEASUREMENTS*

Total length: 560–700mm.
Head/body length: 240–300mm.
Tail length: 320–400mm.
Weight: 750–1,050g. *Estimated measurements

DESCRIPTION & IDENTIFICATION

Originally proposed as a subspecies (L387), recently elevated to a full species (L115). Coloration similar to *H. griseus*, although apparently darker. Upperparts grey to olive-grey with variable russet areas around shoulders and down back. Tail darker grey. Face and underparts slightly paler grey.

A medium-sized active lemur with vertical clinging posture. Sympatric with only one other diurnal species *Eulemur collaris* with which it cannot be confused.

HABITAT & DISTRIBUTION

Found in littoral forest, and

Southern Grey
Bamboo Lemur

lowland and montane rainforest from sea level to at least 1,500m asl (L68). Probable range extends from Mananara River in north, southwards through Midongy-Sud to Anosyenne Mountains and Andohahela in extreme south-east. Type locality Mandena is around 10km north of Tolagnaro (L387; L386). May also be found in Kalambatritra Special Reserve to west of Midongy-Sud, but identity of *Hapalemur* populations here has yet to be determined.

BEHAVIOUR

Limited observations suggest it lives in small groups of up to seven (L193).

Type locality, Mandena Forestry Station, is degraded littoral forest containing considerable marshy areas, dominated by *Pandanus* and Traveller's Tree *Ravenala madagascariensis*. Bamboo occurs but is patchily and sparsely distributed, yet this species achieves quite high densities (L193). Suggests it is not wholly reliant on bamboo and diet contains other significant elements. Studies are required to confirm this.

WHERE TO SEE

Can be seen in Mandena Conservation Zone (part of QMM Titanium Dioxide Development Project), a recently created protected area 12km north of Tolagnaro. Lemurs here not yet habituated and shy. Has also been seen (a group of four) in forest fragments around summit of Pic St Louis outside Tolagnaro.

The more intrepid should visit Malio, the rainforest area of Andohahela National Park (Parcel 1). This area of beautiful forest should become more accessible as ecotourism develops.

Alaotra Reed Lemur.

ALAOTRA REED LEMUR

Hapalemur alaotrensis

Other name: Alaotra Gentle Lemur

MEASUREMENTS

Total length: 770–810mm. Head/body length: 380–400mm. Tail length: 390–410mm. Weight: 1,100–1,380g. (L196)

DESCRIPTION & IDENTIFICATION

Larger than other grey bamboo lemurs with no size difference between sexes (L196; L268). Pelage dense and woolly. Upperparts medium to darkish grey-brown, face and underparts paler grey. Crown and nape chestnut-brown, gradually fades over shoulder region. Head rounded, ears small and unobtrusive.

Medium-sized with rotund body and long tail. In restricted range and unusual habitat, cannot be confused with any other species.

HABITAT & DISTRIBUTION

Unique amongst primates by inhabiting reed and papyrus beds. Confined to marshes of Lac Alaotra in central-east. Probably once present right around lake (largest in Madagascar) and also occurred near Andilamena, at least 35km to north (but disappeared in 1950s when marshes were converted to rice paddies) (L192).

Range further restricted by drainage and destruction of habitat. Stronghold is large area of primary marsh at south-west corner of Lac Alaotra, largely within triangle formed by villages of Andreba, Andilana-Sud and Anororo. Second smaller isolated population occurs in a fragment of marsh on northern shore (L197). Has one of most restricted ranges of any lemur (less than 220km²); only 2,500 to 5,000 animals remain (L268). Survival severely threatened by marsh drainage, burning of reed beds and direct hunting – over 1,000 lemurs have been poached annually in some years (L197).

known populations of Lac Alaotra Reed Lemur

Primary marsh Vegetation

rice cultivation

roads

Alaotra Reed Lemur

BEHAVIOUR

Lives in groups of two to nine, three to five average. Larger groups contain two adult females and up to three adult males. Majority of groups are families – one breeding pair and offspring – but 35% of groups contain two breeding females (L196). Where groups contain two or three males, only one actually breeds (L193).

Territorial; groups occupy exclusive home ranges of 0.6–8ha, a proportion of which may be water that varies seasonally in extent (L205). Group encounters are frequent; home ranges defended by vocalisations, scent-marking and display behaviour. Group cohesiveness maintained by allogrooming – animals sit facing one another, divide partner's fur with their hands and groom with tooth combs (modified lower front dentition)(L189; L190; L191).

Unusually, they are quadrupedal – animals walk up reed stems until they bend over, then walk along to reach next stem. Allows them to cross narrow water channels; wider channels are jumped across in conventional bamboo lemur fashion.

Cathemeral (active day and night); principally active during daylight, with significant bouts of nocturnal activity (lasting 30 minutes or longer) each night. Main periods of activity concentrated around first and last three hours of daylight (L195).

Diet strictly folivorous. Food diversity low – 95% of feeding on four species – major elements are pith of papyrus stems *Cyperus madagascariensis*, young reed shoots *Phragmites communis* and surface grasses *Echinochloa crusgalli* and *Leersia hexandra* (L189; L190). Also plant-part selective; in February to April, they feed predominantly on pith of young papyrus and new shoots of reeds, later in year diet shifts towards older leaves. Diet low quality so lemurs needs to remain active and feed for much of day.

Also spend considerable periods foraging at ground level, particularly during dry season (June–October) when more solid ground is exposed. During wet season, water levels rise but lemurs still descend into floating vegetation (L195).

Births occur between September and February, up to 40% being twins (L196; L193). Young relatively well developed and initially carried on mother's back. Females can swim across open channels while carrying offspring. Infants of one to two weeks are 'parked' by mother in dense thickets of papyrus and left for up to 30 minutes. Both sexes disperse from natal area; females leave before maturity, males delay departure until maturity (L195; L196).

No direct predation observed (other than by humans). Potential threats would be large snakes, raptors and possibly Brown-tailed Mongoose *Salanoia concolor*.

WHERE TO SEE

Very difficult to see in wild. Necessary to travel quietly by pirogue through marginal reed beds around south-west shore of lake and hope for a chance encounter. From eastern shore, leave from village of Andreba and hire a local fisherman with an intimate knowledge of area.

GOLDEN BAMBOO LEMUR

Hapalemur aureus

Other name: Golden Gentle Lemur

MEASUREMENTS

Total length: 720–800mm. Head/body length: 340–380mm. Tail length: 380–420mm. Weight: average 1,250–1,650g. (L345; L346)

DESCRIPTION & IDENTIFICATION

Pelage dense and soft. Upperparts rich olive-chestnut, crown, nape, shoulders, dorsum and upper tail slightly darker. Tail darkens towards tip. Underparts and inner limbs golden-brown. Inner face around eyes dark brown, extending down muzzle, outer face golden-brown. Ears small without tufts and golden-brown.

Medium-sized rotund lemur, intermediate in size between smaller Eastern Grey Bamboo Lemur *H. griseus* and larger Greater Bamboo Lemur *Prolemur simus*. Golden-brown coloration, coupled with size

Alaotra Reed Lemur.

differences should prevent confusion with other bamboo lemurs.

HABITAT & DISTRIBUTION
Primary mid-altitude and higher-altitude rainforest with abundant bamboo (particularly Giant Bamboo *Cathariostachys madagascariensis*), from 600m asl (in Ranomafana) to approximately 1,600m asl (in Andringitra) (L16). Discovered in 1985 at Ranomafana and described two years later (L173). Range extends from northern areas of Ranomafana National Park, south through narrow forest corridor to north-eastern slopes of Andringitra Massif (L336; L161; L112; L267; L131). Total range area around 2,500km², perhaps fewer than 2,000 individuals survive.

BEHAVIOUR
Principally diurnal; activity begins before dawn continuing to mid-morning. Distinct rest period between 09.00 and 13.00, before foraging resumes; they bed down just

Golden Bamboo Lemur

after dusk (L346; L193).

Group size two to six, three to four is the norm, consisting of adult male and female, with slightly smaller subadults and juveniles. Territories are around 30ha, but average daily travel less than 400m (L397; L345; L346).

Vocal; at least two calls identified, first a quiet, resonant *wuulp* with inquisitive inflection (probably a contact call), second is loud, sharp, staccato 'guttural honk' repeated on slowing, descending scale decreasing in volume. Only one individual gives this call, sometimes heard in conjunction with *wuulp* call from others in group. Honk call may be territorial.

Diet exclusively bamboo (around 90%), especially endemic Giant Bamboo *Cathariostachys madagascariensis*. Also eats bamboo creeper and bamboo grass. Highly plant-part selective: bases of young leaves and new shoots preferred. Probably reduces competition with Greater Bamboo Lemur *Prolemur simus*, which prefers inner pith. Young shoots of Giant Bamboo are not consumed by any other lemur – they are protein-rich and contain high levels of cyanide toxins that would normally be lethal (L93; L345; L346). This species has evolved a digestive system to cope,

Golden Bamboo Lemur, Ranomafana National Park.

and so reduces competition for food with other species.

Births occur in November and December; gestation 138 days; a single offspring is produced. During first two weeks infants shelter in dense tangles of vegetation, they are later 'parked' by mother while she forages. Young remain in natal group for three years before becoming independent (L346).

WHERE TO SEE
Ranomafana National Park is the only accessible locality. The species' discovery brought Ranomafana to the world's attention and prompted the creation of the park in 1991. The best area is Talatakely (the main tourist area), around stands of Giant Bamboo adjacent to main trail. It is essential to seek the assistance of one of the local guides.

GREATER BAMBOO LEMUR genus *Prolemur*

Until recently, the Greater Bamboo Lemur was placed in the genus *Hapalemur*. Recent research has concluded it is sufficiently distinct to be classified in its own monotypic genus *Prolemur* (L115). Like other bamboo lemurs, it has a broadened and short muzzle, but is significantly larger than *Hapalemur* species (L4).

GREATER BAMBOO LEMUR

Prolemur simus

Other names: Greater Gentle Lemur and Broad-nosed Gentle Lemur

MEASUREMENTS
Total length: 850–900mm. Head/body length: 400–420mm. Tail length: 450–480mm. Weight: 2,200–2,500g. (L173; L147; L346)

DESCRIPTION & IDENTIFICATION
Pelage short and dense. Upperparts and tail sooty grey-brown, with russet tinge. Head, neck, shoulders and upper arms more olive-brown. Noticeable chestnut-brown patch in pygal region. Tip of tail very dark grey. Underparts and throat paler creamy-brown. Inner face, nose-bridge and muzzle dark grey; areas just above eyes pale grey. Large prominent pale grey to white ear-tufts distinctive. Populations on Andringitra Massif are predominantly deep russet and may represent a distinct colour morph.

Medium-large, round-bodied lemur and the largest bamboo lemur. Appreciably larger size and distinctive ear-tufts should prevent confusion with other bamboo lemurs.

HABITAT & DISTRIBUTION
Lowland and montane rainforest associated with giant bamboo up to around 1,100m asl (L336; L16). Also seen in plantations with Giant Bamboo adjacent to native forests.

Subfossils indicate was once widespread (L95); remains found at Ampasambazimba east of Antananarivo, Montagne des Français and Ankarana Massif in north, Anjohibe, north-east of Mahajanga and in Bemaraha National Park in west (L97).

Also collected from widely dispersed sites in eastern rainforests during 19th century.

Recently presence suspected in

Greater Bamboo Lemur

forests adjacent to Torotorofotsy Marsh near Andasibe from evidence of its highly distinctive feeding techniques (L57).

Currently only confirmed localities are sites in south-east – Ranomafana and Andringitra National Parks and localised sites in forest corridor connecting the two (L112; L131; L16). Also known from forest fragments to east of Ranomafana including Ifanadiana, Kianjavato and possibly Ambolomava. Further south recorded from Karianga in vicinity of Vondrozo west of Farafangana and Evendra to south-east of Andringitra but north of Manampatrana River (L193; L131). Distribution similar to Golden Bamboo Lemur, although because of specialised microhabitat requirements appears far less numerous. Amongst the 25 most endangered primates in the world (L180).

BEHAVIOUR
Probably cathemeral; most active during day, but regular bouts of nocturnal activity occur throughout year (L346). Groups containing two or more adult males and females are polygynous and range from seven to 11 individuals. Occupy large home ranges, up to 60ha, although they tend to remain in around 20% for up to two weeks before moving on,

presumably in response to diminished resources (L345; L346). Often descend to ground when foraging.

Diet almost exclusively bamboo, particularly Giant Bamboo *Cathariostachys madagascariensis* which constitutes up to 95%. Less selective than *H. aureus* and eats both mature and young leaves. During rainy season (mid-November to March) marked shift towards feeding on sprouting ground shoots of Giant Bamboo, at times these represent 98% of diet. After March, when shoots decline, leaves and branch shoots eaten in increasing quantity. Between July and November they heavy rely on inner pith (L345; L346).

Evidence of destructive feeding.

Other foods include flowers of Traveller's Tree (*Ravenala madagascariensis*), fruits of *Artocarpus*, *Ficus* spp., *Dypsis* spp. and leaves of *Pennisetum clandestinum* (L173).

Has powerful jaws and adept at stripping outer layers off live stalks and breaking through bamboo poles to reach pith. This technique is destructive; ravaged stands of Giant Bamboo are clear evidence of this species' presence.

Mating in May and June, gestation 149 days, females give birth to singleton in October and November. Mothers continuously carry infants until around four months, afterwards they move independently. Does not appear to 'park' infants (L346). Weaning between seven and eight months, offspring disperse from parental group between three and four years. Occasionally predated by Fosa *Cryptoprocta ferox* (L154).

WHERE TO SEE
Ranomafana National Park is the only locality within easy reach. Groups often encountered in Giant Bamboo around main trail in Talatakely. Enlisting the help of a park guide is recommended.

Greater Bamboo Lemur eating Giant Bamboo, Ranomafana National Park.

TRUE LEMURS Family Lemuridae

Subfamily Lemurinae

The subfamily Lemurinae includes the most familiar Malagasy primates, collectively known as the 'true' lemurs. Three genera are recognised: *Lemur*, *Eulemur* and *Varecia* (L116; L323). They are medium to medium-large lemurs that adopt a horizontal body posture and move and leap quadrupedally. All are skilled climbers, but some also spend time on the ground to varying degrees, especially the Ring-tailed Lemur *Lemur catta*. Previously they have been regarded as principally diurnal, but both day- and night-time activity is known in a number of species (cathemeral behaviour). This behaviour is quite widespread and particularly prevalent in the genus *Eulemur*.

RING-TAILED LEMUR genus *Lemur*

A genus containing a single species, the Ring-tailed Lemur *Lemur catta*. There are some morphological similarities between the genera *Lemur* and *Eulemur* (e.g. their skeletons are virtually indistinguishable), but molecular evidence and scent-gland distribution suggest that closer affinities may exist between *Lemur* and *Hapalemur* (L348; L116).

The Ring-tailed Lemur is *the* flagship species, an icon synonymous with its island home. Paradoxically it is far from being typical; it is the most terrestrial of Madagascar's primates, lives in the largest social groups and tolerates a variety of extreme habitats that no other lemurs can (L135).

Ring-tailed Lemur.

RING-TAILED LEMUR

Lemur catta

MEASUREMENTS

Total length: 950–1,100mm.
Head/body length: 385–455mm.
Tail length: 560–625mm. Weight: 2.3–3.5kg. (L348)

DESCRIPTION & IDENTIFICATION

Back usually grey to grey-brown rump, limbs and haunches grey. Underparts off-white or cream. Neck and crown charcoal-grey, contrasting with white outer face and throat. Large triangular dark eye-patches just reach crown. Snout also dark. Ears prominent and paler than crown. Tail long and ringed alternately with 13 to 15 bands, each in black and white (L348). Both sexes have scent glands on wrists.

Individuals from isolated populations on Andringitra Massif vary markedly from typical form previously described. Their fur is more dense and woolly in appearance. Dorsal region, rump and limbs noticeably darker and more rufous-brown than typical form. Tail has fewer dark rings (11 to 12) (L101). All plausible variations brought about by cold climate with high ultra-violet light levels that bleach fur.

Ring-tailed Lemur

Ring-tails living in open sunny areas are typically more rufous than neighbours from shady forest areas.

A medium-sized lemur, often seen on ground and instantly recognisable by its distinctive banded tail. Cannot be confused with any other species.

HABITAT & DISTRIBUTION

Has broadest habitat range of any lemur. Spiny forest, dry scrub, deciduous forest and gallery forest are used throughout majority of range. Bare rock, surrounding moist fire-resistant forest and moist forest frequented in Isalo National Park and exposed rocks, low ericoid bush and subalpine vegetation at higher elevations are habitat of population in Andringitra.

Ranges through south and south-west from Tolagnaro in south-east to Marofihise Forest near Belo-sur-Mer on west coast (L407) and inland to vicinity of Ambalavao and western edges of Kalambatritra (L204; L129). Generally occurs at lower

Female Ring-tailed Lemur carrying three-week-old infant, Anjampolo Spiny Forest.

intake (L302). Between August and October pregnant and lactating females prefer energy-rich food items. In dry habitats with low annual rainfall, are able to gain water from dew and succulent plants like endemic *Aloe* sp. and introduced prickly pears (*Opuntia* sp.) (L135).

Occurs in larger groups than any other Malagasy primate – from six to around 25 individuals, 13 to 15 is average but over 30 recorded (L302; L135). Groups contain equal numbers of adult females and males, plus immature and juvenile animals. Group's core is matriline of females; males migrate from natal group at maturity and frequently move from one group to another during adult life (L344; L301).

A well-defined and maintained hierarchy exists within troop; females are completely dominant over males and alpha female forms focal point for group as a whole (L300; L135, L136). Males have own strict hierarchy, but always subordinate to females. The 'central' male interacts with females more often than other group males (L342; L343).

Groups not strictly territorial but do have preferred home range, size of which determined by habitat and resources within. Seasonal changes mean home ranges vary from 6ha to over 30ha. Scent-marking important in demarcating ranges. Females leave genital smears, males use wrist gland armed with horny pad to gouge scent into bark of saplings. High degree of overlap between home ranges of neighbouring groups. When groups meet, dominant females are primarily responsible for defence confronting members of other groups by staring, lungeing approaches and occasional physical aggression. After agonistic encounters, group members retreat towards centre of their home range (L138; L302).

Courtship and mating highly synchronous, occurring in a two-

elevations with apparently isolated population remaining in Andringitra on south-eastern plateau – recorded above tree line to altitudes exceeding 2,600m, where it sleeps in caves at night (L101). Ranges further in to interior highlands than any other lemur, but patchily distributed throughout range.

BEHAVIOUR

Diurnal and semi-terrestrial; spends more time on ground than any other lemur (L135). Tendency probably dictated by semi-arid environments

they inhabit, where vegetation is not always continuous and resources may be sparse and unevenly distributed.

Diet very varied, consisting primarily of fruit, leaves, flowers, bark and sap. Occasionally (but avidly) eat large insects (e.g. locusts and cicadas) and even small chameleons (L208). Fruits always preferred and proportion in diet varies with habitat and season, e.g. in gallery forests in October and November fruits and new leaves of Kily Tree *Tamarindus indica* constitute majority of food to three-week period between mid-April and mid-May. Females in oestrus for only four to six hours during this period. Males establish a hierarchy throughout the year. They anoint their tails with secretions from wrist glands and waft scent in direction of opposing males. These 'stink fights' are normally sufficient to establish rank. But during court-ship they compete vigorously for females – bouts of aggression to establish dominance involve 'jump fights' where rivals leap in air slashing downwards with their upper canines (L135). Male dominance is transient, and females may have several mates, although priority of conception is generally first male to mate (L234).

Troop of Ring-tailed Lemurs calling.

Females pregnant during austral winter, when resources are limited. Fat stored during preceding wet season crucial to female's ability to successfully bear and feed offspring (L135). Gestation around 135 days, young born mainly in September,

with a few in October (L159). Twins often produced, but singletons more common. Initially infants cling to mother's underside, but move to ride on her back after one to two weeks. Weaning in February, when food most abundant (L299; L135). Infant mortality high: about 50% die in first

year and only 30% reach adulthood. Females sexually mature at three years and most give birth each year. Males leave natal groups after maturation, and established males transfer between groups every three to five years (L141).

Young predated by raptors, e.g. Madagascar Harrier-Hawk *Polyboroides radiatus* and Madagascar Buzzard *Buteo brachypterus*. Adults and young predated by Fosa *Cryptoprocta ferox* and very occasionally by introduced Small Indian Civet *Viverricula indica* and Feral Cats *Felis silvestris* (L99). Also two exceptional records of infants being eaten by a Red-fronted Brown Lemur *Eulemur rufus* (L241; L136).

WHERE TO SEE

Most easily seen at Berenty Reserve west of Tolagnaro, where they are completely habituated so viewing is easy. To see Ring-tails in spiny forest visit Anjampolo north of Berenty. Also possible to see in Isalo National Park, where habitat is very different; lemurs may be seen clambering over impres-sive rock formations. Another alterna-tive is the community park at Anjà near Ambalavao on northern edge of Andringitra Massif. Here the lemurs have thick coats and are particularly beautiful and can be seen bounding around on huge granite boulders.

Ring-tailed Lemur in octopus tree, Anjampolo Spiny Forest.

Recent revisions have elevated a number of taxa within this genus to full species; formerly the Brown Lemur (*Eulemur fulvus*) was divided into six subspecies, but these taxa are all now considered specifically distinct (L115). As a result ten species of 'typical' lemur are recognised within the genus *Eulemur* and one, *E. macaco*, is further divided into two subspecies.

Eulemur are characteristically medium-sized, weighing 2–3kg, sexually dichromatic to varying extents and cathemeral. Scent-marking, particularly with the ano-genital region, is frequent in both sexes.

MONGOOSE LEMUR

Eulemur mongoz

MEASUREMENTS

Total length: 750–830mm. Head/body length: 300–350mm. Tail length: 450–480mm. Weight: 1.1–1.6kg. (L348; L220)

DESCRIPTION & IDENTIFICATION

Sexually dichromatic. **Males**: Upperparts grey-brown with darker tail tip, underparts paler creamy-grey. Some brownish tinges around shoul-

ders and a dark grey pygal patch. Face grey, muzzle pale grey with dark nose. Cheeks, beard, forehead and back of neck distinctively rufous-brown. Mature males sometime have triangular bald patch on crown caused by excessive head rubbing when scent-marking. **Females**: Upperparts grey (generally paler than males) with some faint brownish tinges on rear flanks and rump and a dark grey pygal patch. Tail tip darker, underparts creamy-grey. Face dark slate-grey fading to pale grey or white around muzzle. Cheeks and beard form creamy-grey to white ruff continuous

with throat and underparts. Eyes in both sexes reddish-orange.

Medium-sized lemur with long tail and horizontal body posture that moves quadrupedally. Possibly confused with Common Brown Lemur *E. fulvus* or Red-fronted Brown Lemur *E. rufus* – this species is smaller and pelage predominantly grey not brown.

HABITAT & DISTRIBUTION

In Madagascar inhabits dry deciduous forest and secondary forest. Introduced populations on Comoros Islands inhabit more humid forest. Natural range restricted to northwest, from region west of Mahavavy River in vicinity of Mitsinjo (including Tsiombikibo Forest and Lac Kinkony (L202)) to region of Boriziny, including coastal areas like Antrema at Katsepy on west side of Betsiboka River and Mariarano Classified Forest north-east of Mahajanga (L12). Introduced to Anjouan and Moheli in the Comoros; also a few feral individuals on Grande Comoro (L348; L350).

BEHAVIOUR

Lives in small groups, comprising monogamous pair and one to three dependent offspring (L49). Social bonds within family units strong; groups are cohesive when feeding, travelling, resting and sleeping. Home ranges not large, with extensive overlap between ranges of neighbouring groups. Inter-group encounters infrequent but cause considerable agitation, vocalisation and scent-marking when they occur (L50). Does tolerate close proximity

Female Mongoose Lemur.

of Red-fronted Brown Lemur *Eulemur rufus* (sympatric in some areas); the two species sometimes seen in mixed groups (L404).

Cathemeral during both wet and dry seasons. During warm wet months (December to April) considerably more diurnal (or crepuscular) activity. With onset of dry season in May a shift occurs towards nocturnal behaviour, which becomes predominant (L52). At this time, groups travel and feed between dusk and 22:00 hours, then rest for two to four hours before resuming foraging and continuing until just before dawn when they return to sleep sites in dense foliage or tangled vines at tops of trees. Foraging at night, when temperatures are low, allows them to conserve energy. Also, foliage cover at its lowest at this time; nocturnal activity may help reduce risk of predation from diurnal raptors.

During both seasons fruit dominates the diet. In wet season may be complemented by flowers, particularly Kapok *Ceiba pentandra*, and nectar. During dry season, leaves form significant dietary elements, and beetles and insect grubs are also eaten (L49; L50).

Females give birth each year; young are born in October and November, and are weaned at six

Male Mongoose Lemur, Tsiombikibo Forest.

to seven months. Female primarily responsible for infant care, but males do contribute some of the time (L50). Adult size and coloration attained between 14 and 16 months, sexual maturation takes longer.

WHERE TO SEE

Ampijoroa (Ankarafantsika National Park), south-east of Mahajanga, is most accessible site. They are less frequently seen than other lemurs and can require effort and patience to track down. Some more remote locations can offer a better chance of success e.g. areas around Mitsinjo, including Tsiombikibo Forest and forest patches adjacent to the town and around nearby Lac Kamonjo and Lac Kinkony; alternatives are forests around Anjamena on east (north) bank of Mahavavy River and Mariarano Classified Forest north-east of Mahajanga.

Mongoose Lemur

CROWNED LEMUR

Eulemur coronatus

MEASUREMENTS

Total length: 750–850mm. Head/body length: 340–360mm. Tail length: 410–490mm. Weight: 1.5–1.8kg. (L353)

DESCRIPTION & IDENTIFICATION

Sexually dichromatic. **Males**: Upperparts grey-brown, more brown to chestnut-brown on flanks and towards extremities of limbs. Underparts pale creamy-grey, with brown/chestnut wash. Tail grey-brown and slightly darker than body. Face and ears pale grey to white, tip of muzzle black. Conspicuous and distinctive chestnut-orange crown above eyebrow line and by side of ears, forming prominent V-shape with dark charcoal-grey patch on crown. Chestnut-orange coloration also extends around face to form bushy cheeks. **Females**: Upperparts, flanks and limbs mid-grey, underparts pale grey to creamy-white. Tail mid-grey darkening towards tip. Face and ears pale grey to white, tip of muzzle dark grey, nose black. Top of head and cheeks mid-grey with distinctive chestnut-orange crown above

Female Crowned Lemur, Ankarana Special Reserve.

eyebrow line, forming a V-shape with mid-grey area on top of head.

Medium-sized lemur adopting a horizontal body posture. Can only be confused with Sanford's Brown Lemur *Eulemur sanfordi*, as both species are sympatric throughout majority of their ranges. Distinctive chestnut-orange crown and very marked sexual dichromatism of this species should prevent misidentification.

HABITAT & DISTRIBUTION

Dry and semi-dry deciduous forests preferred, but also occurs in some primary and secondary humid forests

(L122) up to 1,400m asl. Restricted to island's northern tip, precise range limits ill-defined. In north-west, southern limit probably Mahavavy du Nord River south of Ambilobe; in north-east range does not extend further south than Manambato River. North of these apparent boundaries found all the way to Cap d'Ambre Peninsula. Recent research in Analamera and Anakrana suggests densities of 21–25 individuals/km² (L25).

BEHAVIOUR

Cathemeral, remaining active both day and night throughout year (L77).

Crowned Lemur

Male Crowned Lemur, Ankarana Special Reserve.

30% of each day, particularly during wet season when resources are abundant (L77). There is little interspecific aggression but Sanford's Brown Lemurs are normally dominant.

Diet dominated by fruit, around 80-90%, during both wet and dry seasons. In dry season flowers and young leaves also taken, together with invertebrates. In wet season greater diversity of plant species is utilised (L77).

Circumstantial evidence suggests may also take eggs from birds' nests: an adult Hook-billed Vanga *Vanga curvirostris* close to its nest violently mobbed a female Crowned Lemur with a small infant, causing the infant to fall to the ground.

Mating occurs during late May and June, gestation around 125 days, births occur from mid-September through October. In captivity twins and singletons equally common (L144). Infants initially carried on mother's front, then moves around to ride on back. Adult size and sexual maturity reached well into second year.

Predated by the Fosa *Cryptoprocta ferox* and in Ankarana may also

Lives in groups of 5–15, five or six is norm (L76), containing several adult females and males plus infants and juveniles. In humid forests average group size is smaller than in dry forests. When feeding, large groups may split into subunits of two to four. Guttural grunts used to maintain contact with adjacent subgroups. Occupy home range of 10–15ha, with considerable overlap between home ranges of neighbouring groups. Travel between 800 and 1,000m per day while foraging (L77).

Foraging takes place from ground level up to the canopy, with a preference for lower levels and understorey, including treelets and bushes. This reduces competition with Sanford's Brown Lemur that prefers the upper levels. The two species do aggregate into mixed foraging groups for 20-

Crowned Lemur

remaining forest cover
known distribution
roads

be eaten by crocodiles *Crocodylus niloticus* (L99) and hunted by immigrant miners.

WHERE TO SEE

A relatively easy species to see, especially in Ankarana Special Reserve in Canyon Forestière and around Campement Anilotra (Camp des Anglais), Campement d'Andrafiabe (Camp des Américans) and Lac Vert. Also seen in Montagne d'Ambre National Park near main campsite, around Station Roussettes and at viewpoint overlooking Grande Cascade.

For the more adventurous, the valley of Bobakindro River in Analamera Special Reserve and forests around village of Andranotsimaty near Daraina are particularly rewarding.

RED-BELLIED LEMUR

Eulemur rubriventer

MEASUREMENTS

Total length: 780–930mm. Head/body length: 350–400mm. Tail length: 430–530mm. Weight: 1.6–2.4kg.

DESCRIPTION & IDENTIFICATION

Sexually dichromatic. **Males**: Pelage

Male Red-bellied Lemur, Ranomafana National Park.

Red-bellied Lemur

long and dense. Upperparts, chest and underparts rich dark chestnut-brown, tail noticeably darker, often almost black. Top of head, face and muzzle darker, often slate-grey. Conspicuous patches of white skin forming teardrops beneath eyes. No ear-tufts, but fur around ears is dense and gives head a squarish look. **Females**: Upperparts rich chestnut-brown, chest and underparts creamy-white. Tail dark grey to black. Head less squarish than males and crown not darkened. Face and muzzle dark

slate grey, with bare patches of white skin dramatically reduced and absent in some individuals. Lower cheeks and beard creamy-white.

A medium-sized lemur with horizontal posture and rich dense coat. Occurs sympatrically with several other *Eulemur* species, all broadly similar in size and shape. Distinguishing *E. rubriventer* is straightforward: its coat is more dense and richly coloured. Also encountered in small family groups, rather than larger multi-adult troops of congeners.

Female Red-bellied Lemur, Ranomafana National Park..

home range of 10–20ha which is defended, although some observations suggest neighbouring groups rarely show aggressive behaviour towards one another. Aggressive behaviour between two males within a group has been observed. Instigated and led by dominant female, groups travel 400–500m per day. Distance varies seasonally according to food availability; in times of shortage they may travel more than 1,000m per day (L210; L214).

Cathemeral, with activity patterns varying according to seasons and food availability (L217). Fruits are mainstay of diet, including introduced species like Chinese Guava *Psidium cattleyanum*. When fruits are unavailable, flowers and leaves also taken and feeding bouts often continue after dark. Utilises nearly 70 different plant species in a year. Invertebrates, especially millipedes, constitute a small but important element in diet (L211; L213).

Single young born in September and October. Breeding timed so peak lactation costs coincide with maximum fruit availability (L399). Initially carried on mother's belly, later moves around to ride on back. Infants also carried by males, who may form a focus for other infants too (L215). After around 35 days female stops carrying offspring, although male may continue to do so until around 100 days of age. Occasionally predated by Fosa (*Cryptoprocta ferox*) and large raptors (L154).

HABITAT & DISTRIBUTION

Primary lowland, mid-altitude and high-altitude rainforest and occasionally secondary growth on edge of primary habitat. Apparently sparsely distributed throughout eastern rainforests from Manampatra River (south of Andringitra Massif) in south (L131) to Tsaratanana Massif in north, not including Masoala Peninsula. Recorded from 70m to 2,400m asl (Tsaratanana), although middle to high elevations are preferred. Occurs in relatively low numbers, e.g. in Ranomafana National Park estimates vary between 30 individuals/km^2 (L210) and 5 individuals/km^2 (L131).

BEHAVIOUR

Lives in family units of two to six, comprising an adult pair and dependent offspring; some larger groups contain more than one adult of each sex (L215). Groups occupy

WHERE TO SEE

Ranomafana National Park, where groups are habituated, is the best location to see this species. During late April and May, when Chinese Guava are fruiting, they can be particularly easy to find (together with *E. rufus*). Alternatively, they can also be seen in Andasibe-Mantadia or Marojejy National Parks (generally above Camp Marojejia).

COMMON BROWN LEMUR
Eulemur fulvus

MEASUREMENTS

Total length: 845–1,010mm.
Head/body length: 430–500mm. Tail
length: 415–510mm. Weight: 2–3kg.

DESCRIPTION & IDENTIFICATION

Males and females similarly coloured.
Pelage short but dense. Upperparts
uniform brown to grey-brown,
underparts paler and slightly greyer.
Face, muzzle and crown dark grey
to black (females slightly paler than
males), with paler faint eyebrow
patches and paler brown-grey fur
around moderately prominent ears,
cheeks and underneath chin. Eyes
rich orange-red. Tail long and slightly
bushy towards tip.

A medium-sized lemur with long
tail and horizontal posture which
moves quadrupedally on ground and
in canopy.

In east, might be confused with
Red-bellied Lemur *E. rubriventer*,
which is very much more reddish,
males have distinctive white teardrops beneath eyes, while females
have creamy-white throat, chest and
belly. In north-west *E. fulvus* is distinguished from Mongoose Lemur *E.
mongoz* by its uniform brown, rather
than grey, coloration.

HABITAT & DISTRIBUTION

Occurs in variety of habitats including
lowland rainforest, montane rainforest,
moist evergreen forests (Sambirano)
and dry deciduous forest.

Three isolated populations
remain: in east occurs in rainforests
north of Mangoro River to probably
Anove River south of Mananara. In
north-west found in dry deciduous
forest north of Betsiboka River
continuing north to vicinity of Baie
of Loza and Maevaranao River.
Another population is centred on

Common Brown Lemur from western deciduous forest, Ankarafantsika National Park.

Manongarivo in Sambirano region,
possibly extending north to Mahavavy
du Nord River and perhaps including
some of Tsaratanana Massif.

Between north-western
and eastern blocks, *E. fulvus*
survives in isolated forest
remnants in central highlands, e.g.
Tampoketsa Analamaitso between

Ankarafantsika and Marotandrano
and Ambohitantely north-west of
Antananarivo (L325). When forests
were intact, these populations would
have been continuous (L352). Also
an introduced population on island of
Mayotte in Comoros (L348; L350).

BEHAVIOUR

Lives in troops of five to 12, with

Common Brown Lemur

eight to nine being average (L216). On island of Mayotte groups of 29 recorded (L348). Groups contain several adult males and females plus subadults, juveniles and infants. Agonistic interactions seem infrequent and there are no discernible dominance hierarchies.

Active during the day, spending virtually all time in canopy; feeding and movement often continues after dark. Extent of nocturnal activity may be influenced by lunar cycle: when moon is full, nocturnal activity reaches its peak.

Home range size strongly influenced by habitat: in dry forests around 7–8ha, in rainforests up to 20ha has been recorded. Groups scent-mark territory but some overlap between ranges occurs: loud vocalisations help groups avoid one another.

Diet varied, consists of leaves, buds, shoots, flowers and fruits, proportions varies seasonally (L80; L216). In north-west they eat cicadas, when insects emerge to breed (L29). In east has been observed feeding in plantations on flowers of introduced pine and eucalyptus trees (L78) and also seen eating an orb-web spider (L56).

Mating between May and June, gestation around 120 days, births occur in September and October (L216). A single offspring is usual, twins have been recorded. Weaning occurs at four to five months, sexual maturity reached around 18 months.

WHERE TO SEE
In west, the best location is Ampijoroa, within Ankarafantsika National Park. A number of troops occupy territories adjacent to campsite and other groups are encountered on walks through the forest in Jardin Botanique A and Jardin Botanique B. Alternatively, most accessible location in eastern rainforests is Andasibe-Mantadia National Park where readily seen close to park entrance or along main ridge where habituated Indri groups also live.

SANFORD'S BROWN LEMUR
Eulemur sanfordi

MEASUREMENTS
Total length: 880–950mm. Head/body length: 380–400mm. Tail length: 500–550mm. Weight: 2–2.5 kg.

DESCRIPTION & IDENTIFICATION
Sexually dichromatic. **Males:** Upperparts and tail medium-brown, slightly darker grey-brown along back and towards tip of tail. Underparts pale brown-grey. Pronounced creamy-grey beard and prominent ear-tufts give males a 'maned' appearance. Crown also long and generally brown-grey. Nose-bridge and snout black. Between dark areas and mane are patches of creamy-white short hair on cheeks and above eyes. **Females:** Upperparts and tail grey-brown, darker areas at tip of tail. Underparts

Common Brown Lemur from eastern rain forest, Andasibe-Mantadia National Park.

Male Sanford's Brown Lemur.

Analamera population densities are 3.5 to 5.5 individuals km². In Ankarana and Analamera this species is less abundant than broadly sympatric Crowned Lemur. It is also hunted by immigrant miners.

BEHAVIOUR

Group size related to habitat: in rainforest areas four to seven, in dry forest regions up to 15. Troops contain several unpaired adult males and females plus offspring. Home ranges are around 15ha, with considerable overlap. Agonistic interactions are rare (L122; L77).

Cathemeral. Prefers to forage in middle understorey and forest canopy. Fruit constitutes up to 90% of diet together with shoots, flowers and some invertebrates, like millipedes and spiders. In wetter months, when fruit is scarce, a greater variety of plant species are utilised than in dry season when favoured resources predominate. In wet season regularly forms mixed-species foraging groups with Crowned Lemurs for up to 30% of day with very little interspecific aggression (L77).

Births occur in late September/ early October, gestation 120 days. Infant clings to mother's belly for first month before transferring to ride on her back.

WHERE TO SEE

Montagne d'Ambre National Park is the most accessible location. Groups often encountered close to Station Roussettes and Petite Cascade and along botanical trail. Ankarana Special Reserve is another rewarding locality; fairly common around both Campement Anilotra (Camp des Anglais) and Campement d'Andrafiabe (Camp des Américains). Forests around village of Andranotsimaty near Daraina also good, where Crowned Lemurs and Golden-crowned Sifakas can also be seen.

Female Sanford's Brown Lemur.

paler grey. Face and head completely grey – this colour extending over crown, down neck and onto shoulders. Females lack ear-tufts and beard. Some individuals have slightly paler areas above eyes.

Medium-sized lemur with long tail; adopts horizontal posture and moves quadrupedally. Shares range with similar sized Crowned Lemur *E. coronatus*, but coloration is completely different. Male Crowned Lemurs are orangey-brown, females are grey and both sexes have distinctive orange-brown V-shape on crowns. Female Sanford's and female White-fronted Brown Lemurs *E. albifrons* are very similar; where ranges of two taxa meet, differentiation can be problematic, but males of two species are distinctive.

HABITAT & DISTRIBUTION

Primary and secondary rainforest, dry deciduous forest and partially degraded forest up to 1,400m asl; elevations between 800m and 1,000m are preferred in Montagne d'Ambre (L77).

Restricted to far north; range extends from Cap d'Ambre Peninsula west of Antsiranana south to Manambato River in east and Mahavavy du Nord River in west. Remaining populations of *Eulemur* south of Manambato River and north of Bemarivo River (northern limit of *E. albifrons*) require investigation to determine taxonomic status. In

Sanford's Brown Lemur

Male White-fronted Brown Lemur.

WHITE-FRONTED BROWN LEMUR

Eulemur albifrons

MEASUREMENTS

Total length: 890–960mm. Head/body length: 390–420mm. Tail length: 500–540mm. Weight: 2–2.6kg.

DESCRIPTION & IDENTIFICATION

Sexually dichromatic. Exhibits greatest pelage differences between sexes in any brown lemur. **Males**: Upperparts and tail rich mid- to dark brown becoming darker and more reddish towards rear. Underparts pale grey, becoming more creamy-white around chest and throat. Head creamy-white with bushy cheeks, muzzle and nose bridge black. Eyes red-orange. **Females**: Upperparts and tail mid- to dark brown, darkening towards rear and on tail, underparts grey. Head, face and muzzle dark grey, nose slightly darker. Unlike males, cheeks not bushy.

A medium-sized lemur with horizontal posture and long tail. Could be confused with Red-bellied Lemur *E. rubriventer*, but highly distinctive white head of male *E. albifrons* makes this unlikely.

HABITAT & DISTRIBUTION

Primary and secondary rainforest up to 1,670m asl. Restricted to north-east from Bemarivo River north of Sambava, south to region of Mananara (probably Anove River), including Masoala Peninsula. At north-eastern limits of range, populations may extend into forest corridor connecting Anjanaharibe-Sud/Marojejy and Tsantanana, but surveys are required to substantiate this.

An introduced population occurs on Nosy Mangabe and an isolated population is found in Betampona Reserve, considerably further south of the defined range. Anecdotal evidence suggests these animals may have been introduced. On Masoala Peninsula population densities of 15 individuals/km² have been estimated (L266).

White-fronted
Brown Lemur

BEHAVIOUR

Group size between four and 13, but eight to nine seems average (L266). Almost exclusively arboreal, feeding on fruits (ripe and unripe), to a lesser extent leaves and millipedes, spiders and insects occasionally (L374; L375; L376). Fruits of *Grewia* trees and various *Ficus* species are particularly relished. Nectar also eaten when fruits are less evident.

Vocalisations heard around dawn and dusk and also recorded well into the night, suggesting cathemeral behaviour. Other aspects of behaviour are probably similar to other brown lemurs inhabiting rainforest areas (see *E. fulvus* and *E. rufus*).

On Nosy Mangabe occasionally predated by Madagascar Ground Boa *Acrantophis madagascariensis*. On mainland the lemur's behaviour strongly suggests the Fosa *Cryptoprocta ferox* is a major predator.

WHERE TO SEE

Nosy Mangabe, near Maroantsetra in the Bay of Antongil, is a good place to see this lemur. Groups live in close proximity to the campsite and are often very approachable. Alternatively, the forests near Lohatrozona on Masoala Peninsula or Marojejy National Park are rewarding localities.

RED-FRONTED BROWN LEMUR
Eulemur rufus

MEASUREMENTS

Total length: 800−1,030mm. Head/body length: 350−480mm. Tail length: 450−550mm. Weight: 2−2.75kg.

DESCRIPTION & IDENTIFICATION

Sexually dichromatic, with noticeable variations between individuals and between eastern and western populations. **Males:** Upperparts and tail grizzled grey to grey-brown, underparts pale creamy-grey. Extremities of limbs sometimes tinged brown. Face, muzzle and mid-forehead dark grey to black, with thin dark line extending up and dividing rich russet-brown crown. Prominent white eyebrow patches and distinctive bushy white cheeks and beard. Ears not prominent and eyes orange-red. **Females:** Considerable regional variation. Upperparts and tail grizzled grey-brown to rufous-brown, even orange/cinnamon-brown (western populations more orange: those around Mitsinjo very rich orange/cinnamon brown, with head, cheeks and throat almost totally white), underparts pale grey. Face and muzzle dark grey to black, with dark line extending up forehead to grizzled grey crown. Large white eyebrow patches and creamy-coloured cheeks, although less bushy than in males.

Medium-sized lemur with a long tail, adopts horizontal posture and moves quadrupedally. In rainforest areas may be confused with Red-bellied Lemur *Eulemur rubriventer*, but latter far more russet-red and lacks very pale cheeks and eyebrow patches. In western areas this species is unmistakable and is not sympatric with another *Eulemur* species.

Female White-fronted Brown Lemur.

Male Red-fronted Brown Lemur from eastern rainforest, Ranomafana National Park.

of *E. rufus* south of Pic d'Ivohibe (south of Andringitra).

In west found from areas just south of the Fiherenana river near Toliara, north as far as the Betsiboka River. Populations north of Tsiribihina River are genetically distinct from those further south and may warrant taxonomic distinction (L223).

BEHAVIOUR

Cathemeral throughout the year (L217) and almost totally arboreal, only occasionally descending to ground, sometimes to lick and eat soil. Troops contain several adult females and males plus younger animals at various stages of matura-tion. Average group size is eight to ten, although varies between four and 18 (L215). In western forests aggregations between 30 and 100 individuals reported feeding in a single large fruiting fig tree (*Ficus grevei*).

Group cohesiveness maintained through grunts, contact calls and vocalisations, but no dominance hierarchies are apparent, although

HABITAT & DISTRIBUTION

Occurs in primary and secondary rainforest and dry deciduous forest. Now found in two distinct popula-tions in the east and west. In east, northern limit is a line formed by Onive and Mangoro Rivers, extending south to northern slopes of Andringitra. Further south situation is complex. On south-eastern slopes of Andringitra Massif, ranges of *E. rufus* and *E. albocollaris* meet and there is a 60km-wide zone of hybridisation around Iantara River (headwaters of Manampatrana River) (L131). Also appears to be an isolated population

Red-fronted Brown Lemur

Female Red-fronted Brown Lemur from eastern rainforest, Ranomafana National Park.

females take the lead. Home range size heavily influenced by habitat and season. During wet season in western forests may be as small as one hectare and groups rarely move more than 125–150m in a day. In dry season when food is scarcer and more dispersed, home ranges expand to 12–15ha, with a corresponding increase in daily distances travelled (L341).

In rainforests territories are much larger, up to 100ha, with daily travel distances between 150 and 2,000m; this correlates with seasonal food availability and density of fruiting trees. Neighbouring territories overlap extensively and there is peaceful movement of individuals between social units. Aggressive inter-group encounters can occur and loud vocalisations help maintain group spatial separation to avoid this (L212; L214).

Diet varies with habitat, but in both dry deciduous forests and rainforests is dominated by fruit. *E. rufus* are important agents for seed dispersal (L85). In western areas,

Male Red-fronted Brown Lemur from western forest, Kirindy.

leaves also important, along with pods, stems, flowers and sap (L341). In eastern areas fruit is the mainstay, including introduced species like Chinese Guava *Psidium cattleyanum*. Leaves less important, but fungi, insects and other invertebrates like millipedes also eaten. Millipedes are first tossed from hand to hand to induce secretion of toxins; these are then washed off with saliva before

the millipede is wiped and dried on lemur's tail – only then is it eaten (L211; L213).

Infants born September or early October, gestation about 120 days (L216). Breeding timed so peak fruit availability coincides with maximum lactation costs to mother (L399). Birth weight around 75g. Initially infants carried on mother's belly, after a month or so begin to move about, transferring to ride on her back. They travel independently around three months. Sexual maturity is reached at two to three years.

Regularly predated by Fosa *Cryptoprocta ferox* in rainforest and dry deciduous forest areas. Large raptors, e.g. Henst's Goshawk *Accipiter henstii* and Madagascar Harrier-Hawk *Polyboroides radiatus* also predators (L99; L154).

WHERE TO SEE

In eastern rainforests, Ranomafana National Park is the best place to see this lemur. April and May is a particularly good time, when Chinese Guava is in fruit, and lemurs tend to congregate. Kirindy Forest north-east of Morondava is the best locality in dry deciduous forest. Alternatives are Tsiombikibo Forest near Mitsinjo or Anjamena on the banks of Mahavavy River.

Female Red-fronted Brown Lemur from western forest, Kirindy.

WHITE-COLLARED BROWN LEMUR

Eulemur albocollaris

MEASUREMENTS

Total length: 890–950mm. Head/body length: 390–400mm. Tail length: 500–550mm. Weight: 2–2.5kg.

DESCRIPTION & IDENTIFICATION

Sexually dichromatic. **Males**: Upperparts grey-brown, tail and lower limbs darker. Underparts paler grey. Head and face predominantly grey, with dark grey crown grading to paler grey down neck and shoulders. Cheeks and beard white, bushy and pronounced. **Females**: Upperparts and tail brown-grey and more rufous than males. Underparts similar but slightly paler. Feet darker. Head and face grey with darker crown, cheeks less bushy than males and similar colour to upperparts.

A medium-sized lemur with horizontal posture. Known range does not overlap with any other *Eulemur* species, but range limits with Red-fronted Brown Lemur remain unclear and where the two meet, confu-

Male White-collared Brown Lemur.

sion is possible. Females very similar but grey face of *E. albocollaris* and white eyebrow patches of *E. rufus* help distinguish. Males differ more; *E. albocollaris* has white not creamy cheeks and *E. rufus* has a distinctive orangey-brown forehead.

HABITAT & DISTRIBUTION

Lowland and mid-altitude eastern rainforest. Range is most restricted of any *Eulemur* species, probably covering no more than 700km² (L131).

Occurs only in central south-east in thin band from an area just north of Manampatrana River, south to Mananara River (L140). Main block of remaining forest within range is Vevembe. Also a small isolated population in forests of Manombo (perhaps fewer than 80 adults).

On south-eastern slopes of Andringitra Massif, ranges of *E. albocollaris* and *E. rufus* meet producing a 60km-wide hybridisation zone around Iantara River (headwaters of Manampatrana River). In Vevembe population densities are ten individuals/km², but probably much lower in other parts of range (L131). This is one of the world's 25 most threatened primates (L180).

BEHAVIOUR

Only studies are from forests of Vevembe. Cathemeral throughout year, with no obvious seasonal

Female White-collared Brown Lemur.

White-collared Brown Lemur

variation in activity patterns. Diet dominated by fruit, but leaves, flowers, fungi and invertebrates also eaten occasionally; flowers particularly important during dry season (L139).

Lives in relatively large groups containing several adult males and females, but no evidence to date suggests females are dominant.

WHERE TO SEE

Seeing this lemur is a challenge, as its limited range is difficult to reach. The best location is Manombo Special Reserve, south of Farafangana. Access is difficult in wet season when local rivers swell and cut off portions of forest. Alternatively, Vevembe offers a reasonable chance of success.

COLLARED BROWN LEMUR

Eulemur collaris

MEASUREMENTS

Total length: 890–950mm. Head/body length: 390–400mm. Tail length: 500–550mm. Weight: 2.25–2.5kg.

DESCRIPTION & IDENTIFICATION

Sexually dichromatic. **Males**: Upperparts brownish-grey, tail darker. Underparts pale brown-grey. Muzzle, forehead and crown dark slate-grey

to black, extending and becoming paler down neck. A dark stripe runs down spinal ridge. Eyebrow patches pale creamy-grey but vary between individuals. Cheeks and beard thick, bushy and orange to rufous-brown. **Females**: Upperparts browner than males, sometimes rufous. Underparts pale creamy-grey. Head and face grey, with faint grey stripe extending over crown. Cheeks rufous-brown, but less bushy than males. Eyes of both sexes orange-red.

Medium-sized, adopts horizontal posture and moves quadrupedally. Range does not overlap with any other *Eulemur* species so confusion is unlikely.

HABITAT & DISTRIBUTION

Found in lowland, mid-altitude and high altitude primary and secondary rainforest and fragments of littoral forest by coast. Recorded from sea level to 1,875m in rainforests of Andohahela (L68).

Restricted to extreme south-east, from Mananara River south through Midongy du Sud to Andohahela. Western limits of range appear to be forests of Kalambatritra.

Collared Brown Lemur

Female Collared Brown Lemur.

Male Collared Brown Lemur.

BEHAVIOUR

Not yet studied in the wild. Thought to be cathemeral throughout year and is assumed to be primarily frugivorous. Groups consist of several adult females and males, and range in size from three to seven (L68).

Females have offspring between October and December. One infant is the norm and some male involvement with youngsters has been observed (L68).

WHERE TO SEE

The most accessible locality is Mandena Conservation Zone (part of the QMM Titanium Dioxide Development Project), a recently protected area 12km north of Tolagnaro; being new, the lemurs have yet to become completely tolerant. For the more intrepid it is worth visiting Malio, the rainforest area of Andohahela National Park (Parcel 1). This is a good place to see truly wild populations in stunning forest. This area should become more accessible as ecotourism is developed.

BLACK LEMUR

Eulemur macaco

Two subspecies of Black Lemur are recognised: the nominate race, simply known as the Black Lemur *E. m. macaco* and the Blue-eyed Black Lemur *E. m. flavifrons*. They are the most extreme sexually dichromatic Malagasy primates.

BLACK LEMUR

Eulemur macaco macaco

MEASUREMENTS

Total length: 900–1,100mm. Head/body length: 390–450mm. Tail length: 510–650mm. Weight: 1.8–2.0kg.

DESCRIPTION & IDENTIFICATION

Sexually dichromatic. **Males**: Pelage

Male Black Lemur.

varies from dark chocolate-brown to almost black (in bright sunlight actually appears reddish-brown to dark chocolate-brown). Ears lavishly tufted with long black hair. Eyes yellow-orange to deep orange. **Females**: Upperparts variable from golden-brown to mid-brown or rich chestnut-brown, becoming paler on flanks and limbs. Tail often darker rich chestnut-brown, particularly towards tip. Feet slate-grey to dark brownish-black. Throat and chin pale brown, gradually changing to pale grey-brown and even off-white on belly. Face and muzzle dark grey, top of head and temples pale grey. Ears extravagantly tufted with long white hair extending

around cheeks and changing to orangey-chestnut beard. Eyes yellow-orange to deep orange.

A population from extreme south of range (forests of Kapany and Lavalohalika, 12km north of Maromandia) differs from typical form because ear-tufts and beard are less well developed and females' throat, chin, top of head and temples are completely white (L317; L316).

A medium-sized lemur with long tail and distinctive coloration. Confusion unlikely as it is allopatric with congeners through most of range. At southern and eastern limits of range (Manongarivo and Tsaratanana) it is sympatric with *E.*

fulvus; distinctive pelage and extreme sexual dichromatism of *E. macaco* should prevent confusion.

HABITAT & DISTRIBUTION
Adaptable; occurs in moist Sambirano forests, similar humid forests on offshore islands and some modified secondary habitats, including timber, coffee and cashew nut plantations. Recorded up to 1,600m asl.

Restricted to Sambirano region and adjacent offshore islands in north-west. Northern limit is Mahavavy du Nord River, east to vicinity of Ambilobe, southern limit is the Andranomalaza River.

To south and east of the Manongarivo Massif, distributional limits become unclear as *E. m. macaco* hybridises with *E. m. flavifrons* (L179; L259; L10). Extent of integration yet to be clarified. Further west, range includes Ampasindava Peninsula and islands of Nosy Be and Nosy Komba. To the east the limits are again unclear, but it certainly reaches the Tsaratanana Massif.

BEHAVIOUR
Live in groups of two to 15, with seven to ten the norm. Larger groups are associated with modified rather than primary habitats (L44). Groups comprise several adult males and females in roughly equal numbers,

Female Black Lemur.

Black Lemur

plus dependent offspring. Group activities dictated by a dominant female, and cohesiveness is maintained by regular guttural grunts and contact calls from all members. Home ranges average 5–6ha, with considerable range overlap between neighbouring groups. By day groups remain separate, but may come together after dark.

Cathemeral: daytime activity is concentrated around early morning and late afternoon, the extent of nocturnal activity varies seasonally with the lunar cycle. During middle of dry season (June–July) populations on Nosy Be are completely inactive at night, and mornings are spent sunning at top of canopy. In contrast, at end of dry period (October–December) nocturnal activity predominates, coinciding with fruiting of favourite large

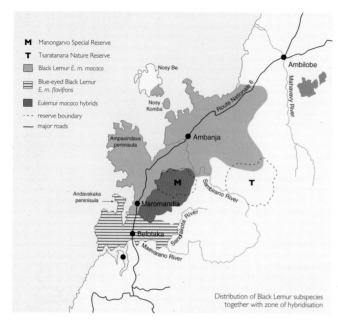

M Manongarvo Special Reserve

T Tsaratanana Nature Reserve

□ Black Lemur *E. m. macaco*

▤ Blue-eyed Black Lemur
   E. m. flavifrons

▓ *Eulemur macaco* hybrids

- - - reserve boundary

—— major roads

Distribution of Black Lemur subspecies
together with zone of hybridisation

trees, e.g. Ramy *Canarium madagas-cariensis* (L14).

On the mainland, the lunar phase is a major influence on activity patterns – when moon is waxing, full nocturnal activity reaches its peak, probably related to increased light and the lemur's improved night-time visual acuity. Nocturnal activity also occurs year-round, but diurnal activity reaches its peak during early part of wet season (December–January) (L45; L46).

Foraging is concentrated in middle and upper canopy. Diet varied, but dominated by ripe fruit, with flowers, leaves, fungi and occasionally inverte-brates like millipedes and insects e.g. cicadas (L29). In dry season nectar also important, probably making the species an important pollinator (L30; L31).

In degraded habitats they descend to ground and forage in leaf-litter for fallen fruit and fungi, and even eat soil. By day they feed mainly in understorey rather than canopy and move from one resource patch to the next with greater regularity. At night, foraging efforts are concen-trated in canopy (when daytime avian predators are not active) and the lemurs travel less (L28).

Mating takes place in late April and May, gestation around 125 days, births occur between late August and early October. A single infant is normal. Young infants have been observed in December, suggesting the breeding season may be more protracted in some areas. Infanticide has also been observed; one female killing the infant of another and consequently assuming dominant status within that group (L13). Thought to be extremely rare; observed in modified habitat with troop in stressful circumstances.

WHERE TO SEE

Easy to see in buffer zone on north-east edge of Lokobe on Nosy Be. From Ambatozavavy take a pirogue around the coast to Ampasipohy. The modified forest area (secondary growth and some crops like vanilla) where troops can easily be seen is a short walk inland. Also a good

place to see Hawk's Sportive Lemur *Lepilemur tymerlachsoni*.

An alternative is the neighbouring island of Nosy Komba where groups are totally habituated and live in highly degraded forest on edge of the village. Local people sell bananas to tourists to feed the lemurs. The 'eco-tourist experience' created in these places is contrived and unfulfilling and is not the sort of development to be encouraged elsewhere.

BLUE-EYED BLACK LEMUR

Eulemur macaco flavifrons

Other name: Sclater's Black Lemur

MEASUREMENTS

Total length: 900–1,100mm. Head/body length: 390–450mm. Tail length: 510–650mm. Weight: 1.8kg.

DESCRIPTION & IDENTIFICATION

Sexually dichromatic. **Males:** Pelage shorter than *E. m. macaco* and has softer appearance. Normally entirely black, but sometimes dark brown tinges are apparent. A distinct ridge of hair on forehead forms a short crest. No ear-tufts. Eyes charac-teristic blue-grey to blue. **Females:** Upperparts and tail pale rufous-tan, sometimes rufous-grey. Underparts creamy-white to grey. In sunshine appears golden-orange. Hands and feet dark grey. Crown rufous-tan, face pale grey around eyes, darkening to slate-grey around muzzle and brown around nose. No ear-tufts. Eyes blue to blue-grey. Females noticeably paler than *E. m. macaco*.

A medium-sized lemur with long tail and distinctive coloration; adopts horizontal posture and moves quadrupedally. Allopatric with all other *Eulemur* species and should not be confused with any other species. Other than human beings, the only blue-eyed primate!

Female Blue-eyed Black Lemur.

HABITAT & DISTRIBUTION
Inhabits more or less disturbed sub-humid forest in Sud-Sambirano, a zone of transition between Sambirano to north and typical western dry-deciduous forest to south. Also lives in adjacent coffee and citrus plantations (L317).

Blue-eyed Black Lemur

Recorded from sea level to 1,200m (L271).

Range in north-west extremely restricted: occurs only on Sahamalaza Peninsula and narrow strip of forest on adjacent mainland. Northern limit is the Andranomalaza River, southern limit is the Maevarano River (L179). To the east range is bounded by the Sandrakota River. In the southern limits of Manongarivo Massif (north of Andranomalaza River, but south of Manongarivo River, including part of Manongarivo Special Reserve) hybridises with *E. m. macaco*; individuals are similar in appearance to pure-bred *E. m. flavifrons*, but have pale brown eyes (L259; L10; L271).

BEHAVIOUR
'Rediscovered' to science in 1983 (L157; L158); studies in the wild have only recently begun. Appears a generalist feeder and adapts to forests with limited resources, degraded by human activity. Diet principally ripe fruit and leaves, but insects, insect exudates, flowers and fungi also eaten periodically and small vertebrates are taken occasionally.

Infant Blue-eyed Black Lemur.

Cathemeral, the degree of nocturnal activity appears linked to the lunar cycle (L316).

Average group size five to seven (L271; L315; L316), females appear dominant (L55). In other respects behaviour probably resembles the nominate race.

WHERE TO SEE
Because of very limited and inaccessible range, this is a difficult lemur to see in the wild. Efforts are best concentrated on the Sahamalaza Peninsula. A protected area encompassing the peninsula, some mainland forests to north and east and the Radama Islands (Aire Protégée Marine et Cotière Sahamalaza-Iles Radama) has been created and declared a UNESCO Biosphere Reserve (L164; L317). This lemur can easily be observed in Ankarafa Forest – one hour by boat from Analalava to Marovato, then a two-hour walk inland. The Sahamalaza Peninsula can also be reached by pirogue from Maromandia. At the beginning of 2005 a local guide association was formed.

Male Blue-eyed Black Lemur.

RUFFED LEMUR genus *Varecia*

Ruffed lemurs are confined to eastern rainforest regions and appear to be uncommon to rare throughout their range. They are the largest extant members of the family Lemuridae and there is no difference in size or pelage coloration between the sexes (L377). They are primarily diurnal and the most frugivorous of lemurs, relying heavily on large fruiting trees in primary forest (L374), something which makes them particularly vulnerable to habitat disturbance (L24). Ruffed lemurs are polygamous and have the shortest gestation period and largest litters within the family Lemuridae (L372). Their large size and distinctive coloration should prevent confusion with all other lemur taxa.

In the past, a single species was recognised that was divided into two subspecies: the Black-and-White Ruffed Lemur and the Red Ruffed Lemur. Recent research indicates that each warrants full species status (L379). Further, there are proposed subspecific divisions within Black-and-White Ruffed Lemur *Varecia variegata* (L116) but their recognition is not entirely conclusive (L379).

Black-and-white Ruffed Lemur.

BLACK-AND-WHITE RUFFED LEMUR

Varecia variegata

MEASUREMENTS

Total length: 1,030–1,220mm.
Head/body length: 430–570mm.
Tail length: 600–650mm. Weight:
2.6–4.1kg. (L184; L32; L23; L377)

DESCRIPTION & IDENTIFICATION

Pelage is primarily black and white, with considerable variation in proportions across geographic range (L379). Muzzle long, giving face a rather 'dog-like' appearance. Tail strikingly long (average 60cm) and lavishly furred. Body fur is luxuriant, and predominantly consists of different-sized patches of black and white. In general, tail, hands and feet, inner surfaces of limbs, shoulders, face, muzzle and top of head are black, while the back (or a portion of it), flanks, rump and majority of hindlimbs are white. Ears white and lavishly tufted; long hair forms a continuous white 'ruff' around cheeks and under chin (L377).

Overall pattern varies throughout range; in very general terms from north to south, the proportion of black reduces as white areas increase. This pelage variation has prompted the description of different forms (L348), with apparent correlation to geographic range that has led to subspecies recognition (L115). Attempts to confirm these divisions in the field are, to date, inconclusive (L379) and their recognition, particularly with respect to location, must be treated with caution. The proposed forms are:

V. v. 'subcincta' (northern extreme of range): black areas dominate dorsally, especially over lower back and outer thighs, white patches being restricted to lower forearms, a saddle

Black-and-white Ruffed Lemur.

tentative subspecies distributions

V. v. 'subcincta'

V. v. 'editorum'

V. v. 'variegata'

Black-and-white Ruffed Lemur

over the shoulders and rear surfaces of hindquarters.

V. v. 'editorum' (mainly central populations): large swathes of white over lower back and flanks; black areas are restricted to shoulders, upper arms and fronts of thighs, with black shoulder patches sometimes meeting to form a mantle.

V. v. 'variegata' (mainly southern extreme of range): black patches occur only on shoulders, upper arms, nape and head and on fronts of upper thighs. Nape, upper and lower back and flanks are white.

Horizontal posture, long tail and utterly distinctive coloration means this species can not be confused with any other lemur.

HABITAT & DISTRIBUTION

Found in primary lowland and mid-altitude rainforest; recorded from sea level up to 1,300m (L377). Very patchily distributed throughout range, but can survive in isolated forest fragments, e.g. Kianjavato and Manombo (L276). Distribution and range of forms, 'subcincta', 'editorum' and 'variegata' is confused. The north-south trends indicated here follow Vasey and Tattersall (2002).

Varecia variegata 'subcincta'

Northern limit is the Antainambalana River north-west of Maroantsetra (*V.*

rubra occurs on the opposite side of river), the range extends south to the Anove River south of Mananara-Nord. Known sites include Mananara, Marotandrano, the Makira Forest and probably the animals introduced onto Nosy Mangabe. The approximate area of remaining forests where this lemur occurs is perhaps less than 4,000km^2.

Varecia variegata 'editorum'

Occurs south of Anove River to a region between Betampona and Zahamena, although a southern limit is ill-defined. Known localities include Zahamena National Park, Betampona and Ambatovaky Reserves. The status of populations south of the region between Betampona and Zahamena, down to Mantadia have yet to be determined.

Varecia variegata 'variegata'

Northern limits very unclear, perhaps the region of Mantadia; occurs south as far as Manombo. Known sites

include Mantadia National Park, Maromahiza, Ranomafana National Park, Kianjavato, Vatovavy, Lakia and Manombo Reserve. Area of remaining forests where this lemur occurs is probably not more than 2,700km^2.

Total area of all known localities for *V. variegata* is probably less than 8,000km^2. Its populations have declined massively in the recent past and it is now extremely endangered.

BEHAVIOUR

Almost exclusively diurnal, most active early in morning and in late afternoon/evening. Principally a high-canopy dweller, preferring areas of forest with tall trees. Diet dominated by fruit (74–90%), supplemented with nectar, flowers and small quantities of leaves (L184; L22; L23). Nectar available for only short periods each year but constitutes dominant food source when flowers in bloom. *Varecia* use their

Black-and-white Ruffed Lemur.

long snouts and tongues to reach deep inside flowers and lick nectar; they do not destroy the inflorescence, but collect pollen on their muzzles and fur and transport this between flowers of different plants. Suspensory postures frequently adopted when feeding (L33).

Traveller's Tree *Ravenala madagascariensis* is a favourite; size and structure of inflorescences, coupled with lemur's selectivity and method of feeding, strongly suggest that *Varecia* is a major pollinator of *Ravenala*, this pollination system is due to co-evolution (L160).

Group size and social system appear to vary considerably. In mainland rainforests (at Ranomafana), multimale, multifemale groups of four to nine are territorial and occupy home ranges of 100 to 150ha (L23). On Nosy Mangabe, groups are larger, consisting of eight to 16 adults with home ranges around 30ha (L184; L185). Studies at Betampona on the mainland suggest it forms monogamous groups of two to five individuals (adults with offspring) in home ranges of 16 to 43ha (L32). Variations may reflect seasonality and/or habitat.

The strongest social bonds develop between females; those between males are much weaker. On Nosy Mangabe, group composition and ranging behaviour are seasonally variable: during warm wet season (November–April) females range widely either singly or in groups up to six; in cool dry season (May–October) smaller, more stable core groups occupy concentrated areas (L184; L185; L186).

Highly vocal; loud raucous calls can carry up to a kilometre (L377), allowing groups to communicate and maintain spacing in forest.

Mating occurs between May and July, gestation 90–102 days, most offspring born in September and October (L183; L272). Breeding

timed so peak lactation requirements coincide with maximum fruit availability (L399). Normal litter size two or three, but up to five recorded. Young weighing just under 100g at birth (L37). Births occur in well-concealed nests constructed of twigs, leaves and vines, generally 10–20m above ground. Young remain within nest for 7–14 days (L187). Later mother begins to carry young in her mouth, and leave them in concealed spots in canopy, sometimes for several hours, allowing her to forage more efficiently during high-cost period of lactation (L183).

The milk is rich (compared with other lemurs) (L366) and young develop more rapidly than other lemurs. At three weeks are capable of following mother while regularly exchanging contact calls. Begin eating solid food from 40 days, weaned at five to six months, but may continue to suckle until seven to eight months (L182; L183). By four months young are three-quarters grown and as active and mobile as adults (L234; L235). Infant mortality is high, in some years 65% fail to reach three months; some die from accidental falls and related injuries. Sexual maturity reached after 18–20 months in females, 32–48 months in males (L75; L183; L184).

Recorded predation by Fosa *Cryptoprocta ferox* (L35; L36), but these animals were captive-bred and restocked into wild. Predation of truly wild animals appears very rare, perhaps because they are high canopy specialists and difficult to catch. *Varecia* has different alarm calls that are specific to potential ground or aerial predators (L377).

WHERE TO SEE
Readily seen on island of Nosy Mangabe in Bay of Antongil. This is easily reached by boat; a number of hotels in Maroantsetra arrange this. Guides are available from Masoala

Project offices. At reserves on mainland this lemur is more difficult to see. The two most likely sites are Ranomafana National Park and Mantadia National Park, especially around PK 15. Here *V. variegata* are quite often heard, but less often seen. Considerable patience, strenuous hiking and luck may be needed to ensure success.

RED RUFFED LEMUR
Varecia rubra

MEASUREMENTS
Total length: 1,000–1,200mm*. Head/body length: 500–550mm*. Tail length: 600–650mm* (L181). Weight: 3.3 – 3.6kg. (L377) *Estimates

DESCRIPTION & IDENTIFICATION
Pelage dense and luxuriant. Upperparts, legs and belly vary from deep chestnut-red, to red-orange, to honey-blonde. Distinctive ear-tufts, ruff around cheeks and throat also rich chestnut-red to honey-blonde. Inner limbs, belly, feet, long tail (average 60cm), top of head, face and muzzle are black. Nape usually white. In some individuals further white, honey-blonde or pale red areas occur around wrists and ankles, rump and muzzle (L377).

Large size and distinctive coloration make confusion with any other species impossible.

HABITAT & DISTRIBUTION
Found in primary lowland rainforest from sea level up to perhaps 1,000m. Appears restricted to Masoala Peninsula and areas immediately to north of peninsula. Western and northern limits are ill-defined, but the Antainambalana River probably forms western limit (*V. variegata* occurs on opposite side). Historically a zone of 'hybridisation' may have occurred

Red Ruffed Lemur, Andranobe, Masoala National Park.

around confluence of Mahalevona, Vohimara and Antainambalana watersheds (L379). Historical accounts suggest *V. rubra* once ranged north as far as Antalaha and Ankavanana River (L349). *Varecia* loud calls are frequently heard in forests south of Anjanaharibe-Sud (L91), but identity of these populations has yet to be confirmed.

Population density estimates vary from 31 to 53 individual/km^2 at Andranobe (L371) to 21 to 23 animals/km^2 at Ambatonakolahy (L279). Total range is probably no more than 4,000km^2.

BEHAVIOUR

Primarily diurnal and almost exclusively a high-canopy dweller; over 90% of time is spent in crowns of tall trees (L374). Lives in multimale/multifemale communities that appear to vary seasonally and with locality. At Ambatonakolahy groups of five to six animals occupy home ranges of around 23ha, in which there are core areas (around 10% of overall home range) where lemurs spend majority of their time. Core areas show close correlation to location of largest fruiting trees within forest (L279; L280).

At Andranobe the community contains 18 to 31 individuals with

Red Ruffed Lemur, Masoala National Park.

a home range approaching 58ha (L378). The structure of this community varies seasonally. Males reside year-round within core areas, while females remain within core areas during cold wet season (June-August), but range more widely through the communal territory during hot rainy season (January-March). Smell also important in territorial defence; females scent-mark with anogenital glands, males primarily use glands on muzzle, neck and chest by embracing branches and repeatedly rubbing themselves back and forth (L377).

Highly vocal with a repertoire that varies seasonally; loud calls more frequent during hot summer when animals are more active, range widely and interact more regularly with dispersed members of their communities (L377). Still widely hunted on Masoala, and the lemur's calls convey their whereabouts to hunters. The onset of loud calling brings an increase in hunting pressure (L377).

Primarily frugivorous: around 88% of diet is fruit, the remainder made up of leaves and flowers (L376). A wide variety of plants are eaten throughout the year: over

130 species recorded (L375). Often hang upside-down by hindfeet to reach fruit and flowers (suspension feeding) (L373). Females eat a greater proportion of leaves (protein) during pregnancy and lactation, reflecting increased energy costs of reproduction (L374, 2002).

Constructs a nest of twigs and leaves and gives birth to litters of one to five, although twins and triplets are most common (L377). Young remain in nest during early stages of development and are moved to different locations by the mother by being carried in her mouth (L372; L374). At 70 days they can move around the canopy completely independently.

WHERE TO SEE

Not a difficult lemur to see but reaching suitable sites on the Masoala Peninsula requires time and effort; take a boat from Maroatsetra. The best sites are Andranobe, Lohatrozona and Tampolo. Camping is required at Lohatrozona; there are basic lodges at Tampolo. Andranobe can only be visited for the day. At each site trails lead into forest, but the terrain is steep and tough.

Red Ruffed Lemur

AVAHIS, SIFAKAS AND THE INDRI Family Indridae

This family contains 14 species arranged between three genera. Two genera, *Indri* and *Propithecus*, are diurnal and the largest extant Malagasy prosimians. *Avahi* is considerably smaller and nocturnal. All indrids are saltatory and characterised by long powerful hindlimbs (35% longer than forelimbs) and prefer to cling to, and leap between, vertical trunks and branches. Using both arms and legs they can hang from finer branches. The hands and feet are narrow and elongate and the thumb and big toe are both slightly opposed to the other digits, providing good grasping ability. The palms and soles are padded. All indrids are strictly vegetarian.

AVAHIS OR WOOLLY LEMURS genus *Avahi*

The only nocturnal genus within the Indridae. With recent taxonomic revisions and descriptions of new forms, four species are recognised: Eastern Avahi *Avahi laniger*, Western Avahi *A. occidentalis*, Sambirano Avahi *A. unicolor* and Cleese's Avahi *A. cleesei* (L359; L360). Closer investigation of the Eastern Avahi may also reveal differences between populations that justify the description of new taxa (L357).

Avahi exhibits some unusual traits. They are unique amongst nocturnal prosimians in moving and feeding as a cohesive family group containing an adult pair and offspring (all other nocturnal prosimians tend to be solitary). Also females carry their infants throughout the activity period, rather than 'parking' them, like other species (L357). *Avahi* may be secondarily nocturnal, meaning that they were formerly diurnal and that the gregarious lifestyle has been retained (L188). Due to their small size and nocturnal habits, members of this genus cannot be mistaken for any other indrid. The generic name *Avahi* derives from their typical high-pitched calls (*wo-he, va-hii, vou-hii*) and is often also used as the vernacular name as it is here.

EASTERN AVAHI

Avahi laniger

Other name: Eastern Woolly Lemur

MEASUREMENTS

Total length: 590–675mm. Head/body length: 250–295mm. Tail length: 315–370mm. Weight: 880–1,400g (males), 1,100–1,600g (females). (L94; L293).

DESCRIPTION & IDENTIFICATION

Pelage thick, curled and woolly in texture. Upperparts greyish-brown with reddish tinges, becoming paler towards rump. Tail more rufous than body and often rusty-red. Chest and underparts pale grey, insides of thighs have distinctive white patches. Head rounded with small hidden ears, muzzle short and dark. Facial disc brown with lighter cream eyebrow patches. Eyes large. Overall effect gives this species rather 'owl-like' appearance.

A medium-small lemur adopting

Eastern Avahi, Andasibe-Mantadra National Park.

vertical posture. Because of similar size and posture, confusion with *Lepilemur* species is possible; *Avahi* generally larger with concealed, not prominent, ears and characteristic white/cream thigh patches and eye-patches.

HABITAT & DISTRIBUTION

Inhabits primary and secondary lowland, mid-altitude and montane rainforest up to at least 1,625m asl (Andringitra) (L336). Occurs throughout eastern rainforest belt, from Sambava in north (Marojejy and Anjanaharibe-Sud) to near Tolagnaro in south (Andohahela). An isolated population remains in a forest frag-ment at Ambohitantely in central highlands. Rainforest populations currently considered as one species, future investigation may prompt amendments to taxonomy (L357).

May attain high population densities – in Analamazaotra Special Reserve (mid-altitude eastern rainforest) 72 to 100 individuals/km^2 estimated, but unlikely the species is so abundant throughout its range. May become more abundant in secondary growth and disturbed areas (L80).

BEHAVIOUR

Nocturnal and lives in family groups up to five individuals – an adult pair

Eastern Avahi, Ranomafana National Park.

Eastern Avahi

plus offspring from previous years. Day spent concealed in thick foliage 3–4m off ground, usually sitting on branch and lodged against a vertical trunk (L119). Occasionally rests alone, but more usually pairs and offspring sleep tightly huddled together.

Activity begins after dusk; families spend some time grooming themselves or each other before moving off to forage. Foraging occurs as a cohesive family group. Most activity takes place during first and last two hours of darkness but may continue for short periods inbetween. Intervening time spent

resting and grooming when family reunites. When apart individuals keep in close contact with regular high-pitched whistles. They return to sleep sites just before first light (L119; L293).

Pairs occupy home range of 1–2ha, aggressively defended by calling (distinctive 'wo-he' or 'va-hii' call) followed by chasing intruders (L119). Does not range widely, trav-elling around 300–500m per night. Diet young and mature leaves from variety of tree species, plus small quantities of fruit and flowers (L78; L293). Reduces competition with sympatric *Lepilemur* by concentrating on better-quality vegetation, restricting *Lepilemur* to leaves of lower nutritional value.

Mating in April or May, single infant born September or October. Initially carried on mother's underside, when older rides on her back. Females produce offspring each year (L357).

Regularly predated by Fosa *Cryptoprocta ferox*, Henst's Goshawk *Accipiter henstii* and Madagascar Harrier-Hawk *Polyboroides radiatus* (L395; L99; L154). Not widely hunted by humans, but in Mikira Forest and other northern areas (e.g. Mananara) local communities do hunt *Avahi* with spears and sling-shots (L98).

WHERE TO SEE

Easily seen in Andasibe-Mantadia National Park, east of Antananarivo. Night walks along road between village, main park entrance and Hotel Feon'ny ala regularly produce sightings. Along road in Mantadia is also very productive. Alternatively Ranomafana National Park is very good, too. Local guides are adept at finding day-time sleep sites.

Western Avahi with infant, Ankarafantsika National Park.

WESTERN AVAHI

Avahi occidentalis

Other name: Western Woolly Lemur

MEASUREMENTS

Total length: 560–660mm. Head/body length: 250–295mm. Tail length: 310–365mm. Weight: 700–1,005g. (L381; L359)

DESCRIPTION & IDENTIFICATION

Pelage dense, slightly curled and woolly. Upperparts light to medium-grey with sandy-brown or olive-brown tinges that fade towards rear. Tail greyish with reddish-ochre tinges near base. Underparts and throat sparsely furred, pale grey to light beige,

tinged with apricot. Pygal area has distinctive triangle of cream or pale beige fur. Inner thighs clearly white. Face rounded and whitish-cream to pale grey, forming characteristic mask contrasting in both colour and texture. Distinct darker triangle above black hairless nose. Ears small and unobtrusive, eyes brown-yellow and encircled with black eye-rings.

A medium-small lemur that clings to vertical trunks or branches. Smaller and paler than *A. laniger*. Round face, concealed ears and visible white inner thigh, help distinguish from similar sized *Lepilemur*.

HABITAT & DISTRIBUTION

Dry deciduous forests and secondary forests. Restricted to west and north-west, but precise limits of range are unclear. Area north and east of

Betsiboka River from Ankarafantsika National Park to region of Bay of Narinda is its stronghold (L359). Recorded in Mariarano Classified Forest, north-east of Mahajanga

Western Avahi

Western Avahi, Ankarafantsika National Park.

(L12). Northern limit possibly Mahajamba River.

BEHAVIOUR

Lives in small family groups of two to four, consisting of adult pair with dependent offspring, up to two years old (groups of five have been seen, but composition uncertain). Family units occupy almost exclusive home ranges of 1–2ha, containing a central core area where most time is spent. There is modest overlap between ranges of adjacent social units, but territories are defended with piercing 'va-hii' call (L383).

Almost exclusively nocturnal; family spends day resting huddled close together in dense clumps of foliage or lianas, 3–13m above ground. Families have several favoured sleep sites and may move during day if initially chosen site becomes exposed to sun (L382). Become active around dusk, but spend time grooming prior to vacating sleep site. Family unit largely remains together when foraging, individuals maintain contact with gentle purring calls. Foraging follows a regular itinerary, animals often revisit same feeding sites night after night (L383; L357).

Much of the night is spent travelling; average distance covered is 750–1,200m (L383; L357). Feeding mainly concentrated into first half of night. Returns to sleep sites before dawn, but during dry season (May–October) when foliage is reduced, they sometimes remain active after sunrise (L384; L385).

Diet consists of leaves (over 70%) – at certain times of year they are almost exclusively folivorous. Other food includes flowers, leaf buds and young leaf shoots and can be highly selective, choosing to feed predominantly on a small number of species (L381; L355).

Mating occurs in April and May, a single offspring is born from September to October. Infants cling to mother's belly for first three weeks or so, then move round to ride on her back. Offspring remain with parents until following breeding season and occasionally longer (L357).

WHERE TO SEE

Common and easy to find on night walks at Ampijoroa (Ankarafantsika National Park), south-east of Mahajanga.

SAMBIRANO AVAHI

Avahi unicolor

Other name: Sambirano Woolly Lemur

MEASUREMENTS*

Total length: 560–650mm. Head/body length: 250–290mm. Tail length: 310–360mm. Weight: 700–1,000g. *Estimated measurements cf. A. occidentalis

DESCRIPTION & IDENTIFICATION

Head and body light sand brown/grey, fur curled and woolly. Face paler than head; indistinct facial mask result of differences in fur texture (short and straight opposed to curled). Tail darker grey-brown to reddish-brown. Triangle of creamy light beige fur in pygal region. Fur on chest, belly and inside of upper limbs pale grey, thin and downy. Inside lower limbs whitish. Eyes maroon with obvious dark rings (L359).

Distinguished from A. occidentalis in lacking white facial mask and broad dark eye-rings.

Should not be confused with Lepilemur because of round face, concealed ears and white inner thighs.

HABITAT & DISTRIBUTION

Found in sub-humid transitional forest and moist lowland forest up to around 700m asl. Recently described; probably restricted to western Sambirano region, including Ampasindava Peninsula. Southern and northern range limits are unclear; southern limit possibly Andranomalaza or Maevarano Rivers, northern boundary perhaps Sambirano River (L359). Recorded on western, but not north-eastern, slopes of Manongarivo Massif (L278; L104).

Avahi recorded further north in dry forests of Ankarana are very rare (L122); their taxonomic status requires verification.

Face variation in western woolly lemur (Avahi) species: A. Cleese's Woolly Lemur (Avahi cleesei); B. Western Woolly Lemur (Avahi occidentalis); C. Sambirano Woolly Lemur (Avahi unicolor). Redrawn from Thalmann and Geissmann 2000 (L359).

Sambirano Avahi

BEHAVIOUR
Nocturnal. Not yet studied in wild. Behaviour probably similar to *A. occidentalis*.

WHERE TO SEE
Restricted range is difficult to reach. Forests on Ampasindava Peninsula probably provide the best opportunity.

CLEESE'S AVAHI

Avahi cleesei

Other name: Cleese's Woolly Lemur

MEASUREMENTS
Total length: 560–650mm*. Head/body length: 250–290mm*. Tail length: 310–360mm*. Weight: 830g**. *Estimated measurements cf. *A. occidentalis* **Single specimen

DESCRIPTION & IDENTIFICATION
Head and upperparts brown/grey, fur curled and woolly with flecked appearance. Inner thighs white. Underparts pale grey and sparsely furred. Tail beige to brown-grey and slightly reddish where it joins base of back. Face slightly paler than forehead and crown, with upper line of face mask indented upwards towards crown, rather than downwards towards nose (as seen in *A. occidentalis* and *A. unicolor*). Forehead above

Cleese's Avahi, Tsingy de Bemaraha National Park.

face mask is blackish and forms dark chevron pattern. Eyes maroon with narrow dark rings. Snout very dark, areas immediately surrounding nose and mouth whitish (L360).

Distinguished from *A. occidentalis* in lacking white facial mask and broad dark eye-rings, and from both *A. occidentalis* and *A. unicolor* by dark chevron pattern on forehead.

Should not be confused with *Lepilemur* because of round face, concealed ears and white inner thighs.

Named after British comic actor John Cleese, in recognition of his support for lemur conservation.

HABITAT & DISTRIBUTION
Sub-humid dry deciduous forest restricted to limestone karst ('tsingy') areas. Recently described and known only from region of Bemaraha National Park, north of

Cleese's Avahi

Manambolo River (L360). Recorded at only three sites: two within the park, Ankindrodro and type locality (forest 3–4 km ENE of Ambalarano); and one outside park in disturbed forest near village of Ankinajao (L359). Forest at latter site has now completely disappeared (L361). Wider surveys of similar forests in region have failed to locate the species elsewhere.

BEHAVIOUR

Studied only briefly. Nocturnal, forming groups (presumably family units like other *Avahi*) with home range around 2ha. Diet consists of buds, shoots and young leaves. Most active just after dark, for a period before midnight and again before dawn. Very vocal like other *Avahi* (L361).

WHERE TO SEE

Based on current knowledge, can only be seen in forests within Bemaraha National Park.

SIFAKAS genus *Propithecus*

All sifakas (called simponas in rainforest regions) are diurnal and arboreal. They move through the canopy with bounding leaps between vertical trunks and branches but are also capable of descending to the ground and bouncing bipedally across open spaces (more common in species from western and southern regions).

Formerly three species were recognised: *P. diadema* from eastern and north-eastern areas; *P. verreauxi* from the drier southern and western regions; and *P. tattersalli* from a small enclave of forest in the north. *P. diadema* and *P. verreauxi* were each further divided into four subspecies – *P. d. diadema, P. d. edwardsi, P. d. candidus, P. d. perrieri* and *P.v. verreauxi, P. v. coquereli, P. v. deckeni, P. v. coronatus*. These subspecies are now considered full species (L170; L181), such that *Propithecus* currently encompasses nine species, each with apparently distinct ranges.

DIADEMED SIFAKA

Propithecus diadema

MEASUREMENTS

Total length: 940–1,050mm.
Head/body length: 500–550mm.
Tail length: 440–500mm. Weight: 6–8.5kg (L92; L163). In southern extreme of range (Tsinjoarivo): 4.75–5.75kg.

DESCRIPTION & IDENTIFICATION

Pelage moderately long and silky. Considerable variation in coloration across species' range. Typically, head principally white with black crown extending down nape. Face bare and dark grey to black with rich red-brown eyes. Shoulders and upper back deep slate-grey fading to silver-grey on lower back. Lower body and tail pale grey to white and often a golden-yellow area around pygal region. Arms and legs rich orange to yellow-gold, hands and feet black. Chest and belly off-white to pale grey.

Diademed Sifaka, Mantadia National Park.

Diademed Sifaka, Mantadia National Park.

Distinctive colour variant of Diademed Sifaka from forests near Tsinjoarivo.

At south-western extreme of range (vicinity of Tsinjoarivo), animals sometimes much darker – black on head and shoulders, slate-grey on upper body and upper arms, rich orange limbs, black hands and feet and small white areas around face. These may warrant subspecific recognition.

A large, vertically clinging and leaping lemur widely regarded as the most beautiful of Malagasy primates. Largest of the sifakas and second largest extant lemur after the Indri. Confusion between these two species extremely unlikely; marked differences in coloration and morphology – Indri is black and white with virtually no tail, all *Propithecus* species have long tails.

HABITAT & DISTRIBUTION

Primary mid-altitude rainforest up to around 1,700m asl.; elevations above 700m preferred. Restricted to rainforests of east and north-east; precise limits are unclear. Northern limit probably the region of Mananara River, west to the Marotandrano Massif. Southern limit extends from Tsinjoarivo northwards and corre-

sponds to west–east line formed by Onive River and lower reaches of Mangoro River.

BEHAVIOUR

Diurnal, living in multimale/multfemale groups of up to eight or more. Initial studies suggested males immigrate into a group from neighbouring groups and are unrelated, whereas females, which are socially dominant, remain within their natal group (L256). Recent studies indicate both sexes migrate between groups,

Diademed Sifaka

although females only emigrate if resident male is their father.

Groups occupy home ranges of 25 to 60ha (25-35ha in forest fragments; 50-60ha in continuous forest); defended primarily by scent-marking with occasional inter-group aggression (L256).

Daily distance travelled is 500m to 1,700m. Group spends time moving through all levels of the canopy, occasionally descending to ground to search for fallen fruits, eat fungi and soil and indulge in bouts of play-wrestling (L256).

Diet primarily immature leaves, fruit seeds, whole fruits and flowers; respective proportions vary with seasonal abundance. Over 25 different plant species regularly utilised each day. Minimal overlap in species eaten by this sifaka and broadly sympatric Indri. This reduces food competition to a minimum (L257).

Mating occurs between January and March, gestation is 170 to180 days, births occur in June. The single offspring initially clings to mother's lower belly, progressing to riding on her back when older.

Vocalisations not used as primary means of territorial advertisement; rather to maintain group cohesion, signal alarm and convey aggression. Vocal repertoire not varied (compared to some other lemurs e.g. *Lemur* or *Varecia*), but several different calls have been identified (L230). When alarmed by potential terrestrial threats, adults give intense sneeze-like 'zzuss' call; when threatened from overhead (large raptors), call is loud resonant 'honk-honk-honk' or roar.

Infants and adults are predated by the Fosa *Cryptoprocta ferox*; no records of successful raptor predations.

WHERE TO SEE

Such is its beauty all reasonable attempts should be made to see this lemur. The most accessible locality is

Mantadia National Park, 15km north of Andasibe. Some groups are habituated and good sightings are increasingly common but not certain. Also occasionally seen in Special Reserve at Andasibe where a small population has been translocated. These animals remain shy. Tsinjoarivo south-east of Ambatolampy is an alternative site for the more adventurous.

MILNE-EDWARDS'S SIFAKA
Propithecus edwardsi

MEASUREMENTS
Total length: 830–995mm. Head/body length: 420–520mm. Tail length: 410–475mm. Weight: 5–6.5kg. (L94; L163)

DESCRIPTION & IDENTIFICATION
Pelage soft and dense; varies from dark chocolate-brown to almost black on head, upper body, limbs and tail. Chest and belly also dark, but more sparsely furred. Face bare, dark grey to black, eyes orange-red. Lower flanks and back form creamy-white saddle with reddish-brown at margins grading into main dark brown regions. A thin dark area runs down spine to base of tail.

Large, dark, vertically clinging and leaping lemur. Cannot be mistaken for any other species within range.

HABITAT & DISTRIBUTION
Middle to high altitude primary and slightly degraded rainforests up to around 1,700m asl. Restricted to southern portion of eastern rainforest belt: from west–east line formed by Onive River and lower reaches of Mangoro River, range extends south to eastern slopes of Andringitra Massif (southern limit may be Iantara and Rienana Rivers). Populations north of Ranomafana National Park

Milne-Edwards's Sifaka, Ranomafana National Park.

Milne-Edwards's Sifaka

extremely sparsely distributed and widely hunted (L131).

Population densities vary reflecting habitat differences and effect of hunting pressure. Ranomafana almost certainly constitutes the species' stronghold: within the park densities are around eight individuals/km², but in areas south of park this drops to three individuals/km² (L391; L131).

BEHAVIOUR

Diurnal and arboreal. Lives in groups of three to nine containing two or more mature members of each sex. Females are dominant (L243).

Groups largely stable: adults and offspring remain together throughout year. Adults may remain resident for up to 12 years and breeding relationships are stable over six to ten years (L392; L394). Periodically, both females and males migrate between groups (L242).

Diet varied; mainly equal amounts of leaves, fruits, seeds and flowers – over 25 different species are eaten in a day. In spring (October–November) new leaves and shoots, rich in protein, are preferred. Timing high-quality resources is vital for females, corresponding to late lactation/early weaning period when energy costs are highest. During

foraging they move and feed at all heights within forest canopy, occasionally descending to ground level to eat soil – this may provide vital trace nutrients or help detoxify poisons accumulated from their regular diet (L391; L124; L125; L126; L17).

Groups maintain exclusive home ranges with virtually no overlap. These are large – 45 to 55ha – and their boundaries consistent, even if group size fluctuates. Both sexes regularly scent-mark – a function linked to territorial defence and conveying information on status to other group members (L245; L246). Daily distances travelled also considerable, usually between 650m and 1,250m. At home range boundaries, neighbouring groups sometimes approach within a few metres of one another with no apparent aggression or vocalisations, but increased scent-marking activity; group intermingling has even been observed (L391; L245; L246). Sleep sites normally associated

with ridge tops, preferring branches 8–10m above ground, probably to reduce predation (L392).

Infants typically born in June and July (peak in June), gestation 180 days (L244). Breeding timed so maximum lactation costs coincide with peak fruiting season, suggesting, even for primarily leaf-eating sifakas, fruit is key resource to reproductive success (L399). Birth weight around 150g. For first month young hold onto mother's belly, later transferring to ride on back. At two to three months they begin taking solid food; by six months over half infant's nourishment comes from non-milk foods. Mothers sleep with offspring for up to two years. Females breed every other year, except when infant is lost when they again breed the following year (L394; L244). Females can reproduce into their late 20s (L242) although survival rates for young of older females are reduced (L156).

Infant mortality very high – over

Milne-Edwards's Sifaka, Ranomafana National Park.

40% die in first year; around 65% fail
to reach sexual maturity (L244). Most
infants (and some adults) predated,
mainly by Fosa *Cryptoprocta ferox*, or
possibly large raptors (L398; L395).
Some are victims of infanticide by
immigrating adult males and females
(L394; L395).

At one year, individuals weigh
around 50% of adult body weight.
Sexual maturity reached at four in
females and five in males. Females
either remain in natal group and begin
breeding or move to an adjacent
group; males may move out between
five and ten years of age to take up
residence elsewhere. Life expectancy
in the wild is 27 to 30 years.

WHERE TO SEE
Ranomafana National Park is the
best place to see this lemur. Some
groups are well habituated and it is
often possible to approach individuals
closely. Local guides are very good
at finding these and other lemurs,
and their services should always be
sought.

An alternative is Forêt Ialatsara
(Lemur Forest Camp), north of
Ambohimahasoa on Route National
7. This small forest fragment is
home to several lemur species and
sifakas can normally be found and
approached.

SILKY SIFAKA
Propithecus candidus

MEASUREMENTS
Total length: 930–1,050mm.
Head/body length: 480–540mm.
Tail length: 450–510mm. Weight:
5–6.5kg.

DESCRIPTION &
IDENTIFICATION
Pelage long, silky and uniformly
creamy-white, sometimes with tints
of silver-grey around crown, back
and limbs. Pygal area (lower back
and base of tail) sometimes darker

Male Silky Sifaka with curious lack of skin pigmentation particularly around face,
Marojejy National Park.

and discoloured. Adult males also
have large brown 'chest patch'
– consequence of scent-marking with
sternal-gular gland; patch enlarges
with increased scent-marking during
breeding season (L227). Face bare,
slate-grey to black, eyes deep orange-
red. Some individuals (in Anjanaharibe-
Sud and Marojejy) lack skin pigment
on faces and other areas to varying
extents; areas appear totally pink or
mixture of pink and slate-grey.

A large, vertically clinging and
leaping lemur with very distinctive all-
white coloration. Cannot be mistaken
for any other lemur.

HABITAT & DISTRIBUTION
Primary mid-altitude and montane
rainforest; elevations above 700m asl
preferred, observed up to approximately 1,600m asl (L310; L335).
Found only at northern extremity of
eastern rainforest belt. Range extends
from Marojejy in north, around
Andapa Basin to Anjanaharibe-Sud
and then south possibly to region of
Ambodivoahangy. Covers an area no
more than 2,250km².

Silky Sifaka

Female Silky Sifaka in forest above Camp Marojejia, Marojejy National Park.

Hunted for food, particularly around northern and western parts of Marojejy and other areas around Andapa Basin (L58; L232). One of 25 most threatened primates in the world (L180).

BEHAVIOUR

Diurnal. Lives in multimale/multifemale groups of two to nine individuals (L58; L226). Smaller groups of three to four consist of adult pairs plus offspring; larger groups constitute mutually familiar foraging units containing more than one breeding pair plus juveniles. Home ranges are up to 44ha, groups travel around 700m per day, sometimes ascending over 500m vertically up slopes (L226; L297). Group movements are led by females.

Foraging activity begins at dawn; poor weather often delays this. Approximately 45% of day spent resting in canopy, 16% engaged in social behaviour, 22% feeding and remainder travelling between foraging sites (L155; L226; L297). When feeding, females are dominant, although male submissive signals are not always apparent (L224). During rest, there is regular social interaction such as grooming and play between preferred partners; play bouts on ground may last over 30 minutes.

Primarily folivorous: brief studies suggest over 75% of diet is mature or young leaves, fruit and seeds 15%, flowers 7%, remainder bark and soil consumed very occasionally (L155). Mating between November and January, young born in June or July. Infants initially grasp the mother's belly and later ride on her back. Offspring sleep with mothers, until maturity approaches. All group members interact with infants – grooming, playing, carrying and nursing. Mothers observed nursing their own and other offspring simultaneously (L228).

Moderately vocal: several distinct adult calls have been recognised. When disturbed, general response is repeated 'zzuss' call that also conveys identity and sex of caller to other group members (L230; L231; L233). Also give 'aerial disturbance' roars when large raptors fly overhead (L228).

Communicates extensively through smell. Females scent-mark tree trunks with ano-genital region, males scent-mark with chest and ano-genital region. Scent-marking generally occurs within core area of home range, rather than boundaries of territory (L227).

Predated by the Fosa *Cryptoprocta ferox* (L225) and hunted by local communities (L232).

WHERE TO SEE

A difficult lemur to see. Only accessible location is Marojejy National Park: best looked for between Camp Marojejia (Camp 2) and Camp Simpona (Camp 3). Camp Marojejia is five- to six-hour walk from Manantenina (on Sambava to Andapa road); Camp Simpona a further three hours. Well-maintained rustic huts with bunk beds, toilets and showers at each camp. Terrain tough, hills steep and often very wet, but experience is one of the best in Madagascar. Worth staying at Camp Marojejia for view alone.

PERRIER'S SIFAKA

Propithecus perrieri

MEASUREMENTS

Total length: 850-920mm. Head/body length: 430-470mm. Tail length: 420-460mm. Weight: 3.7-5kg. (L163, L270)

DESCRIPTION & IDENTIFICATION

Sexes similar. Pelage dense and uniformly black, sometimes tinged with russet-brown around chest and lower abdomen. Face bare and dark grey-black, eyes deep orange-red, ears small and largely concealed.

A large, vertically clinging and leaping lemur with jet black pelage. Largest lemur within its range. Distinctive coloration makes misidentification impossible.

HABITAT & DISTRIBUTION

Dry deciduous and semi-humid forests from near sea level to around 400m. Most restricted range of any *Propithecus* species. Occurs only in north-east in narrow area lying between Lokia River to the south and Irodo River to the north, centred on Analamera Massif and including Andrafiamena Classified Forest (L270). Once occurred in nearby Ankarana (L122), but has now disappeared from these forests (due to hunting).

Occurs at very low densities throughout range – around three animals/km^2 (L25). Total area of suitable habitat probably less than 400km^2 (20km x 20km) with probably fewer than 1,000 individuals remaining; the effective population size (potential breeding adults) unlikely to exceed 230 animals (L25). Many live in small isolated forest fragments; long-term viability is extremely questionable. Hunting by immigrant

Perrier's Sifaka

Perrier's Sifaka, Analamera.

to cross open areas (sometimes over 500m wide) between forest fragments and to drink water from river beds (L169). This makes them particularly vulnerable to predation, especially by Fosa *Cryptoprocta ferox* (L169) and occasionally feral dogs.

At end of dry season (November) groups may move into ribbons of more humid forest bordering dry river beds and feed for considerable periods in introduced mango trees *Mangifera indica*.

Distinctive alarm call, '*zzuss*', is given to human intruders and potential predators. Reacts in highly agitated manner to the Fosa: when predator is on ground all group members gather into adjacent trees, watch intently and alarm call. They then quickly bound away through canopy.

WHERE TO SEE
A challenging lemur to see. The best locality is the forest along the Bobakindro River flowing through Analamera, particularly from October to November when mango trees are

miners is serious and increasing (L177; L176; L25). Considered to be amongst 25 most endangered primates in the world (L180).

BEHAVIOUR
Group size relatively small, normally two to six, probably consisting of adult males and females, in varying proportions plus offspring. Home range around 30ha (L177; L169). Within a group only one adult pair reproduces each year (L176). Infants born in June and July.

Diet mainly mature leaves, unripe fruit, leave petioles, young shoots and flowers (L162). When feeding a group may be spread out in trees more than 50m apart, but individuals maintain contact with one another through regular quiet calls.

Regularly descends to ground

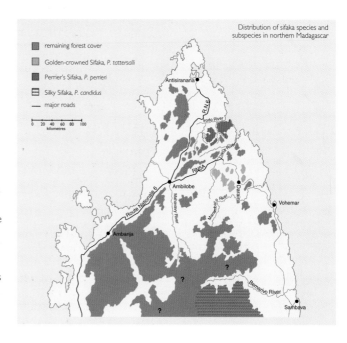

Distribution of sifaka species and subspecies in northern Madagascar

- remaining forest cover
- Golden-crowned Sifaka, *P. tattersalli*
- Perrier's Sifaka, *P. perrieri*
- Silky Sifaka, *P. candidus*
- major roads

0 20 40 60 80 100
kilometres

fruiting. Area best approached from village of Menagisy at northern edge of reserve. Good areas are 15-20km south of the village. Consult staff at ANGAP office in Anivorano-Nord before visiting.

VERREAUX'S SIFAKA

Propithecus verreauxi

MEASUREMENTS

Total length: 900–1,075mm.
Head/body length: 400–475mm.
Tail length: 500–600mm. Weight:
3–3.5kg. (L348; L147; L292)

DESCRIPTION & IDENTIFICATION

Pelage longish, thick and soft. Overall colour, including tail, white, with dark brown crown extending down nape. Ears white, tufted and prominent. Face and muzzle very dark grey to black, eyes vivid yellow. Fur on chest, belly and underarms is sparse, allowing grey skin to show through. Gives underparts a darker appearance. Upper chest in males sometimes tinged with reddish-brown from glandular secretions.

Considerable variation exists: some individuals in Isalo, Zombitse and Andohahela National Parks have

Verreaux's Sifaka, Andohahela National Park.

Verreaux's Sifaka

dark brown areas on back, chest, upper arms, upper thighs and tail (L289). Others almost completely white, and mixed groups containing both 'normal' individuals and variants are known.

A medium-large, vertically clinging and leaping lemur, impossible to confuse with any other species within its range.

HABITAT & DISTRIBUTION

A broad habitat tolerance: occurs in dry deciduous forest in west, xerophytic spiny forest and gallery forests in south and occasionally rainforest at extreme south-east of range (western edge of humid forest

regions of Andohahela). Found from sea level to around 450m (Parcel I of Andohahela) (L68).

Range extends from Tsiribihina River in west, south to Tolagnaro area in south-east and inland to Isalo Massif. Most widely distributed and abundant *Propithecus* species. In gallery forest (Berenty) densities approach 200 individuals/km² (L207), and at Antserananomby the equivalent of over 400 individuals/km² (L340). Densities in spiny forest dramatically lower, 37 individuals/km² (L289).

BEHAVIOUR

Diurnal. Lives in mixed (multimale/ multifemale) groups of up to 14, four

Female Verreaux's Sifaka carrying infant and feeding on leaves of octopus tree (Didierea trolli), Anjampolo Spiny Forest.

to eight is average. Larger groups contain more than one breeding female, but unusual for more than one infant to survive annually. Smaller groups (six or less) represent family units, larger groups comprise mutually familiar foraging parties. At least one and sometime all females are socially dominant over males, and displace adult males at feeding sites (L290; L287; L289).

In spiny forests home ranges are 7–8ha; in gallery forests, with more abundant resources, ranges are around 2–3ha (L137). In dry deciduous forest, home ranges are between 12 and 25ha (L41). The increase is correlated with more intense competition, as this habitat supports a greater density and diversity of other lemur species.

Home ranges constrict when females give birth. Ranges overlap, often considerably, but the core territory remains exclusive to the group. Territories defended by scent-marking; boundary disputes generally

Female Verreaux's Sifaka with two-month-old infant.

resolved with few or no vocalisations (L137; L286).

Activity varies with habitat and season: in cool dry season often remain inactive for up to two hours after sunrise then move into canopy to sunbathe. Afterwards foraging almost continuously until mid-afternoon before settling down for night; rarely travel more than 500m in a day.

In warm wet season regularly active before sunrise and stop foraging by mid-morning, then rest during middle of day and resume foraging by late afternoon, sometimes continuing after sunset – often travelling more than 1,000m in the day (L137).

Movement involves leaping between vertical trunks, even amongst the viciously thorned trees of spiny forest. May also descend to ground and cross open spaces by bounding on hindlegs with arms held aloft for balance.

Diet principally leaves, fruits, seeds and flowers, with seasonal variation in proportions eaten. Leaves predominate in dry season, with a shift to fruit, seeds and flowers during wet season. Can tolerate prolonged drought conditions – groups inhabiting spiny forest areas appear to gain

Verreaux's Sifaka resting in Allaudia procera, *Anjampolo Spiny Forest.*

necessary moisture from leaves of Didiereaceae. In dry season, when heavy dews are common, they lick moisture from their own coats (L284; L285).

Mating season brief and highly synchronous: females in oestrus between late January and early February. Around 45% of females breed each year, remainder every other year. Males move from female to female in group to find a receptive mate and sometimes roam between neighbouring groups (L281; L291). Fights between males common (bouts of cuffs and bites) occasionally resulting in serious injury.

Single offspring born between July and August, gestation around 162–170 days. Initially, infants carried on mother's belly, later shift to ride on her back. Independence reached shortly after six months (L283; L289). Adults particularly vigilant when group has young, always keeping an eye out for predators.

Alarm call for ground predators is characteristic nasal bark – 'si-fak, si-fak, si-fak', at same time individuals throw back their heads in a jerky motion. Potential aerial predators induce a loud bellow or roar.

Infant predation is high: in dry deciduous forests around 30% are taken by Fosa Cryptoprocta ferox (L275; L99), smaller numbers taken by large raptors, e.g. Madagascar Harrier-Hawk Polyboroides radiatus (L153).

Sexual maturity reached between three and five years; where conditions are harsh, majority of breeding females are over six years (L202). Adult females remain within natal group, males are encouraged by established group members to leave prior to maturity and transfer to a neighbouring group. Groups often slow to accept incoming males, which are forced to spend time on periphery. Resident males also initially hostile towards newcomers.

Males move between groups several times within their lifetime (L291; L292; L287; L288). Life expectancy is around 25 years (L289).

WHERE TO SEE
Easily seen at several places. At Berenty Private Reserve groups are completely habituated and close encounters are guaranteed. Most groups live in gallery forest. This is also the best place to see them 'dancing' across open spaces. To see them in spiny forest visit Anjampolo north of Berenty or Mangatsiaka or Ihazofotsy on western edge of Andohahela National Park.

Easy to see in deciduous forest at Kirindy and in Zombitse and Isalo National Parks.

COQUEREL'S SIFAKA
Propithecus coquereli

MEASUREMENTS
Total length: 925–1,100mm. Head/body length: 425–500mm. Tail length: 500–600mm. Weight: 3.5–4.3kg. (L147)

DESCRIPTION & IDENTIFICATION
Pelage dense; mostly white on head, body and tail, with distinctive deep maroon patches on thighs and arms, extending across chest. Some individuals have brown to silvery-grey area at base of back. Inner face black, surrounded by white fur around cheeks and crown extending from forehead down nose to muzzle. Ears black and prominent. Eyes vivid yellow.

A medium-large, vertically clinging and leaping lemur with highly distinctive coloration. Cannot be confused with any other species within its range.

HABITAT & DISTRIBUTION
Dry deciduous and semi-evergreen

Coquerel's Sifaka

forest up to around 500m asl. Also sightings in coastal mangroves on Baie de Mahajamba.

Restricted to north-west: range extends from region of Ambato-Boeni and Betsiboka River north to areas south of Baie of Loza in north-west and Befandriana Nord in north-east. Hunting by local people is widespread, including in and around Ankarafantsika National Park (L90).

BEHAVIOUR
Diurnal. Lives in groups of three to ten, but four or five most common (L282; L2). Smaller groups are family units rarely containing more than one infant; larger groups have variable age and sex composition and are probably mutually familiar foraging units.

Home ranges are 4–8ha, but group spends over 60% of time in an exclusive core area of 2–3ha. Considerable overlap of home ranges around periphery. Boundary encounters with other groups rarely aggressive, but rather mutual avoidance (L282).

Diet primarily mature leaves, buds and occasionally bark in dry season: in wet season proportion of young leaves (in particular), flowers and fruits increases: known to eat nearly 100 different plant species, but 12 of these form 65% of diet.

Coquerel's Sifaka, forests near Anjajavy.

Coquerel's Sifaka feeding in typical suspensory posture, Ankarafantsika National Park.

DECKEN'S SIFAKA
Propithecus deckeni

MEASUREMENTS
Total length: 925–1,075mm.
Head/body length: 425–475mm.
Tail length: 500–600mm. Weight:
3.5–4.5kg. (L348)

DESCRIPTION & IDENTIFICATION
Typical pelage creamy-white all over, sometimes washed with tinges of yellow-gold, silver-grey or pale brown on neck, shoulders, back and limbs. Face entirely black. Appears slightly more rounded and blunt-muzzled than similar species like *P. verreauxi*.

Melanistic variants known from several localities: Bongalova, Analabe region west of Mahavavy River and east of Lac Kinkony and Réserve Spéciale Kasijy (L51; L364). These differ from typical form as entire head and nape are dark brown to black, areas on upper arms, shoulders and upper back are light brown to silvery-grey. Under surface of arms and chest dark brown, inner thighs light brown or silvery-grey. Upper surfaces of forearms and legs white.

Medium-large, vertically clinging and leaping lemur. Confusion with any other lemur highly improbable.

Foraging occupies 30% to 40% of day, with seasonal changes in times of principal activity (L285). During wet season feeding regularly begins before sunrise and peaks before mid-morning. After a rest period, activity begins again in afternoon and continues until early evening. Average daily distance travelled around 1,000m. In dry season feeding starts later and ends earlier, with shorter rest period around midday. Daily distance covered around 750m.

Single offspring is born in June and July, gestation around 160 days. Infant initially clings to mother's front. After three to four weeks, transfers to ride on her back and may continue doing so to six months. Adult size reached at around one year (L283).

WHERE TO SEE
Ampijoroa (Ankarafantsika National Park) is the best place to see this stunningly beautiful lemur. Several groups live within close proximity of the campsite; the trail network is well maintained and good views are almost guaranteed.

For those wishing to watch sifakas and enjoy beautiful coastal surroundings a trip to Anjajavy is recommended. Alternatively, the more adventurous might visit Mariarano Classified Forest north-east of Mahajanga.

Decken's Sifaka

Decken's Sifaka, forests near Mitsinjo.

At southern and eastern extreme of range (Bongolava) distinction from Crowned Sifaka may be required; *P. deckeni* is all white, whereas *P. coronatus* has dark brown to black head.

HABITAT & DISTRIBUTION

Dry deciduous forest. Restricted to parts of west but precise limits of range are unclear. Found between Manambolo River to south and Mahavavy River to north, including western edge of Bongolava Massif (L362; L364). In some areas occurs sympatrically with *P. coronatus* with possible zones of hybridisation.

BEHAVIOUR

Group size ranges from two to ten individuals; troops between three and six appear most common (L51; L202). Groups containing two adult females, both with young have been observed. Seems able to survive in quite degraded habitat, e.g. around Mitsinjo and Tsiombikibo Forest.

Other aspects of behaviour probably similar to *P. verreauxi* inhabiting dry deciduous forest.

WHERE TO SEE

Readily seen in Tsingy de Bemaraha National Park, where locally common and relatively easily located. Forests close to Bekopaka are worth exploring. Locally common further north, in the region of Antsalova. Often seen in forests along western bank of Mahavavy River and areas around Mitsinjo. These include Tsiombikibo Forest, forests adjacent to Lac Kamonjo and forests around Lac Kinkony.

CROWNED SIFAKA

Propithecus coronatus

MEASUREMENTS

Total length: 870–1,020mm.
Head/body length: 395–455mm.

Tail length: 475–565mm. Weight: 3.5–4.3kg.

DESCRIPTION & IDENTIFICATION

Overall colour creamy-white, with head, neck and throat dark chocolate-brown to black. Upper chest, shoulders, upper forelimbs and upper back variably tinted with golden-brown that lightens to golden-yellow lower down torso and fades out to creamy-white by abdomen. This discoloration due to secretions from glands on chest; more noticeable in males. Hindlimbs and tail creamy-white. Face bare, mainly dark grey to black: sometimes a paler grey to white patch across bridge of nose and whitish ear-tufts. Muzzle more blunt and face more squarish than other similar *Propithecus*.

A medium-large, predominantly white, vertically clinging and leaping lemur. 'Typical' form (as above) cannot be confused with any other lemur in its range. Some colour variation has been observed; relationships and distinctions between this species and Decken's Sifaka *P. deckeni* yet to be fully established (L51; L364).

Crowned Sifaka

HABITAT & DISTRIBUTION

Dry deciduous forest. Also been seen in mangroves at Antrema, although probably does not stay within this habitat permanently.

Range lies between Mahavavy and Betsiboka Rivers in north-west. Previously assumed that Mahavavy River is boundary between this species and Decken's Sifaka, while Betsiboka River separates this lemur from Coquerel's Sifaka.

P. coronatus known to occur on Bongolava Massif and in isolated areas to south. The situation in Bongolava where ranges of *P. coronatus* and *P. deckeni* meet will remain unclear until thorough surveys are undertaken (L362; L364).

BEHAVIOUR

Group size seems variable. At Anjahamena groups between two and eight individuals with variable sex and age composition have been observed (L51), probably representing mutually familiar foraging parties.

Home ranges appear very small, around 1.2–1.5ha, and even within this group members spend around

75% of time in a core area of little more than 0.3ha. Groups are territorial and defend home ranges aggressively (L51; L202).

Forage principally in upper canopy; rarely seen on forest floor, although they occasionally eat soil. During dry season, diet primarily buds and unripe fruits, but also includes significant proportion of mature leaves with high fibre content. No dietary data available for wet season.

In dry season, groups active for over nine hours; foraging occupying 30–40% of day and average distance covered is around 600m. Remainder of day principally spent resting, grooming and socially interacting with

group members. At Anjahamena, groups choose tall trees (over 20m), optimally exposed to sunlight and located close to major river (Mahavavy) to sleep in (L201; L51; L202).

WHERE TO SEE

Most accessible site is Antrema, the forest below the lighthouse north of Katsepy (opposite side of Betsiboka estuary from Mahajanga). There are few trails although sifakas are quite common and easy to see. An alternative location is Anjamena on eastern bank of Mahavavy River, around two to three hours' walk from road between Katsepy and Namakia.

Crowned Sifaka.

GOLDEN-CROWNED SIFAKA

Propithecus tattersalli

Other name: Tattersall's Sifaka

MEASUREMENTS

Total length: 870−940mm. Head/body length: 450−470mm. Tail length: 420−470mm. Weight: 3.4−3.6kg. (L174; L163)

DESCRIPTION & IDENTIFICATION

Pelage moderately long. Head and body predominantly creamy-white. Crown rich yellow-orange with similar tinges on shoulders, upper arms, across chest and rump. Ears tufted, giving head a triangular shape. Face mainly bare, dark grey-black with white hairs extending underneath eyes onto cheeks. Eyes are orange. Smallest *Propithecus*, first observed in 1974, later described as new species (L318).

A medium-large, vertically clinging and leaping lemur. Impossible to confuse with any other species within its very limited range.

HABITAT & DISTRIBUTION

Found in dry deciduous, gallery and semi-evergreen forests. Also one record from Analabe coastal forest,

Female Golden-crowned Sifaka with five-month-old infant, forests near Daraina.

Golden-crowned Sifaka

probably an animal in transit. Does not occur above 700m asl; marked preference for elevations below 500m (L177; L368).

Confined to very small area primarily between Manambato and Loky Rivers in north-east. Town of Daraina, 55km north-west of Vohemar, lies at centre of range (L175; L176).

At north-western limits of range has been recorded in three forest fragments on western side of Loky River around Antanimarazoko. Easternmost locations are forest patches within Amporaha Mountains (L368). Within this limited area, forests highly fragmented and cover an area no greater than 44,000ha. Within remaining forests, including small fragments, *P. tattersalli* is often common; total population of breeding adult is probably 2,400 to 4,000 animals (L368).

Golden-crowned Sifaka, forests near Andranotsimaty.

BEHAVIOUR

Primarily diurnal, although seen moving before dawn and after dusk during rainy season (December–March). At night sleeps in taller trees. Group size varies between three and ten, most often five or six; consisting of two or more mature members of each sex. Only one female within a group breeds successfully each year. Males move between neighbouring groups during mating season (L174).

Home ranges vary seasonally between 6 and 12ha (9–12ha the norm); groups travel between 400 and 1,200m daily – greater distances during drier months when food is less abundant (L174; L175).

Diet a variety of unripe fruits, seeds, shoots, mature leaves and flowers. Bark may also be eaten during dry season. Immature leaves are particularly favoured; will forage over a wider area than normal in search of them.

Responds to large raptors, e.g. Madagascar Harrier-Hawk *Polyboroides radiatus*, with characteristic 'mobbing' alarm calls; more familiar 'si-fak' call directed at terrestrial threats, e.g. Fosa *Cryptoprocta ferox*, a known predator (L99).

Mating takes place in January, births occur in July, gestation around 170 days. Infants sparsely covered in hair when born and initially carried by mother on her belly, before later moving to ride on her back. Weaning at around five months (November–December), coinciding with increased abundance of high-quality immature leaves. Following weaning, mother repeatedly refuses all attempts by infant to suckle and only rarely tolerates dorsal riding for brief periods, for instance during predator scares. By one year, young animals attain around 70% of normal adult body weight. Females breed every two years (L178).

WHERE TO SEE

The vicinity of Daraina; various patches of forest where sifakas live can be reached from the town. Perhaps best are those close to village of Andranotsimaty, 5km north-east of Daraina. Here there are several habituated groups of sifakas. Before visiting, contact the conservation organisation FANAMBY, who have an office in Daraina and can offer advice.

INDRI genus *Indri*

A monotypic genus containing one of the most familiar and charismatic lemurs. The Indri is the largest surviving prosimian. Its characteristic eerie wailing song is unforgettable and provides an abiding memory after a visit to this species' rainforest home. The range of the Indri largely coincides with that of the Betsimisaraka tribe, whose name for the animal is *'Babakoto'* literally meaning 'Ancestor of Man' or 'Father of Man'.

INDRI

Indri indri

MEASUREMENTS

Total length: 640–720mm. Head/body length: 640–720mm. Tail length: 40–50mm. Weight: 6.5–9.5kg. (L92, L181)

DESCRIPTION & IDENTIFICATION

Characterised by very long hindlimbs (equivalent to head/body length) and vestigial tail (only 5cm). Only virtually tail-less lemur. Pelage very dense, coloration mixture of black and white with considerable variation over range.

Has been suggested animals from southern part of range have more obvious white areas and individuals from north are predominantly black.

Southern individuals typically described as black with creamy-white patches on crown, nape

Indri

and throat, base of back, forearms, thighs and lower legs – these areas may be tinged with silver-grey or pale creamy-yellow. Face and muzzle black. Ears round, tufted and prominent. Eyes yellow-green. Such descriptions based largely on familiar individuals in Analamazaotra Reserve.

At northern extreme of range (Anjanaharibe-Sud) base colour again black, but pale grey and white regions far less evident. Inner face black, surrounded by white facial disc extending down throat. Also white areas on sides of abdomen extending under armpits. A white pygal triangle at base of back continues to rump and includes vestigial tail. Heels also pale grey or yellowish-white. White areas completely absent on forearms and upper hindlimbs.

These two forms have been proposed as subspecies (L115), with a transition occurring in region of Mananara-Nord (L363). Now known that dark individuals are also widespread in southern areas and that mixed groups occur in many localities, e.g. Mantadia and Zahamena National Parks. It is likely the Indri is simply highly variable and subspecific divisions are unjustified (L258).

A large, highly distinctive, vertically clinging and leaping lemur. Within its range, only Diademed Sifaka is comparable in size; it is much paler with a long tail. Black-and-White Ruffed Lemurs *Varecia variegata* are similarly coloured, but smaller and adopt a horizontal posture.

HABITAT & DISTRIBUTION

Inhabits primary and secondary lowland and mid-altitude rainforest from near sea level to around 1,800m (exceptionally) (L100); lower altitudes, below 1,000m, are strongly preferred.

Confined to central-eastern and north-eastern rainforests. Range extends from Anosibe An'ala region in south to south-west of Andapa

The territorial call of the Indri is one of the most memorable sounds in the natural world.

Indri can leap prodigious distances through the canopy.

in north (near the northern limit of Anjanaharibe-Sud). Does not reach Marojejy nor does its range extend into the Masoala Peninsula.

Population densities low; in large forest tracts e.g. Mantadia, around five adults/km^2 (L256); in restricted forest fragments, e.g. Analamazaotra, around 23 individuals/km^2 (L249).

Subfossil evidence indicates range was once more extensive: remains have been found in caves in Ankarana Massif in the north plus several central highland locations (L142; L96).

BEHAVIOUR

The most strictly diurnal lemur; moves at night only during bad weather or when flushed by a predator (during breeding season often calls at night). Lives in small family groups of two to six animals, comprising a monogamous pair with maturing offspring of varying ages. Female is dominant and has priority at food resources (L251). Animals seek new partner only after death of their mate. In unbroken forest, group size is small – an adult pair and a single youngster (L256). In fragmented forests groups may contain several generations of maturing offspring (L247; L248), probably because of lack of uninhabited areas into which young animals can disperse (L258).

Occupy territories between 17 and 40ha, defended by their melodic calls. Smaller territories typical in isolated pockets of forest like Analamazaotra (L250); larger territories associated with expansive undisturbed tracts of forest, e.g. Mantadia National Park (L256).

Indri's song is its hallmark. It carries one to two kilometres and is generally answered sequentially by neighbouring groups, and so maintains group spatial distribution in forest and prevents significant overlap of home ranges. Most calling bouts occur between 06:00 and 13:00 hours, peak period from 07:00 to 11:00 hours. Daily call frequency increases around September and peaks in October and November, when groups may also call at night (L256).

Call typically introduced with communal 'roar' lasting several seconds before song proper begins. All group members contribute, except very young offspring. Calling bouts last around 45 seconds but may continue up to three minutes. Pairs often synchronise their calls and sing 'duets' (L258). Call's primary function assumed to be proclamation of territory; may also maintain group cohesion and possibly communicate reproductive potential (L252). Elements of the song closely resemble those of White-handed

Adult Indri, Andasibe-Mantadia National Park.

seeds. Foraging takes place in trees at all levels within canopy. Feeding bouts punctuated by periods of rest, before group moves on to next feeding site. Preferred leaves and seeds are different from those eaten by largely sympatric Diademed Sifaka *Propithecus diadema*, thus reducing feeding competition (L257).

Reach sexual maturity between seven and nine years. Females able to give birth only every third year; the capacity for population growth is very slow. Mating occurs between December and March, single offspring is born in May/June, occasionally as late as August. Gestation estimated at 150 days. Initially, infant carried on mother's lower stomach, but transfers to her back after four months. Young capable of moving independently at eight months, but remains in close proximity to mother until well past its second year. Mother and infant always sleep together for the first year, but afterwards do so only sporadically (L249).

WHERE TO SEE

No visit to Madagascar would be complete without seeing this spectacular creature. Analamazaotra, part of Andasibe-Mantadia National Park, is the best location: two family groups are habituated and good sightings are virtually guaranteed (although reserve is home to over 30 groups and a total of around 130 individuals). Be in the forest between 07:00 and noon to hear the Indri call.

Also relatively common in Mantadia National Park, but more time and effort are often required to locate them. Families in forest at PK14 are reasonably habituated and can be approached once found.

It is also worth trying to see dark variants in Anjanaharibe-Sud Special Reserve at the species' northern extreme. Indris here are not habituated so are much more difficult to find.

Female Indri with five-month old infant, Andasibe-Mantadia National Park.

Gibbon *Hylobates lar* (L363). Repeated 'roar' call used to warn of potential aerial predators, while a repeated klaxon-like '*honk*' alerts others to ground predators, like the Fosa *Cryptoprocta ferox* (L258).

Active for five to 11 daylight hours, depending on season and weather conditions; on average around eight hours are spent resting (L250; L256). Daily range averages 770m (in large forest tracts). They patrol majority of territory within eight to 14 days (L256). Can move through canopy with spectacular bounds up to 10m between vertical branches and trunks. Sometimes scent-mark branches and trunks with ano-genital region or cheek glands or both (L258). Prior to dusk, groups settle in a sleep tree, 10–30m off ground. Females sleep in contact with infants or subadult offspring, males typically sleep 2–50m away. If males approach too close to sleeping female, they often get cuffed.

Diet largely young leaves and leaf buds (72%), also fruit seeds and whole fruits (16%) and some flowers (7%) (L256). Soil also regularly eaten; thought to help neutralise toxins that accumulate from leaves and

AYE-AYES Family Daubentoniidae

A family containing a single extant species, the Aye-aye *Daubentonia madagascariensis*. Such is the bizarre appearance of the Aye-aye that, when first discovered, it was classified as a squirrel-like rodent; not until around 1850 was the species widely accepted as a primate.

AYE-AYE genus *Daubentonia*

Daubentonia possesses a variety of peculiar morphological traits setting it apart from all other primates: an unusual dentition – incisors that grow continually, very large ears, clawed digits, a skeletally thin middle finger that can rotate 360° and mammary glands low on the torso (L333). The Aye-aye's morphology is so unusual that determining its closest relatives amongst other lemurs and primates has proved extremely difficult (L329) although recent molecular evidence confirms that the Aye-aye is derived from the same original colonising ancestor as all other lemurs (L401). This species must be regarded as one of the most unusual mammals on Earth.

A second species, the Giant Aye-aye *D. robusta* is known only from subfossil remains found in southern and south-western Madagascar; it is estimated to have been 2.5– 5 times heavier than *D. madagascariensis* (L320; L95).

There is much local folklore and contradictory superstition surrounding the Aye-aye. Local taboos or '*fady*' differ from village to village, even within the same region. The majority regard the Aye-aye as an omen of evil, sickness or death. Some villages in the far north even think Aye-ayes eat people! Extreme reactions to one being seen or, worse, entering a village, include having to kill the animal or even burn down the village and move on. Slaughtered animals are sometimes hung on poles at crossroads outside the village in the belief that passing travellers will carry the evil and ill-fortune away. Conversely, in some areas the Aye-aye is believed to be the embodiment of ancestral spirits and is bestowed the same rites as a grand chief after death (L334; L322).

Aye-aye.

AYE-AYE

Daubentonia madagascariensis

MEASUREMENTS

Total length: 740–900mm. Head/body length: 300–370mm. Tail length: 440–530mm. Weight: 2.4–2.5kg. (L67)

DESCRIPTION & IDENTIFICATION

Sexes similar. Dark grey-brown head, upperparts, legs and tail brindled with white flecks. Effect produced by long coarse dark grey-black guard hairs, with white tips, overlaying dense but short pale grey to creamy-white undercoat. Ears black, very large, leathery in appearance and mobile. Snout very short and blunt, nose pink. Striking yellow/orange eyes surrounded by dark rings, rest of face and throat pale grey. Tail long and very bushy. Hands highly distinctive: all digits elongated with curved claw-like nails (only first toe has a flat nail). Middle finger extraordinarily thin – simply skin, tendons and bone. Incisors particularly long and rodent-like. Females have two inguinal mammary glands located abdominally. Males have a penis bone.

The largest nocturnal lemur. Suite of peculiar features – huge ears, bushy tail, long shaggy coat and skeletal 'probe-like' middle finger – make it absolutely unmistakable.

HABITAT & DISTRIBUTION

Adaptable; found in variety of habitats – low and mid-altitude rainforests

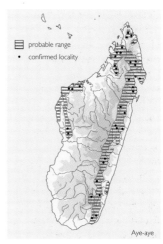

probable range
• confirmed locality

Aye-aye

Aye-aye.

(L79; L86), dry deciduous forests (L134) and some degraded and cultivated areas like coconut and lychee plantations (L5; L8).

Once thought confined to lowland rainforests of north-east in vicinity of Mananara (L1). Now known to be widely distributed. Recorded at localities covering entire extent of eastern rainforest belt, from Ampanefana in north to Andohahela in south. Also found in moist forests of Sambirano region in north-west, drier forests further south in vicinity of the Manasamody Hills, deciduous forests of Ankarana and Analamera and humid forests of Montagne d'Ambre in far north. Recorded at isolated localities in west, most notably Tsiombikibo Forest near Mitsinjo, region south-east of Soalala,

Tsingy de Bemaraha National Park and forests south of Manambolo River (L319; L332: L333; L262). No confirmed records south of Tsiribihina River or in south-western spiny forests. Probably the most broadly distributed primate species on the island.

BEHAVIOUR
Strictly nocturnal, largely solitary but does sometimes forage in pairs (L338). Day spent tucked away in nest constructed from interwoven twigs and dead leaves, located towards the canopy (between 7 and 20m) in dense tangles of vines or branches. Nest occupied for several days and frequently refreshed with new vegetation. High nest turnover rate: in one study, eight Aye-ayes used over 100 nests in two years;

different Aye-ayes use same nest on different occasions. Large trees contain up to six nests (L327).

Male Aye-ayes have large home ranges, between 125 and 215ha. There is considerable overlap – common area may be occupied by both males simultaneously; interactions occur, sometimes agonistic. Males capable of travelling 2–4km per night. Female home ranges much smaller, generally 30 to 50ha and do not overlap with one another, but do overlap with home range of at least one male (L327; L330). Females interact rarely and are invariably aggressive towards one another. Males and females interact for brief periods, often when foraging in tandem. Scent-mark regularly through urination and rubbing ano-genital region, neck and cheeks directly onto branches (L338).

Activity begins up to 30 minutes before sunset, but may not begin until three hours after. Males often active before females. Vocalisations frequent at this time, typically a short 'cree-cree-cree' lasting two to three seconds (known as signature 'eeep' call). Up to 80% of night spent travelling and foraging in upper canopy. Foraging bouts punctuated by rest periods lasting up to two hours. Can move quite nimbly around branches and leaps and climbs vertically with ease; horizontal movements more deliberate. Also descends to ground and sometimes covers large distances. Outside breeding periods, three to four individuals recorded travelling together and feeding at favoured sites (L338).

Diet specialised. Consists mainly of interior of Ramy nuts *Canarium madagascariensis*, nectar from Traveller's Tree *Ravenala madagascariensis*, some fungi and insect grubs. Also raids coconut, lychees and mango plantations. Hard exteriors of Ramy nuts and coconuts gnawed through with chisel-like incisors, before thin middle digit is used to scoop out pulp (L134; L331; L106). Insect grubs are winkled out of bark and rotting wood, their cavities having first been located by Aye-aye tapping on wood with middle finger and listening for movement beneath (L62; L63; L64). Spend considerable periods in search of insect grubs, suggesting they are particularly nutritious and energy-rich (L339).

No fixed breeding season: at onset of oestrus (once a year, lasting only a few days), females move rapidly around home range advertising with distinctive calls (L326; L330; L338). Attracts attention of several males simultaneously, who gather around female and fight one another for access. Copulation lasts around an hour. Afterwards female moves

to another location and repeats her advertisement call. Males and females may mate with several partners.

A single offspring born, gestation around 160 to 170 days. At birth infant weighs approximately 100g. Infant remains with mother for long period, allowing them to learn the complex foraging techniques needed for survival. Females begin breeding at three or four years; probably two to three year intervals between births (L327; L66).

WHERE TO SEE

Encountered very infrequently and assumed to occur at very low densities. One of the most difficult lemurs to see in the wild. The best place is Ile Mon Désir (Roger's or Aye-aye Island) near Mananara. This is not an idyllic pristine wilderness, quite the contrary – the island is mainly overgrown plantation (coconut and lychee) gradually being reclaimed by forest. Several Aye-ayes were introduced and are free-ranging. Sightings are frequent, but – be warned – the animals never stop moving and are difficult to follow!

Nosy Mangabe in the Bay of Antongil is an idyllic wilderness where Aye-ayes were introduced (in 1966–67) and have since thrived. They are seen, but not with the regularity they once were and not because the population has diminished, but because favoured feeding

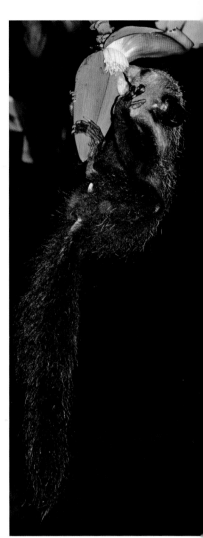

Aye-aye feeding on a banana flower, Aye-aye Island near Mananara.

The evidence of feeding Aye-ayes is seen more often than the animals.

trees along the main trail behind the beach have blown down in cyclones. So their feeding habits are now far less predictable. Also very, very occasionally seen at other localities, like Daraina, Andasibe-Mantadia, Ranomafana and Tsingy de Bemaraha National Parks. In all localities, evidence of Aye-aye presence – gnawed holes in tree trunks, *Canarium* nuts with tell-tail teeth marks or nests in canopy – is far more likely to be seen than the animal itself.

CIVET-LIKE CARNIVORES AND MONGOOSES

Order Carnivora

Madagascar is home to a remarkable assemblage of carnivores. Remarkable for two reasons: first, there is a smaller number of native species than might be expected – the island's total of eight is impoverished when compared with the diversity shown by carnivores in Africa and Asia; and, second, because of the considerable morphological and ecological diversity that exists amongst them.

Established thinking places the Malagasy carnivores in two families: the civet-like carnivores in the family Viverridae, and the mongooses in the family Herpestidae (C7; C53). Recent molecular research, however, indicates that all Malagasy carnivores are derived from a common 'mongoose-like' ancestor (so are monophyletic) that arrived on Madagascar 30 to 20 million years ago (C55; C56; C16). The taxonomy of this group is, therefore, currently under review and relationships amongst all species have yet to be fully resolved.

MALAGASY CARNIVORES

Family Eupleridae

Confirmation that the Malagasy carnivores can be traced to a single ancestor has resulted in the former subfamily Euplerinae being elevated to a full family Eupleridae that now contains all eight species of endemic carnivores.

More precise relationships within the Eupleridae are still being investigated and no new subfamily divisions have yet been proposed beyond the traditionally recognised Galidiinae clade. However, for convenience the group is divided here into civet-like carnivores and mongooses.

CIVET-LIKE CARNIVORES

The three endemic civet-like carnivores, *Fossa fossana*, *Eupleres goudotii* and *Cryptoprocta ferox*, are amongst the most peculiar and extreme members of the family. All belong to monotypic genera, although a second species of Fosa, *Cryptoprocta spelea*, is known from the Holocene and is now extinct (C21).

All are primarily nocturnal native forest-dwellers and show considerable degrees of morphological and ecological specialisation. They are the largest of the island's endemic carnivores, ranging in weight from 1.5kg (*Fossa fossana*) to around 10kg (*Cryptoprocta ferox*).

Fosa.

Fanaloka, Ranomafana National Park.

FANALOKA

Fossa fossana

Other Name: Malagasy Civet

MEASUREMENTS

Total length: 615–710mm. Head/body length: 400–450mm. Tail length: 215–265mm. Weight: males up to 1.9kg, females up to 1.75kg. (C24; C34)

DESCRIPTION & IDENTIFICATION

Pelage dense and light brown with greyish areas around head and along back. Two blackish largely complete mid-dorsal lines and on flanks, two irregular rows of black spots which often merge forming broken stripes. Also irregular scattered spots on thighs. Underparts, including under neck and chin, much paler and have few markings: often light grey or cream but can tend towards pale orange (C34). Snout pointed, ears rounded. Tail cylindrical and similar colour to main body, with faint darker bands and diffuse spots sometimes extending along from back. Tail and dorsal markings more distinct in young animals than adults (C34). Legs shortish and delicate with small paws and medium-sized claws. Obviously digitigrade (walks on toes) (C34).

A small fox-like carnivore approximately the size of a domestic cat with conspicuous body markings. Confusion possible with similarly marked introduced Small Indian Civet *Viverricula indica*, but Fanaloka smaller, with thinner legs, a chunky body and unmarked tail; *Viverricula* larger, longer-bodied with clearly ringed tail. Also Fanaloka ears are far apart at their base, while Small Indian Civet's are close together. *Fossa* distinguished from *Eupleres goudotii* by less stocky build, spotted/striped flanks and blunter snout.

HABITAT & DISTRIBUTION

Found throughout lowland and mid-altitude rainforest areas of east and north, from sea level to 1,600m, including Sambirano region in north-west (C2; C20; C24) and littoral forests near Tolagnaro in south (C34). Also occurs in isolated humid forests of Montagne d'Ambre and less humid deciduous forests of Ankarana in far north. Not seen outside native forest areas.

Fanaloka

BEHAVIOUR

Shy and nocturnal, forages on forest floor and in low vegetation for rodents, small tenrecs, reptiles, frogs and invertebrates, including freshwater crabs (C1; C5; C34; C28). Sleeps during day in tree holes, under fallen logs or in rocky crevices.

Male and female live as a pair and share a territory up to 0.5km² (C34). Boundaries marked with scent from glands around anus and on cheeks and neck. Areas around streams and marshes may be preferred (C34). Vocalisations are few, involving occasional faint cry or groan or more characteristic *coq-coq* call, only heard when two or more individuals are together (C5).

Courtship occurs in August and September with single young born in austral summer after gestation period of 82 to 89 days (C5). Births occur in a secluded den. Young are very well developed at birth (unusual amongst carnivores, but similar to *Eupleres*), weigh 60–70g, have eyes open, and are fully furred (C5). Can walk after three days, but progress relatively slowly after this. Meat eaten after a month, but not fully weaned until two to three months. Probably independent when one year of age and begin breeding at two.

Fanaloka lays down fat reserves, especially in its tail, in preparation for austral winter (June–August) when food is scarce and foraging difficult. These may constitute 25% of animal's body weight (C5).

WHERE TO SEE

Chance encounters during night walks are rare. Individuals regularly seen at Ranomafana National Park near *Belle Vue* at a 'feeding station' where they are tolerant. *Fossa* also seen in Ankarana Special Reserve around Campement Anilotra (Camp des Anglais), but here they are very shy.

Falanouc.

FALANOUC

Eupleres goudotii

Other name: Malagasy Small-toothed Civet

MEASUREMENTS

Total length: 670–910mm. Head/body length: 450–650mm. Tail length: 220–260mm. Weight: 2.5–4.5kg.

DESCRIPTION & IDENTIFICATION

Pelage dense and soft. Upperparts vary from grey to sombre rufous-brown or light brown, with (sometimes) russet spots and tinges around the thighs. Underparts pale grey-brown. Head and tail grey. Tail large, broad at base, tapering to a point, and covered with longer hairs, giving bushy appearance. May also be faint brown bands along flanks. Forepaws and claws formidable and well developed for digging (C5).

A medium-sized carnivore (larger than a domestic cat) with stocky body, small delicate head, large ears, elongate snout and highly distinctive fat cylindrical tail. Larger size and very distinct pointed muzzle should prevent confusion with other small carnivores.

HABITAT & DISTRIBUTION

Found in humid forests of east and dry forests of west. Throughout range sparely and patchily distributed. Always uncommon and appears closely associated with riverine, swampy and marshy areas (C5).

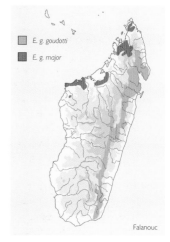

E. g. goudotii

E. g. major

Falanouc

Falanouc.

Two subspecies have been proposed. Eastern Falanouc *E. g. goudotii* from eastern lowland rainforests from Andohahela region in south to Marojejy Massif in north (C20; C12; C24).

Western Falanouc *E. g. major* recorded in Sambirano region in north-west, Ankarafantsika area, Tsiombikibo forests near Mitsinjo (local name 'falanoucy'), and Soalala/Baly Bay region (local name 'jabady')(C29).

Also found in humid forests of Montagne d'Ambre in far north and has been recorded in drier deciduous forests of Ankarana.

BEHAVIOUR

Probably Madagascar's most specialised carnivore. Elongate snout and tiny conical teeth (resembling an insectivore) have evolved to predate earthworms on which *Eupleres* feeds almost exclusively (C5). Other small invertebrates are eaten occasionally (C12). Forages in leaf-litter, digging up morsels using strong forepaws and long claws. Claws held above ground when walking.

Mainly solitary (C12), although small groups (possibly families) have been observed. Probably crepuscular and nocturnal, the day spent sleeping under logs or in rock crevices.

Occasional sightings during daylight suggest some diurnal activity (C24). Defends a large territory, marking with scent glands around anus and neck (C5). Few vocalisations recorded.

Courtship and mating occur in July and August; offspring born between November and January. Litter size one or two (C3). Gives birth to extremely well-developed, fully furred young (pelage darker than adult, sometimes almost black) with open eyes, weighing around 150g. Can follow foraging mother within two days. Weaned after nine weeks.

Stores large amounts of fat (up to 800g) in tail (C5), helping survival during austral winter when earthworms are harder to find (C12). Hunted for its meat in some areas (C47). Also predated by domestic and feral dogs.

WHERE TO SEE

Rare or even very rare over most of its range. Shy, secretive and nocturnal, so a very difficult species to observe. In Montagne d'Ambre National Park individuals can very occasionally be seen at night close to the Station Roussettes.

FOSA

Cryptoprocta ferox

Other name: Fossa

MEASUREMENTS

Total length: 140–170cm. Head/body length: 75–80cm (males), 65–70cm (females). Tail length: 70–90cm. Weight: 6–10kg (males), 5–7kg (females) (C31; C32).

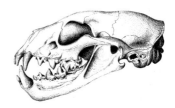

DESCRIPTION & IDENTIFICATION

Slender and elongate with short powerful legs; shoulder height is up to 35cm. Head relatively small, short muzzle, prominent round ears and large eyes with vertical pupils. Feet large and tail very long and slender. Pelage short, smooth and dense. Upperparts sepia brown blending to creamy underparts. In males underparts, especially between forelimbs and hindlimbs, are stained with orange secretion (C32). Unconfirmed reports of melanistic (black) variants (known locally as 'fosa mainty', or black *Cryptoprocta*) from some rainforest areas (C27).

Shows several adaptations to an arboreal lifestyle: long tail acts as counterbalance when climbing (but is not prehensile) (C36; C37), paw pads extend almost to heel, claws decurved and semi-retractile and ankles are 'reversible' (C32). When walking, gait is distinctive and can be either plantigrade or digitigrade (C32).

Close morphological similarities (e.g. retractile claws, dental traits, facial resemblance) have led to past comparison with the cat family (Felidae) (C48). *Cryptoprocta* has attained such cat-like traits through convergent evolution.

Largish sleek low-slung carnivore with very long, slender tail. Largest carnivore and largest native terrestrial mammal on Madagascar. Cannot be confused with any other species.

Pug mark consists of five evenly spaced pads around large central pad, c.f. dog's paw mark has only four outer pads, with middle two closer together and claws often visible. Fosa scats also characteristic grey cylinders with twisted ends and around 10–14cm in length (C32).

HABITAT & DISTRIBUTION

Widely, but sparsely, distributed throughout native forest regions from sea level to 2,600m (Andringitra Massif) (C26). Even in deciduous forest areas where it is regarded as relatively common, population densities are very low, 0.26 individuals km^2 (C33). In rainforests densities are probably even lower (C11; C13).

Generally not found outside intact forests; observations in degraded areas and wooded savannas, probably represent transient, not resident individuals. No longer found in central highlands where virtually all native forest cover has been removed.

BEHAVIOUR

Solitary outside the breeding season. Active both day and night (cathemeral): peak activity usually under cover of darkness, although this varies seasonally (C32). No regular sleep sites, instead use a variety of locations: caves or hollowed-out termite mounds, but most frequently prefers trees, usually resting on large branches. Extremely agile climbers, equally at home hunting in trees or on ground, but large distances rarely covered in canopy. 'Reversible' ankles enable it to grasp both sides of slender tree trunk with hindfeet when ascending or descending (head first) or leaping to an adjacent trunk (C32).

Occupies and hunts in very large territories: in western forests, males up to 26km^2 and females up to 13km^2 (C31). Female ranges are exclusive, but male ranges overlap considerably with one another and those of females with considerable seasonal fluctuation. May cover large distances – well over 7km in a day (C32) and in mountainous regions like Andringitra daily climbs of at least 600m in altitude are known (C26). Territorial boundaries marked using pungent scent from glands in anogenital region (C32).

Mammals are mainstay of diet, although relative abundance and

Male Fosa in western forest.

Fosas mating in the canopy, Zombitse National Park.

size of prey taken reflects habitat and location. In high mountains like Andringitra small prey such as shrew tenrecs *Microgale* predominate (C26). In forests larger prey are preferred; lemurs may comprise more than half the diet (C31) and are often ambushed at night while sleeping (C54). Larger species like sifakas

Fosa

Propithecus are regularly taken, but also *Varecia, Eulemur, Hapalemur* and *Lepilemur* and most members of family Cheirogaleidae (C10; C21). In deciduous forests near Morondava, Giant Jumping Rat *Hypogeomys antimena* is a major food (C42). Here, Fosas also take introduced Bush Pigs *Potamochoerus larvatus* and even smaller native carnivores like Narrow-striped Mongoose *Mungotictis decemlineata*.

Tenrecs (*Tenrec* and *Echinops* spp.) are eaten year round. During dry season while aestivating these animals are excavated from burrows or hideaways, as are Dwarf Lemurs *Cheirogaleus* (C32). Birds, reptiles, amphibians and invertebrates also taken on occasion (C26), but constitute a much smaller proportion of overall diet. In forests close to villages Fosas have a reputation for taking smaller domestic livestock, especially fowl (C32).

Front paws used to pin larger

prey down before a fatal bite is administered to throat or back of head (C10). Victim often eviscerated and vital organs eaten first (C54). Observations from eastern rain-forest raise the possibility that pairs hunt cooperatively at times (C17), although this may be mothers hunting with older offspring (C32).

Courtship is between October and December; a single female in oestrus attracts the attention of several males (up to eight in a day) (C32) which stay in close proximity, although female remains in same place, often a favoured tree (used year on year), for up to a week (C31; C32). She may mate with several different males during this time. Copulation is noisy, with both sexes purring, snorting and shrieking and, if uninterrupted by other males, can last several hours (C32).

Gestation six to seven weeks (C32). Litter between two and four (six has been recorded) and females raise offspring alone (C5). Den usually a hollow tree, hollowed termite mound or similar. At birth, young very pale grey, fully furred but toothless and blind and weigh around 100–150g. Eyes open after 15 to 16 days; development is relatively slow. After two months young leave den for first time and make initial attempts at climbing. First solid food taken around three months and weaning occurs between four and five months. Independence is reached after one year (C2) (less than 50% survival to this stage), with physical and sexual maturity not reached until three or four years. Infants stay with mothers for 12 months or more, so females can breed only every other year.

Much local folklore surrounds the Fosa, some suggesting they pose a threat to humans: there is no evidence and stories have become exaggerated over time. However, Fosas certainly behave in an irregular and erratic manner on occasion and without provocation. For instance, even in remote forest areas they have walked into field camps, entered unoccupied tents and ransacked the contents, chewing metal objects, leather boots, rucksacks and even eating soap (C14).

WHERE TO SEE
Common nowhere and consequently very difficult to see. Best looked for in western deciduous forest, particularly Kirindy, where sometimes seen during the day, particularly in dry season when coming to drink at pools. Also seems less wary during breeding season (October and November). Also seen with greater frequency in Ankarana. Encounters in rainforest areas like Mantadia, Ranomafana and Masoala National Parks are rare and fleeting.

MONGOOSES Subfamily Galidiinae

The Malagasy mongooses have a variety of morphological traits that set them apart from mongooses in Africa and Asia (C53) and form their own subfamily, Galidiinae. New research indicates their closest allies are in fact the civet-like carnivores on Madagascar (C55; C56), so these mongooses are now placed in the family Eupleridae. It has yet to be established whether additional subfamily divisions exist beyond the Galidiinae.

Currently, five species of mongoose are recognised. However, fieldwork in inaccessible areas may bring new taxa to light.

RING-TAILED MONGOOSE

Galidia elegans

MEASUREMENTS
Total length: 550–690mm. Head/body length: 300–390mm. Tail length: 250–300mm. Weight: 900–1,080g (males), 760–890g (females). (C15; C22).

DESCRIPTION & IDENTIFICATION
Upperparts, thighs and legs rich russet-chestnut. Head, throat and chin more olive-grey to olive-brown. Tail bushy and ringed with five to seven (six most common) alternate bands of russet-chestnut and black. Head small, snout pointed, ears rounded. Moderately sexually dimorphic; males slightly larger than females.

Three subspecies recognised: eastern race *G. e. elegans* is darkest with dark brown to black feet; northern race *G. e. dambrensis* has lighter chestnut upperparts and belly; western race *G. e. occidentalis* has light chestnut upperparts blending to dark

Key:
- G. e. elegans
- G. e. dambrensis
- G. e. occidentalis
- Ssp uncertain

Ring-tailed Mongoose

belly and legs and paws black (C22).

A small carnivore of 'typical' mongoose shape. Might be confused with Brown-tailed Mongoose; more russet coat and distinctively marked tail, should prevent misidentification.

HABITAT & DISTRIBUTION
Commonest and most widespread of Malagasy mongooses (C22). Found widely in intact forests of east, north and west from sea level to around 1,950m (Andringitra Massif) (C20). More abundant in forests below 1,500m. Primary habitats preferred, but able to survive in secondary forests and forest edge bordering cultivation (C22).

Three subspecies occur in distinct areas: eastern race *G. e. elegans* found throughout eastern rainforests from Andapa Basin in north to Tolagnaro in south; western race *G. e. occidentalis* restricted to deciduous forests

Eastern Ring-tailed Mongoose, Camp Simpona, Marojejy National Park.

between Manambolo River in south and Soalala to north, particularly around karst formations at Bemaraha and Namoroka; northern race *G. e. dambrensis* found in moist forests of Montagne d'Ambre and drier forests around Ankarana and between Ambanja and Ambilobe. Unclear which form occurs in Sambirano to south of this.

BEHAVIOUR

Largely diurnal, with occasional activity at dusk and after dark. Can be solitary but more often in pairs or family groups up to five (two adults, three offspring) (C22). Dens excavated at base of large trees or stream banks. These have a number of entrances/exits (C15). Den sites changed frequently (every few days), to avoid predation and reduce parasites like fleas.

Very versatile, equally at home on ground or in trees. Regularly climbs nimbly up trunks, along vines or in branches. Seen in canopy over 15m above ground (C22). Often rips open epiphytes when foraging. An adept swimmer that regularly hunts along forest streams (C15; C22).

Diet includes small lemurs (particularly *Microcebus* and *Cheirogaleus* spp.), rodents (C46), small tenrecs (*Hemicentetes* and *Microgale* spp.), adult and young birds (mainly terrestrial species), eggs, smaller reptiles, frogs, invertebrates and even fish (C22; C24). Victims dispatched by bite to back of neck. Large eggs and snails broken in typical mongoose fashion – holding item between forepaws and kicking it against a hard surface with hindfeet. Is persecuted in forests bordering habitation because

Northern Ring-tailed Mongoose, Ankarana Special Reserve.

it predates domestic chickens (C18). Not averse to scavenging at forest research camps.

Family groups occupy territories between 20ha and 25ha (C5). Scent-marking important in defining and maintaining these. Scent smeared from large anal glands against rocks, tree-trunks and branches (C15). Can be vocal. Contact calls are high-pitched 'peeping' whistles that keep family together while foraging. Muffled 'meows' and soft 'mews' emitted during prey capture; louder shrieks and growls heard when disputes break out; alarm calls are low moans or grunts (C8).

Gestation just under three months, births occur between November and January (C5). Newborn weigh around 50g and are fully furred. Eyes do not open until seventh or eighth day. Female initially raises young alone in burrow and does not allow male to approach. After a month male allowed access to infants.

Development is slow: young take first steps at 12 to 14 days, can take small amounts of meat at one month, not fully weaned until two to three months. Physically mature at around one year, but do not leave parents, and attain sexual maturity, until 18 months to two years.

WHERE TO SEE

The.most regularly seen native carnivore. Eastern race readily encountered at Ranomafana National Park and less frequently in Marojejy and Mantadia National Parks. Northern race easily seen in Montagne d'Ambre National Park and Ankarana, especially around Campement Anilotra. Western race is difficult to see because it inhabits remote locations; southern end of Bemaraha National Park is best place to try.

NARROW-STRIPED MONGOOSE
Mungotictis decemlineata

MEASUREMENTS

Total length: 450–560mm. Head/body length: 250–320mm. Tail length: 200–240mm. Weight: 400–550g. (C44).

DESCRIPTION & IDENTIFICATION

Pelage short and dense, longer under belly. Upperparts grizzled grey-beige fading to paler beige underparts. Back and flanks marked with eight to ten broadly spaced thin longitudinal dark stripes running from nape to base of tail, often becoming indistinct. Tail similar colour to upper body but often more grey and flecked with darker and lighter areas. It is very bushy and brush-like. Muzzle shortish

Narrow-striped Mongoose, Kirindy Forest.

and pointed, ears short and rounded. Legs short and delicate, feet webbed with long claws (C4). Two subspecies, *M. d. decemlineata* and *M. d. lineata*, proposed on basis of colour differences. This requires investigation (C30).

HABITAT & DISTRIBUTION

Inhabits primary deciduous forests of west and arid spiny forest of the south-west, from sea level to around 125m elevation. Known range restricted to region between Tsiribihina River to north and Fiherenana River to south and inland possibly as far as Mahabo.

If two subspecies do exist, *M. d. decemlineata* may range from Tsiribihina River south to Mangoky River, while *M. d. lineata* occurs south of Mangoky River to banks of Fiherenana River. Rarer at southern extreme of deciduous forests (north of Mangoky River) (C49) and extremely rare in spiny forest south of Mangoky River.

M. d. decemlineata

M. d. lineata

Narrow-striped Mongoose

BEHAVIOUR

Largely diurnal, both terrestrial and arboreal (C44); more often encountered on ground, but an accomplished climber. Forages widely covering distances in excess of 2km per day. Diet dominated by insects, especially larvae, which are

dug up or excavated from decaying wood (C41). These are particularly important during drier months. Diet more varied in rainy season, includes small mammals, reptiles, worms and other invertebrates. Larger prey like mouse lemurs *Microcebus* spp. and dwarf lemurs *Chierogaleus* and *Mirza* spp., may be hunted cooperatively (C41; C21).

Social and lives in family units, preferring areas of forest with dense undergrowth (C44). Behaviour varies seasonally. In warm wet season (December–May) groups consist of six to eight (up to 12 have been observed) including males, females and young, occupying a range up to 100ha. More arboreal at this time, often spending night in tree holes up to 10m off the ground (C44).

In cool dry season (June–October) groups of three to five maintain ranges between 12 and 18ha (C44). Preferring to den in abandoned ant nests or collapsed ant burrows at this time, then at onset of rainy season (November) switch to holes in fallen trees. However, at no time are shelters fixed; sleep sites change regularly to avoid predation and parasites (C44). Dens mainly situated around periphery of territory. Boundaries of adjacent territories may overlap. Within common areas scent-marking very intense (C44).

Mating in August and September. Gestation 74 to 106 days (C44). A single infant is born weighing around 50g (C57). Initially, mother may carry young in her mouth, especially when moving between dens and sleep sites.

WHERE TO SEE

Kirindy, north-east of Morondava, is best place to see this mongoose. Here it is locally quite common. During a two or three day stay the chances of success are good.

BROAD-STRIPED MONGOOSE
Galidictis fasciata

MEASUREMENTS

Total length: 540–640mm. Head/body length: 560–630mm. Tail length: 250–295mm. Weight: 520–750g. (C23)

DESCRIPTION & IDENTIFICATION

Base colour grey-beige extending down legs and lower tail; underparts paler creamy-white. Tail slightly less than half body length, bushy and creamy-white over distal two-thirds. Head grizzled grey-brown with cheeks, chin and throat noticeably paler. Several distinctive longitudinal dark brown stripes on flanks running from nape to base of tail. These broader than grey-beige inter-stripe spaces. Muzzle short and slightly rounded, ears small. Digits and claws long, but webbing less developed than in *G. grandidieri* and *Galidia elegans* (C23).

A medium-sized mongoose with conspicuous creamy-white tail and distinctive body markings. Much smaller than *Fossa fossana* or *Viverricula indica* and difficult to confuse with other species within range.

HABITAT & DISTRIBUTION

Inhabits eastern lowland and mid-altitude rainforests, occurring at low densities at all locations. Majority of records from elevations below 700m, but has been seen up to 1,500m (C24). Range extends from Andohahela in south to region of Anjanaharibe-Sud and Marojejy in north.

BEHAVIOUR

Appears strictly nocturnal (C23). Most observations are of lone individuals or pairs foraging.

Morphology is the most robust of small native carnivores; able to tackle

Broad-striped Mongoose, Andringitra National Park.

largest prey relative to body size. Diet mainly small vertebrates, like rodents, reptiles and amphibians and occasionally invertebrates. Forages on the forest floor, often with tail held vertically upwards (C23). Observed climbing up and down fallen logs and into lower branches of undergrowth to 1.5m (C6).

Broad-striped Mongoose

Generally shy and occurs at very low densities. Yet individuals occasionally seen around forest research camps can be tolerant and sometimes raid camp food stores (C20).

WHERE TO SEE
A very difficult species to see. Very occasionally seen at Ranomafana National Park (e.g. along road between park entrance and village). Other possible localities are Masoala, Zahamena, and Andohahela National Parks.

GIANT-STRIPED MONGOOSE

Galidictis grandidieri

Other name: Grandidier's Mongoose

MEASUREMENTS
Total length: 680–720mm. Head/body length: 380–405mm. Tail length: 300–315mm. Weight: 1.0–1.5kg. (C23)

DESCRIPTION & IDENTIFICATION
Described in 1986 and until 1989 known only from two museum specimens (C50; C51). Largest of Madagascar's mongooses. Upperparts grizzled beige-grey, with back and flanks marked with dark brown longitudinal stripes from neck to base of tail – inter-stripe spaces broader than stripes (C23). Top of head darker grey, underparts creamy-grey. Tail less than half body length, off-white in colour and bushy.

Large and distinctively marked, with prominent ears and pale bushy tail. Introduced Small Indian Civet *Viverricula indica* is only broadly similar species within same range, but is larger and has obvious ringed tail.

Giant-striped Mongoose

HABITAT & DISTRIBUTION

Inhabits spiny forest and known only from narrow band of habitat on western edge of Mahafaly Plateau in south-west Madagascar (C39) in vicinity of Lac Tsimanampetsotsa. Seen both in pristine habitat and degraded areas on edge of spiny forest (C23). Subfossils indicate it was probably once more widespread (C19).

BEHAVIOUR

Strictly nocturnal and terrestrial (C23). Sleeps in natural cavity, burrow or hole in peculiar fissured limestone terrain that dominates its habitat (C52). Burrows are up to 2m deep and probably help keep mongooses cool when daytime temperatures are very high. Emerges after dusk, generally returning before dawn. Do not use same burrow each night and different mongooses may use same sleep site on successive nights.

Forages singly or in pairs within a small area (approximately 0.8 to 1.3km²). Diet mainly invertebrates like hissing cockroaches and scorpions, but its powerful skull and massive teeth suggest larger prey are tackled (C52).

Evidence suggests able to breed year-round (C23), surprising given the degree of seasonal variation in climate within its range.

Defecates at specific latrine sites, mostly on exposed rocks or similar prominent places, suggesting these are territorial markers (C52). In optimum habitat apparently occurs at higher densities than other similar small carnivores. Wary when first approached, but very docile and soon becomes accustomed to human presence (C23).

WHERE TO SEE

Only known from Lac Tsimanampetsotsa National Park, 80km south of Toliara. Best looked for in Euphorbiaceae scrub on the eastern side of lake. Here locally common and easily seen at night (C52, C23).

BROWN-TAILED MONGOOSE

Salanoia concolor

MEASUREMENTS

Total length: 490–570mm. Head/body length: 300–350mm. Tail length: 190–220mm. Weight: 550–750g.

DESCRIPTION & IDENTIFICATION

Pelage short, dense and dark brown, flecked with paler guard hairs along back and flanks. Area below ears to around throat is paler reddish-brown. Under chin and around mouth is whitish-grey. Underparts are reddish-brown. Ears relatively large and rounded. Muzzle thickly furred, and sharply pointed. Snout protrudes over lower jaw. Whiskers short. Tail uniformly dark brown and bushy. When alarmed long tail hairs become erect. Claws long and relatively straight.

A small delicate carnivore, noticeably smaller and more gracile than similar Ring-tailed Mongoose. Also has more rounded ears and shorter tail (with no banding) (C8).

HABITAT & DISTRIBUTION

Prefers intact lowland rainforest (all records between 300m and 700m). Occasionally seen in secondary forest and cultivated land adjacent to forest (C9).

Information on distribution scant. Probably restricted to north-east Madagascar, north of Mangoro River to south of Andapa Basin, including Masoala Peninsula.

Recently trapped in reed beds around Lac Aloatra (has also been observed swimming).

BEHAVIOUR

Strictly diurnal, activity peaks early in morning and late in afternoon. Sleeps in burrows or hollow trees.

Giant-striped Mongoose, Tsimanampetsotsa.

insects in leaf-litter. Generally silent, when foraging but can be heard making soft throaty squeaks and growls (C9).

Nervous when encountered and growl loudly with alarm, sometimes rearing onto hindlegs before fleeing rapidly: also gait becomes more stiff-legged and tail hair erect.

WHERE TO SEE

Shy and secretive; sightings are very rare indeed. Information here based primarily on sightings from the Betampona Reserve, where species appears to be common (C9).

Brown-tailed Mongoose

The rarely seen Brown-tailed Mongoose, Betampona Reserve.

Primarily terrestrial; appears to prefer ridge tops (90% of observations at Betampona); occasionally seen climbing trees to around 2m (C9). Solitary or in pairs; groups of three to five presumed to be parents with offspring (C8). Mating between August and October, gestation 74 to 90 days, young born from November to January. Infants left concealed while mother is away foraging.

Diet mainly beetle larvae excavated from rotting wood using long straight claws (C9); also catch other

INTRODUCED CARNIVORES

Apart from two domesticated species, the dog and cat, only a single species of wild carnivore has been introduced to Madagascar. When the introduction of the Small Indian Civet *Viverricula indica* occurred is uncertain (C27), although it may have arrived from the Indo-Malay region with the early human settlers, around 1,500 to 2,000 years ago. The civet's gradual spread from north to south across the island mirrored that of humans, as the species is regularly associated with settlements.

TRUE CIVETS

Family Viverridae

Restricted to the Old World, the Viverridae is one of the most diverse carnivore families and includes the civets, genets, linsangs and their allies.

Subfamily Viverrinae

A subfamily containing seven genera and 19 species, of true civets, linsangs and genets. They are distributed throughout Africa and Asia. *Viverricula* is a monotypic genus whose single representative is spread widely through southern Asia. It has also been introduced onto a number of islands.

What influence the Small Indian Civet has on native carnivores is unclear. Where ranges overlap, some competition probably occurs but to what degree is uncertain.

SMALL INDIAN CIVET

Viverricula indica

MEASUREMENTS

Total length: 750–1,060mm. Head/body length: 450–630mm. Tail length: 300–430mm. Weight: 2–4kg. (C40)

DESCRIPTION & IDENTIFICATION

Pelage short and coarse. Upperparts brownish-grey to beige, underparts slightly paler and greyer. Head and rounded face slightly darker with few markings, except dark areas around eyes. Legs and feet very dark brown-grey, sometimes almost black. Forequarters covered in small dark spots, which gradually increase in size towards rear and fuse to form six to eight longitudinal stripes down flanks. Tail has six to nine dark rings, broader than inter-ring spaces.

A medium-sized viverrid with conspicuous body markings.

Small Indian Civet.

Small Indian Civet

Generally larger than all but two of native carnivores, *Cryptoprocta* and *Eupleres*. Confusion between smaller individuals and Fanaloka *Fossa fossana* is possible, but boldly ringed tail of this species should differentiate.

HABITAT & DISTRIBUTION

Originates from Indian subcontinent, Indochina, mainland South-east Asia and islands of Sumatra, Java, Bali, Hainan and Taiwan (C40). Also introduced to Comoros Islands and Socotra in Indian Ocean.

In Madagascar, widely distributed and recorded in most of major habitat types (C24; C27). Does not appear to penetrate dense primary rainforest, more often associated with degraded areas, secondary forests and marsh-land. Regularly found in and around human settlements and agricultural areas including those on high plateau.

BEHAVIOUR

Usually solitary and nocturnal, but may be active during day in areas away from disturbance. Terrestrial, but capable of climbing. Normally sleeps in shallow burrows that it excavates (C45), or in clumps of dense vegetation. In urban areas, frequents disused buildings and drainage ditches (C38).

Diet consists of small verte-brates, including small lemurs (in Ankarafantsika a known predator of *Microcebus* spp.) and larger species like Ring-tailed Lemur (C25), carrion, insects, grubs, fruits, roots and tubers. In rural areas regularly predates domestic poultry and in urban areas often scavenges around refuse tips. Is trapped and killed as a pest.

Males and females probably pair during austral winter when mating occurs. Litter of two to five born between September and December in a burrow or similar safe area on ground.

WHERE TO SEE

Because of association with human settlement may be encountered at night patrolling perimeter of rural villages and field camps or urban fringe areas, especially where there is rubbish. Seen in Berenty Private Reserve, especially between October and December when they scavenge for fallen eggs and chicks beneath colonies of breeding Cattle Egrets.

Giant Jumping Rat, Kirindy Forest.

RATS AND MICE
Order Rodentia

OLD WORLD RATS AND MICE Family Muridae

Madagascar has a rich and diverse rodent fauna, split between two subfamilies within the broadly defined family Muridae (R9; R41).

Native forms all belong to the subfamily Nesomyinae and constitute a remarkable assemblage, which displays a diversity of body forms and lifestyles (R33). Their evolutionary affinities and taxonomy have been contentious as, on the face of it, their only common feature appears to be the cohabitation of Madagascar. However, recent molecular analysis reaffirms that the Malagasy rodents constitute a classic example of adaptive radiation from a single ancestral species (R36).

The second subfamily, Murinae is represented by three introduced species: the Black Rat *Rattus rattus*, Brown Rat *Rattus norvegicus* and House Mouse *Mus musculus*. As in most other parts of the world, these live as human commensals.

MALAGASY RATS AND MICE Subfamily Nesomyinae

The endemic subfamily Nesomyinae currently contains 24 species split between nine genera. There are significant differences between the genera, but also close relationships within them. For an island of its size, Madagascar has fewer rodent species than might be expected (islands slightly larger than Madagascar like Borneo and New Guinea support 55 to 60 species) (R4). There are two possible explanations for this apparent paucity. Either the rodent fauna of Madagascar is relatively impoverished or the inventory is incomplete. While it is certain new species await discovery, it seems unlikely rodent diversity on Madagascar will match islands like Borneo and New Guinea (R33).

Recent surveys (within the past decade) have discovered two new genera – *Monticolomys* and *Voalavo* – (R3; R4) and many new species of rodent, several of which still await formal description. It seems probable further new species will come to light; however, the currently anticipated eventual total is still only 30 to 35 indigenous forms (R33).

The Malagasy rodents are exceptionally diverse in their morphology and ecology: there are great differences in body size, form and behaviour. This striking variety is underlined by the comparisons that have been drawn to their appearance, some of the genera being likened to gerbils (*Macrotarsomys*), voles (*Brachyuromys*), arboreal dormice (*Eliurus*) and even rabbits (*Hypogeomys*). Nevertheless, they do share certain features: all prefer native habitats and the majority appear to be predominantly nocturnal.

The humid forests of the east harbour the greatest diversity with seven genera (*Brachytarsomys, Brachyuromys, Eliurus, Gymnuromys, Monticolomys, Nesomys* and *Voalavo*), while the deciduous forests of the west are home to three genera (*Eliurus, Macrotarsomys* and *Hypogeomys*) and arid spiny forests of the south just two genera (*Macrotarsomys* and *Eliurus*). Further survey work, particularly in the west and the south is sure to reveal new species and perhaps even genera.

GIANT JUMPING RAT genus *Hypogeomys*

A distinctive genus containing a single extant species, *H. antimena*; this is the largest living rodent on Madagascar. A second larger species *H. australis* is known from the subfossil record (R21).

GIANT JUMPING RAT

Hypogeomys antimena

MEASUREMENTS

Total length: 540–585mm. Head/body length: 305–345mm. Tail length: 215–240mm. Weight: 1.1–1.3kg.

DESCRIPTION & IDENTIFICATION

Fur short and dense. Upperparts medium/dark brown to light brown-grey, reddish tinges on some individuals. Head usually darkest area. Underparts paler, creamy-grey or off-white. Sometimes darker V-shaped area on top of nose. Snout blunt and ears highly conspicuous (50–65mm long). Tail muscular, dark and covered in short stiff hairs. No sexual dimorphism. Juveniles have greyer upperparts, paler underparts (R61).

A rotund rabbit-like rodent with conspicuous large ears.

HABITAT & DISTRIBUTION

Historically more widespread, but now restricted to narrow coastal zone of deciduous forest (roughly 20km x 40km) north of Tomitsy River and south of Tsiribihina River (R61). Area characterised by sandy soils and dry leaf-litter (R12). Current range may not exceed 800km².

In good habitat, population densities reach 50 individuals/km², in most areas densities much lower. Populations declining (R14).

BEHAVIOUR

Nocturnal and monogamous, the latter a very rare trait in rodents (R58). Pair bonds last more than one

Giant Jumping Rat.

breeding season and persist outside this, normally until one mate dies or is predated. Predation rates are high, mainly from Fosa *Cryptoprocta ferox* and Madagascar Ground Boa *Acrantophis madagascariensis* (R51; R61). After a death, remaining mate normally develops new pair bond within a few days or weeks (R58). Infanticide does not occur: after taking over new burrow, males tolerate infants sired by previous male (R61).

Moves on all fours or 'kangaroo-like' hops on hindlegs, particularly when nervous (R12; R57; R58). Forages alone or in pairs, on forest floor for fallen fruit, seeds and leaves. Also strips bark from saplings and digs for roots and tubers. Food held in forepaws and manipulated while sitting semi-upright (like a rabbit) (R61).

Births begin at start of rainy season (late November) this corresponds to a reduction in parents' home range. Litter size one or two. Young remain in burrow for first four to six weeks; when first venturing out stay close to entrance.

Female offspring remain with parents for two to three years, then leave to breed; males leave at around one year. Males sometimes establish a territory and mate within a short period, but normally this takes two years (R60).

Family unit occupies territory of 3–4ha (larger in dry season when food is scarce). Specific latrine sites important in demarcating territorial boundaries (R61). Home ranges of neighbouring pairs are mutually exclusive.

Family burrow situated on slightly elevated area of bare soil. Adults and offspring spend the day within. Burrow is complex of tunnels (around 45cm diameter) up to 5m across that has between one and seven entrance holes; only one to three in use at one time, others blocked by soil and leaves. Entrances in use are 'plugged' with barrier of soil, at depth of around 50cm, that must be excavated to allow passage in and out (R57).

Burrows provide protection against predators and the elements (heat and heavy rain). At night,

individuals, including recently independent males, use unoccupied burrows as temporary refuges. After death of a resident, new immigrants readily occupy empty burrows (R59).

Giant Jumping Rat

WHERE TO SEE
Kirindy Forest, 60km north-east of Morondava. Animals can readily be encountered in some areas of main trail network, but it may require persistent searching over two or three nights. Jumping Rats probably more active on moonless nights.

RED FOREST RATS genus *Nesomys*

Nesomys contains three species of medium-sized, diurnal, terrestrial forest-dwelling rats. All are chestnut-brown or reddish-brown in colour. Diurnal rodents are rare in tropical forests: such behaviour patterns probably developed in *Nesomys* because of reduced predator pressure in Malagasy forests (compared with other tropical forests). Diurnal activity may also reduce competition with other Nesomyine species that are all nocturnal.

EASTERN RED FOREST RAT

Nesomys rufus

MEASUREMENTS
Total length: 310–370mm. Head/body length: 170–190mm. Tail length: 140–180mm. Weight: 125–205g; female average 150g; male average 175g. (R54).

DESCRIPTION & IDENTIFICATION
Pelage longish, soft and smooth. Upperparts reddish-brown, flecked with darker brown and darker guard hairs. Around cheeks, flanks and rump may be hint of reddish-chestnut. Underparts slightly paler rufous-brown; chin and throat may be whitish. Ears prominent (20–25mm) and rounded, whiskers fine and black.

Tail medium-long (90% of head/body length), narrow, moderately covered in hair, sometimes white at the tip, but no suggestion of a terminal tuft.

A medium-sized, robust forest rat, bearing resemblance to Brown Rat *Rattus norvegicus*, but appreciably smaller and reddish in colour.

HABITAT & DISTRIBUTION
Found throughout middle and high-

Eastern Red Forest Rat, Andasibe-Mantadia National Park.

altitude (800–2,300m) rainforest regions from mountains around Andapa Basin, south to Andohahela region (R18; R19; R5). *Nesomys* also known from Tsarantanana Massif and Sambirano region (Manongarivo), assumed to be *N. rufus* (R22).

Near Anjozorobe, in central-east, has been recorded outside forest in agricultural areas where it feeds on crops (R54).

BEHAVIOUR

Strictly terrestrial and diurnal. Activity begins prior to sunrise, males often becoming active before females (R53). Foraging is more intense in early morning and late afternoon and to lesser extent around midday. Average daily distance travelled around 400m. Forages in dense vegetation, leaf-litter and around dead logs. Diet mainly seeds and fallen fruits. Adept scavenger around

research camps and associated rubbish pits (R18).

Males and females occupy home ranges around 0.5ha (male range generally slightly larger), which appear constant year to year (R53). Home ranges non-exclusive and may be shared with several other individuals. Considerable overlap between ranges of males and females and between neighbouring individuals of same sex.

Home range contains a number of dispersed burrows or dens, all in regular use, although one is often preferred. Burrows generally located under fallen logs and brush piles; each has several entrances (R53). They are multi-chambered: upper chambers lined with freshly clipped grass and used as food storage caches, deeper chambers lined with deep beds of shredded palm fronds or similar and used for sleeping (R53). Occasionally

males and females share a den.

Little known about reproduction. In higher altitude areas, reported to be reproductively active mid-October to December (R18; R19; R31). At lower elevations reproductive activity observed between July and early

Eastern Red Forest Rat

September (R53). Litter size probably one or two.

Predated especially by Ring-tailed Mongoose *Galidia elegans*, also Fosa *Cryptoprocta ferox* and diurnal raptors (R54).

WHERE TO SEE

Encountered in many eastern rainforest parks. Often seen in Ranomafana National Park, particularly in late April or early May when fallen Chinese Guava are plentiful on forest floor. Andasibe-Mantadia and Marojejy National Parks also good places.

LOWLAND RED FOREST RAT

Nesomys audeberti

MEASUREMENTS

Total length: 350–410mm. Head/ body length: 180–205mm. Tail length: 170–205mm. Weight: 155–250g; females average 210g; males average 225g. (R54).

DESCRIPTION & IDENTIFICATION

Very similar to *N. rufus*, but generally larger. Upper pelage reddish-brown flecked with darker guard hairs. Throat, chest and belly are paler, often off-white. Tail has a white tuft at tip (R54).

Large robust forest rat, broadly similar to Brown Rat *Rattus norvegicus*, but obviously reddish in colour with distinctive white underparts.

HABITAT & DISTRIBUTION

Prefers elevations below 800m in eastern-lowland rainforests, from Masoala Peninsula in north to around Manantantly, near Tolagnaro in south (R10; R31). Distribution appears patchy (R54). Recorded at elevations up to 1,000m; sympatric with *N. rufus* at some localities between 800m and 1,000m, e.g., Ranomafana (R54).

BEHAVIOUR

Terrestrial, foraging on forest floor for seeds and fallen fruits, but also capable of climbing amongst fallen logs. Night spent in multi-chambered burrow, located under tangle of roots, a fallen log or similar. Burrows similar to *N. rufus*: multi-chambered with several entrances, deeper chambers used for sleeping.

Activity begins around sunrise and continues through the morning. Declines after midday and rats return to burrow before dark. Male home ranges up to 1.4ha and appear more active than females, whose home ranges are smaller, around 0.5ha (R54). Home ranges are non-exclusive. Daily travel no more than 400–500m (R54).

Reproductive activity recorded

Lowland Red Forest Rat

during July and August. Litter size of one or two suspected.

WHERE TO SEE

Can be encountered at lower elevations in Ranomafana National Park, where it is sympatric with *N. rufus*. Forests at Lohatrozona and Tampolo on Masoala Peninsula are also likely places.

WESTERN RED FOREST RAT

Nesomys lambertoni

MEASUREMENTS*

Total length: 380–400mm. Head/body length: 200–210mm. Tail length: 180–190mm. Weight: 220–245g. *Based on two specimens (R25).

DESCRIPTION & IDENTIFICATION

Known from only a handful of specimens and a few recent observations in wild (R25). Similar appearance to *N. rufus*, but dorsal pelage is darker reddish-brown, underparts are paler, with obvious orange tinge. Tail long and conspicuously hairy with very obvious tuft at tip.

HABITAT & DISTRIBUTION

Known only from deciduous forest areas south of Antsalova in Tsingy de Bemaraha National Park.

Lowland Red Forest Rat, Ranomafana National Park.

Western Red Forest Rat, Tsingy de Bemaraha National Park.

BEHAVIOUR

Largely unknown. Observed foraging on forest floor amongst leaf-litter between limestone karst formations in Bemaraha. Also seen climbing over the smaller rocky formations and eating seeds.

WHERE TO SEE

A very difficult species to see. Occasionally seen in forests at southern end of Bemaraha National Park, near village of Bekopaka.

• confirmed locality

Western Red Forest Rat

TUFT-TAILED RATS genus *Eliurus*

The Tuft-tailed Rats are Madagascar's most diverse group of rodents (R2). On pristine Madagascar, the genus was probably ubiquitous and today *Eliurus* are found wherever there are significant patches of primary forest (R33). Population densities are highest in pristine forests and some species are able to tolerate minor forest degrada-tion. However, *Eliurus* soon disappear when disturbance becomes substantial (R15).

Tuft-tailed Rat.

Tuft-tailed Rats are strictly nocturnal, small to medium in body size and share various distinctive morphological features associated with a scansorial (climbing) way of life; most noticeable are broad hindfeet and a long tail. In all species the tail length exceeds the head/body length (about 115–130%). The tail is sparsely haired over its proximal portion and ends in a conspicuous terminal tuft or pencil that covers the distal half to quarter of the tail (R2).

In all species the pelage is soft and fine, consisting of a thick coat of cover hairs, inter-spersed with longer, darker, coarse guard hairs. The dorsal pelage is usually longer and denser than the ventral pelage. Overall, upperparts appear a shade of brown to brownish-grey, while underparts are generally creamy-grey to buff. The transition between the two is quite abrupt. In two species (*E. majori* and *E. penicillatus*), this is not always so and dorsal and ventral fur may be similar shades with no pronounced lateral line. Dark hairs around the eye often give the impression of an eye-ring, and facial vibrissae are well developed. The sexes are similar in size.

Tuft-tailed Rats are adept climbers and are routinely found well above the ground amongst lianas, branches and vines. However, they are also seen much lower down amongst boulders, tree buttresses, fallen logs, tangled roots and even leaf-litter.

At present ten species are recognised (although new species await description): eight species from eastern rainforest regions and two (*E. myoxinus* and *E. antsingy*) from the dry forests and scrub of the west and south (R11, R2). External differences between species are principally in size, relative tail length, colour and texture of the fur, and the colour, extent and characteristics of the tail tuft.

Birds of prey and mammalian carnivores prey heavily upon Tuft-tailed Rats. In some areas they constitute around 60% of the diet of some owls (R28; R26). The remains of *Eliurus* have also been found in the scats of the Fosa *Cryptoprocta ferox* (R30).

The nocturnal and arboreal habits of the Tuft-tailed Rats make them a difficult group to observe in the wild. However, they may sometimes be seen climbing in vegetation on night walks in places like Andasibe-Mantadia, Ranomafana, Marojejy, Masoala and Ampijoroa. The majority of records are from specimens caught in traps placed in the lower branches of the forest understorey.

GRANDIDIER'S TUFT-TAILED RAT

Eliurus grandidieri

MEASUREMENTS
Total length: 255–350mm. Head/body length: 110–165mm. Tail length: 145–185mm. Weight: 40–60g. (R2)

DESCRIPTION & IDENTIFICATION
Medium-sized. Dorsal pelage sleek, fine in texture and sooty-brown to charcoal-grey. Underparts medium to dark grey: distinct but not contrasting with upperparts. Tail relatively long (130% of head/body length), tuft is not well developed and extends only over final 30% of tail. Tuft composed principally of white hairs, making it distinctive.

possible range
confirmed locality

Grandidier's Tuft-tailed Rat

Grandidier's Tuft-tailed Rat tail.

HABITAT & DISTRIBUTION
Known from dispersed localities in middle and upper montane forests (1,250–1,875m) of eastern central highlands. Particularly abundant at lower levels within elevational range (R5; R19). Also found as low as 410m in some localities. Southerly limit appears to be Tsinjoarivo area, northerly limits are forest around the Andapa Basin (Anjanaharibe-Sud and Marojejy). Occurs sympatrically with *E. majori*, *E. minor* and *E. tanala* (R2).

BEHAVIOUR
Probably least scansorial *Eliurus*; climbs infrequently. Prefers environs on forest floor, around tree roots, fallen logs and rocks. Frequently trapped in front of hollows and tunnels, suggesting it may occupy burrows (R5).

Evidence from Anjanaharibe-Sud and Marojejy suggest reproduction is between October and November. Litter size two or three (R5; R19).

MAJOR'S TUFT-TAILED RAT

Eliurus majori

MEASUREMENTS
Total length: 315–375mm. Head/body length: 145–170mm. Tail length: 170–205mm. Weight: 75–125g. (R2)

DESCRIPTION & IDENTIFICATION
Probably largest-bodied *Eliurus* (along with *E. tanala*). Pelage soft, dense and woolly. Upperparts and underparts sombre slate-grey to blackish-brown, with little or no contrast between them. Occasionally, underparts are slightly paler. Distinct dark eye-ring. Tail relatively short (approximately 115% head/body length) and pencillate. Tuft less developed than in congeners – simply gradual increase in length and density of dark hairs towards tail tip.

Dark coat, uniform coloration and less developed tail tuft should prevent confusion with all congeners, except perhaps *E. penicillatus*. Pelage colour and morphology of *E. majori* and *E. penicillatus* are remarkably similar but latter species has characteristic white tail tip.

Major's Tuft-tailed Rat tail.

HABITAT & DISTRIBUTION
Restricted to montane forest and

possible range
confirmed locality

Major's Tuft-tailed Rat

upland sclerophyllous vegetation (mossy forest) (R2). Recorded at elevations between 1,000 and 2,000m. Distribution unlikely to be continuous, but recorded from montane locations stretching extent of eastern highland ranges, from Montagne d'Ambre in north to Andohahela in south, including Anjanaharibe-Sud, Marojejy, Ambohimitambo and Andringitra (R52; R18, IR19; R31; R3).

Sympatric with *E. grandidieri, E. minor* and *E. tanala*, plus single record of sympatry with *E. webbi* from Montagne d'Ambre (R2).

BEHAVIOUR
Principally arboreal, with occasional forays to ground level. At middle elevations (1,210m) most specimens are caught in vines, lianas or tangled lower branches. At higher altitudes (1,625m), most animals still captured above ground, but some caught on forest floor (R18, R19; R31).

Breeding and births probably occur between October and December. Litter size three or four.

WHITE-TIPPED TUFT-TAILED RAT
Eliurus penicillatus

MEASUREMENTS
Total length: c. 325mm. Head/body length: c. 150mm. Tail length: c. 175mm. Weight: c. 100g. (R10)

DESCRIPTION & IDENTIFICATION
Size, proportions and coloration very similar to *E. majori*. Dorsal pelage often more brownish than greyish. Tail tuft slightly more developed and has a conspicuous white tip covering final third of tuft.

White-tipped Tuft-tailed Rat tail.

- confirmed locality

White-tipped Tuft-tailed Rat

HABITAT & DISTRIBUTION
Known only from type locality – montane rainforest in vicinity of Ambositra (Ampitambe forest). Specimen collected at elevation of 900m (R10). Sympatric with *E. minor*.

BEHAVIOUR
Unknown.

TANALA TUFT-TAILED RAT
Eliurus tanala

MEASUREMENTS
Total length: 290–355mm. Head/body length: 140–160mm. Tail length: 150–195mm. Weight: 65–100g. (R2)

DESCRIPTION & IDENTIFICATION
Distinctive; along with *E. majori*, probably largest member of genus. Upperparts dark greyish-brown, flanks slightly paler. Back noticeably darker in some individuals. Underparts light buffy-grey, creamy-grey in some individuals. Feet also white or pale grey. Tail relatively long (120–130% head/body length); pencil thin and relatively short, covering final third of tail. Terminal tuft bushy, white and conspicuous. This differentiates this

species from similar sized *E. majori* and *E. webbi*.

Tanala Tuft-tailed Rat tail.

HABITAT & DISTRIBUTION
Prefers rainforest at middle elevations (775–1,000m) (R2), but recorded up to 1,625m. Range extends full length of eastern highlands from Anjanaharibe-Sud and Marojejy in north to Andohahela in south (R18; R19; R31; R5).

▦ possible range
- confirmed locality

Tanala Tuft-tailed Rat

BEHAVIOUR
Utilises a variety of microhabitats including grassy glades, herbaceous growth, tangles of vines along watercourses, stands of tree ferns and bamboo thickets. Collected in lower branches, lianas and vines (suggesting partially scansorial), but also at ground level, particularly at higher elevations (R18; R19: R31; R5).

Breeding noted in November and December. Litter size two to four.

ELLERMAN'S TUFT-TAILED RAT
Eliurus ellermani

MEASUREMENTS
Total length: around 330mm**.

- ▥ possible range
- • confirmed locality

Ellerman's Tuft-tailed Rat

Head/body length: 152mm**. Tail length: 177mm**. Weight: c. 100g*. *Estimated measurement **Measurements taken from a single specimen.

DESCRIPTION & IDENTIFICATION

Moderately large. Upperparts drab dark grey-brown, underparts dull creamy-buff. Pelage longish and relatively coarse. Noticeably dark eye-ring and upper incisors are bright orange. Tail moderately long (115% head/body length) and tail tuft extends over final third. Tuft is well developed (hairs 9–11mm long) and dark all the way to tip. Resembles robust version of *E. tanala*, except tail is completely dark to the tip.

Ellerman's Tuft-tailed Rat tail.

HABITAT & DISTRIBUTION

Known only from two localities, suggesting it occurs in lowland and mid-altitude rainforest (400–850m) in north-east (R1). Type specimen collected around 40km north-west of Maroantsetra. Other record from vicinity of Lohariandava in central-east. Probably sympatric with *E. minor* and *E. webbi*.

BEHAVIOUR

Unknown.

LESSER TUFT-TAILED RAT

Eliurus minor

MEASUREMENTS

Total length: 220–265mm. Head/body length: 100–125mm. Tail length: 120–140mm. Weight: 20–50g. (R2)

DESCRIPTION & IDENTIFICATION

Upperparts light greyish-brown to rich cinnamon-brown. Underparts grey to darkish grey, but paler than upperparts: transition is abrupt. Tail tuft dark brown to blackish and well developed, covering 60% of tail length, increasing in density at tip. Easily recognisable by small size (smallest *Eliurus*), longish tail (120% head/body length) and well-developed dark tail tuft.

Malagasy Mountain Mouse *Monticolomys koopmani* similar in size: *E. minor* distinguished by heavier build, shorter tail and conspicuous tail tuft.

There is considerable variation within the taxon and *E. minor* may be differentiated into subspecies or even species (R2).

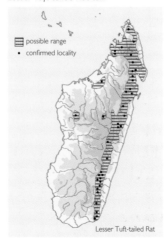

Lesser Tuft-tailed Rat tail.

- ▥ possible range
- • confirmed locality

Lesser Tuft-tailed Rat

HABITAT & DISTRIBUTION

Most extensive range within *Eliurus*, covering entire eastern rainforest belt, from Montagne d'Ambre in north to Anosyenne Mountains in south (R2). Most ecologically versatile *Eliurus* with greatest altitude tolerance of any Nesomyine rodent; recorded from sea level to around 1,875m, but middle elevations preferred. Sympatric with all congeners except *E. petteri* (from east) and *E. myoxinus* and *E. antsingy* (from west and south) (R18; R19; R31; R5).

BEHAVIOUR

Utilises wide variety of terrestrial and arboreal microhabitats. Forages at ground level and amongst vines and lianas in understorey. Observed climbing to several metres (R18; R19; R31; R5).

Probably breeds in November and December. Litter two to four.

WEBB'S TUFT-TAILED RAT

Eliurus webbi

MEASUREMENTS

Total length: 255–345mm. Head/body length: 105–160mm. Tail length: 150–185mm. Weight: 55–90g. (R2)

DESCRIPTION & IDENTIFICATION

Moderately large but lighter build than other large congeners, *E. majori* and *E. tanala*. Pelage soft and quite long, particularly over dorsal region and flanks. Upperparts buffy-brown to grey-brown, underparts dull yellowish-grey; transition is abrupt. Regional variation in ventral pelage colour exists. Tail relatively long (120–130% head/body length); tuft entirely dark brown to blackish-brown, well-developed (hairs 10–12mm long) covering distal two-fifths of tail.

Tuft-tailed Rat, possibly Eliurus webbi, *Andasibe-Mantadia National Park.*

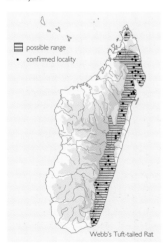

Webb's Tuft-tailed Rat tail.

HABITAT & DISTRIBUTION

Found mainly in undisturbed lowland rainforest, including stands of littoral forest along portions of the east coast (R2). Occurs from Montagne d'Ambre in north to Tolagnaro region on south-east coast. Majority of localities between sea level and 850m. Exceptional records from Andringitra Massif at 1,500m (R18; R19; R31; R5).

Between 700m and 900m sympatric with *E. minor, E. tanala* and *E. majori.*

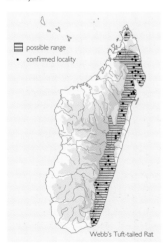

Webb's Tuft-tailed Rat

BEHAVIOUR

Primarily scansorial (R2); observed and trapped in lianas and lower branches. Evidence suggests may live in monogamous pairs occupying ground burrows up to one metre in depth. Inhabit chamber at rear of burrow also used to store seeds (*Cryptocarya* [Lauraceae] have been recorded). When exiting clogs entrance with soil and leaf-litter (R16). Probably nests and forages at different levels in forest.

Recorded sharing same burrow system as nesting Scaly Ground-roller *Brachypteracias squamiger* (R16); ground-roller nest located in principal tunnel of burrow system, while rats' food cache was at rear, so rats had to climb over birds' nest when entering and exiting.

Time of breeding may vary across the range (R18; R19; R31; R5). Litter two to three.

PETTER'S TUFT-TAILED RAT

Eliurus petteri

MEASUREMENTS

Total length: 305–320mm. Head/body length: 130–135mm. Tail length: 175–185mm. Weight: *c.* 75g. (R2)

DESCRIPTION & IDENTIFICATION

Moderately sized with very long tail. Pelage longish, soft with sleek appearance. Upperparts dark grey-brown, may vary from charcoal-grey to paler grey-brown. Underparts conspicuous bright white (distinguishes from all congeners). Distinct line between dorsal and ventral coloration. Tail tuft weakly developed, covers final quarter of tail. Tuft hairs light brown or greyish-brown and relatively short (8–10mm). Longest tail in *Eliurus* – around 135% head/body length.

Petter's Tuft-tailed Rat tail.

HABITAT & DISTRIBUTION

Known only from few localities in lowland forests in central east, between 450m and 640m. Suggests restricted distribution, but lack of information means full extent cannot be determined (R1). Probably sympatric with *E. minor, E. tanala* and *E. webbi.*

BEHAVIOUR

Unknown.

Petter's Tuft-tailed Rat

Western Tuft-tailed Rat.

WESTERN TUFT-TAILED RAT

Eliurus myoxinus

MEASUREMENTS

Total length: 240–205mm. Head/body length: 115–135mm. Tail length: 125–170mm. Weight: 50–75g. (R2).

DESCRIPTION & IDENTIFICATION

Upperparts light sandy-brown, underparts pale grey to creamy-grey. Tail relatively short (105–110% head/body length), proximal third scaled, distal part covered in brown hair (12–15mm long), forming thick dark brush. Head stocky and squarish, upper incisors distinctive deep orange.

Currently only known *Eliurus* with broad range in drier forests of west and south.

Western Tuft-tailed Rat tail.

HABITAT & DISTRIBUTION

Found in western deciduous forests and south-western and southern spiny forests, from Ankarafantsika in north-west to Tolagnaro region in south-east. More common in deciduous forests than spiny forests

Western Tuft-tailed Rat

(R2). Also found in forest regenerating after fire (R50). Recorded from sea level to 1,250m.

BEHAVIOUR
Totally arboreal, rarely, if ever, descending to ground level (R2). Nests in tree holes. In Andohahela National Park feeds on fruits of locally endemic Three-cornered Palm *Dypsis decaryi* (R2). Gestation period 24 days, litter size one to three.

WHERE TO SEE
Night walks at Ampijoroa and Kirindy offer best chance. Often seen running along branches at all levels in canopy.

TSINGY TUFT-TAILED RAT
Eliurus antsingy

MEASUREMENTS
Total length: 300+mm. Head/body length: 150+mm. Tail length: 150-169mm. Weight: no figures available (R11)

DESCRIPTION & IDENTIFICATION
Recently described. Characterised by large size. Pelage soft and fine. Upperparts drab brown to blackish-grey, underparts medium grey. Tail tuft well developed, covering distal 40-50% (longest hairs 12mm). Tuft noticeably dark towards tip. Head large and domed. Hindfeet broad (R11).

Distinguished from *E. myoxinus*

Tuft-tailed Rat, possibly Eliurus antsingy, *Tsingy de Bemaraha National Park.*

by drab, rather than pale brown, coloration and less well-developed tail tuft.

Tsingy Tuft-tailed Rat tail.

HABITAT & DISTRIBUTION
Known only from deciduous forests associated with limestone karst (*tsingy* in Malagasy) formations in Bemaraha and possibly Namoroka in west (R11).

BEHAVIOUR
Unknown.

• confirmed locality

Tsingy Tuft-tailed Rat

VOALAVO genus *Voalavo*
A recently described genus (R4) currently containing a single species, *V. gymnocaudus*. Characterised by its diminutive size (the smallest endemic rodent from rainforest regions) and very long tail (R36). It appears to occupy a similar niche to the genus *Monticolomys*, although as far as is known from current information, the ranges of these two genera do not overlap.

VOALAVO

Voalavo gymnocaudus

MEASUREMENTS
Total length: 210–215mm. Head/
body length: 85–90mm. Tail length:
125mm. Weight: 20–25g.

DESCRIPTION & IDENTIFICATION
Fur soft, short and dense. Upperparts
smokey grey with brownish tinges on
flanks. Underparts from throat also
grey but slightly paler than upperparts
with no sharp contrast. Whitish-grey
beneath chin and throat. Vibrissae
medium-long and white. Ears short
and rounded. Tail long (135% of head/
body), mainly dark and virtually naked,
except for final third that is much

· confirmed locality

Voalavo

paler and finely haired but not tufted.
Closely resembles small *Eliurus*
species, but is darker grey in colour

and lacks discernible tail tuft.

HABITAT & DISTRIBUTION
Known only from montane and dwarf
upper-montane/sclerophyllous forest
areas around Andapa Basin, specifically Anjanaharibe-Sud and Marojejy
(R19; R5). Habitat is typified by lush
epiphytic growth with profuse moss
coverage and regular drenching cloud
cover. Trapped at elevations between
1,260m and 1,950m, appears more
abundant higher up.

BEHAVIOUR
Primarily terrestrial but can climb.
Prefers environs close to ground level
with dense tangles of roots. Uses
natural tunnels and runways between
roots. Also trapped on branches
1.5m above ground (R19; R5).

VOALAVOANALA genus *Gymnuromys*

A distinctive monotypic genus. Since its discovery and description in 1896, *Gymnuromys roberti* has remained mysterious
with virtually nothing known of its behaviour and ecology. Surveys carried out during the past decade have begun to
shed light on the species' distribution and natural history (R7).

VOALAVOANALA

Gymnuromys roberti

MEASUREMENTS
Total length: 325–370mm. Head/
body length: 149–175mm. Tail
length: 176–197mm. Weight:
100–155g, average 120–140g. (R7)

DESCRIPTION & IDENTIFICATION
Medium-sized typical rat-like rodent
with stout body and relatively long
tail (around 110–115% head/body).
Pelage short and sleek: upperparts
dark grey to slate-grey, underparts
grey-white with silvery sheen. Ears
oval and protrude. Vibrissae dark and
long (50–60mm). Tail sparsely haired
and bicoloured – dark grey on top
and pale grey to white underneath;
final 25–30% often completely white.
There is no terminal tuft (R7).

Superficially resembles young

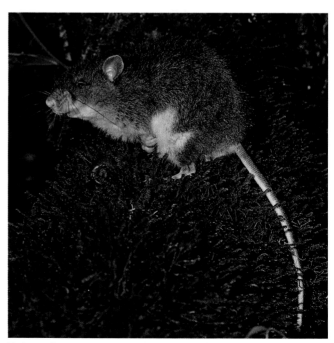

Voalavoanala.

Rattus rattus and possibly some members of *Eliurus*, particularly *E. majori*. Fur of *E. majori* is woollier and tail appreciably longer (120+% head/body) ending in bushy tuft (R7).

HABITAT & DISTRIBUTION

Known from lowland and montane forest locations ranging the length of eastern flank of central highlands, from Anjanaharibe-Sud and Marojejy in north (R10; R62; R19; R5) to Anosyenne Mountains in south (R31). Majority of sites between 900m and 1,625m. Some records from lower altitudes in lowland rainforest: 720m in Andringitra National Park (R18) and 500m on foothills west of Vondrozo (R49).

Never recorded outside native forests but some records from non-pristine environments (R7).

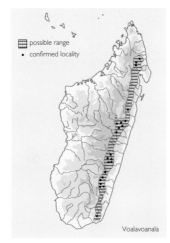

possible range
• confirmed locality

Voalavoanala

BEHAVIOUR

Exclusively terrestrial and nocturnal. Probably forages for fallen seeds and fruits in leaf-litter, amongst roots,

trunks and fallen logs (R7). Lives in burrows up to one metre deep, often under fallen logs. Tunnel relatively straight and ends in small chamber used for food storage: one chamber examined contained 22 Canarium fruits, 21 of which were gnawed open and cotyledons eaten (R7).

Breeding biology largely unknown; males suspected of being reproductively active between October and December (R7). Litter sizes are small. Probably suffers increasing competition from intro-duced *Rattus* species.

WHERE TO SEE

Nocturnal habits make observation difficult: a chance of sightings on night walks in Marojejy, Andasibe-Mantadia and Ranomafana National Parks.

MALAGASY TREE RATS OR WHITE-TAILED TREE RATS genus *Brachytarsomys*

A genus containing two species of large nocturnal arboreal rats exhibiting a number of traits betraying their scansorial habits – most notably a long flexible tail for counterbalance, and exceptionally short but broad feet with narrow sharp claws. Both species have thick, soft woolly fur. The upperparts are brownish-grey to dark grey and the underparts are grey-white to almost pure white. The tail is obviously longer than the head/body and is distinctive in that the distal portion is white. The ears are round and relatively tiny, hardly protruding above the surrounding fur (R6).

The two species are distinguished mainly by size, *B. villosa* being substantially larger, but also by the colour and shade of the upperparts and more subtle tail characteristics.

During the day, holes and hollows in standing trees (usually within 2.5m of the ground) are used for sleeping. They are thought to feed mainly on fruit. Because of their nocturnal and arboreal habits, the Malagasy Tree Rats are not commonly encountered in the wild (R6).

WHITE-TAILED TREE RAT

Brachytarsomys albicauda

MEASUREMENTS

Total length: 410–500mm. Head/body length: 200–240mm. Tail length: 210–260mm. Weight: 175–285g, average 200–220g. (R6)

DESCRIPTION & IDENTIFICATION

Upperparts greyish-brown, more rufous on flanks, underparts and feet off-white. Head more tawny to buffy brown. Tail appears naked and scaly (but covered in short fine hairs); dark towards base but white over most of length. Snout quite short, giving head rather blunt appearance. There are five rows of longish dark whiskers.

Eyes largish and sometimes bulbous. Claws prominent and hindfoot has extra-long fifth digit (R6).

Typical 'rat-like' appearance, similar to *Nesomys* but with shorter snout, very pale underparts and exclusively arboreal habits (whereas *Nesomys* is terrestrial). Distinguished from *B. villosa* by smaller size, more rufous-brown upperparts and hair-less tail (R6).

White-tailed Tree Rat.

HABITAT & DISTRIBUTION

Broadly distributed in lowland and mid-altitude montane rainforest, from Marojejy and Anjanaharibe-Sud Massifs south to vicinity of Andringitra Massif (R10; R19; R32). Circumstantial evidence suggests this extends south to Andohahela (R31). Recorded only patchily at localities ranging from 455m to 1,600m in elevation (R6).

BEHAVIOUR

Nocturnal and probably totally arboreal, making nest in tree holes up to 2.5m above ground (R6). Tree holes close to dense tangles of lianas and vines allowing easy access to canopy preferred. If disturbed may appear at hole entrance and chatter. Diet mainly various canopy fruits and perhaps seeds. Litters of six produced in captivity (R6).

WHERE TO SEE

Very rarely seen, although widely distributed and probably present in most rainforest reserves within its range.

DESCRIPTION & IDENTIFICATION

Upperparts, including head, dark charcoal-grey contrasting noticeably with pale cream to white underparts. Long tail very distinctive – bushy and densely covered in soft hairs of uniform length (6–8mm). Hairs very dark over proximal half and white over distal half (R6).

Outwardly similar to *Rattus*. Has

possible range
• confirmed locality

White-tailed Tree Rat

HAIRY-TAILED TREE RAT

Brachytarsomys villosa

MEASUREMENTS

Total length: 490–515mm. Head/body length: 230–245mm. Tail length: 260–270mm. Weight: 235–350g, average 290–300g. (R6)

• confirmed locality

Hairy-tailed Tree Rat

shorter snout, smaller ears and very pale underparts. White tail tip distinctive. Larger than *B. albicauda* and darker grey. Tail also very obviously haired.

HABITAT & DISTRIBUTION
Recently found at two localities on western slope of Anjanaharibe-Sud Massif in mid-altitude montane forest (at 1,200m and 1,600m)

(R32). Previously known only from single specimen from unknown locality.

B. albicauda also trapped in Anjanaharibe-Sud, but only on eastern slopes of massif. Possible dark grey form (*B. villosa*) is restricted to western side of massif and brownish-red variety (*B. albicauda*) lives only on eastern side (R32). More fieldwork is

required to establish geographic limits of these species.

BEHAVIOUR
Nocturnal and arboreal. Probably feeds on fruit. Males in reproductive condition in November (R6). Other behaviour unknown, but probably similar to *B. albicauda*.

SHORT-TAILED RATS OR MALAGASY VOLES genus *Brachyuromys*

Brachyuromys shows remarkable resemblance in body form, particularly small ears and short tail, and ecology to some voles (subfamily Arvicolinae), although they are not closely related. For this reason they are often referred to as Malagasy voles or vole rats.

The head is broad with inconspicuous, small, rounded ears and small eyes; the body is compact. The legs are short with relatively narrow hindfeet. The tail is noticeably shorter than the head/body length – around 50–60%. The pelage is fine, but dense and soft in texture. Dorsally, *Brachyuromys* species are rich reddish-brown or yellowish-brown with a darker undercoat visible beneath. The venter is similarly coloured with no obvious transition. The uniformly dark tail is sparsely haired on the dorsal surface, but has a dense covering on the lower surface (R37).

They inhabit marshy areas or abandoned rice paddies on the edge of native forests or in moist meadows above the tree-line, especially in areas of matted grasses and reeds (R37). Beneath such vegetation they construct networks of runways, the vegetation above often being so dense that no sunlight penetrates. Within these 'tunnel' systems, they appear to be active at all hours, both day and night, feeding predominantly on grass. *Brachyuromys* may also live in the same areas as *Microgale*, *Eliurus* and introduced *Rattus* species.

Brachyuromys may provide one of the few examples in which a native mammal benefits from human-induced habitat alteration. Abandoned rice paddies appear to create ideal habitat. In such areas they may still suffer competition from introduced *Rattus*: during studies in the Ranomafana area, *Brachyuromys* was trapped only in the centre of disused rice fields, whereas *Rattus* dominated the edges (R37).

The fossorial nature of these species makes observations extremely difficult, unless they are trapped.

GREGARIOUS SHORT-TAILED RAT

Brachyuromys ramirohitra

MEASUREMENTS
Total length: 282–293mm. Head/body length: 165–169mm. Tail length: 110–117mm. Weight: 117–129g. (R37)

DESCRIPTION & IDENTIFICATION
Pelage thick and soft. Upperparts reddish-brown with blackish tinges.

Underparts more reddish but no obvious distinction between the two. Snout blunt, head broad and rounded. Tail short and dark. Larger *Brachyuromys* species, differentiated from congener by longer more reddish coat.

HABITAT & DISTRIBUTION
Known from three localities in south-eastern highlands: Ampitambe (the type locality), Amboasary and Andringitra Massif (R10; R18). Also recently recorded on western slopes of Anjanaharibe-Sud (R37).

In southerly localities occurs in

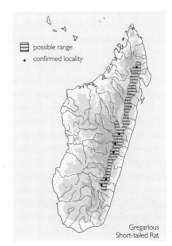

possible range
confirmed locality

Gregarious
Short-tailed Rat

Gregarious Short-tailed Rat.

close proximity to *B. betsileoensis*, although actual zone of sympatry is limited. *B. ramirohitra* prefers montane and sclerophyllous forest between 1,200m and 1,960m (R27), corresponding to a lower elevational zone preferred by its congener (R37).

BEHAVIOUR

In Andringitra, specimens caught on ground close to extensive natural tunnel networks associated with tangled roots (R18).

BETSILEO SHORT-TAILED RAT

Brachyuromys betsileoensis

MEASUREMENTS

Total length: 223–258mm. Head/body length: 140–163mm. Tail length: 83–97mm. Weight: 86–144g. (R37)

DESCRIPTION & IDENTIFICATION

Very similar appearance to *B. ramirohitra*, but noticeably smaller. Dorsal and ventral pelage plain brown and lacks rich reddish tones of its congener. Pelage also shorter and less luxuriant than *B. ramirohitra*.

☰ possible range
• confirmed locality

Betsileo Short-tailed Rat

HABITAT & DISTRIBUTION

Found in grassland, marshes, mossy upper-montane (sclerophyllous) forest above 1,900m and heathland above tree line up to 2,450m. Also survives in open grassland outside forest, where sometimes common (R39). Recorded at several locations in central highlands, from Lac Alaotra area, south to Andringitra Massif (R10; R18; R45).

BEHAVIOUR

Active both day and night; utilises networks of tunnels through the dense matted meadow vegetation. In Ranomafana, reproductive activity during July. Litter size two. Eaten by Fosa *Cryptoprocta ferox*; skeletal remains found in scats in heathland areas at elevations of 2,000m to 2,100m (Andringitra) (R30).

MOUNTAIN MICE genus *Monticolomys*

A recently named monotypic genus characterised by its small size, dense pelage, rounded ears and relatively long tail (R3). Within the Nesomyinae from eastern humid forest regions, only the new genus *Voalavo* is similarly small, although based on current known ranges, these two genera are allopatric and apparently occupy a similar upper montane niche. *Monticolomys* is probably more closely related to the Big-footed Mice *Macrotarsomys* from western Madagascar, than to other species from eastern regions (R38).

MALAGASY MOUNTAIN MOUSE

Monticolomys koopmani

MEASUREMENTS

Total length: 205–240mm. Head/body length: 84–101mm. Tail length: 116–143mm. Weight: 18.5–27.5g. (R3; R29).

DESCRIPTION & IDENTIFICATION

Pelage fine, soft and relatively thick. Upperparts sombre dark brown

with black guard hairs, underparts, including chin and throat, dark grey. Ears short, rounded and densely furred both inside and out. Tail uniformly grey, very long (about 140% of the head/body) and covered in fine brown hairs. No terminal tuft (R3).

Within its range and ecotone, small size and mouse-like appearance of *M. koopmani* should distinguish it from other sympatric rodents. Only *Eliurus minor* is similarly diminutive, but in comparison *M. koopmani* is lighter in build and has a longer tail, which lacks a terminal tuft.

☰ possible range
• confirmed locality

Malagasy Mountain Mouse

HABITAT & DISTRIBUTION

Inhabits upper montane/sclero-phyllous forest regularly covered in cloud and mist: these forests often dominated by dense stands of bamboo and similar species, encrusted with mosses, lichens and epiphytes. Currently known only from three widely dispersed high mountain locations: Ankaratra Massif between 1,800m and 2,000m, Andringitra Massif at 1,625m and Andohahela at 1,875m (R3; R31).

BEHAVIOUR

Probably predominantly terrestrial but also an adept climber and caught on narrow lianas around 2m above ground (R3; R31). Long tail and enlarged claws suggest partially scansorial.

MALAGASY BIG-FOOTED MICE genus *Macrotarsomys*

This genus contains three species of small forest mice, including a species very recently described, *Macrotarsomys petteri* (R23). They are strictly nocturnal and outwardly show resemblance to some African gerbils (Gerbillinae). All have soft, fine textured fur and similarly coloured light brown dorsal and white ventral pelage. *Macrotarsomys* appears to be restricted to the dry deciduous forest areas of western Madagascar and can be quite common and readily observed in some areas.

Western Big-footed Mouse, Kirindy Forest.

WESTERN BIG-FOOTED MOUSE

Macrotarsomys bastardi

MEASUREMENTS

Total length: 185–245mm. Head/ body length: 86–102mm. Tail length: 100–142mm. Weight: 21–38g. (R8)

DESCRIPTION & IDENTIFICATION

Upperparts light brown to fawn with more greyish under fur showing through. Underparts and legs paler cream or yellowish-white. Ears oval in shape and relatively large (20–25mm). Eye also relatively large. Tail moderately long (around 135% head/body), quite stiff with slight dark terminal tuft (R8).

A small gerbil-like rodent with large ears and long tail. Can only be confused with its congener *M. ingens*.

M. b. bastardi
M. b. occidentalis

Western
Big-footed Mouse

are rarely deep and have closed concealed outlets. Reproductive activity peaks in April and May (but probably occurs throughout the year). Litter size two or three, gestation period around 24 days.

Preyed upon by owls (possibly *Asio, Otus* and *Ninox* spp.), and Fosa *Cryptoprocta ferox* (R8).

WHERE TO SEE
Readily seen on night walks in Kirindy Forest near Morondava and Ampijoroa, part of Ankarafantsika National Park.

LONG-TAILED BIG-FOOTED MOUSE
Macrotarsomys ingens

MEASUREMENTS
Total length: 305–390mm. Head/body length: 115–150mm. Tail length: 193–240mm. Weight: 54–73g. (R8)

DESCRIPTION & IDENTIFICATION
Dorsal pelage light sandy brown,

M. bastardi has proportionally shorter tail and is more likely to be seen on ground.

HABITAT & DISTRIBUTION
Found in deciduous forests and arid spiny forests from Ankarafantsika National Park in north-west to southern tip of island and east to foothills of Anosyenne Mountains near Tolagnaro (R10; R31). Two subspecies are proposed: nominate race, *M. b. bastardi* from open savanna and bush areas (750–915m) in central south-west; and *M. b. occidentalis* from Parcel 2 in Andohahela National Park in extreme south to deciduous forests of Ankarafantsika in north-west. Found at elevations from sea level to 915m (R8).

BEHAVIOUR
Strictly nocturnal and largely terrestrial. Moves on forest floor, often in pairs, in typical gerbil-like fashion – a slightly erect posture, hopping with forelimbs off ground and using tail as counterbalance (R8). Hopping becomes more pronounced when covering larger areas of bare ground. Diet consists of seeds, fruits, berries, roots and some plant stems.

Pairs spend day in long burrows (up to 1.5m) excavated under large rocks or tree stumps. These

Long-tailed Big-footed Mouse, Ankarafantsika National Park.

confirmed locality

Long-tailed
Big-footed Mouse

metres above ground (R8). Often pauses and rests in small forks in branches.

Lives in burrows recognisable by small piles of soil thrown up outside entrance (R44). Entrance always kept closed.

Preyed upon by diurnal raptors (possibly *Accipiter* spp.), nocturnal owls (possibly *Asio*, *Otus* and *Ninox* spp.) and Fosa *Cryptoprocta ferox* (R8).

WHERE TO SEE
Ampijoroa within Ankarafantsika National Park is only known site this species can be seen. On night walks it is worth searching narrow branches and tangles of vines; gives faint reflective eye-shine in torch beam.

ventral pelage creamy-white; transition is abrupt. Ears large, oval and obvious. Tail exceptionally long (up to 170% of head/body) and lightly haired. Hairs longer and denser at tail tip forming a modest tuft (not as well developed as *Eliurus*) (R8).

Similar in appearance to *M. bastardi*, but appreciably larger with much longer tail. Extreme length of tail should distinguish from *Eliurus myoxinus* that is also arboreal.

HABITAT & DISTRIBUTION
Currently known only from the deciduous forests of Ankarafantsika and its immediate vicinity in the north-west (R43; R10).

BEHAVIOUR
Nocturnal and probably solitary. Scansorial; rarely observed low down and generally seen amongst narrow branches and vines, often several

confirmed locality

Petter's Big-footed Mouse

PETTER'S BIG-FOOTED MOUSE

Macrotarsomys petteri

MEASUREMENTS*
Total length: 390mm. Head/body length: 150mm. Tail length: 238mm. Weight: 105g. (R23). *Based on single specimen

DESCRIPTION & IDENTIFICATION
Dorsal fur short, soft and dense with agouti appearance. Flanks mid-brown with obvious dark brown dorsal ridge. Underparts buff-white, with sharp transition on lower flank. Tail is long (160% head/body length) and

partially naked; dark over proximal half and off-white distally. Terminal tuft well developed, covering 25% of tail and becomes increasingly bushy towards tip (R23).

Large, stocky *Macrotarsomys* (noticeably larger than congeners) with long hindfeet, short forelimbs, long ears (32mm), long vibrissae (60+mm) and considerable weight.

HABITAT & DISTRIBUTION
Currently known only from Forêt d'Andaladomo within extensive Mikea Forest, south of Lac Ihotry in south-west Madagascar (R23). Area constitutes a unique zone of transition between deciduous forest and xerophytic spiny bush formations (R55).

BEHAVIOUR
Morphology suggests it is terrestrial (R23). Other behaviour unknown.

INTRODUCED SPECIES

Three rodents have been introduced to Madagascar. The Black Rat *Rattus rattus*, Sewer Rat *R. norvegicus* and House Mouse *Mus musculus* have been introduced to most parts of the planet and, with the exception of humans, must be the most widely distributed and prolific mammal species. It is not known when the introductions to Madagascar occurred but maybe initial colonisations happened when the first human colonists arrived around 2,000 years ago (R13). Since then, other waves of introduction may have taken place, and the frequency of these has probably increased in recent times.

OLD WORLD RATS AND MICE Subfamily Murinae

Due to their ability to survive and adapt to change, capacity to reproduce quickly and history of spectacular diversification, this large subfamily is regarded as one of the most successful groups of mammals: the subfamily Murinae is naturally distributed throughout the Old World south of the Arctic Circle (although not in Madagascar) and contains more than 542 species divided between at least 118 genera (R56).

OLD WORLD RATS genus *Rattus*

Rattus is one of the largest mammalian genera, containing over 50 species found throughout the Old World. The two species mentioned here are the most familiar because of their constant association with humans. However, they are not representative of the genus as a whole: most species are more specialised, prefer natural forests, have restricted ranges and often avoid human habitation (R42). All *Rattus* species are omnivorous and eat a wide variety of animal and plant matter. Seeds, grains, nuts, fruits and vegetables are preferred by most species.

The earliest records of *Rattus* in Madagascar are somewhere between the 11th and 14th centuries (R48), although even earlier arrival on Madagascar is suspected. Since then it has spread dramatically throughout the island and penetrates all native habitats, achieving greater densities in eastern humid areas (R13).

There is considerable overlap in the diets of the endemic Nesomyine rodents and *Rattus*, and there is increasing evidence that *Rattus* are displacing the endemic taxa from some native forests through resource competition and also direct predation (R17; R37; R54). An increasing *Rattus* population may also have a devastating effect on endemic birds, particularly ground dwellers and nesters such as mesites (Mesitornithidae) and ground rollers (Brachypteraciidae).

BLACK RAT

Rattus rattus

MEASUREMENTS

Total length: 310–480mm. Head/body length: 150–230mm. Tail length: 160–250mm. Weight: 85–280g.

DESCRIPTION & IDENTIFICATION

Upperparts dark slate-grey (almost black) to dark brown, underparts and throat paler. Pelage appears coarse due to long dark guard hairs. Ears relatively long, pinkish and hairless. Dark eye prominent. Tail long (up to 115%

head/body), thin and lacks hairs.

Immature Black Rats could be confused with any endemic species – particularly *Gymnuromys* and possibly *Nesomys* or the larger members of *Eliurus*.

HABITAT & DISTRIBUTION

Widely distributed throughout

Black Rat.

Madagascar; more common in humid eastern areas, than in west and south. Associated with rural villages, degraded areas and wherever native forests have been replaced by agriculture. Also penetrates deep into pristine native forest areas and throughout elevational zones to over 2,500m, including offshore islands like Nosy Mangabe (R33).

BEHAVIOUR

Predominantly nocturnal. Diet consists mainly of vegetables, fruits, seeds, grains and nuts. Also takes birds' eggs including endemic species. Adept scavenger (R42).

Territorial, defending its entire home range, which is usually small. Two or more females are generally subordinate to dominant male, but are themselves dominant over other group members.

Now widespread in many rain-forest areas and probably a severe competitor to sympatric endemic rodents: broad dietary overlap between Rattus and Nesomyine species, and direct predation may also occur. In some isolated forest patches, native species have been extirpated already, while in other native forests areas Rattus may be the most abundant rodent species. Endemic rodents suffering most

Brown Rat.

directly are Brachyuromys (R37) and Nesomys and Eliurus to a lesser extent. R. rattus is eaten by Fosa Cryptoprocta ferox (R30; R34).

WHERE TO SEE

Often seen in towns and villages around rubbish and where there are rice and grain stores. Also seen around more permanent forest camps.

BROWN RAT

Rattus norvegicus

MEASUREMENTS

Total length: 385–510mm. Head/body length: 215–280mm. Tail length: 170–230mm. Weight: c. 275–520g.

DESCRIPTION & IDENTIFICATION

Dorsal pelage various shades of brindled brown-grey, overall appearance from mid-brown to dark grey. Ventral pelage paler grey, sometimes creamy-white on throat and chest. Ears short, hairy and partially obscured. Tail relatively short (around 80% head/body), thick, hairless and bicoloured – dark on top, pale underneath.

HABITAT & DISTRIBUTION

Most restricted range of introduced rodents; limited mainly to ports and larger towns in central highlands (R13). Also trapped well away from human habitation in some areas, particularly along coast.

Timing of arrival in central highlands unknown, but thought to be relatively recent, perhaps within past 50 years. Colonisation of suitable areas has been dramatic; in Antananarivo accounts for 95% of all rodents trapped (R13).

BEHAVIOUR

Nocturnal, although day-time activity

Black Rat

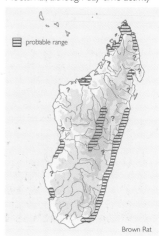

probable range

Brown Rat

is not uncommon. Terrestrial, but also occurs in semi-aquatic environments. Omnivorous, feeding on a variety of seeds, nuts, fruits, invertebrates and smaller vertebrates. Will also eat any foodstuff associated with humans. In native forests may also predate eggs and chicks of native birds.

In urban environments range is small, rarely moving more than 70–80m. In open areas may travel 3–4km per night. Colonies develop from pair or single pregnant female. Very large aggregations the result of several smaller units (clans) coming together (R42).

In native forest areas may compete with endemic Nesomyine species, although current influence less serious than *R. rattus*.

WHERE TO SEE
Can be seen around waste ground, sewers and refuse tips in urban areas.

OLD WORLD MICE genus *Mus*

A large genus containing around 40 species distributed throughout the Old World (R42). Most dwell in natural habitats like forests and savannas and have restricted distributions. The House Mouse *M. musculus* and a few closely related species have spread dramatically in association with humans. The earliest records on Madagascar are from an Islamic port dated between the 11th and 14th centuries (R48) and suggest colonisation via Arabia (R35).

HOUSE MOUSE

Mus musculus

MEASUREMENTS
Total length: 150–200mm. Head/body length: 75–100mm. Tail length: 75–100mm. Weight: 12–20g.

DESCRIPTION & IDENTIFICATION
Upperparts uniform grey-brown, underparts similar but slightly paler.

Ears rounded and relatively small. Eyes small. Tail prominently ringed, moderately long, usually equal to head/body length.

Smaller than all endemic rodents. Found principally in association with humans, rather than in native forests.

HABITAT & DISTRIBUTION
Found throughout the island in association with human habitation from rural villages and agricultural areas to major towns and cities.

BEHAVIOUR
Mainly nocturnal. Omnivorous, with preference for cereals and seeds. Home range size varies with habitat and locality – within farmyards, buildings or similar may be as little as 4m², while field-dwelling populations may be semi-nomadic and cover 1–2km². Lives in territorial family units that become aggressive towards one another at higher densities. Breeding can be prolific, with between five and ten litters per year each containing between four and eight young (R42).

WHERE TO SEE
Often seen in villages, especially where there is grain or cereal.

House Mouse.

House Mouse

NON-ENDEMIC MAMMALS

Unlike many other islands, Madagascar has not (yet) suffered a major intrusion of species, accidentally or intentionally, introduced by humans. Nonetheless, a number of non-endemic mammal species are now established. These include species that live as human commensals, e.g. Black Rat *Rattus rattus*, Sewer Rat *R. norvegicus*, House Mouse *Mus musculus* and Asian Musk Shrew *Suncus murinus*. Others include domestic species like Dogs *Canis lupus*, Cats *Felis silvestris*, Goats *Capra hircus*, Sheep *Ovis aries*, Pigs *Sus scofa* and Zebu Cattle *Bos taurus*, and some are introduced wild animals that have become naturalised. These latter species include ungulates like Fallow Deer *Dama dama*, Rusa or Timor Deer *Cervus timorensis* and the Bush Pig *Potamochoerus larvatus*, plus one carnivore, the Small Indian Civet *Viverricula indica* (NE2).

For details on *Rattus*, *Mus*, *Suncus* and *Viverricula* refer to the respective sections in the Rodent, Insectivore and Carnivore chapters. This is a summary of information relating to the other introduced mammals.

DOMESTIC STOCK

There are no firm records as to when the various species of domestic stock were introduced. The bone remains of all four species, Goats *Capra hircus*, Sheep *Ovis aries*, Pigs *Sus scofa* and Zebu Cattle *Bos taurus*, have been unearthed in village middens at Mahilaka (NE9).

The Malagasy cow or Zebu is an ancestor of an Asian breed (NE11) formerly named *Bos indicus*, although this is now a synonym of the domestic cow *Bos taurus* (NE2).

Feral Zebu live in, and around, native forests in many parts of the island, including within the bounds of protected areas. It is frequent to come across their dung pats on forest trails in parks such as Mantadia, Ranomafana and Masoala, even if the animals themselves are not seen. The impact of these animals on the forest environment and how this affects native species is unclear.

DEER

Between 1928 and 1935 two species of deer were introduced: Fallow Deer *Dama dama* and Rusa or Timor Deer *Cervus timorensis* (NE5). Fallow Deer were first released near the Ankaratra Massif and Rusa Deer were released near Station Forestière d'Analamazaotra (Périnet). Even though there is little forest remaining in Ankaratra and hunting pressure from local communities is high, a small population of Fallow Deer does persist (NE2). Populations of Rusa Deer, on the other hand, perhaps survived into the early 1960s but have since been hunted out completely (NE5).

DOGS AND CATS

The Domestic Dog *Canis lupus* is found in association with humans throughout the island and in places is used to hunt native species such as Common Tenrec *Tenrec ecaudatus* and Greater Hedgehog Tenrec *Setifer setosus*. It is also probable that some live feral on the edge of native forest and prey on some endemic mammals and birds (NE2).

The presence of cats on Madagascar poses fascinating questions. They were introduced in both domestic and 'wild' forms, although when is unclear; remains have been found in subfossil deposits, but these were thought to be recent remains (NE2).

In 1792 a cat was described as '*Fel. Catus madagascariensis*' (NE6), the author noting that, 'this is a beautiful variety, which inhabits the island of Madagascar'. This form is now considered synonymous with the domestic form, *Felis silvestris*.

Feral cats still survive in many forest areas and appear more common in drier western regions (NE2). They resemble wild cats in appearance, and are often distinctly larger than domestic cats. Typically large animals have been trapped in Ankarafantsika in the north-west. What impact these have on the native fauna is unclear, although it seems certain they prey on small mammals and birds. Lemurs such as *Eulemur* and *Propithecus* spp. also perceive them as threats and alarm call vociferously when a cat is seen.

BUSH PIGS

There is conjecture as to how the Bush Pig arrived on the island. There are suggestions the species is native and arrived under its own steam. On mainland Africa, Bush Pig are known to venture frequently into extensive papyrus beds, which may become detached, float downriver and out to sea. In this manner Bush Pigs might have reached Madagascar naturally. Alternatively they may be introduced and have become naturalised.

Introductions may have coincided with the arrival of the first humans around 2,000 years ago, in which case it is supposed Bush Pigs were at least partially domesticated before they reached Madagascar and there is evidence for this in some parts of Africa (NE1).

There are no known remains in subfossil deposits and the earliest known written reference is from the mid-17th century (NE2). The lack of evidence until recent times suggests the species is a relatively recent addition to the Malagasy fauna and that it is introduced. It is nonetheless an important component of the island's biota so is afforded more extensive treatment here.

BUSH PIGS genus *Potamochoerus*

A genus containing two species, Red River Hog *P. porcus* and Bush Pig *P. larvatus*. They are distributed through the equatorial regions of sub-Saharan Africa: Red River Hog being found in West Africa from Senegal to eastern Zaïre and as far south as northern Angola; Bush Pig's range is limited to eastern and south-eastern Africa and Madagascar (NE4).

The Malagasy people generally consider Bush Pigs as harmful animals. The devastation they cause is very apparent in agricultural areas, where they can quickly destroy crops of cassava, sweet potatoes, corn, sugar cane and even rice (NE1).

BUSH PIG

Potamochoerus larvatus

MEASUREMENTS
Head/body length: 900–1,200mm*.
Tail length: 300–400mm*. Shoulder height: 600–800mm*. Weight: females up to 55kg*, males up to 70kg*. (NE7)
*Estimated measurements for Malagasy specimens.

DESCRIPTION & IDENTIFICATION
Hair covering entire body, including head and face, long and bristly but relatively sparse. Distinct dorsal crest from between ears running down length of spine. Snout elongate, ears tufted with extended pinnae. Cheeks of males in particular bushy and beard-like. Males have small tusks, barely visible but used for defence. Coloration variable: generally face and head predominantly grey, extending over nape and part-way down dorsal crest. A darker broad band surrounds muzzle. Upperparts are reddish-brown to greyish-brown and grade to darker grey-brown underparts and limbs.

A medium-sized wild pig with shaggy appearance. The largest free-living mammal on island and cannot be confused with any other species.

HABITAT & DISTRIBUTION
An adaptable species; occurs in all major habitat types from rainforests to dry deciduous forests, spiny forests and even open savanna. Its presence dependent more on water and food availability and less on vegetation cover, so it occurs in many secondary and degraded habitats and cultivated areas, providing hunting levels are not high (NE12; NE1). It reaches highest densities in protected areas with little hunting pressure (NE3). Appears absent from deforested central highlands and the proximity of major urban areas.

Divided into four subspecies: *P. l. larvatus* is described from western Madagascar and the Comoros (despite being introduced); *P. l. hova* is recognised from eastern regions of Madagascar, although some regard this division as questionable; while mainland Africa populations comprise *P. l. hassama* from East Africa as far north as Ethiopia and *P. l. koiropotamus* from northern Tanzania, east to Angola and south to Mozambique. There is also an apparently isolated population of this race on the Cape coast in South Africa (NE4).

Recognition of two races in Madagascar is contentious. Few specimens have been examined, so

P. l. larvatus
P. l. hova

Bush Pig

differentiation may not withstand closer scrutiny. Populations from rainforest regions appear to be larger and greyer, while those from the west are smaller and distinctly reddish.

BEHAVIOUR

Lives in groups of two to ten individuals but four to six is average in Madagascar. Groups contain a dominant male and female, the only reproducers within a group. Predominantly nocturnal, possible tendency towards diurnal activity in remote areas away from human disturbance. Day is spent in self-excavated burrows or similar natural secluded hideaways like large roots systems. Average home ranges are between four and ten square kilometres (NE1).

Births occur between October and December, gestation around 120 days, litter size one to four (NE12). Females construct deep nest of vegetation to protect the piglets, and they are given considerable care and attention not only by sow but also by dominant boar. Dispersal from family group begins around eight months (NE3) and sexual maturity is reached around 20 months.

Omnivorous. Diet varies according to season and food availability, mainly roots, tubers, rhizomes, berries, fallen fruit and some grass, but also animal matter like reptile eggs, small vertebrates, a variety of invertebrates, carrion and excrement (NE1). May take advantage of fruit discarded by lemurs feeding in canopy. When feeding, powerful snout used as a plough to dig up subsoil matter; tusks also used to help dig deeper. This is highly destructive method of feeding, in short periods of time a group can strip an area of most plants; also does considerable damage to crops.

Has been an influential factor contributing to rapid decline of some native tortoise species. For instance, nests of Anogonoka *Geochelone yniphora* (probably world's most endangered tortoise restricted to small area around Soalala in western Madagascar) are regularly predated (both eggs and hatchlings) (NE8). It is likely other endemic reptiles and possibly ground-nesting birds suffer in a similar fashion.

Widely hunted by humans, sometimes with aid of dogs. Smaller individuals also predated by the Fosa *Cryptoprocta ferox* (NE10).

WHERE TO SEE

Widespread and common, but rarely seen due to their shyness and mainly nocturnal habits. Indications of their presence are often seen in forested regions, in form of large excavated areas on forest floor, droppings and hoof prints. Animals occasionally encountered on forest walks at night, but soon disappear when startled.

Bush Pig.

CONSERVATION AND PROTECTED AREAS

Madagascar's unique biodiversity faces numerous and ever-increasing threats, the most immediate being habitat destruction and degradation – sadly factors that affect floral and faunal communities throughout the forests of the world, especially in tropical regions.

In Madagascar habitat destruction is severe. The majority of people live in rural communities that depend heavily on the land and native forests for their livelihood. Methods of traditional subsistence agriculture involve slash-and-burn (*tavy*) cultivation, where forests are felled and then torched to clear the land and subsequently plant crops – mainly rice and manioc, but also coffee, vanilla, cloves and other spices. The soil cannot sustain food crops for more than two or three years; without the protection of the trees above, it is quickly eroded and washed away, especially on slopes, resulting in rivers and streams becoming clogged with silt. Within a short space of time, the cleared land is reduced to a sterile and barren moonscape, so farmers move on to clear more forest, and the sad destructive cycle is reinforced.

Humans are comparative newcomers to Madagascar: they arrived as recently as 1,500 to 2,000 years ago (mainly from South-east Asia, Arabia and later mainland Africa). It is bewildering to contemplate that in the relatively short time that our species has been resident around 90% of the native forest cover has been lost (G20). In the past 50 years alone, there has been a 50% decline in the extent of the eastern rainforests. Perhaps as much as 100,000ha of rainforest are felled each year, an area approximately half the size of the island's largest national park!

Barren deforested hills dominate the Central Plateau.

Spiny forest near Ifaty remains unprotected; large areas are cut and burned annually.

As if the destruction of the forests were not enough, many of Madagascar's mammals (and other species) face a more direct threat from hunting. With an ever-expanding human population there is an increased demand for food, and protein in particular – a demand that the beleaguered agricultural system struggles to meet. In many remaining forest tracts a variety of species are hunted remorselessly for food, or for their skins, to supply the animal trade or even for superstitious reasons, despite being officially protected by law. This particularly affects many of the large lemurs, but also some of the carnivores, larger tenrecs, rodents and fruit bats (G14).

Forest clearance to plant hill rice remains the most significant threat in eastern regions. Near Andasibe-Mantadia National Park.

So what can be done to try to reduce the rate of depletion? In the past the simple creation of a protected area has not been enough. More often than not this has been little more than a line-drawing exercise on a map. The local people have continued to cut wood, clear forests and hunt wildlife within the area, unaware that legislation had been implemented. And even if they were aware, it has made little difference since they have had no alternatives to supplement their livelihood.

In many past instances, in other parts of the world, the human populations living adjacent to protected areas have been regarded as the first line of attack. Exclusion was seen as the answer, leaving the area as a preserve solely for wildlife. However, attempts to exclude local people from these areas have proved futile and disastrous in the long term. When the people's very survival is dependent on utilising the natural environment, no protective force will be sufficient to stop them, and they will find ways to circumvent even the strictest laws. Consequently, there has been a growing realisation amongst the conservationists that the issue needs to be addressed from the opposite perspective: if conservation activities are to succeed in the long run, they must *involve* the local people.

In essence the principles are simple. Conservation needs to be linked to incentives that help improve the standards of living for local people, but in ways that reduce the pressures they place on their local environment to the point where they ultimately become sustainable. In this way the rate of destruction may be slowed and eventually halted. However, if these initiatives are to succeed, they must above all else give the local people both a say and a personal stake in the project. By becoming aware that their very existence is inextricably linked to the quality and integrity of their environment, local people have the strongest possible incentive to help ensure that its conservation is a success. No longer are they considered the first line of attack, but rather the last line of defence.

These ideas are now germane to the conservation efforts in Madagascar. The Malagasy Government, working in conjunction with a number of international conservation organisations and funding agencies, has now implemented numerous projects that integrate the conservation of biodiversity with the development of local communities (Integrated Conservation and Developments Projects). A number of fundamental principles underpin the majority of these projects.

In order to devise sustainable (long-term) economic alternatives to forest clearance it is vital to understand the interrelationships of the fauna and flora within the forest. To this end biodiversity research, involving a wide spectrum of taxonomic groups, focuses on how each species fits into the forest community as a whole and its interdependence on other species. This information can then be integrated with indigenous knowledge from the local communities.

Armed with this knowledge, it is then possible to devise, implement and support sustainable agricultural techniques that are sympathetic to the local environment. For instance, in rainforest areas alternatives such as aquaculture, apiculture and horticulture of important native species have been encouraged, whilst attempting to find ways of maximising production from existing land under rice cultivation (by application of fertilisers, using more suitable seed varieties, and improved irrigation systems). This then reduces the need for the expansion of *tavy* cultivation and hence maintains the integrity of the remaining forests and watershed.

Healthcare is also a vital component. Local communities generally acknowledge this to be their primary concern. It involves improved preventative measures, sanitation and family planning, and wherever possible incorporates both traditional medicines based on forest products (those that can be cultivated or sustainably harvested) as well as modern western techniques. If improved health results in better child survivorship, then there is less incentive to have a large family, eventually leading to a slowing of population growth.

Of course education and training run hand-in-hand with all of these measures. Education and conservation awareness programmes are designed to increase literacy and provide access to educational facilities for local residents. Local people also work closely with both Malagasy and western scientists to gain a better understanding of the precarious nature of their environment: some become full-time researchers and others park officials.

Once all the above are in place, the remaining piece of the jigsaw can be slotted into place – ecotourism. The recreational use of protected areas, by both Malagasy nationals and foreign visitors, creates more jobs for the local people and increases revenue for the community. Local people, who may have once relied for their livelihood on harvesting forest products, are then able to earn a living in connection with the park or reserve. Furthermore, tourists require accommodation and guides, so employment is created in local hotels and other secondary service industries.

This is not to say that ecotourism is a panacea for Madagascar's environmental ills. It is not. There is always a great danger of cultural identity and integrity being lost when simple indigenous communities are exposed to materialistic western cultures. However, if the approach is cautious and the system carefully managed, there is every reason to believe that ecotourism has a vital role to play in the conservation of Madagascar's biological riches.

PARKS AND RESERVES

Madagascar has an extensive network of protected areas, the origins of which date back to 1927 and French colonial administration. For years the system was underfunded, inadequately manned and stagnant, offering only cursory protection against habitat destruction, disturbance and hunting. However, the situation has changed over recent years.

The National Association for Management of Protected Areas (*Association Nationale pour la Gestion des Aires Protégées* – ANGAP) is now responsible for the administration of Madagascar's protected areas, and ANGAP work in conjunction with a number of high-profile international conservation agencies to enhance the management of the island's protected areas network.

Today there are 46 legally protected areas (including 18 National Parks and 23 Special Reserves) that cover an area of just under 1.7 million hectares (G28). However, in 2003 at the 5th World Parks Congress in Durban, South Africa, President Marc Ravalomanana announced his government's intention to triple the extent of the national parks and reserves to six million hectares over the next five years, representing an increase from the current 3% of the country's total area to 10%. This has become known as 'The Durban Vision'.

Because of Madagascar's large size and modest road infrastructure, a large number of these parks and reserves have in the past been difficult to reach without serious logistical back up. This has been a frustrating limitation to the visiting naturalist. However, substantial development has taken place over the past decade with improvements in the transport network. Many of the island's major 'wildlife hotspots' are now within easy, or relatively easy, reach for visitors, and these include areas that were until very recently virtually inaccessible.

All parks and reserves require entry permits, which are issued by the ANGAP and are easily obtainable from their main offices in Antananarivo or from the regional offices close to the protected area in question. Some of the more frequently visited parks and reserves issue tickets at the entrance. It is vital that a ticket be obtained every time an area is visited, as 50% of the money is ploughed back into conservation and local community development around the protected area. In this way the local population becomes aware of the sustainable benefits to be gained by maintaining the integrity of their forest areas.

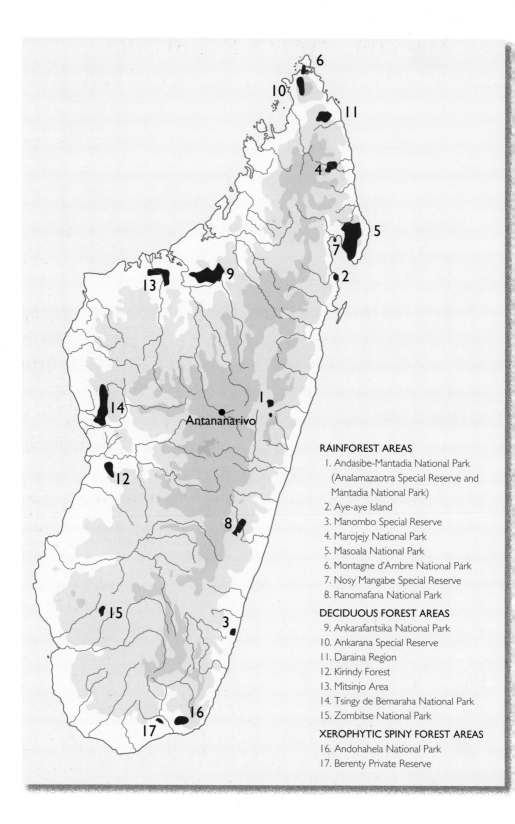

RAINFOREST AREAS

1. Andasibe-Mantadia National Park
   (Analamazaotra Special Reserve and
   Mantadia National Park)
2. Aye-aye Island
3. Manombo Special Reserve
4. Marojejy National Park
5. Masoala National Park
6. Montagne d'Ambre National Park
7. Nosy Mangabe Special Reserve
8. Ranomafana National Park

DECIDUOUS FOREST AREAS

9. Ankarafantsika National Park
10. Ankarana Special Reserve
11. Daraina Region
12. Kirindy Forest
13. Mitsinjo Area
14. Tsingy de Bemaraha National Park
15. Zombitse National Park

XEROPHYTIC SPINY FOREST AREAS

16. Andohahela National Park
17. Berenty Private Reserve

TOP MAMMAL-WATCHING SITES

Sites have been chosen, first, because they offer very good wildlife, and particularly mammal-watching experiences and, second, because they represent a cross-section of different habitat types and so cover the broadest breadth of mammal diversity. Most selected sites are also accessible for both organised groups and independent travellers, but some more 'off-the-beaten-track' locations might only suit the more adventurous.

Each account contains a list of the main mammal species that have been recorded at the site. Species in **bold** indicate that observations can be particularly rewarding, and correspond to the recommended sites suggested in the 'Where to See' section of the species accounts.

Rainforest Areas

The eastern rainforests are perhaps the most exciting region for naturalists as they support the greatest diversity of animal and plant species. Around 80% of species are endemic to this habitat. It can also be the most infuriating, as animals, and in particular mammals, can be very difficult to find. However, several key parks and reserves in widely distributed localities are now accessible and some of the wildlife, particularly lemurs, has become habituated. Visits to three or four of these areas would offer ample mammal-watching opportunities to see a wide cross-section of species.

Andasibe-Mantadia National Park

Location and Access: Consists of two discrete sections. The smaller area (Analamazaotra Special Reserve) lies adjacent to village of Andasibe, 30km east of Moromanga and 145km east of Antananarivo (three to four hours' drive). Mantadia lies around 12–18km north of Andasibe on a well-maintained dirt road (around 50 minutes' drive).

Habitat and Terrain: Analamazaotra is a reasonable example of mid-altitude montane rainforest covering 810ha. Many of the largest trees have been removed and canopy rarely exceeds 20–25m. Dominant trees include, *Tambourissa*, *Symphonia*, *Dalbergia* and *Weinmannia* species. Also numerous tree ferns (*Cyathea* spp.) and epiphytes. Reserve centred on small lake (*Lac Vert*), with moderately steep forested slopes rising around it. Average annual rainfall is 1,700mm.

Mantadia is excellent primary mid-altitude montane rainforest, covering over 10,000ha. Numerous huge trees and canopy in valleys averages 25–30+m. Understorey dominated by tree ferns (*Cyathea* spp.) and *Pandanus* species near watercourses; orchids and other epiphytes common. A hilly area with little flat ground. Some slopes are steep and difficult. Rainfall averages 1,500mm to 2,000mm per year.

Key Mammal Species

Lemurs: Indri *Indri indri*, **Diademed Sifaka** *Propithecus diadema*, **Black and White Ruffed Lemur** *Varecia variegata (editorum?)*(Mantadia only), **Common Brown Lemur** *Eulemur fulvus*, Red-bellied Lemur *Eulemur rubriventer*, **Eastern Grey Bamboo Lemur** *Hapalemur griseus*, **Weasel Sportive Lemur** *Lepilemur mustelinus*, **Eastern Avahi** *Avahi laniger*, **Furry-eared Dwarf Lemur** *Cheirogaleus crossleyi*, **Hairy-eared Dwarf Lemur** *Allocebus trichotis*, **Goodman's Mouse Lemur** *Microcebus lehilahytsara* and Aye-aye *Daubentonia madagascariensis*.

Carnivores: Fanaloka *Fossa fossana*, Fosa *Cryptoprocta ferox* and Eastern Ring-tailed Mongoose *Galidia elegans elegans*.

Tenrecs: Common Tenrec *Tenrec ecaudatus*, **Greater Hedgehog Tenrec** *Setifer setosus*, **Lowland Streaked Tenrec** *Hemicentetes semispinosus*, Hova Mole Tenrec *Oryzorictes hova* and several shrew tenrecs *Microgale* spp., including *M. cowani*, *M. talazaci* and *M. gracilis*.

Rodents: **Eastern Red Forest Rat** *Nesomys rufus*, Voalavoanala *Gymnuromys roberti*, White-tailed Tree Rat *Brachytarsomys albicauda* and tuft-tailed rats *Eliurus* spp.

Bats: Commerson's Leaf-nosed Bat *Hipposideros commersoni*.

Season: Accessible all year; best times for wildlife are September to December and April to May.

Facilities: Comfortable lodges in vicinity of Andasibe (Hotel Feon'ny ala, Hotel Eulophiella, Hotel de la Gare) and a better quality hotel (Vakona Lodge) on way to Mantadia. An extensive network of paths runs through reserve at Andasibe. There is a good selection of more difficult trails in Mantadia, where slopes are steeper and conditions often wet.

Recommendations: One of Madagascar's top sites, with potential to see ten or more lemur species. Two days with night walks is adequate to see Andasibe. With patience, really good views of Indri are almost guaranteed. Mantadia warrants more time, ideally two or three early morning trips. Areas close to PK14 are renowned for many species, including Diademed Sifaka and Indri. Either side of road at PK15 is best place to look for Black and White Ruffed Lemurs, although

Grey Bamboo Lemurs are regularly seen at forest edges and from the road in Andasibe-Mantadia National Park.

they can often be very tough to track down. Local guides from the Association des Guides d'Andasibe are always on hand to offer assistance.

Aye-aye Island or Ile Roger

Location and Access: Small island (30ha) in river mouth, just outside town of Mananara. Monsieur Roger arranges boat trips at night. Mananara best reached by flights from Maroantsetra or Toamasina. Access by road difficult.

Habitat and Terrain: Once a coconut, banana and lychee plantation, now partially reclaimed by secondary forest. Mainly flat but vegetation is tangled and dense in places.

Key Mammal Species

Lemurs: **Aye-aye** *Daubentonia madagascariensis*, White-fronted Brown Lemur *Eulemur albifrons*, Eastern Grey Bamboo Lemur *Hapalemur griseus* and Eastern Avahi *Avahi laniger*.

Season: Accessible year round, but better to avoid very wet cyclone season, January to March.

Facilities: None on island. Pleasant rustic accommodation at Aye-aye Hotel near the air-strip in Mananara.

Recommendations: Only worth visiting after dark. Aye-ayes (13 animals) and other lemurs have been introduced. Aye-ayes are seen most nights but can be difficult to follow as they move quickly.

Although not a pristine wilderness, Aye-aye Island is the best place to see Madagascar's most bizarre mammal.

Manombo Special Reserve

Location and Access: Approximately 30km south of Farafangana down Route Nationale 12 on south-east coast. From village of Manombo routes into forest require four-wheel drives or walking. Best areas are 6 to 7km from village.

Habitat and Terrain: Lowland rainforest and littoral forest covering around 3,000ha (although reserve is 5,000ha).

Key Mammal Species

Lemurs: **White-collared Brown Lemur** *Eulemur albocollaris*, Black and White Ruffed Lemur *Varecia variegata* (*variegata*), Eastern Grey Bamboo Lemur *Hapalemur griseus*, Eastern Avahi *Avahi laniger*, **James' Sportive Lemur** *Lepilemur jamesi*, Greater Dwarf Lemur *Cheirogaleus major* and Brown Mouse Lemur *Microcebus rufus*.

Season: Access difficult during heavy rain. September to December or April/May are best times.

Facilities: None at reserve.

Recommendations: Visits arranged by local hotels, e.g. Les Cocotiers and Hotel Austral. Permission required from local ANGAP office, where guides can be arranged. A two-day stay is recommended.

Marojejy National Park

Location and Access: The park lies between the towns of Sambava and Andapa at the northern extremity of the eastern rainforest belt. Manantenina is the initial point of access some 60km from Sambava and 40km from Andapa, from here the park boundary is around a two-hour walk.

Habitat and Terrain: Lowland, mid-altitude rainforest, high-altitude cloud forest and high-altitude montane scrub near peaks, covering 60,050ha. Extremely rich with high proportion of locally endemic species.

Marojejy spans a considerable elevational range, with an unbroken transect from lowland rainforest through to high montane scrub. Below 750m asl canopy reaches 30+m with large buttress trees like *Canarium*; typical mid-altitude montane rainforest between 750m and 1,400m asl, canopy averaging 20m to 25m; above 1,400m is high-altitude cloud forest; where altitudes exceeds 1,800m mainly stunted bush dominated by family Ericaceae. At lower elevations annual rainfall averages around 3,000mm, rising to over 4,000mm at higher altitudes. Slopes often steep and there are many deep valleys with fast-flowing streams.

The view from Camp Marojejia, Marojejy National Park.

Key Mammal Species

Lemurs: **Silky Sifaka** *Propithecus candidus*, White-fronted Brown Lemur *Eulemur albifrons*, **Red-bellied Lemur** *Eulemur rubriventer*, **Eastern Grey Bamboo Lemur** *Hapalemur griseus*, Eastern Avahi *Avahi laniger*, **Seal's Sportive Lemur** *Lepilemur seali*, **Greater Dwarf Lemur** *Cheirogaleus major*, Brown Mouse Lemur *Microcebus rufus*, Hairy-eared Dwarf Lemur *Allocebus trichotis* and Aye-aye *Daubentonia madagascariensis*.

Carnivores: Fanaloka *Fossa fossana*, Fosa *Cryptoprocta ferox*, **Eastern Ring-tailed Mongoose** *Galidia elegans elegans* and Broad-striped Mongoose *Galidictis fasciata*.

Tenrecs: Common Tenrec *Tenrec ecaudatus*, Greater Hedgehog Tenrec *Setifer setosus*, Lowland Streaked Tenrec *Hemicentetes semispinosus* and various shrew tenrecs *Microgale* spp., including *M. dobsoni*, *M. talazaci*, *M. soricoides* and *M. gymnorhyncha*.

Rodents: Eastern Red Forest Rat *Nesomys rufus*, White-tailed Tree Rat *Brachytarsomys albicauda*, tuft-tailed rats *Eliurus* spp.

Bats: Amongst the richest sites for bats in eastern region: at least 13 species recorded including, Madagascar Flying Fox *Pteropus rufus*, Madagascar Rousette *Rousettus madagascariensis*, **Commerson's Leaf-nosed Bat** *Hipposideros commersoni*, Eastern Sucker-footed Bat *Myzopoda aurita*, Peters's Sheath-tailed Bat *Emballonura atrata*, Mauritian Tomb Bat *Taphozous mauritianus*, Malagasy Mouse-eared Bat *Myotis goudoti*, Little Free-tailed Bat *Chaerephon pumilus* and others.

Season: Avoid rainy season between late December and March. Months prior to this (September to November) offer best combination of mammal watching (especially for Silky Sifaka) and tolerable weather conditions.

Facilities: Three excellent campsites, each with cabins containing beds and bedding and sheltered eating areas. All lie on main summit trail. Camp Mantella (450m, six cabins) is a two-hour walk from park boundary (four hours from Manantenina), Camp Marojejia (775m, four cabins) is two further hours' walk and Camp Simpona (1250m, two cabins) is three hours beyond Camp Marojejia. Other than the main summit path, trails are minimal and slopes are steep or very steep. Walking, particularly at higher elevations, is tough and walk to summit is very strenuous (but worth it).

Recommendations: A fantastic wilderness experience that should not be rushed. Guides, porters and minor provisions can be arranged through Park Bureau in Manantenina (www.marojejy.com). Supplies should be brought in Andapa or

Silky Sifaka, Marojejy National Park.

A walk in lowland rainforest, Masoala National Park.

Sambava. Fee structure for guides, porters and camping is administered through Park Bureau. Minimum stay of three nights recommended to see Silky Sifaka (two nights at Camp Marojejia), four or five days are required to reach summit. A complete excursion package can be arranged through Sambava Voyages in Sambava.

Masoala National Park

Location and Access: Lies to east of Maroantsetra and forms northern coastline of Bay of Antongil. Western side of park is best reached by boat from Maroantsetra and takes around two to three hours to Lohatrozona or Tampolo, the best points of access. From these good areas of forest are easily reached.

Habitat and Terrain: Largest and best remaining area of coastal/lowland rainforest on Madagascar, often extending down to shore. Peninsula covers total area in excess of 400,000ha, the park occupies 230,000ha primarily on western side. Canopy is between 25m and 30+m with few emergent trees. Understorey characterised by abundant palms (*Dracaena* spp.) and tree ferns, with many epiphytes and orchids. Slopes often steep, numerous clear, fast-flowing streams and small rivers. Annual rainfall exceeds 3,500mm with no discernible dry season.

Key Mammal Species

Lemurs: Red Ruffed Lemur *Varecia rubra*, White-fronted Brown Lemur *Eulemur albifrons*, Western Grey Bamboo Lemur (?) *Hapalemur occidentalis*, sportive lemurs *Lepilemur* spp., Eastern Avahi *Avahi laniger*, Greater Dwarf Lemur *Cheirogaleus major*, **Eastern Fork-marked Lemur** *Phaner furcifer*, Brown Mouse Lemur *Microcebus rufus*, Hairy-eared Dwarf Lemur *Allocebus trichotis* and Aye-aye *Daubentonia madagascariensis*.

Carnivores: Fanaloka *Fossa fossana*, Falanouc *Eupleres goudotii*, Fosa *Cryptoprocta ferox*, Broad-striped Mongoose *Galidictis fasciata*, Ring-tailed Mongoose *Galidia elegans* and Brown-tailed Mongoose *Salanoia concolor*.

Tenrecs: Common Tenrec *Tenrec ecaudatus*, Greater Hedgehog Tenrec *Setifer setosus*, Lowland Streaked Tenrec *Hemicentetes semispinosus*, mole tenrecs *Oryzorictes* spp. and shrew tenrecs *Microgale* spp.

Rodents: Eastern Red Forest Rat *Nesomys rufus*, **Lowland Red Forest Rat** *Nesomys audeberti* and tuft-tailed rats *Eliurus* spp.

Bats: One of richest rainforest areas for bats, with at least 14 species including; **Madagascar Flying Fox** *Pteropus rufus*,

Madagascar Straw-coloured Fruit Bat *Eidolon dupreanum*, Madagascar Rousette *Rousettus madagascariensis*, Eastern Sucker-footed Bat *Myzopoda aurita* and **Commerson's Leaf-nosed Bat** *Hipposideros commersoni*.

Season: Wet throughout year. Avoid cyclone season (January to March).

Facilities: Hotels in Maroantsetra (Relais du Masoala and Coco Beach) can arrange boat trips with equipment and guides. Modest lodges, with basic facilities at Andranobe, Lohatrozona and Tampolo. Trail network is limited and paths can be steep.

Recommendations: Takes time and effort to reach and enjoy fully: a visit of at least three or four days is recommended. Red Ruffed Lemurs regularly seen in accessible areas of forest, as are White-fronted Brown Lemurs. Eastern Fork-marked Lemurs often seen on night walks near Lohatrozona. Local guides from Association des Guides Ecotouristiques de Maroantsetra (AGEM) are essential.

Montagne d'Ambre National Park

Location and Access: Towards island's northern tip, 30km south from Antsiranana (Diego Suarez). Less than one hour's drive on good road to Ambohitra (Joffreville) and then a pot-holed dirt road for last 7km.

Habitat and Terrain: An isolated patch of montane rainforest covering 18,200ha. Name derived from resin that oozes from trunks of large trees like 'Ramy' *Canarium madagascariense* and 'Rotra' *Eugenia rotra*. Canopy height averages 25m to 30m. Numerous Bird's Nest Ferns *Asplenium nidus*, tree ferns *Cyanathea* spp., orchids *Angraecum* spp. and lianas. Two waterfalls – La Grande Cascade and La Petite Cascade – form the focal points and there are also crater lakes (Lac de la Coupe Verte and La Grande Lac) and several viewpoints over the forest and surrounding area.

Key Mammal Species

Lemurs: **Sanford's Brown Lemur** *Eulemur sanfordi*, **Crowned Lemur** *Eulemur coronatus*, **Ankarana Sportive Lemur** *Lepilemur ankaranensis*, **Amber Mountain Fork-marked Lemur** *Phaner electromontis*, Greater Dwarf Lemur *Cheirogaleus major*, **Northern Rufous Mouse Lemur** *Microcebus tavaratra* and Aye-aye *Daubentonia madagascariensis*.

Carnivores: **Falanouc** *Eupleres goudotii*, Fanaloka *Fossa fossana*, Fosa *Cryptoprocta ferox* and **Northern Ring-tailed Mongoose** *Galidia elegans dambrensis*.

Tenrecs: Common Tenrec *Tenrec ecaudatus*, **Greater Hedgehog Tenrec** *Setifer setosus*, **Lowland Streaked Tenrec** *Hemicentetes semispinosus* and various shrew tenrecs *Microgale* spp.

Lowland Streaked Tenrec.

Rodents: Eastern Red Forest Rat *Nesomys rufus*.

Bats: **Commerson's Leaf-nosed Bat** *Hipposideros commersoni*.

Season: Accessible all year: October to April is more rewarding, avoid January to March because of heavy rain.

Facilities: A modest cabin with dormitory-style accommodation and a campsite within the park. Equipment and provisions must be taken. Or two very nice lodges near Ambohitra (Joffreville) – Nature Lodge and Doamain de Fontenay. Numerous well-maintained broad trails link all the main areas of interest. Trails less frequently used tend to become overgrown. Some of these follow steep slopes, so walking can be difficult and tiring.

Recommendations: Day trips from Antsiranana possible, but better to stay within vicinity or camp for at least one night and preferably two or three. Areas around, and within easy walking distance from, the campsite (Les Roussettes) are good for several mammals (e.g. Sanford's Brown Lemur, Crowned Lemur and Northern Ring-tailed Mongoose). Nocturnal walks are excellent especially for Ankarana Sportive Lemur, Amber Mountain Fork-marked Lemur and Northern Rufous Mouse Lemur.

Nosy Mangabe Special Reserve

Location and Access: Lies 5km off Maroantsetra in Bay of Antongil. Boat ride takes about 30 minutes.

Habitat and Terrain: Lowland rainforest covers entire island, an area of 520ha. Forest has largely regenerated after considerable human activity 200 to 300 years ago. Large buttress-rooted trees reach 35m or more in height. Typical species are *Ravensara, Canarium, Ocotea, Ficus* and *Tambourissa*. Tree ferns, ferns, epiphytes and orchids also common. Slopes rise steeply from sea to summit.

Key Mammal Species

Lemurs: **Aye-aye** *Daubentonia madagascariensis*, **Black and White Ruffed Lemur** *Varecia variegata (subcincta)*, **White-fronted Brown Lemur** *Eulemur albifrons*, Greater Dwarf Lemur *Cheirogaleus major* and **Brown Mouse Lemur** *Microcebus rufus*.

Male White-fronted Brown Lemurs, Nosy Mangabe Special Reserve.

The Fanaloka is regularly seen after dark in Ranomafana National Park.

Tenrecs: **Greater Hedgehog Tenrec** *Setifer setosus* and Hova Mole Tenrec *Oryzorictes hova*.
Rodents: Introduced Black Rats *Rattus rattus*.
Bats: **Commerson's Leaf-nosed Bat** *Hipposideros commersoni*.

Season: Accessible all year, but avoid cyclone season (January to March).
Facilities: Well-maintained campsite, with covered tent platforms, shower (fed from waterfall) and flushing toilets. All equipment and provisions must be taken from Maroantsetra. The network of footpaths is extensive and gradually being improved. Many trails are steep; flat trails with wooden walkways/bridges around campsite and behind beach.
Recommendations: Day trips from Maroantsetra are possible. To fully appreciate this beautiful island a longer camping trip of two days/nights is recommended and necessary for nocturnal walks that offer the chance of seeing an Aye-aye.

Ranomafana National Park

Location and Access: Approximately 65km north-east of Fianarantsoa and adjacent to village of Ranomafana. Access along Route Nationale 25, which bisects the park and continues to Mananjary on east coast. From Fianarantsoa it takes between 1½ and 2½ hours depending on road conditions. Also possible to drive from Antananarivo in a day, but this takes more than ten hours.
Habitat and Terrain: Excellent mid-altitude rainforest and higher altitude montane cloud forest covering 39,200ha. Dominated by Namorona River, fed by many streams flowing from hills, and plunges off eastern escarpment near park entrance. Steep slopes covered with a mixture of primary and secondary forest, where canopy averages 30m. Much of secondary growth in main tourist zone at Tanatakey is dominated by dense areas of introduced Chinese Guava *Psidium cattleyanum*. Stands of Giant Bamboo *Cathariostachys madagascariensis* are also a prominent feature. Average annual rainfall 2,600mm.

Key Mammal Species
Lemurs: **Golden Bamboo Lemur** *Hapalemur aureus*, **Greater Bamboo Lemur** *Prolemur simus*, **Eastern Grey Bamboo Lemur** *Hapalemur griseus*, **Milne-Edwards's Sifaka** *Propithecus edwardsi*, **Red-bellied Lemur** *Eulemur rubriventer*, **Red-fronted Brown Lemur** *Eulemur rufus*, **Black and White Ruffed Lemur** *Varecia variegata (variegata)*, **Eastern Avahi** *Avahi laniger*, Small-toothed Sportive Lemur *Lepilemur microdon*, **Greater Dwarf Lemur** *Cheirogaleus major*, **Brown Mouse**

Discovery of the Golden Bamboo Lemur helped prompt the creation of Ranomafana National Park.

Lemur *Microcebus rufus* and Aye-aye *Daubentonia madagascariensis*.

Carnivores: **Fanaloka** *Fossa fossana*, Falanouc *Eupleres goudotii*, Fosa *Cryptoprocta ferox*, **Eastern Ring-tailed Mongoose** *Galidia elegans elegans* and Broad-striped Mongoose *Galidictis fasciata*.

Tenrecs: Aquatic Tenrec *Limnogale mergulus*, Greater Hedgehog Tenrec *Setifer setosus*, **Lowland Streaked Tenrec** *Hemicentetes semispinosus* and several shrew tenrecs *Microgale* spp.

Rodents: **Eastern Red Forest Rat** *Nesomys rufus*, **Lowland Red Forest Rat** *Nesomys audeberti*, Voalavoanala *Gymnuromys roberti*, White-tailed Tree Rat *Brachytarsomys albicauda* and tuft-tailed rats *Eliurus* spp.

Bats: Madagascar Straw-coloured Fruit Bat *Eidolon dupreanum*, Malagasy Mouse-eared Bat *Myotis goudoti* and members of the genera *Eptesicus*, *Miniopterus*, *Mormopterus*, *Tadarida* and others.

Season: Most vibrant during austral summer rainy season from December to March, but access and conditions can be difficult. Otherwise, the periods either side of main rains are most rewarding – April/May (when fruiting Chinese Guava attracts lemurs) and September to November.

Facilities: Several pleasant lodges near village of Ranomafana (Setam Lodge, Centrest Sejour, Domain Nature), all around 6km from park entrance. At park gate Gite Rain'ala has dormitory rooms and a snack bar. Also a good campsite at Park gate. An extensive system of well-maintained trails and paths runs through best wildlife areas, but many are up and down steep and often muddy slopes.

Recommendations: One of the best mammal sites, especially for Bamboo Lemurs (*Hapalemur* and *Prolemur*), Milne-Edwards's Sifaka, Red-bellied Lemur and Fanaloka. Minimum of two or three days is recommended, with at least two day-time excursions to Tanatakely and one night-time visit to Belle Vue and surrounding forest. Higher elevation forests at Vohiparara also well worth exploring for Small-toothed Sportive Lemur. Local guides generally very knowledgeable and helpful.

Deciduous Forest Areas

The deciduous forests of western and northern Madagascar are less diverse than the rainforests of the east, but nonetheless contain a wealth of fauna and flora of great importance with very high levels of endemicity (around 90%). Canopy height and tree density are lower than eastern rainforests, giving the forests a more 'open' feel. This makes wildlife watching easier. Several major protected areas exist within deciduous forest regions: while some are remote and remain difficult for visitors to reach, others are amongst the most popular and rewarding wildlife-watching localities on the island.

Of particular note are parks incorporating limestone massifs that have been eroded into spectacular pinnacle formations known as karst or locally as 'tsingy'. Rivers flowing through these areas have eroded underground passages and caves, some having subsequently collapsed to form canyons. Within these, deciduous forest flourishes, often supporting isolated faunal communities unlike any others on the island. Mammal watching can be particularly rewarding in such areas: the main examples are at Ankarana, Bemaraha and Namoroka, although only the first two are readily accessible.

Ankarafantsika National Park (Ampijoroa Forestry Station)

Location and Access: Ampijoroa lies either side of Route Nationale 4, approximately 120km south-east of Mahajanga (two to three hours). Also possible to drive directly from Antananarivo, but this takes 12 to 14 hours.

Habitat and Terrain: A mixture of dry deciduous forest and a karstic limestone plateau covering 65,520ha. Ampijoroa is towards centre of reserve and covers 20,000ha. Immediate area dominated by Lac Ravelobe, on northern side of Route Nationale 4. On sandy soils around lake, grows typical deciduous forest where canopy reaches 15m to 20m. Understorey sparse, with virtually no epiphytes. On higher plateau areas canopy averages 5m to 10m with very little understorey. In open rocky areas succulents like *Pachypodium rosulatum rosulatum* and *Aloe* species grow. Terrain gently undulating or flat, with occasional shallow ridge. Annual rainfall 1,000mm to 1,500mm.

Key Mammal Species

Lemurs: **Coquerel's Sifaka** *Propithecus coquereli*, **Mongoose Lemur** *Eulemur mongoz*, **Common Brown Lemur** *Eulemur fulvus*, **Western Avahi** *Avahi occidentalis*, **Milne-Edwards's Sportive Lemur** *Lepilemur edwardsi*, **Fat-tailed Dwarf Lemur** *Cheirogaleus medius*, **Grey Mouse Lemur** *Microcebus murinus* and **Golden-brown Mouse Lemur** *Microcebus ravelobensis*.

Carnivores: Fosa *Cryptoprocta ferox*. Also introduced Small Indian Civet *Viverricula indica*.

Tenrecs: Common Tenrec *Tenrec ecaudatus* and **Greater Hedgehog Tenrec** *Setifer setosus*.

Rodents: **Western Tuft-tailed Rat** *Eliurus myoxinus*, **Western Big-footed Mouse** *Macrotarsomys bastardi* and **Long-tailed Big-footed Mouse** *Macrotarsomys ingens*.

Bats: **Commerson's Leaf-nosed Bat** *Hipposideros commersoni* and **Mauritian Tomb Bat** *Taphozous mauritianus*.

Season: Accessible year-round, but roads difficult in very wet season (January to March), especially from Antananarivo. During austral summer can be extremely hot.

Facilities: Six well-appointed bungalows with en-suite facilities overlooking Lac Ravelobe, plus more rustic rooms with shared toilet facilities (Gite de Ampijoroa) (all must be pre-booked with ANGAP). Also a large campsite with water and small toilet block and modest restaurant that serves all. Nearby village of Andranofasika has small shops for basic supplies.

Trails are wide and walking easy on both sides of road (Jardin Botanique A and B). Very good guides available at ANGAP bureau by campsite.

Recommendations: Perhaps best remaining examples of deciduous forest. At least two or three days, including two night walks, are recommended. At least seven lemur species are easily seen by day and night, only Mongoose Lemur is sometimes elusive. Night walks also good for Western Big-footed Mouse, Long-tailed Big-footed Mouse and Commerson's Leaf-nosed Bat.

Ankarana Special Reserve

Location and Access: Approximately 110km south of Antsiranana, reserve lies predominantly to west of Route Nationale 6. Access on foot is via Mahamasina on main road or by four-wheel drive on track south of Anivorano Avaratra. Also possible to approach from Ambilobe in south, but road is poor and four-wheel drive essential.

Habitat and Terrain: Reserve constitutes majority of Ankarana Massif covering 18,225ha. Dominated by impressive formations of pinnacle karst or '*tsingy*' (Malagasy for 'to walk on tiptoes') that form an almost impenetrable fortress in places. Extensive cave systems with underground rivers and canyons. Deciduous forest grows around periphery and penetrates into larger canyons. Also isolated pockets of forest growing within karst where caves have collapsed. Canopy reaches 25m, dominant trees include *Cassia sp.*, *Dalbergia sp.*, *Ficus sp.* and baobab *Adansonia madagascariensis*. In canyon bottoms terrain is undulating but most areas, especially karst formations, are very rugged and potentially hazardous. Annual rainfall averages 1,800mm.

A male Crowned Sifaka crosses razor sharp 'tsingy', Ankarana Special Reserve.

Key Mammal Species

Lemurs: **Crowned Lemur** *Eulemur coronatus*, **Sanford's Brown Lemur** *Eulemur sanfordi*, Western Grey Bamboo Lemur *Hapalemur occidentalis*, **Avahi** *Avahi* spp., **Ankarana Sportive Lemur** *Lepilemur ankaranensis*, **Amber Mountain Fork-marked Lemur** *Phaner electromontis*, Fat-tailed Dwarf Lemur *Cheirogaleus medius*, **Northern Rufous Mouse Lemur** *Microcebus tavaratra* and Aye-aye *Daubentonia madagascariensis*.

Carnivores: **Northern Ring-tailed Mongoose** *Galidia elegans dambrensis*, **Fosa** *Cryptoprocta ferox* and **Fanaloka** *Fossa fossana*.

Tenrecs: **Greater Hedgehog Tenrec** *Setifer setosus*.

Bats: One of richest bat sites on island. At least 16 species recorded including: Madagascar Flying Fox *Pteropus rufus*, Madagascar Straw-coloured Fruit Bat *Eidolon dupreanum*, **Madagascar Rousette** *Rousettus madagascariensis*, Madagascar Slit-faced Bat *Nycteris madagascariensis*, **Commerson's Leaf-nosed Bat** *Hipposideros commersoni*, Trouessart's Trident Bat *Triaenops furculus*, Malagasy Mouse-eared Bat *Myotis goudoti* and the long-fingered bat *Miniopterus manavi*.

Season: Only accessible during the drier months from May to November. Can be very hot during day, but cool at night.

Facilities: No lodges, camping only: all equipment and provisions must be taken.

Campsite at Mahamasina entrance gives access on foot to some forest and caves (for bats); two- to three-hour walk through reserve to other campsites. Two main campsites are Campement Anilotra (formerly des Anglais) in the Canyon Grande and Campement d'Andrafiabe (formerly des Americains) at foot of western-facing escarpment. Water is scarce, but available from underground streams near camps. Reasonable trails around Canyon Grande but remote areas are much more challenging to explore.

Recommendations: Camping excursions arranged through tour operators in Antsiranana. Minimum stay of two or three nights is recommended. To explore reserve fully it is best to spend nights at different campsites. Local guides essential. Campement Anilotra is best for Crowned Lemur, Sanford's Brown Lemur, Ankarana Sportive Lemur, Northern Rufous Mouse Lemur, Northern Ring-tailed Mongoose and Fanaloka. Areas close to camp at Mahamasina can be good for Fosa.

Daraina Region

Location and Access: Around 70km west of Iharana (Vohemar) in far north-east. Road is poor and drive from Iharana takes around three hours. Also accessible from opposite direction via Ambilobe. Due to become an official protected area in near future, so permits may be required.

Habitat and Terrain: Covering rolling hills, a mosaic of dry deciduous forest, semi-evergreen forest and gallery forest, interspersed with degraded grassland, dry scrub and agricultural land. Within region forests highly fragmented covering total area no greater than 44,000ha; individual forest blocks range from one to 14,000ha.

Denuded hillsides and forest fragments characterise the Daraina area.

Key Mammal Species

Lemurs: **Golden-crowned Sifaka** *Propithecus tattersalli*, Crowned Lemur *Eulemur coronatus*, Sanford's Brown Lemur *Eulemur sanfordi*, **Daraina Sportive Lemur** *Lepilemur milanoii*, Fork-marked Lemur *Phaner* spp., Dwarf Lemur *Cheirogaleus* spp., Mouse Lemur *Microcebus* spp. and Aye-aye *Daubentonia madagascariensis*.

Carnivores: Fosa *Cryptoprocta ferox*.

Tenrecs: Greater Hedgehog Tenrec *Setifer setosus*.

Season: Accessible during drier months from May to December. Can be very hot during day.

Facilities: No facilities within forest, self-sufficient camping only option. Very basic hotels in Daraina.

Recommendations: Go to village of Andranotsimaty, 5km north-east of Daraina, where there are several habituated groups of sifakas that are easy to see. Day visits are possible, camping is better as night-walks can be very good for Fork-marked Lemurs, Dwarf Lemurs and occasionally even Aye-aye. For advice contact conservation organisation FANAMBY (www.fanamby.org.mg), who have an office in Daraina.

Kirindy Forest

Location and Access: Approximately 60km north-east of Morondava and 20km inland from west coast: situated to east of road to Belo sur Tsiribihina, north of village of Marofandilia. From Morondava drive takes two to three hours.

Habitat and Terrain: Typical dry deciduous forest growing on sandy soils covering around 12,000ha. Canopy averages 12–15m, but may reach 20–25m in more humid areas along watercourses. Often a dense understorey and intermediate layer. Three species of baobab also present, *Adansonia fony, A. za* and *A. grandidieri* which is the largest baobab in Madagascar and reaches heights of 30+m. Annual rainfall averages 700mm to 800mm, majority falling between December and March.

Key Mammal Species

Lemurs: **Verreaux's Sifaka** *Propithecus verreauxi verreauxi*, **Red-fronted Brown Lemur** *Eulemur rufus*, **Madame Berthe's Mouse Lemur** *Microcebus berthae*, **Grey Mouse Lemur** *Microcebus murinus*, **Red-tailed Sportive Lemur** *Lepilemur rufi-caudatus*, **Pale Fork-marked Lemur** *Phaner pallescens*, **Coquerel's Giant Dwarf Lemur** *Mirza coquereli* and **Fat-tailed Dwarf Lemur** *Cheirogaleus medius*.

Carnivores: **Fosa** *Cryptoprocta ferox* and **Narrow-striped Mongoose** *Mungotictis decemlineata*. Also the introduced Small Indian Civet *Viverricula indica*.

Tenrecs: **Common Tenrec** *Tenrec ecaudatus*, **Greater Hedgehog Tenrec** *Setifer setosus*, Lesser Hedgehog Tenrec *Echinops telfairi* and **Large-eared Tenrec** *Geogale aurita*.

Rodents: **Giant Jumping Rat** *Hypogeomys antimena*, Western Tuft-tailed Rat *Eliurus myoxinus* and **Western Big-footed Mouse** *Macrotarsomys bastardi*.

Kirindy Forest remains the best place to see Fosas.

Bats: One of most diverse sites in western regions with at least 17 species including; Madagascar Flying Fox *Pteropus rufus*, Madagascar Straw-coloured Fruit Bat *Eidolon dupreanum*, **Commerson's Leaf-nosed Bat** *Hipposideros commersoni*, Rufous Trident Bat *Triaenops rufus*, Madagascar House Bat *Scotophilus borbonicus*, Little Free-tailed Bat *Chaerephon pumilus*, *Mops leucostigma* and members of the genus *Pipistrellus*.

Season: Marked dry season May to October with virtually no rain. Wettest months in austral summer. Wildlife watching best in spring and summer (October to April), particularly after rain. Road conditions can be difficult during wetter months and temperatures very high. In winter forests may appear quite lifeless and nights can be cold.

Facilities: A basic field camp, comprising rustic bungalows and permanent tent pitches. When camping, all equipment must be taken. A snack bar serves

Giant Jumping Rat, Kirindy Forest.

cool drinks and simple good-value meals. Paths through forest are wide and walking flat and easy. Trails arranged in grid system which makes navigation straightforward. Local guides are available.

Recommendations: Perhaps the premier nocturnal site in Madagascar. The only site to see Giant Jumping Rat plus six nocturnal lemurs. Verreaux's Saifaka, Red-fronted Brown Lemur and Narrow-striped Mongoose readily seen during day. Also best place to see Fosa (especially in October and November). Day trips and excursions organised by several hotels in Morondava (e.g. Baobab Café and Hotel Chez Maggie). Two or three nights' camping is recommended. Between Morondava and Kirindy is famous Avenue of Giant Baobabs (*Baobab Allé*) which is well worth stopping at.

Mitsinjo Area: Tsiombikibo Forest, Lac Kinkony and Anjamena

Location and Access: Mitsinjo town lies west of Mahajanga and the Betsiboka River estuary and south of Mahavavy River delta. About 65km by road from Katsepy, which takes around three to four hours by taxi-brousse. Three nearby forest areas are renowned sites for lemurs: the Tsiombikibo Forest to the west of the town; vicinity of Lac Kinkony some 15km south; and Anjamena on the eastern bank of the Mahavavy River.

Habitat and Terrain: All three areas are typical western dry deciduous forest similar to those at Ankarafantsika and Kirindy.

Key Mammal Species

Lemurs: Decken's Sifaka *Propithecus deckeni* (Tsiombikibo and Lac Kinkony only), **Crowned Sifaka** *Propithecus coronatus* (Anjamena only), **Mongoose Lemur** *Eulemur mongoz*, **Red-fronted Brown Lemur** *Eulemur rufus*, **Western Grey Bamboo Lemur** *Hapalemur occidentalis* (Tsiombikibo only), **Red-shouldered Sportive Lemur** *Lepilemur aeeclis* (Anjamena only), **Ahmanson's Sportive Lemur** *Lepilemur ahmansoni* (Tsiombikibo only) and Fat-tailed Dwarf Lemur *Cheirogaleus medius*.

Season: Road between Katsepy and Mitsinjo often impassable during wet season. Best time to visit is May to December.

Facilities: No facilities at forest locations. Mitsinjo has a modest hotel (Hotely Salama) offering basic accommodation and good food. Camping excursions can be arranged through tour operators in Mahajunga or Antananarivo.

Recommendations: An exciting area best suited to the adventurous mammal watcher. A stay of three or more days visiting at least two sites is recommended. Mahavavy Delta and Lac Kinkony also internationally important birdwatching sites and some operators organise tours where several lemurs are also regularly seen.

The Manambolo Gorge at the southern edge of Tsingy de Bemaraha National Park. Decken's Sifakas and Red-fronted Brown Lemurs are often seen in these forests.

Tsingy de Bemaraha National Park

Location and Access: North of Manambolo River in central west. Reached by dirt road from Belo sur Tsiribihina (and Morondava). In four-wheel drive, journey from Belo takes five hours and from Morondava ten hours. Access is close to village of Bekopaka on north bank of Manambolo River.

Habitat and Terrain: A World Heritage Site covering 152,000ha, the southern 66,630ha is the National Park. Majority of limestone massif has been eroded into largest and most impressive pinnacle karst ('*tsingy*') formations in Madagascar. In between rock formations grows typical dry deciduous forest dominated by *Dalbergia, Commiphora* and *Hildegardia* species. Numerous succulents include *Kalanchoe* and *Pachypodium* species. In shady canyons species like *Pandanus* and various ferns flourish.

A network of trails and boardwalks over *tsingy* begins at park entrance near Bekopaka. Paths form circuits of varying lengths from around two to eight hours' walking. The best wildlife areas lie in forest areas close to entrance.

Key Mammal Species

Lemurs: **Decken's Sifaka** *Propithecus deckeni*, Red-fronted Brown Lemur *Eulemur rufus*, **Cleese's Avahi** *Avahi cleesei*, **Randrianasolo's Sportive Lemur** *Lepilemur randrianasoli*, Fat-tailed Dwarf Lemur *Cheirogaleus medius*, **Grey Mouse Lemur** *Microcebus murinus*, **Western Rufous Mouse Lemur** *Microcebus myoxinus* and Aye-aye *Daubentonia madagascariensis*.
Carnivores: **Western Ring-tailed Mongoose** *Galidia elegans occidentalis* and Fosa *Cryptoprocta ferox*.
Tenrecs: Common Tenrec *Tenrec ecaudatus* and Greater Hedgehog Tenrec *Setifer setosus*.
Rodents: **Western Red Forest Rat** *Nesomys lambertoni*.
Bats: Together with Ankarana, possibly the richest single site for bats on Madagascar. Documenting this diversity is just beginning, but probably more than 50% of island's bat species occur.

Season: Access only feasible during dry season (May to December) when road conditions are passable. During spring and summer (October onwards) it is very hot.

Facilities: Well-maintained campsite close to park entrance. All equipment must be provided. A snack bar serves basic meals and drinks. Excursions organised by tour operators in Morondava. Hotel Relais de Tsingy has beautifully situated bungalows overlooking the lake and serves good food. Guides are available at entrance.

Recommendations: Considerable effort is required to reach Bemaraha, so stay for at least three nights. Only site for

Cleese's Avahi and Randrianasolo's Sportive Lemur. Forest walks good for Decken's Sifaka; also take boat trip up gorge of Manambolo River where groups of sifakas can be seen in the trees close to river (www.tsingy-madagascar.com).

Zombitse National Park

Location and Access: Straddles Route Nationale 7, 25km east of Sakaraha. Drive from Ranohira takes one and a half hours, from Toliara it takes around three hours.

Habitat and Terrain: With adjacent forests of Vohibasia, Zombitse constitutes last remnant of transition forest between western and southern floristic domains. Similar in appearance to western deciduous forests and shares many tree species along with some species normally associated with areas further south. Two baobabs, *Adansonia madagascariensis* and *A. za*, are present, canopy averages 15m. Covers 17,240ha – in past edges and forest margins were continually eroded by fires and spread of agriculture, but creation of park has slowed this. Terrain fairly flat. Annual rainfall averages 700mm. Long dry season (May to October) with no permanent watercourses.

Key Mammal Species

Lemurs: **Verreaux's Sifaka** *Propithecus verreauxi*, Ring-tailed Lemur *Lemur catta*, Red-fronted Brown Lemur *Eulemur rufus*, **Hubbard's Sportive Lemur** *Lepilemur hubbardi*, **Pale Fork-marked Lemur** *Phaner pallescens*, **Coquerel's Giant Dwarf Lemur** *Mirza coquereli*, Fat-tailed Dwarf Lemur *Cheirogaleus medius* and Grey Mouse Lemur *Microcebus murinus*.
Carnivores: Fosa *Cryptoprocta ferox*. Also the introduced Small Indian Civet *Viverricula indica*.
Tenrecs: Common Tenrec *Tenrec ecaudatus*, Greater Hedgehog Tenrec *Setifer setosus*, Lesser Hedgehog Tenrec *Echinops telfairi* and Large-eared Tenrec *Geogale aurita*.
Rodents: Western Tuft-tailed Rat *Eliurus myoxinus* and Western Big-footed Mouse *Macrotarsomys bastardi*.
Bats: Mauritian Tomb Bat *Taphozous mauritianus*, Madagascar House Bat *Scotophilus robustus*, Peters's Goblin Bat *Mormopterus jugularis* and Midas Mastiff Bat *Mops midas*.

Season: Accessible year round. Best during austral spring and summer, October to April. Forests relatively lifeless during winter months.

Facilities: Very basic camp facilities; must be entirely self-sufficient (including water supplies). Easily walked trails originate at park office and lead into forest on southern side of main road. Guides available at park office.

Recommendations: Most visitors stop briefly en route between Isalo National Park and Toliara. Sometimes possible to see lemurs such as Verreaux's Sifakas and Ring-tailed Lemurs in trees close to road. Enthusiasts, should camp for one or two nights, to see the best this intriguing and unusual forest has to offer: good for Pale Fork-marked Lemur, Coquerel's Giant Dwarf Lemur, Fat-tailed Dwarf Lemur and sometimes even Fosa.

Xerophytic Spiny Forest Areas

Perhaps the most bizarre and unusual areas in Madagascar. They occupy the harshest and most arid regions and consequently the faunal and floral diversity is much reduced in comparison with other areas, but the rates of endemicity remain very high. Vegetation comprises a type of deciduous thicket dominated by members of the Didiereaceae and Euphorbiaceae families and commonly referred to as 'spiny forest' or 'thorn thicket'.

Mammal diversity is reduced in this region, but that is not to say it is an area the mammal-watcher should overlook as some sites offer some of the closest and most intimate mammal-watching experiences Madagascar has to offer, particularly with two species the island is perhaps most famous for, Ring-tailed Lemur and Verreaux's Sifaka.

Andohahela National Park

Location and Access: A complex of three separate forest areas (Parcels) to the north and west of Tolagnaro. Parcel 3 (see below) is relatively easy to visit, Parcels 1 and 2 are more difficult and require four-wheel drives to reach.
Habitat and Terrain: Particularly notable as it spans rainforest regions in Anosyennes Mountains and arid spiny forest regions in rain shadow to west of these mountains. Habitat diversity corresponds to rich mammal diversity.

Parcel 1 covers 63,100ha of lowland, medium altitude and high elevation rainforest up to 2,000m asl. and represents southernmost tip of humid forest belt. Amongst the most southern 'tropical forests' in the Old World.

Parcel 2 covers 12,420ha, largely supporting typical spiny and gallery forest. Communities are dominated by Didiereaceae and Euphorbiaceae families. With proximity of humid forest, this area acts as transition zone for many species and is one of the most biologically diverse forest areas in the south.

Parcel 3 covers just 500ha on the Ambolo Massif and is a representative fragment of 'transition forest', largely set aside to protect locally endemic Triangle Palm *Dypsis decaryi*, but is also home to many other species. For instance, troops of Ring-tailed Lemurs can sometimes be seen, even from the road.

Key Mammal Species
Lemurs: **Parcel 1** – Verreaux's Sifaka *Propithecus verreauxi*, Collared Brown Lemur *Eulemur collaris*, **Southern Grey Bamboo Lemur** *Hapalemur meridionalis*, Eastern Avahi *Avahi laniger*, Fleurete's Sportive Lemur *Lepilemur fleuretae*, Fork-marked Lemur *Phaner* spp., Greater Dwarf Lemur *Cheirogaleus major*, Furry-eared Dwarf Lemur *Cheirogaleus crossleyi*, Brown Mouse Lemur *Microcebus rufus* and Aye-aye *Daubentonia madagascariensis*.

Parcel 2 & 3 – **Verreaux's Sifaka** *Propithecus verreauxi*, Ring-tailed Lemur *Lemur catta*, White-footed Sportive Lemur *Lepilemur leucopus*, Fat-tailed Dwarf Lemur *Cheirogaleus medius*, Grey-brown Mouse Lemur *Microcebus griseorufus* and Grey Mouse Lemur *Microcebus murinus*.

Carnivores: Eastern Ring-tailed Mongoose *Galidia elegans elegans*, Broad-striped Mongoose *Galidictis fasciata*, Fosa *Cryptoprocta ferox*, Fanaloka *Fossa fossana* and Falanouc *Eupleres goudotii* (all Parcel 1 only, with the exception of *Cryptoprocta* which may occur in spiny forest). The introduced Small Indian Civet *Viverricula indica* is found in both rain-forest and arid forest areas.

Tenrecs: Common Tenrec *Tenrec ecaudatus*, Greater Hedgehog Tenrec *Setifer setosus*, Lesser Hedgehog Tenrec *Echinops telfairi* and numerous Shrew Tenrecs *Microgale* spp..

Rodents: Eastern Red Forest Rat *Nesomys rufus*, Voalavoanala *Gymnuromys roberti*, Malagasy Mountain Mouse *Monticolomys koopmani* and several species of Tuft-tailed Rat: *Eliurus majori, E. minor, E. tanala* and *E. webbi*.

Bats: At least 12 species have been recorded including Madagascar Flying Fox *Pteropus rufus*, Madagascar Straw-coloured Fruit Bat *Eidolon dupreanum*, Madagascar Rousette *Rousettus madagascariensis*, Commerson's Leaf-nosed Bat *Hipposideros commersoni*, Mauritian Tomb Bat *Taphozous mauritianus*, Malagasy Mouse-eared Bat *Myotis goudoti* and the Eastern Sucker-footed Bat *Myzopoda aurita*.

Season: Parcels 2 and 3 accessible most of year. Parcel 1 better visited outside rainy season. The best months are during austral spring and early summer, September to December.

Facilities: There are basic camping facilities in Parcel 1 at Malio and a modest network of trails. In Parcel 2, three areas have been developed for tourists, Hazofotsy in the north-west and Tsimelahy and Mangatsiaka in the south-east. All have basic camping site facilities, although it is necessary to be entirely self-sufficient (including water supplies). Mangatsiaka is relatively easy to reach being only 4km off the main Tolagnaro to Amboasary-Sud road, while Tsimelahy is 15km from the same road.

Recommendations: Malio (Parcel 1) is off the regular rainforest circuit, but for the committed mammal enthusiast is worth visiting. Lemur watching, especially for Verreaux's Sifaka, is excellent at Ihazafotsy and Mangatsiaka (both Parcel 2), which are also good places for White-footed Sportive Lemur and Grey-brown Mouse Lemur. Day trips to both Ihazafoty and Mangatsiaka are possible. Tsimelahy (Parcel 2) is not good for mammal watching, but is nonetheless a beautiful place and has a rich diversity of unusual plants and reptiles.

Berenty Private Reserve

Location and Access: Located on banks of Mandrare River, 80km west of Tolagnaro and approximately 10km north of Amboasary-Sud. Journey from Tolagnaro takes around three hours.

Habitat and Terrain: A small (25ha) isolated patch of riverine gallery forest dominated by huge Tamarind Trees *Tamarindus indica*, which may exceed 20m. Adjacent to gallery forest are much smaller parcels of spiny forest dominated by *Alluaudia procera* and *A. ascendens*. Terrain is flat and walking very easy.

North of Berenty are more pristine spiny forest parcels at Anjampolo. Here forest is dominated by various species of Didiereaceae including *Didierea madagascariensis, D. trolli, Alluaudia procera* and *A. ascendens*.

Key Mammal Species
Lemurs: **Verreaux's Sifaka** *Propithecus verreauxi*, **Ring-tailed Lemur** *Lemur catta*, Red-fronted Brown Lemur *Eulemur rufus* (introduced), **White-footed Sportive Lemur** *Lepilemur leucopus*, **Grey-brown Mouse Lemur** *Microcebus griseorufus* and Grey Mouse Lemur *Microcebus murinus*.

Carnivores: The introduced **Small Indian Civet** *Viverricula indica*.

Tenrecs: **Lesser Hedgehog Tenrec** *Echinops telfairi* and Common Tenrec *Tenrec ecaudatus*.

Rodents: Not known.

Bats: **Madagascar Flying Fox** *Pteropus rufus*.

Female Ring-tailed Lemur with infant.

Season: Accessible year round. September and October are good for baby lemurs.

Facilities: Comfortable bungalows with a restaurant adjacent to reserve. An excellent network of wide paths and trails covers the gallery forest. Guides arranged through the Hotel Le Dauphin.

Recommendations: Day trips from Tolagnaro are possible, but a stay of at least one or two days and nights is recommended. *The* place to see Verreaux's Sifakas 'dancing' across open ground. Intimate encounters with troops of Ring-tailed Lemurs gauranteed. Also make the effort to visit Anjampolo, where beautiful Ring-tailed Lemurs and Verreaux's Sifakas can be seen in spiny forest.

Lesser Hedgehog Tenrec, Andohahela National Park.

GLOSSARY

Adaptive Radiation A burst of evolution, where an ancestral form undergoes rapid diversification into many new forms, resulting in the exploitation of an array of habitats (cf. Convergent Evolution).

Aestivate In tropical environments where animals seasonally enter a state of dormancy or torpor in response to periods of water and/or food shortage usually corresponding with hot dry climatic conditions (cf. Hibernate).

Agouti Referring to pelage: a grizzled coloration resulting from alternate light and dark barring of each hair.

Allopatry The occurrence of populations of different species (or higher taxonomic units) in different geographical areas i.e. with non-overlapping ranges or distributions (cf. Sympatry).

Altricial Applied to young animals that are born in a rudimentary state of development and, therefore, require an extended period of nursing by the parents (cf. Precocial).

Anthropogenic Applied to habitats and environments that are primarily a consequence of interference by man.

Arboreal Refers to animals that spend the majority of their lives living in trees.

Austral Of the southern hemisphere.

Cathemeral Applied to animals that are active both day and night. The relative proportions of daytime and night-time activity may vary with the seasons (cf. Diurnal and Nocturnal).

Carnivore Generally applied to any primarily flesh-eating organism. More specifically refers to members of the taxonomic order Carnivora.

Class A taxonomic category that is subordinate to phylum and superior to order, e.g. the mammals are class Mammalia in phylum Chordata (see Taxonomy).

Cline A graded sequence of differences within a species across its geographical distribution.

Commensal Refers to an animal that lives side by side with another species, sharing its food. Often applied to species that live in close association with humans, e.g. rats and mice.

Congener Individuals from the same or different species that belong to the same genus.

Conspecific Individuals that belong to the same species.

Convergent Evolution The independent acquisition through evolution of similar characteristics in unrelated taxonomic groupings that lead similar ways of life, as opposed to the possession of similarities by virtue of descent from a common ancestor.

Crepuscular Of twilight: the term applies to animals that are primarily active around dusk.

Cursorial Applied to an animal possessing limbs adapted for running.

Dichromatic Where individuals of the same species exhibit two noticeably different colour patterns, e.g. sexually dichromatic refers to differences between adult males and females, while maturationally dichromatic refers to differences between immature and adult individuals.

Digitigrade Applied to the gait in which only the digits, and not the heel, make contact with the ground (cf. Plantigrade).

Diurnal Applied to animals that are primarily active during the day time (cf. Nocturnal and Cathemeral).

Dorsal The upper or top side or surface of an animal (cf. Ventral).

Endemic Where a species or other taxonomic grouping is naturally restricted to a particular geographic region: such a taxon is then said to be endemic to that region. In this context, the size of the region will usually depend on the status of the taxon: thus, all other factors being equal, a family will be endemic to a larger area than a genus or a species. For instance the family Lemuridae is endemic to the island of Madagascar as a whole, while the Crowned Lemur is endemic to the very northern tip of the island (cf. Indigenous and Exotic).

Exotic Refers to a taxonomic grouping (usually a species) that has been accidentally or deliberately introduced to a region in which it does not occur naturally (cf. Indigenous).

Family A taxonomic category that is subordinate to order and superior to subfamily, e.g. the mongooses – family Herpestidae (see Taxonomy).

Folivore Applied to an animal that feeds primarily on leaves.

Fossorial Applied to an animal with a burrowing lifestyle.

Frugivore Applied to an animal that feeds primarily on fruit.

Genus (plural **Genera**) A taxonomic category that is subordinate to subfamily and superior to species, e.g. the sifakas – genus *Propithecus* (see Taxonomy).

Gestation The period of development within the uterus.

Glabrous Smooth and lacking hairs.

Hallux The 'great toe'. In mammals: on the pentadactyl hindlimb, the digit on the tibial side which is often shorter than the other digits.

Hibernate In cold environments where animals become dormant over the winter months: during this deep sleep the metabolic rate is dramatically reduced and the animal survives on stored fat reserves that have been built up during the favourable summer months (cf. Aestivate).

Hybrid An offspring produced by parents which are genetically unlike, e.g. belonging to different species or subspecies.

Indigenous Applies to species or other taxonomic groupings that occur naturally in a specified area or region and have, therefore, not been introduced either deliberately or accidentally by humans. This term is synonymous with Native (cf. Endemic and Exotic).

Inguinal Refers to the groin region.

Monogamy A mating system where individuals have only one partner per breeding season. This is often extended to mean the pair mate for life (cf. Polygamy and Polygyny).

Niche The functional position or role of an organism (usually applied to a species) within its community and environment, defined in all aspects of its lifestyle, e.g. food, competitors, predators and other resource requirements. Also referred to as Ecological Niche.

Nocturnal Applied to animals that are primarily active during the night (cf. Diurnal and Cathemeral).

Omnivore Applied to an animal with a varied diet that feeds on both flesh and vegetation.

Order A taxonomic category that is subordinate to class and superior to family, e.g. the rodents – order Rodentia (see Taxonomy).

Pelage The hair covering the body of a mammal. Coat is a synonymous and more popular term.

Pencillate Applied to the tails of mammals that end in a conspicuous brush-like terminal tuft.

Plantigrade Applied to the gait in which the soles of the feet, including the heels, make contact with the ground (cf. Digitigrade).

Polygamy A mating system where individuals of either sex have more than one partner per breeding season (cf. Monogamy and Polygyny).

Polygyny A mating system where males mate with more than one (and generally several) females during a single breeding season (cf. Monogamy and Polygamy).

Post-cranial Refers to all parts of the skeleton behind/below the cranium (skull).

Precocial Applied to young animals that are born in a relatively advanced state of development and, therefore, require only a brief period of nursing by the parents (cf. Altricial).

Prosimian Literally meaning 'before the monkeys': used as a collective term referring to the relatively primitive primates belonging to the suborder Strepsirhini (formerly Prosimii) which includes the lemurs, galagos, pottos and lorises.

Pygal The region at the base of the back where the tail joins the main body.

Quadrupedal Applied to an animal that walks on all four limbs.

Saltatory Applied to animals whose primary mode of movement is leaping.

Scansorial Applied to an animal that is adapted to climbing.

Sclerophyllous Applied to vegetation, typically scrub, but also woodland, in which the leaves of the trees and shrubs are small, hard, thick, leathery with a waxy cuticle and evergreen. These adaptations allow the vegetation to survive a pronounced hot, dry season.

sp. (plural **spp.**) When considering a species, an abbreviation indicating that the genus is known, but not the specific species, e.g. *Eulemur* sp. refers to an unspecified member of the genus *Eulemur*.

Species A taxonomic category that is subordinate to genus and superior to subspecies, e.g. the Ring-tailed Lemur (*Lemur catta*). This is the fundamental unit of taxonomy and is broadly defined as a population of organisms with like morphology that are able to interbreed and produce viable offspring, i.e. they have compatible gametes and share a common fertilisation technique (see Taxonomy).

Speciation The process by which new species arise by evolution. It is widely accepted that this occurs when a single species population becomes divided and then different selection pressures acting on each new population cause them to diverge.

Subfamily A taxonomic category that is subordinate to family and superior to genus, e.g. the Malagasy mongooses – subfamily Galidiinae (see Taxonomy).

Subspecies A taxonomic category that is subordinate to species and denotes a recognisable subpopulation within a single species that typically has a distinct geographical range, e.g. the Black Lemur (*Eulemur macaco*) is divided into the nominate subspecies, *Eulemur macaco macaco* and the blue-eyed subspecies, *Eulemur macaco flavifrons*. Subspecies is interchangeable with the term race (see Taxonomy).

Sympatry The occurrence of populations of different species (or higher taxonomic units) in the same geographical areas, i.e. with overlapping ranges or distributions (cf. Allopatry).

Taxon (plural **Taxa**) A general term for a taxonomic group whatever its rank, e.g. family, genus, species or subspecies.

Taxonomy The science of classifying organisms. In this classification system organisms which share common features are grouped together and are, therefore, thought to share a common ancestry. Each individual is thus a member of a series of ever-broader categories (individual – species – genus – family – order – class – phylum – kingdom) and each of these categories can be further divided where convenient and appropriate (e.g. subspecies, subfamily, superfamily or infraorder).

Terrestrial Refers to animals that spend the majority of their lives living on the ground.

Ventral The lower or bottom side or surface of an animal.

Vibrissae Stiff, coarse hairs, richly supplied with nerves that are especially found around the snout and have a sensory (tactile) function. More commonly referred to as whiskers.

Xerophytic Applies to vegetation, typically a forest, that grows in areas that receive relatively little rainfall. The trees and plants of such forests are generally adapted to protect themselves against browsing animals by having well-developed spines and reduce water loss through transpiration by having small, leathery leaves with a waxy cuticle.

Like the young of all primates, infant Red-fronted Brown Lemurs are altricial i.e. they require prolonged parental care before independence.

BIBLIOGRAPHY
Cited Literature: General, Biogeography, Habitats & Conservation

G1 Andrianjakarivelo, V. (2003) Artiodactyla: *Potamochoerus larvatus*, Bush Pig, *Lambo, Lambodia, Lamboala, Antsanga*. In Goodman, S.M. and Benstead, J.P. (eds) *The Natural History of Madagascar*, pp. 1365 – 1367. The University of Chicago Press, Chicago, USA.

G2 Burney, D.A. and Ramilisonina (1999) The *kilopilopitsofy, kidoky* and *bokyboky*: Accounts of strange animals from Belo-sur-Mer, Madagascar and the mega-faunal 'extinction window'. *American Anthropologist* 100: 957-966.

G3 Carleton, M.D. and Goodman, S.M. (1996) Systematic studies of Madagascar's endemic rodents (Muroidea: Nesomyinae): a new genus and species from the Central Highlands. In Goodman, S.M. (ed) *A Floral and Faunal Inventory of the Eastern slopes of the Réserve Naturelle Intégrale d'Andringitra, Madagascar: with reference to elevational variation. Fieldiana Zoology* 85: 231-256.

G4 Carleton, M.D. and Goodman, S.M. (1998) New Taxa of Nesomyine Rodents (Muroidea: Muridae) from Madagascar's northern highlands, with taxonomic comments on previously described forms. In Goodman, S.M. (ed) *A Floral and Faunal Inventory of the Réserve Spéciale d'Anjanaharibe-Sud, Madagascar: with reference to elevational variation. Fieldiana Zoology* 90: 163-200.

G5 Carleton, M.D., Goodman, S.M. and Rakotondravony (2001) A new species of tufted-tailed rat, genus *Eliurus* (Muridae: Nesomyinae), from western Madagascar, with notes on the distribution of *E. myoxinus*. *Proceedings of the Biological Society of Washington* 114: 972-987.

G6 Dewar, R. E. (1984) Recent extinctions in Madagascar: the loss of the subfossil fauna. In: Martin, P.S. and R.G. Klein (eds.), *Quaternary extinctions: a prehistoric revolution*, pp. 574-593. Uni. Ariz. Press.

G7 Dewar. R. E. (1997) Were People Responsible for the Extinction of Madagascar's Subfossils, and How Will We Ever Know? In: Goodman, S. M. and B. D. Patterson (eds.) *Natural Change and Human Impact in Madagascar*, pp. 364-377. Smithsonian Institution Press, Washington D.C., U.S.A. and London, U.K.

G8 Dufils, J.-M. (2003) Remaining Forest Cover. In Goodman, S.M. and Benstead, J.P. (eds) *The Natural History of Madagascar*, pp. 88 – 96. The University of Chicago Press, Chicago, USA.

G9 Du Puy, D.J. and Moat, J. (1996) A refined classification of the vegetation types of Madagascar, and their current distribution. In: Lourenco, W.R. (ed.) *Biogéographie de Madagascar*, pp. 205-218. Editions de l'ORSTOM, Paris.

G10 Du Puy, D.J. and Moat, J. (2003) Using Geological Substrate to Identify and Map Primary Vegetation Types in Madagascar and the Implications for Planning Biodiversity Conservation. In Goodman, S.M. and Benstead, J.P. (eds) *The Natural History of Madagascar*, pp. 51 – 66. The University of Chicago Press, Chicago, USA.

G11 Fenn, M.D. (2003) The Spiny Forest Ecoregion. In Goodman, S.M. and Benstead, J.P. (eds) *The Natural History of Madagascar*, pp. 1525 – 1530. The University of Chicago Press, Chicago, USA.

G12 Gautier, L. and Goodman, S.M. (2003) Introduction to the Flora of Madagascar. In Goodman, S.M. and Benstead, J.P. (eds) *The Natural History of Madagascar*, pp. 229 – 250. The University of Chicago Press, Chicago, USA.

G13 Godfrey, L.R. (1986) The tale of the *tsy-aomby-aomby*. The Sciences (Jan-Feb): 49-51.

G14 Golden, C. (2005) *Eaten to Endangerment: Mammal Hunting and the Bushmeat Trade in Madagascar's Makira Forest*. Undergraduate Thesis, University of Harvard, USA.

G15 Goodman, S.M. (2003) Checklist to the Extant Land Mammals of Madagascar. In Goodman, S.M. and Benstead, J.P. (eds) *The Natural History of Madagascar*, pp. 1187 – 1190. The University of Chicago Press, Chicago, USA.

G16 Goodman, S.M. and Cardiff, S.G. (2004) A new species of *Chaerephon* (Molossidae) from Madagascar with notes on other members of the family. *Acta Chiropterologica* 69: 75-81

G17 Goodman, S.M. and Langrand, O. (1996) A high mountain population of the ring-tailed lemur, *Lemur catta* on the Andringitra Massif, Madagascar. *Oryx* 30: 259-268.

G18 Goodman, S.M. and Soarimalala, V. (2004) A new species of *Microgale* (Lipotyphla: Tenrecidae: Oryzorictinae) from the Forêt des Mikea of southwestern Madagascar. *Proceedings of the Biological Society of Washington* 117: 251-265

G19 Goodman, S.M., Ganzhorn, J.U. and Rakotndravony (2003) Introduction to the Mammals. In Goodman, S.M. and Benstead, J.P. (eds) *The Natural History of Madagascar*, pp. 1159 – 1186. The University of Chicago Press, Chicago, USA.

G20 Green, G.M. and Sussman, R.W. (1990) Deforestation history of the eastern rainforests of Madagascar from satellite images. *Science* 248: 212-215.

G20a Harper, G., Steininger, M.K., Tucker, C.J. Juhn, D. and Hawkins, A.F.A. (submitted) *Fifty Years of Deforestation and Forest Fragmentation in Madagascar*. PLOS.

G21 Jansa, S.A. and Carleton, M.D. (2003) Systematics and Phylogenetics of Madagascar's Native Rodents. In Goodman, S.M. and Benstead, J.P. (eds) *The Natural History of Madagascar*, pp. 1257 – 1265. The University of Chicago Press, Chicago, USA.

G22 Jury, M.R. (2003) The Climate of Madagascar. In Goodman, S.M. and Benstead, J.P. (eds) *The Natural History of Madagascar*, pp. 75 – 87. The University of Chicago Press, Chicago, USA.

G23 Kremen, C. (2003) The Masoala Peninsula. In Goodman, S.M. and Benstead, J.P. (eds) *The Natural History of Madagascar*, pp. 1459 – 1466. The University of Chicago Press, Chicago, USA.

G24 MacPhee, R. D. E. (1994) Morphology, adaptations and relationships of *Plesiorycteropus*, and a diagnosis of a new order of eutherian mammals. *Bulletin of the American Museum of Natural History* 220.

G25 MacPhee, R. D. E. and D. A. Burney (1991) Dating of modified femora of extinct dwarf *Hippopotamus* from southern Madagascar: implications for constraining human colonisation and vertebrate extinction events. *Journal of Archaeological Science*, 18: 695-706.

G26 Olson, L.E. and Goodman, S.M. (2003) Phylogeny and Biogeography of Tenrecs. In Goodman, S.M. and Benstead, J.P. (eds) *The Natural History of Madagascar*, pp. 1235 – 1242. The University of Chicago Press, Chicago, USA.

G27 Olson, L.E., Goodman, S.M. and Yoder, A. (2004) Illumination of cryptic species boundaries in Long-tailed Shrew Tenrecs (Mammalia: Tenrecidae; *Microgale*), with new insights into

geographic variation and distributional constraints. *Biological Journal of the Linnean Society* 83: 1-22.

G28 Randrianandianina, B.N., Andriamahaly, L.R., Harisoa, F.M. and Nicoll, M.E. (2003) The Role of the Protected Areas in the Management of the Island's Biodiversity. In Goodman, S.M. and Benstead, J.P. (eds) *The Natural History of Madagascar*, pp. 1423 – 1444. The University of Chicago Press, Chicago, USA.

G29 Rasolonandrasana, B. and Grenfell, S. (2003) Parc National d'Andringitra. In Goodman, S.M. and Benstead, J.P. (eds) *The Natural History of Madagascar*, pp. 1489 – 1494. The University of Chicago Press, Chicago, USA.

G30 Schmid, J. and Stephenson, P.J. (2003) Physiological Adaptations of Malagasy Mammals: Lemurs and Tenrecs compared. In Goodman, S.M. and Benstead, J.P. (eds) *The Natural History of Madagascar*, pp. 1198 – 1203. The University of Chicago Press, Chicago, USA.

G31 Yoder, A. D (2003) Phylogeny of the Lemurs. In Goodman, S.M. and Benstead, J.P. (eds) *The Natural History of Madagascar*, pp. 1242 – 1247. The University of Chicago Press, Chicago, USA.

G32 Yoder, A. D. and Flynn, J.J. (2003) Origin of Malagasy Carnivora. In Goodman, S.M. and Benstead, J.P. (Eds) *The Natural History of Madagascar*, pp. 1253 – 1256. The University of Chicago Press, Chicago, USA.

Cited Literature: Order Lypotyphla (Insectivores)

IN1 Ade, M. (1996) Examination of the digestive tract contents of *Tenrec ecaudatus* Schreber, 1777 (Tenrecidae, Insectivora) from western Madagascar. In: Ganzhorn, J.U. and Sorg, J.-P. (eds.) Ecology and Economy of a Tropical Dry Forest in Madagascar, pp. 233-249. *Primate Report*, Special Issue, 46-1(June 1996).

IN2 Ade, M. (1996) Morphological observations on a *Microgale* specimen (Insectivora, Tenrecidae) from western Madagascar. In: Ganzhorn, J.U. and Sorg, J.-P. (eds.) Ecology and Economy of a Tropical Dry Forest in Madagascar, pp. 251-255. *Primate Report*, Special Issue, 46-1(June 1996).

IN3 Barden, T.L., Evans, M.I., Raxworthy, C.J., Razafimahimodison, J.C. and Wilson, A. (1991) The mammals of Ambatovaky Special Reserve. In, Thompson, P.M. and Evans, M.I. (eds.) *A Survey of Ambatovaky Special Reserve, Madagascar*. Madagascar Environmental Research Group. Chapter 5, pp. 1-22 & Appendix 2.

IN4 Benstead, J.P. and Olson, L.E. (2003) *Limnogale mergulus*, Web-footed or Aquatic Tenrec. In Goodman, S.M. and Benstead, J.P. (eds) *The Natural History of Madagascar*, pp. 1267 – 1273. The University of Chicago Press, Chicago, USA.

IN5 Benstead, J.P., Barnes, K.H. and Pringle, C.M. (2001) Diet, activity patterns, foraging movements and response to deforestation of the Aquatic Tenrec, *Limnogale*

mergulus (Lipotyphla: Tenrecidae) in eastern Madagascar. *Journal of Zoology*, London 254: 119-129.

IN6 Eisenberg, J.F. (1975) Tenrecs and Solenodons in captivity. *International Zoo Yearbook* 15: 6-12.

IN7 Eisenberg, J.F. and Gould, E. (1967) The maintenance of tenrecoid insectivores in captivity. *International Zoo Yearbook* 7: 194-196.

IN8 Eisenberg, J.F. and Gould, E. (1970) The tenrecs: a study in mammalian behaviour and evolution. *Smithsonian Contributions to Zoology* 27: 1-137.

IN9 Eisenberg, J.F. and Gould, E. (1984) The Insectivores. In Jolly, A., Oberle, P. and Albignac, R. (eds.). *Key Environments – Madagascar*, pp 155-165. Pergamon Press, Oxford.

IN10 Fowler, P.A. (1986) Aspects of reproduction and heterothermy in seasonally breeding mammals. PhD thesis, University of Aberdeen, Aberdeen, U.K.

IN11 Ganzhorn, J.U., Sommer, S., Abraham, J.-P., Ade, M., Raharivololona, B.M., Rakotovao, E.R., Rakotondrasoa, C. and Randriamarosoa, R. (1996) Mammals of the Kirindy Forest with special emphasis on *Hypogeomys antimena* and the effects of logging on the small mammal fauna. In: Ganzhorn, J.U. and Sorg, J.-P. (eds.) Ecology and Economy of a Tropical Dry Forest in Madagascar, pp. 251-255. *Primate Report*, Special Issue, 46-

1(June 1996).

IN12 Ganzhorn, J.U., Ganzhorn, A.W., Abraham, J.-P., Andriamanarivo, L. and Ramananjatovo, A. (1990) The impact of selective logging on forest structure and tenrec populations in western Madagascar. *Oecologia* 84: 126-133.

IN13 Genest, H. and Petter, F. (1977) Subfamilies Tenrecinae and Oryzorictinae. In Meester, J. and Setzer, H.W. *The Mammals of Africa: an Identification Manual*. Smithsonian Inst. Press, Washington, D.C.

IN14 Godfrey, G.K. and Oliver, W.L.R. (1978) The reproduction and development of the pygmy hedgehog. *Dodo* 15: 38-52.

IN15 Goodman, S.M. (2003) *Oryzorictes*, Mole Tenrec or Rice Tenrec. In Goodman, S.M. and Benstead, J.P. (eds) *The Natural History of Madagascar*, pp. 1278 – 1281. The University of Chicago Press, Chicago, USA.

IN16 Goodman, S.M. and Ganzhorn, J.U. (1994) Les petits mammifères. In: Goodman, S.M. and Langrand, O. (eds.) *Inventaire Biologique Forêt de Zombitse, Recherches pour le Developpement, Série Science Biologiques*, pp. 58-63. No.Spécial 1994. Centre d'Information et de Documentation Scientifique et Technique, Antananarivo, Madagascar.

IN17 Goodman, S.M. and Jenkins, P.D. (1998) The Insectivores of the Réserve Spéciale d'Anjanaharibe-Sud, Madagascar. In Goodman, S.M. (ed) A Floral and Faunal

Inventory of the Réserve Spéciale d'Anjanaharibe-Sud, Madagascar: with reference to elevational variation. *Fieldiana Zoology* 90: 139-161.

IN18 Goodman, S.M. and Thorstrom, R. (1998) The diet of the Madagascar Red Owl (*Tyto soumagnei*) on the Masoala Peninsula, Madagascar. *Wilson Bulletin* 110: 417-421.

IN19 Goodman, S.M. and Jenkins, P.D. (2000) Tenrecs (Lipotyphla: Tenrecidae) of the Parc National de Marojejy, Madagascar. In Goodman, S.M. (ed) A Floral and Faunal Inventory of the Parc National de Marojejy, Madagascar: with reference to elevational variation. *Fieldiana Zoology* 97: 201-229.

IN20 Goodman, S.M. and Rakotondravony, D. (2000) The effects of forest fragmentation and isolation on the insectivorous small mammals (Lipotyphla) on the Central High Plateau of Madagascar. *Journal of Zoology, London* 250: 193-200.

IN21 Goodman, S.M. and Rasolonandrasana, B.P.N. (2001) Elevational zonation of birds, insectivores, rodents and primates on the slopes of the Andringitra Massif, Madagascar. *Journal of Natural History* 35: 285-305.

IN22 Goodman, S.M. and Soarimalala, V. (2002) Les petits mammifères de la Réserve Spéciale de Manongarivo. In Gautier, L and Goodman S.M. (eds) Inventaire floristique et faunistique de la Réserve Spéciale de Manongarivo, Madagascar. *Boissiera* 59: 383-401.

IN23 Goodman, S.M. and Soarimalala, V. (2004) A new species of *Microgale* (Lipotyphla: Tenrecidae: Oryzorictinae) from the Forêt des Mikea of southwestern Madagascar. *Proceedings of the Biological Society of Washington* 117: 251-265

IN24 Goodman, S.M., Langrand, O. and Raxworthy, C.J. (1993) The food habits of the Madagascar Long-eared Owl (*Asia madagascariensis*) in two habitats in southern Madagascar. *Ostrich* 64: 79-85.

IN25 Goodman, S.M., Langrand, O. and Raxworthy, C.J. (1993) The food habits of the Barn Owl (*Tyto alba*) at three sites on Madagascar. *Ostrich* 64: 160-171.

IN26 Goodman, S.M., Raxworthy, C.J. and Jenkins, P.D. (1996) Insectivore Ecology in the Réserve Naturelle Intégrale d'Andringitra, Madagascar. In Goodman, S.M. (ed) A Floral and Faunal Inventory

of the Eastern slopes of the Réserve Naturelle Intégrale d'Andringitra, Madagascar: with reference to elevational variation. *Fieldiana Zoology* 85: 218-230.

IN27 Goodman, S.M., Andrianarimisa, A., Olson, L.E. and Soarimalala, V. (1996) Patterns of elevational distribution of birds and small mammals in the humid forests of Montagne d'Ambre, Madagascar. *Ecotropica* 2: 87-98.

IN28 Goodman, S.M., Rakotondravony, D., Schatz, G. and Wilmé, L. (1996) Species richness of the forest-dwelling birds, rodents and insectivores in a planted forest of native trees: a test case from Ankaratra, Madagascar. *Ecotropica* 2: 109-120.

IN29 Goodman, S.M., Jenkins, P.D. and Langrand, O. (1997) Exceptional records of *Microgale* species (Insectivora: Tenrecidae) in vertebrate food remains. *Kunde: Bonn. Zool. Beiträge* 47: 1-2.

IN30 Goodman, S.M, Langrand, O. and Rasolonandrasana, B.P.N. (1997) The Food Habits of *Cryptoprocta ferox* in the High Mountain Zone of the Andringita Massif, Madagascar (Carnivora, Viverridae). *Mammalia* 61: 185-192.

IN31 Goodman, S.M., Jenkins, P.D. and Pidgeon, M. (1999) Lipotyphla (Tenrecidae and Soricidae) of the Réserve Naturelle Intégrale d'Andohahela, Madagascar. In Goodman, S.M. (ed) A Floral and Faunal Inventory of the Eastern slopes of the Réserve Naturelle Intégrale d'Andohahela, Madagascar: with reference to elevational variation. *Fieldiana Zoology* 94: 187-216.

IN32 Goodman, S.M., Rakotondravony, D., Raherilalao, M.J., Rakotomalala, D., Raselimanana, A.P., Soarimalala, V., Duplantier, J.-M., Duchemin, J.-B. and Rafanomezantsoa (2000) Inventaire biologique de la forêt de Tsinjoarivo, Ambatolampy. *Akon'ny Ala* 27: 18-35.

IN33 Goodman, S.M., Rakotondravony, D., Soarimalala, V., Duchemin, J.-B. and Duplantier, J.-M. (2000) Syntopic occurrence of *Hemicentetes semispinosus* and *Hemicentetes nigriceps* (Lipotyphla: Tenrecidae) on the central highlands of Madagascar. *Mammalia* 64: 113-136.

IN34 Goodman, S.M., Ganzhorn, J.U. and Rakotndravony (2003) Introduction to the Mammals. In

Goodman, S.M. and Benstead, J.P. (eds) *The Natural History of Madagascar*, pp. 1159 – 1186. The University of Chicago Press, Chicago, USA.

IN35 Gould, E (1965) Evidence for echolocation in the Tenrecidae of Madagascar. Proceedings of the American Philosophical Society 109: 352-360.

IN36 Gould, E. and Eisenberg, J.F. (1966) Notes on the biology of the Tenrecidae. *Journal of Mammalogy*. 47: 660- 686.

IN37 Grandidier, G. (1934) Deux nouveaux mammifères insectivores de Madagascar, *Microgale drouhardi* et *Microgale parvula*. *Bull. Mus. Natn. Hist. Nat. Paris (Zool.)* 6: 474-477.

IN38 Hasler, M.J., Hasler, J.F. and Nalbandov, A.V. (1977) Comparative breeding biology of musk shrews (*Suncus murinus*) from Guam and Madagascar. *Journal of Mammalogy* 58: 285-290.

IN39 Hawkins, C.E. (2003) *Cryptoprocta ferox*, Fossa, Fosa. In Goodman, S.M. and Benstead, J.P. (eds) *The Natural History of Madagascar*, pp. 1360 – 1363. The University of Chicago Press, Chicago, USA.

IN40 Hutterer, R. (1993) Order Insectivora. In Wilson, D.E. and Reeder, D.M. (eds) *Mammal Species of the World: A Taxonomic and Geographic Reference*, 69-130. Smithsoniam Institute Press, Washington D.C., USA.

IN41 Hutterer, R. and Tranier, M. (1990) The immigration of the Asian house shrew (*Suncus murinus*) into Africa and Madagascar. In Peters and Hutterer, R. (eds.) *Vertebrates in the Tropics*, pp.309-321. Museum A. Koenig, Bonn.

IN42 Jenkins, P.D. (1988) A new species of *Microgale* (Insectivora: Tenrecidae) from north eastern Madagascar. *American Museum Novitates* 2910; 1-7.

IN43 Jenkins, P.D. (1992) Description of a new species of *Microgale* (Insectivora: Tenrecidae) from north eastern Madagascar. *Bulletin of the Natural History Museum*, London (Zoology) 58: 53-59.

IN44 Jenkins, P.D. (1993) A new species of *Microgale* (Insectivora: Tenrecidae) from eastern Madagascar with unusual dentition. *American Museum Novitates* 3067: 1-11.

IN45 Jenkins, P.D. (2003) *Microgale*,

Shrew Tenrecs. In Goodman, S.M. and Benstead, J.P. (eds) *The Natural History of Madagascar,* pp. 1273-1278. The University of Chicago Press, Chicago, USA.

IN46 Jenkins, P.D. and Goodman, S.M. (1999) A new species of *Microgale* (Lipotyphla, Tenrecidae) from isolated forest in southwestern Madagascar. *Bulletin of the Natural History Museum,* London (Zoology) 65: 155-164.

IN47 Jenkins, P.D., Goodman, S.M. and Raxworthy, C.J. (1996) The Shrew Tenrecs (Microgale)(Insectivora: Tenrecidae) of the Réserve Naturelle Intégrale d'Andringitra, Madagascar. In Goodman, S.M. (ed) *A Floral and Faunal Inventory of the Eastern slopes of the Réserve Naturelle Intégrale d'Andringitra, Madagascar: with reference to elevational variation. Fieldiana Zoology* 85: 191-217.

IN48 Jenkins, P.D., Raxworthy, C. J. and Nussbaum, R.A. (1997) A new species of *Microgale* (Insectivora, Tenrecidae), with comments on the status of four other taxa of shrew tenrec. *Bulletin of the Natural History Museum,* London (Zoology) 63: 1-12.

IN49 MacPhee, R.D.E. (1987) The shrew tenrecs of Madagascar: systematic revision and Holocene distribution of *Microgale* (Insectivora: Tenrecidae). *American Museum Novitates* 2889.

IN50 Major, C.I. Forsyth (1896) Diagnoses of new mammals from Madagascar. *Annals & Magazine of Natural History,* series 6, 18: 318-325.

IN51 Major, C.I. Forsyth (1896) Descriptions of four additional new mammals from Madagascar. *Annals & Magazine of Natural History,* series 6, 18: 461-463.

IN52 Mallinson, J. (1974) Establishing mammalian gestation periods. *J.W.P.T. Report* 9: 62-65.

IN53 Malzy, P. (1965) Un mammifère aquatique de Madagascar: Le *Limnogale. Mammalia* 29: 399-411.

IN54 Morrison-Scott, T.C.S. (1948) The insectivorous genera *Microgale* and *Nesogale* (Madagascar). *Proceedings of the Zoological Society (London),* 118: 817-822.

IN55 Nicoll, M.E. (1982) Reproductive ecology of *Tenrec ecaudatus* (Insectivora: Tenrecidae) in the Seychelles. Ph.D. thesis, University of Aberdeen, UK.

IN56 Nicoll, M.E. (1983) Mechanisms and consequences of large litter production in *Tenrec ecaudatus* (Insectivora: Tenrecidae). Annales de la Musée Royale de l'Afrique Centrale, *Science Zoologiques* 237: 219-226.

IN57 Nicoll, M.E. (1985) Responses to Seychelles tropical forest seasons by a litter foraging mammalian insectivore, *Tenrec ecaudatus,* native to Madagascar. *J. Anim. Ecol.* 54: 71-88.

IN58 Nicoll, M.E. (1986) Diel variation in body temperature in *Tenrec ecaudatus* during seasonal hypothermia. *Journal of Mammalogy* 67: 759-762.

IN59 Nicoll, M.E. (2001) Tenrecs. In MacDonald, D. W (ed) *The New Encyclopedia of Mammals,* pp 728-731. Oxford University Press, UK.

IN60 Nicoll, M.E. (2003) *Tenrec ecaudatus,* Tenrec, *Tandraka, Trandraka.* In Goodman, S.M. and Benstead, J.P. (eds) *The Natural History of Madagascar,* pp. 1283 – 1287. The University of Chicago Press, Chicago, USA.

IN61 Nicoll, M.E., and Racey, P.A. (1985) Follicular development, ovulation, fertilization and fetal development in tenrecs (*Tenrec ecaudatus*). *Journal of Reproduction and Fertility* 74: 47-55.

IN62 Nicoll, M.E. and Langrand O. (1989) *Madagascar: Revue de la Conservation et des Aires Protégées.* WWF, Gland, Switzerland, pp 374.

IN63 Nicoll, M.E. and Rathbun, G.B. (1990) *African Insectivora and Elephant Shrews: An Action Plan for their Conservation.* IUCN, Gland, Switzerland.

IN64 Nicoll, M.E. and Thompson, S.D. (1987) Basal Metabolic Rates and the Energetics of Reproduction in Therian Mammals: Marsupials and Placentals Compared. *Symposium of the Zoological Society,* London 57: 7-27.

IN65 Nowak, R.M. (1991) *Walker's Mammals of the World* (5th edition). Johns Hopkins U.P. Baltimore and London.

IN66 Olson, L.E. and Goodman, S.M. (2003) Phylogeny and Biogeography of Tenrecs. In Goodman, S.M. and Benstead, J.P. (eds) *The Natural History of Madagascar,* pp. 1235 – 1242. The University of Chicago Press, Chicago, USA.

IN67 Olson, L.E., Goodman, S.M. and Yoder, A. (2004) Illumination of cryptic species boundaries in Long-tailed Shrew Tenrecs (Mammalia: Tenrecidae; *Microgale*), with new insights into geographic variation and distributional constraints. *Biological Journal of the Linnean Society* 83: 1-22.

IN68 Poppitt, S.D., Speakman, J.R. and Racey, P.A. (1994) Energetics of reproduction in the lesser hedgehog tenrec, *Echinops telfairi. Physiological Zoology* 976-994.

IN69 Raxworthy, C.J. and Rakotondraparany, F. (1988) Mammals Report. In Quansah, N. (ed.) *Manongarivo Special Reserve, Madagascar 1987/88 Expedition Report.* Madagascar Environmental Research Group. Chapter 7, pp. 121-131.

IN70 Raxworthy, C.J. and Nussbaum, R.N. (1994) A rainforest survey of amphibians, reptiles and small mammals at Montagne d'Ambre, Madagascar. *Biological Conservation* 69: 65-73.

IN71 Soarimalala, V. and Goodman, S.M. (2003) The Food Habits of Lipotyphla. In Goodman, S.M. and Benstead, J.P. (eds) *The Natural History of Madagascar,* pp. 1203 – 1205. The University of Chicago Press, Chicago, USA.

IN72 Stephenson, P.J. (1991) Reproductive energetics of the Tenrecidae (Mammalian: Insectivora). PH.D. thesis, University of Aberdeen, UK.

IN73 Stephenson, P.J. (1993) The small mammal fauna of Réserve Speciale d'Analamazaotra, Madagascar: the effects of human disturbance on endemic species diversity. *Biodiversity and Conservation* 2: 603- 615.

IN74 Stephenson, P.J. (1993) Reproductive biology of the large-eared tenrec, *Geogale aurita* (Insectivora: Tenrecidae). *Mammalia* 57: 553-563.

IN75 Stephenson, P.J. (1994) Small mammal species richness in a Madagascar rainforest. *African Journal of Ecology* 32: 255-258.

IN76 Stephenson, P.J. (1994) Notes on the biology of the fossorial tenrec, *Oryzorictes hova* (Insectivora: Tenrecidae). *Mammalia* 58: 312-315.

IN77 Stephenson, P.J. (1994) Resting metabolic rate and body temperature in the aquatic tenrec, *Limnogale mergulus* (Insectivora: Tenrecidae). *Acta Theriologica* 39: 89-92.

IN78 Stephenson, P.J. (1995) Small mammal micro-habitat use in lowland rainforest of north east

Madagascar. *Acta Theriologica* 40(4): 425-438.

IN79 Stephenson, P.J. (1995) Taxonomy of shrew-tenrecs (*Microgale* spp.) from eastern and central Madagascar. *Journal of Zoology* (London) 235: 339-350.

IN80 Stephenson, P.J. (2003) Liptotyphla (ex Insectivora): *Geogale aurita*, Large-eared Tenrec. In Goodman, S.M. and Benstead, J.P. (eds) *The Natural History of Madagascar*, pp. 1265 – 1267. The University of Chicago Press, Chicago, USA.

IN81 Stephenson, P.J. (2003) *Hemicentetes*, Streaked Tenrecs, *Sora, Tsora*. In Goodman, S.M. and Benstead, J.P. (eds) *The Natural History of Madagascar*, pp. 1281 – 1283. The University of Chicago Press, Chicago, USA.

IN82 Stephenson, P.J. and Racey, P.A. (1992) Basal metabolic rate and body mass in the Tenrecidae: the influence of phylogeny and ecology on the energetics of the Insectivora. *Israel Journal of Zoology* 38: 426.

IN83 Stephenson, P.J. and Racey, P.A. (1993) Reproductive energetics of the Tenrecidae (Mammalia: Insectivora), I: the large-eared tenrec, *Geogale aurita*. *Physiological Zoology* 66: 643-663.

IN84 Stephenson, P.J. and Racey, P.A. (1993) Reproductive energetics of the Tenrecidae (Mammalia: Insectivora), II: the shrew tenrecs, *Microgale* spp. *Physiological Zoology* 66: 664-685.

IN85 Stephenson, P.J. and Racey, P.A. (1994) Seasonal variation in resting metabolic rate and body temperature of streaked tenrecs, *Hemicentetes nigriceps* and *Hemicentetes semispinosus* (Insectivora: Tenrecidae). *Journal of Zoology* (London) 232: 285-294.

IN86 Stephenson, P.J. and Racey, P.A. (1995) Resting metabolic rate and reproduction in the Insectivora. *Comparitive Biochemical. & Physiol.* 112A: 215-223.

IN87 Stephenson, P.J., Racey, P.A. and Rakotondraparany, F (1994) Maintenance and reproduction of tenrecs (Tenrecidae) at Parc Tsimbazaza, Madagascar. *International Zoo Yearbook*. 33: 194-201.

IN88 Stephenson, P.J., Randriamahazo, H., Rakotoarison, N. and Racey, P.A. (1994) Conservation of mammalian species diversity in Ambohitantely Special Reserve, Madagascar. *Biol. Conserv.* 69: 213-218.

IN89 Stephenson, P.J., Speakman, J.R. and Racey, P.A. (1994) Field meta-

bolic rate in two species of shrew tenrec, *Microgale dobsoni* and *Microgale talazaci. Comp. Biochem. & Physiol.* 107A: 283- 287.

IN90 Taylor, A. (1995) The abundance and distribution of small mammals in a Malagasy rainforest in relation to micro-habitat. In Wells, M. *et al.*, Project Madagascar 1994 – Final Report of the 1994 Aberdeen University Expedition to Zahamena Special Reserve, Madagascar. pp. 20-28. Aberdeen University 1995.

IN91 Thomas, O. (1918) On the arrangement of the small Tenrecidae hitherto referred to *Oryzorictes* and *Microgale*. *Annals and Magazine of Natural History* 17: 250-252.

IN92 Wever, E.G. and Herman, P.N. (1968) Stridulation and hearing in the tenrec, *Hemicentetes semispinosus. Journal of Auditory Research* 8: 39-42.

IN93 Yoder, A., Olson, L.E., Hanley, C., Heckman, K.L., Rasoloarison, R. Russell, A.L., Ranivo, J., Soarimalala, V., Karanth, K.P., Raselimanana, A.P. and Goodman, S.M. (2005) A multidimensional approach for detecting species patterns in Malagasy vertebrates. *PNAS* 102 (supplement 1); 6587-6594.

Cited Literature: Order Chiroptera

B1 Baum, D.A. (1995) The comparative pollination and floral biology of baobabs (*Adansonia*: Bombaceae). *Annals of the Missouri Botanical Garden*, 82: 322-348.

B2 Baum, D.A. (1996) The ecology and conservation of the baobabs of Madagascar. In: Ganzhorn, J.U. and J.-P. Sorg (eds.), Ecology and Economy of a Tropical Dry Forest in Madagascar, pp. 311-327. *Primate Report*, Special Issue, 46-1(June 1996).

B3 Bayliss, J. and Hayes, B. (1999) The status and distribution of bats, primates and butterflies from the Mikira Plateau, Madagascar. Fauna and Flora International, Cambridge.

B4 Bergmans, W. (1977) Notes on new material of *Rousettus madagascariensis* Grandidier, 1929 (Mammalia, Megachiroptera). *Mammalia* 41: 67-74.

B5 Bergmans, W. (1990) Taxonomy and biogeography of African fruit bats (Mammalia, Megachiroptera) 3. The genera *Scotonycteris*

Matschie 1894, *Casinycteris* Thomas 1910, *Pteropus* Brisson 1762 and *Eidolon* Rafinesque 1815. *Beaufortia* 40(7): 111-117.

B6 Bergmans, W. (1994) Taxonomy and biogeography of African fruit bats (Mammalia, Megachiroptera) 4. The genus *Rousettus* Gray 1821. *Beaufortia* 44(4): 79-126.

B7 Bollen, A., and L. van Elsacker. 2002. Feeding ecology of *Pteropus rufus* (Pteropodidae) in the littoral forest of Sainte Luce, SE Madagascar. *Acta Chiropterologica* 4:33-47.

B8 Bollen, A., L. van Elsacker, and A. U. Ganzhorn. 2004. Tree dispersal strategies in the littoral forests of Sainte Luc (SE Madagascar). *Oecologia* 139:604-616.

B9 Cheke, A.S. and Dahl, J.F. (1981) The status of bats on Western Indian Ocean islands, with special reference to *Pteropus*. *Mammalia* 45: 205-238.

B10 Cottam, M. and Heath, H. (1999) *Bats of Lac Sahara*: A wetland in northern Madagascar. Report

available from L. Eger.

B11 Cotterill, F.P.D. and Fergusson, R.A. (1993) Seasonally polyestrous reproduction in a free-tailed bat *Tadarida fulminans* (Microchiroptera: Molossidae) in Zimbabwe. *Biotropica* 25(4): 487-492.

B12 DeFrees, S.L. and Wilson, D.E. (1988) *Eidolon helvum*. *Mammalian Species* 312.

B13 Duckworth, J.W. and Rakotondraparany, F. (1990) The mammals of Marojejy. In Safford, R. J. and Duckworth, J.W. (eds.) A Wildlife Survey of Marojejy Nature Reserve, Madagascar, pp.54-60. *Int. Council Bird Preserv. Study Report No. 40*.

B14 Du Puy, B. (1996) Faunal Interactions with the genus *Adansonia* in the Kirindy Forest. In Ganzhorn, J.U. and Sorg, J.-P. (eds.) Ecology and Economy of a Tropical Dry Forest in Madagascar, pp. 329-334. *Primate Report*, Special Issue, 46-1(June 1996).

B15 Eger, J.L. and Mitchell, L. (1996) Biogeography of the bats of Madagascar. In: Lourenco, W.R. (ed.) *Biogéographie de Madagascar*, pp. 321-328. Editions de l'ORSTOM, Paris.

B16 Eger, J.L. and Mitchell, L. (2003) Chiroptera, Bats. In Goodman, S.M. and Benstead, J.P. (eds) *The Natural History of Madagascar*, pp. 1287 – 1298. The University of Chicago Press, Chicago, USA.

B17 Fayenewo, J.O. and Halstead, L.B. (1974) Breeding cycle of the Straw-coloured Fruit Bat, *Eidolon helvum* at Ile Ife Nigeria. *Journal of Mammology* 55: 453-454.

B18 Freeman, P.W. (1981) A multivariate study of the family Molossidae (Mammalia, Chiroptera): morphology, ecology and evolution. *Fieldiana Zoology* 7: 1-173.

B19 Goodman, S.M. (1996) Results of a bat survey of the eastern slopes of the Réserve Naturelle Intégrale d'Andringitra, Madagascar. In Goodman, S.M. (ed) A Floral and Faunal Inventory of the Eastern slopes of the Réserve Naturelle Intégrale d'Andringitra, Madagascar: with reference to elevational variation. *Fieldiana Zoology* 85: 284-288.

B20 Goodman, S.M. (1998) Notes on the Bats of the Réserve Spéciale d'Anjanaharibe-Sud, Madagascar. In Goodman, S.M. (ed) A Floral and Faunal Inventory of the Réserve Spéciale d'Anjanaharibe-Sud, Madagascar: with reference to elevational variation. *Fieldiana Zoology* 90: 223-226.

B21 Goodman, S.M. (1999) Notes on the Bats of the Réserve Naturelle Intégrale d'Andohahela, Madagascar. In Goodman, S.M. (ed) A Floral and Faunal Inventory of the Eastern slopes of the Réserve Naturelle Intégrale d'Andohahela, Madagascar: with reference to elevational variation. *Fieldiana Zoology* 94: 252-258.

B22 Goodman, S.M. and Cardiff, S.G. (2004) A new species of *Chaerephon* (Molossidae) from Madagascar with notes on other members of the family. *Acta Chiropterologica* 6 (2): 227-248.

B23 Goodman, S.M. and Ranivo, J. (2004) The taxonomic status *Neoromicia somalicus malagasyensis*. *Mammalian Biology* 69 (6): 434-438.

B24 Goodman, S.M., Andriafidison, D., Andrianaivoarivelo, R., Cardiff, S. G., Jenkins, R.K.B., Kofoky, A., Mbohoahy, T., Rakotondravony, D., Ranivo, J., Ratrimomanarivo,

F., Razafimanahaka, J. and Racey, P. A. (2005) The distribution and conservation of bats in the dry regions of Madagascar. *Animal Conservation* 8: 153-165.

B25 Goodman, S.M., Jenkins, R. K. B. and Ratrimomanarivo, F. H. (2005) A review of the genus *Scotophilus* (Mammalia: Chiroptera: Vespertilionidae) on Madagascar, with the description of a new species. *Zoosystema* 27: 867-882.

B25a Goodman, S.M., Cardiff, S.G., Ranivo, J. Russell, A. L. and Yoder, A.D. (2006) A New Species of *Emballonura* (Chiroptera: Emballonuridae) from the Dry Regions of Madagascar. *American Museum Novitates* 3538: 1-24.

B25b Goodman, S.M., Rakotondraparany, F. And Kofoky, A. (in press) The Description of a New Species of *Myzopoda* (Myzopodidae: Chiroptera) from Western Madagascar. *Mammalian Biology (2006), doi: 10.1016/j.mambio.2006.08.001*.

B26 Goodman, S.M., Ratrimomanarivo, F. H. and Randrianandrianina, F.H. (in press) A new species of *Scotophilus* (Chiroptera: Vespertilionidae) from western Madagascar. *Acta Chiropterologica*

B27 Göpfert, M.C. and Wasserthal, L.T. (1995) Notes on the echolocation calls, food and roosting behaviour of the Old World sucker-footed bat *Myzopoda aurita* (Chiroptera, Myzopodidae). *International Journal of Mammalian Biology* 60: 1-8.

B28 Griffin, D.R. (1974) Listening in the Dark – the acoustic orientation of bats and men. Dover, New York, USA.

B29 Hill, J.E. (1993) Long-fingered bats of the genus *Miniopterus* (Chiroptera: Vespertilionidae) from Madagascar. *Mammalia* 57: 401-405.

B30 Hutcheon, J.M. (2003) Frugivory by Malagasy Bats. In Goodman, S.M. and Benstead, J.P. (eds) *The Natural History of Madagascar*, pp. 1205 – 1207. The University of Chicago Press, Chicago, USA.

B31 Kearney, T.C., Volleth, M., Contrafatto, G. and Taylor, P. (2002) Systematic implications of chromosome GTG-band and bacula morphology of southern African *Eptesicus* and *Pipistrellus* and several other species of Vespertilionidae (Chiroptera: Vespertilionidae). *Acta Chiropterologica* 40: 55-76.

B31a Kofoky, A.F., Andriafidison,

D., Razafimanahaka, H.J., Rampilamanana, R.L., and Jenkins, R.K.B. (2006) The First Observation of *Myzopoda* sp. Roosting in Western Madagascar. *African Bat Conservation News* 9: 5-6.

B32 Koopman, K.F. (1984) Bats. In: Anderson, S. and Jones, J.K. (eds.) *Orders and Families of Recent Mammals of the World*, pp. 145-186. John Wiley & Sons, N.Y.

B33 Koopman, K.F. (1984) A progress report on the systematics of the African *Scotophilus* (Vespertilionidae). *Proceedings of 6th International Bat Research Conference*, Ile-Ife, Nigeria, p 102-113.

B34 Koopman, K.F. (1993) Order Chiroptera. In: Wilson, D.E. and Reeder, D.M. (eds.), *Mammal Species of the World: A Taxonomic and Geographic Reference*, 2nd edition, pp. 137-241. Smithsonian Inst. Press, Washington, D.C.

B35 Long, E. (1995) Some aspects of the feeding ecology of *Pteropus rufus* in north east Madagascar. In: Wells, M., Long, E., Palmer, G., Taylor, A., Tedd, J. and Grant, I. (eds.) Project Madagascar 1994: Final Report of University of Aberdeen Expedition to Zahamena Nature Reserve, Madagascar, pp. 30-35. Dept. Zoology, University of Aberdeen. Unpublished report.

B36 Long, E. (2002) The Role of *Pteropus rufus* in the pollination and seed dispersal in Madagascar. Ph.D. Thesis, University of Aberdeen, UK.

B37 MacKinnon, J.L., Hawkins, C.E. and Racey, P.A. (2003) Pteropodidae, Fruit Bats, *Fanihy, Angavo*. In Goodman, S.M. and Benstead, J.P. (eds) *The Natural History of Madagascar*, pp. 1299 – 1302. The University of Chicago Press, Chicago, USA.

B38 McHale, M. (1987) The Bats. In: Wilson, J. (ed.), The crocodile caves of Ankarana: Expedition to northern Madagascar 1986, pp. 14. *Cave Sci.: Trans. British Cave Res. Ass.* 14: 107-119.

B39 Mickleburgh, S.P., Hutson, A.M. and Racey, P.A. (1992) *Old World Fruit Bats: An Action Plan for their Conservation*. IUCN/SCC Chiroptera Special Group. IUCN Gland, Switzerland and Cambridge, U.K.

B40 Mutere, F.A. (1967) The breeding biology of equatorial vertebrates: Reproduction in the Fruit Bat,

Eidolon helvum at latitude 0°20'N. *Journal of Zoology* 153: 153-161.

B41 Peterson, R.L. Eger, J.L. and Mitchell, L. (1995) Chiroptères: *Faune de Madagascar*. Vol. 84. Nat. Hist. Mus. Paris.

B42 Pont, S.M. and Armstrong, J.D. (1990) A study of the bat fauna of the Réserve Naturelle Intégrale de Marojejy in north east Madagascar. Report of the Aberdeen University Expedition to Madagascar 1989. Dept. Zoology, University of Aberdeen. Unpublished report.

B43 Racey, P. (2004) 8 Million Bats: Africa's Best-kept Wildlife Secret. *Bats, Journal of Bat Conservation International* 22 (1): 1-5.

B44 Rasolozaka, I.N. (1994) Les Micro-Chiroptères. In: Goodman, S.M. and Langrand, O. (eds.) *Inventaire Biologique Forêt de Zombitse, Recherches pour le Developpement, Série Science Biologiques*, pp. 64-67. No.Spécial 1994. Centre d'Information et de Documentation Scientifique et Technique, Antananarivo, Madagascar.

B45 Ratrimomanarivo, F.H. and Goodman, S.M. (2005) The first records of the synanthropic occurrence of *Scotophilus* spp. on Madagascar. *African Bat Conservation* 6: 3-5.

B45a Razakarivony, V., Rajemison, B. and Goodman, S. M. (2005) The diet of Malagasy Microchiroptera

based on stomach contents. *Mammal Biology* 70: 312-316.

B46 Robbins, C.B., De Vree, F. and Van Cakenberghe, V. (1985) A systematic revision of the African bat genus *Scotophilus* (Vespertilionidae). Annales Musée royal de l'Afrique centrale, *Sciences Zoologiques*, Tervuren, Belgium 246: 51-84.

B47 Russ, J. and Bennett, D. (1999) *The bats of Masoala Peninsula, Madagascar and the use of expansion ultrasound detectors in surveying microchiropteran communities*. Final report of Queen's University, Belfast Masoala Bat Project, Glossop, UK: Viper.

B48 Schliemann, H. and Goodman, S.M. (2003) *Myzopoda aurita*, Old World Sucker-footed Bat. In Goodman, S.M. and Benstead, J.P. (eds) *The Natural History of Madagascar*, pp. 1303 – 1306. The University of Chicago Press, Chicago, USA.

B49 Schliemann, H. and Maas, B. (1978) *Myzopoda aurita*. *Mammalian Species* 116.

B50 Simmons, N.B. (2005) Order Chiroptera. In Wilson, D.E. and Reeder, D.M. (eds) *Mammal Species of the World: A Taxonomic and Geographical Article Reference*, 3rd Edition. Smithsonian Institution Press, Washington DC, USA.

B51 Smithers, R.H.N. (1971) *The Mammals of Botswana*. Trustees of the National Museum of Rhodesia (Zimbabwe).

B52 Skinner, J.D. and Smithers,

R.H.N. (1990) *The Mammals of the Southern African Subregion*. University of Pretoria, South Africa.

B53 Taylor, P.J. (2000) *Bats of Southern Africa*. University of Natal Press, Pietermaritzburg, South Africa.

B54 Van Cakenberghe, V. and DeVree, F. (1985) Systematics of African *Nycteris* (Mammalia: Chiroptera). *Proc. Int. Symp. Afr. Vert., Bonn*, pp. 53-90.

B55 Volleth, M., Bronner, G. Göpfert, M.C., Heller, K.-G., von Helversen, O., and Yong, H.-S. (2001) Karyotype comparison and phylogenetic relationships of *Pipistrellus*-like bats (Vespertilionidae; Chiroptera; Mammalia). *Chromosome Research* 9: 25-46.

B56 Wells, M. (1995) The roost ecology of the Malagasy flying fox (*Pteropus rufus*). In: Wells, M., Long, E., Palmer, G., Taylor, A., Tedd, J. and Grant, I. (eds.) Project Madagascar 1994: Final Report of University of Aberdeen Expedition to Zahamena Nature Reserve, Madagascar, pp. 36-44. Dept. Zoology, University of Aberdeen. Unpublished report.

B57 Yoder, A., Olson, L.E., Hanley, C., Heckman, K.L., Rasoloarison, R. Russell, A.L., Ranivo, J., Soarimalala, V., Karanth, K.P., Raselimanana, A.P. and Goodman, S.M. (2005) A multidimensional approach for detecting species patterns in Malagasy vertebrates. *PNAS* 102 (supplement 1); 6587-6594.

Cited Literature: Order Primates, Infraorder Lemuriformes

L1 Albignac, R. (1987) Status of the aye-aye in Madagascar. *Primate Conservation* 8: 44-45.

L2 Albignac, R. (1981) Lemurine social and territorial organisation in a northwestern Malagasy forest (restricted area of Ampijoroa). In Chiarelli, A.B. and Corruccini, R.S. (eds) *Primate Behaviour and Sociobiology*, pp 25-29. Springer Verlag, Berlin, Germany.

L3 Albignac, R., Justin, and Meier, B. (1991) Study of the first behaviour of *Allocebus trichotis* Gunther 1875 (hairy-eared dwarf lemurs): prosimian lemur rediscovered in the north west of Madagascar (Biosphere Reserve of Mananara-Nord). In: Ehara, A., Kimura, T., Takenaka, O. and Iwamoto, M. (eds.) *Primatology Today*. Elsevier Science, Amsterdam.

L4 Albrecht, G.H., Jenkins, P.D. and Godfrey, L.R. (1990)

Ecogeographic size variation among the living and subfossil prosimians of Madagascar. *American Journal of Primatology* 22: 1-50.

L5 Ancrenaz, M., Lachman-Ancrenaz, I. and Mundy, N. (1994) Field observations of Aye-ayes (*Daubentonia madagascariensis*) in Madagascar. *Folia Primatologica* 62: 22-36.

L6 Andriaholinirina, V.N., Rabarivola, J.C. and Rumpler, Y. (2004) Limites de la zone de répartition de *Propithecus diadema diadema* et *Propithecus diadema edwardsi*. *Lemur News* 9: 18-19.

L7 Andriaholinirina, V.N., Fausser, J.-L., Roos, C., Zinner, D., Thalmann, U., Rabarivola, C., Ravoarimanana, I., Ganzhorn, J. U., Meier, B., Hilgartner, R., Walter, L., Zaramody, A., Langer, C., Hahn, T., Zimmermann, E., Radespiel, U., Craul, M., Tomiuk, J., Tattersall, I. and Rumpler, Y. (2006) Molecular phylogeny and

taxonomic revision of the Sportive Lemurs (*Lepilemur*, Primates). *BMC Evolutionary Biology* 6: 17. http://www.biomedcentral.com/content/pdf/1471-2148-6-17.pdf

L8 Andriamasimanana, M. (1994) Ecoethological study of free-ranging Aye-ayes (*Daubentonia madagascariensis*) in Madagascar. *Folia Primatologica* 62: 37-45.

L9 Andrianarivo, A.J. (1981) Étude comparée de l'organisation sociale chez *Microcebus coquereli*. Establissement d'Enseignement Supérieur de Science, Université de Madagascar.

L10 Andrianjakarivelo V. (2004) Exploration de la zone en dehors de la peninsule Sahamalaza pour l'évaluation rapide de la population d'*E. m. flavifrons*. Report to WCS Madagascar, unpublished. 31 p.

L11 Andriantompohavana, R., Zaonarivelo, J. R., Endberg,

S. E., Randriamampionona, R., McGuire, S. M., Shore, G. D., Rakotonomenjanahary, R., Brenneman, R. A. and Louis, E. E. (2006) Mouse Lemurs of Northwestern Madagascar with a Description of a New Species at Lokobe Special Reserve. *Occasional Papers, Museum of Texas Tech University*, No. 259: 1-24.

L12   Andriantompohavana, R., Zaonarivelo, J. R., Randriamampionona, R., Razafindraibe, J.-F. X., Brenneman, R. A. and Louis, E. E. (2006) A Preliminary Study on Resident Lemur Populations in the Mariarano Classified Forest. *Lemur News*: 11: 21-24.

L13   Andrews, J. (1998) Infanticide by a female Black Lemur *Eulemur macaco macaco* in disturbed habitat on Nosy Be, northwestern Madagascar. *Folia Primatologica* 69: 14-17.

L14   Andrews, J. and Birkinshaw, C. R. (1998) A comparison between the daytime and night-time activity and feeding height of the black lemur, *Eulemur macaco macaco* (Primates: Lemuridae) in Lokobe Forest, Madagascar. In Harcourt, C., Crompton, R. H. and Feistner, A.T.C. (eds.) *Biology and Conservation of Prosimians. Folia Primatologica* 69(supplement):175-182.

L15   Andrews, J., Antilahimena, P. and Birkinshaw, C. R. (1998) Use of a Day Resting Box by Wild Sportive Lemur, *Lepilemur dorsalis*, on Nosy Be, northwest Madagascar. In Harcourt, C., Crompton, R. H. and Feistner, A.T.C. (eds.) *Biology and Conservation of Prosimians. Folia Primatologica* 69 (supplement):18-21.

L16   Arrigo-Nelson, S.J. and Wright, P.C. (2004) Survey results from Ranomafana National Park: New evidence for the effects of habitat preference and disturbance on the distribution of *Hapalemur. Folia Primatologica* 75: 331-334.

L17   Arrigo-Nelson et al. (in press) Milne-Edwards's Sifaka (*Propithecus edwardsi*) in Ranomafana National Park, Madagascar.

L18   Atsalis, S. (1999) Diet of the brown mouse lemur (*Microcebus rufus*) in Ranomafana National Park, Madagascar. *International Journal of Primatology* 20: 193-229.

L19   Atsalis, S. (1999) Seasonal fluctuations in body fat and activity levels in a rain forest species of

mouse lemur, *Microcebus rufus. International Journal of Primatology* 20: 883-910.

L20   Atsalis, S. (2000) Spatial distribution and population composition of the brown mouse lemur (*Microcebus rufus*) in Ranomafana National Park, Madagascar and its implications for social orgainisation. *American Journal of Primatology* 51: 61-78.

L21   Atsalis, S., Schmid, J. and Kappeler, P.M. (1996) Metrical comparisons of three species of mouse lemur. *Journal of Human Evolotion* 31: 61-68.

L22   Balko, E.A. (1996) Foraging ecology of *Varecia variegata variegata* at Ranomafana National Park, Madagascar. *American Journal of Physical Anthropology* 22 (supplement): 64.

L23   Balko, E.A. (1998) A behaviourally plastic response to forest composition and logging disturbance by *Varecia variegata variegata* in Ranomafana National Park, Madagascar. Ph.D. Thesis State University of New York, Syracuse, New York, USA.

L24   Balko, E.A., Chambers, R., Wright, P. and Underwood, B. (1995) The relationship of logging disturbance to forest composition and to population density and distribution of black and white ruffed lemur (*Varecia variegata variegata*) in Ranomafana National Park, Madagascar. In Patterson, B.D., Goodman, S.M. and Sedlock, J.L. (eds.) *Environmental Change in Madagascar*, pp. 36-37. Field Museum of Natural History, Chicago.

L25   Banks, M., Ellis, E.R., Antonio, M. and Wright, P.C. (in press) Census results for lemurs of northern Madagascar, including low populations numbers for the Critically Endangered *Propithecus perrieri. Animal Conservation.*

L26   Barre, V., Lebec, A., Petter, J-J. and Albignac, R. (1988) Etude du Microcébe par radiotracking dans la forêt de l'Ankarafantsika. In Rakotovato et al (eds), *L'Equilibre des ecosystémes forestiers a Madagascar: actes d'un séminaire international.* Gland and Cambridge, IUCN.

L27   Baum, D.A. (1996) The ecology and conservation of the baobabs of Madagascar. In Ganzhorn, J.U. and Sorg, J.-P. (eds.) Ecology and Economy of a Tropical Dry Forest in Madagascar, pp. 311-327.

Primate Report, Special Issue, 46-1 (June 1996).

L28   Birkinshaw, C. R (1999) The importance of the Balck Lemur (*Eulemur macaco macaco*) for seed dispersal in Lokobe Forest, Nosy Be. In Rakotosamimanana, B., Rasammimanana, Ganzhorn, J.U. and Goodman, S.M. (eds) *New Directions in Lemur Studies*, pp 189-199. Kluwer Academic Press/Plenum, New York.

L29   Birkinshaw, C. R (2003) Exploitation of the cicada (*Pycna madagascariensis*) for food by black lemurs (*Eulemur macaco macaco*) and brown lemurs (*Eulemur fulvus fulvus*). *Lemur News* 8: 3.

L30   Birkinshaw, C. R. and Colquhoun, I.C. (1998) Pollination of *Ravenala madagascariensis* and *Parkia madagascariensis* by *Eulemur macaco* in Madagascar. *Folia Primatologica* 69: 252-259.

L31   Birkinshaw, C. R. and Colquhoun, I.C. (2003) Lemur Food Plants. In Goodman, S.M. and Benstead, J.P. (eds) *The Natural History of Madagascar*, pp. 1207-1220. The University of Chicago Press, Chicago, USA.

L32   Britt, A. (1997) Environmental influences on the behavioural ecology of Black and White Ruffed Lemurs (*Varecia variegata variegata*). PH. D. Thesis, University of Liverpool.

L33   Britt, A. (2000) Diet and feeding behaviour of the Black and White Ruffed Lemurs (*Varecia variegata variegata*) in the Betampona Reserve, eastern Madagascar. *Folia Primatologica* 71: 133-141.

L34   Britt, A., Welch, C. and Katz, A. (2000) Ruffed Lemur restocking and conservation program update. *Lemur News* 5: 36-38.

L35   Britt, A., Welch, C. and Katz, A. (2001) The impact of *Cryptoprocta ferox* on the *Varecia variegata variegata* Reinforcement Project at Betampona. *Lemur News* 6: 35-37.

L36   Britt, A., Iambana, B.R. Welch, C. and Katz, A. (2003) Restocking of *Varecia variegata variegata* in the Réserve Naturelle Intégrale de Betampona. In Goodman, S.M. and Benstead, J.P. (eds) *The Natural History of Madagascar*, pp. 1545-1551. The University of Chicago Press, Chicago, USA.

L37   Brockman, D. K., Willis, M.S. and Karesh, W.B. (1987) Management and husbandry of ruffed lemurs, *Varecia variegata*, at the San Diego Zoo. II. Reproduction, pregnancy, parturition, litter size, infant care and reintroduction of hand raised infants. *Zoo Biology* 6: 349-363.

L38 Buesching, C., Heistermann, M. Hodges, J. and Zimmerman, E. (1998) Multimodal oestrus advertisement in a small nocturnal prosimian, *Microcebus murinus*. *Folia Primatologica* 69: 295-308.

L39 Burney, D.A. (1997) Theories and facts regarding Holocene environmental change before and after human colonization. In Goodman, S.M. and Patterson, B.D. (eds) *Natural Change and Human Impact in Madagascar*, pp75-89. Smithsonian Institute Press, Washington D.C.

L40 Burney, D.A. (1999) Rates, patterns and processes of land-scape transformation and extinc-tion in Madagascar. In MacPhee, R.D.E. (ed) *Extinctions in near time*, 145-164. Kluwer Academic Press/Plenum, New York

L41 Carrai, V. and Lunardini, A. (1996) Activity patterns and home range use of two groups of *Propithecus v. verreauxi* in the Kirindy Forest. In Ganzhorn, J.U. and Sorg, J.-P. (eds.), Ecology and Economy of a Tropical Dry Forest in Madagascar, pp. 275-284. *Primate Report*, Special Issue, 46-1 (June 1996).

L42 Ceska, V., Hoffman, H.-U. and Winkelsträter, K.-H. (1992) *Lemuren im Zoo*. Verlag Paul Parey, Berlin.

L43 Charles-Dominique, P. and Petter, J.-J. (1980) Ecology and social life of *Phaner furcifer*. In Charles-Dominique, P., Cooper, H.M., Hladik, A., Hladik, C.M., Pagès, E., Pariente, G.F., Petter-Rousseaux, A., Petter, J.-J. and Schilling, A. (eds.) *Nocturnal Malagasy Primates: Ecology, Physiology and Behaviour*, pp. 75-96. Academic Press, N.Y.

L44 Colquhoun, I.C. (1993) The socioecology of *Eulemur macaco*: a preliminary report. In Kappeler, P.M. and Ganzhorn, J.U. (eds.) *Lemur Social Systems and their Ecological Basis*, pp. 11-23. Plenum Press, London & N.Y.

L45 Colquhoun, I.C. (1996) Variation in seasonal dietry shifts among *Eulemur macaco macaco* groups at Ambato Massif, Madagascar. *American Journal of Physical Anthropology* 22 (supplement): 88.

L46 Colquhoun, I.C. (1998) Cathemeral behaviour of *Eulemur macaco macaco* at Ambato Massif, Madagascar. In Harcourt, C., Crompton, R. H. and

Feistner, A.T.C. (eds.) *Biology and Conservation of Prosimians. Folia Primatologica* 69 (Supplement 1): 22-34.

L47 Constable, I.D., Mittermeier, R.A., Pollock, J.I., Rat-sirarson, J. and Simons, H. (1985) Sightings of aye-ayes and red ruffed lemurs on Nosy Mangabe and the Masoala Peninsula. *Primate Conservation* 5: 59-62.

L48 Corbin, G.D. and Schmid, J. (1995) Insect secretions determine habitat use pattern by a female Lesser Mouse Lemur (*Microcebus murinus*). *Amererican Journal of Primatology* 37: 317-324.

L49 Curtis, D.J. and Zaramody, A. (1998) Group size, home range use and seasonal variation in the ecology of *Eulemur mongoz*. *International Journal of Primatology* 19: 811-835.

L50 Curtis, D.J. and Zaramody, A. (1999) Social structure and seasonal variation in the behav-iour of *Eulemur mongoz*. *Folia Primatologica* 70: 79-96.

L51 Curtis, D.J., Velo, A., Raheliarisoa, E.-O., Zaramody, A. and Müller, P. (1998) Surveys on *Propithecus verreauxi deckeni*, a melanistic variant, and *P. v. coronatus* in north west Madagascar. *Oryx* 32 (2): 157-164.

L52 Curtis, D.J., Zaramody, A. and Martin, R.D. (1999) Cathemerality in the Mongoose Lemur *Eulemur mongoz*. *American Journal of Primatology* 47: 279-298.

L53 Curtis, D.J, Zaramody, A. and Rabetsimialona, O.D. (1995) Sighting of the western gentle lemur *Hapalemur griseus occiden-talis* in north-west Madagascar. *Oryx* 29: 215-217.

L54 Dausmann, K.H., Glos, J., Ganzhorn, J.U. and Heldmaier, G. (2005) Hibernation in the tropics: lessons from a primate. *Journal of Comparative Physiological Biology* 175: 147-155.

L55 Digby, L.J. and Kahlenberg, S.M. (2002) Female dominance in blue-eyed black lemurs (*Eulemur macaco flavifrons*). *Primates* 43 (3): 191-199.

L56 Dolch, R. (2006) Spider-catcher – Predation of *Eulemur fulvus* on an orb-web spider. *Lemur News*, 11: 41-42.

L57 Dolch, R., Hilgarter, R.D., Ndriamiary, J.-N., and Randriamahazo, H. (2004) The grandmother of all bamboo lemurs – evidence for the occur-rence of *Hapalemur simus* in the

fragmented rainforest surrounding the Torotorofotsy marshes, Central Eastern Madagascar. *Lemur News* 9; 24-26.

L58 Duckworth, J.W.Evans, M.I., Hawkins A.F.A., Safford, R.J., and Wilkinson, R.J. (1995). The lemurs of Marojejy Strict Nature Reserve, Madagascar. A status overview with notes on ecology and threats. *International Journal of Primatology* 16(3): 545-559.

L59 Du Puy, B. (1996) Faunal Interactions with the genus *Adansonia* in the Kirindy Forest. In Ganzhorn, J.U. and Sorg, J.-P. (eds.) Ecology and Economy of a Tropical Dry Forest in Madagascar, pp. 329-334. *Primate Report*, Special Issue, 46-1 (June 1996).

L60 Eberle, M and Kappeler, P.M. (2002) Mouse Lemurs in space and time: a test of the ecological model. *Behaviour, Ecology and Sociobiology* 51: 131-139.

L61 Engqvist, A. and Richard, A. (1991) Diet as a possible determinant of cathemeral activity patterns in primates. *Folia Primatologica*, 57: 169-172.

L62 Erickson, C.J. (1991) Percussive foraging in the Aye-aye (*Daubentonia madagascariensis*). *Animal Behaviour* 41: 793-801.

L63 Erickson, C.J. (1995) Perspective on percussive foraging in the Aye-aye (*Daubentonia madagas-cariensis*). In Alterman, L. Doyle, G.A. and Izard, K. (eds.) *Creatures of the Dark: the Nocturnal Prosimians*, pp. 251-259. Plenum Press, London & N.Y.

L64 Erickson, C.J. (1998) Cues for Prey Location by Aye-ayes (*Daubentonia madagascariensis*). In Harcourt, C., Crompton, R. H. and Feistner, A.T.C. (eds.) *Biology and Conservation of Prosimians. Folia Primatologica* 69 (Supplement 1): 35-40.

L65 Fausser, J.-L., Prosper, P., Donati, G., Ramanamanjato, J.-B. and Rumpler, Y. (2002) Phylogenetic relationships between *Hapalemur* species and subspecies based on mitochondrial DNA sequences. *BMC Evolutionary Biology* 2:4.

L66 Feistner, A.T.C. and Sterling, E.L. (eds.) (1994) The aye-aye: Madagascar's most puzzling primate. *Folia Primatologica* 62 (1-3).

L67 Feistner, A.T.C. and Sterling, E.L (1995) Body mass and sexual dimorphism in the aye-aye. *Dodo* 31: 73-76

L68 Feistner, A.T.C. and Schmid, J. (1999) Lemurs of the Réserve Naturelle Intégrale d'Andohahela, Madagascar. In Goodman, S.M. (ed) A Floral and Faunal Inventory of the Eastern slopes of the Réserve Naturelle Intégrale d'Andohahela, Madagascar: with reference to elevational variation. *Fieldiana Zoology* 94: 269-283.

L69 Fietz, J. (1998) Body mass in the wild *Microcebus murinus* over the dry season. In Harcourt, C., Crompton, R. H. and Feistner, A.T.C. (eds.) *Biology and Conservation of Prosimians.Folia Primatologica* 69 (supplement): 183-190.

L70 Fietz, J. (1999) Mating system of *Microcebus murinus. American Journal of Primatology* 48: 127-133.

L71 Fietz, J. (1999) Demography and floating males in a population of *Cheirogaleus medius*. In Rakotosamimanana, B., Rasammimanana, Ganzhorn, J.U. and Goodman, S.M. (eds) *New Directions in Lemur Studies*, pp 159-172. Kluwer Academic Press/Plenum, New York.

L72 Fietz, J. (1999) Monogamy as a rule rather than exception in nocturnal lemurs: The case of the Fat-tailed Dwarf Lemur, *Cheirogaleus medius. Ethology* 105: 259-272.

L73 Fietz, J. (2003) Primates: *Cheirogaleus*, Dwarf Lemurs or Fat-tailed Lemurs. In Goodman, S.M. and Benstead, J.P. (eds) *The Natural History of Madagascar*, pp. 1307-1309. The University of Chicago Press, Chicago, USA.

L74 Fietz, J. and Ganzhorn, J.U. (1999) Feeding ecology of the hibernating primate *Cheirogaleus medius*: how does it get so fat? *Oecologia* 121: 157-164.

L75 Foerg, R. (1982) Reproductive behaviour in *Varecia variegata. Folia Primatologica* 38: 108-121.

L76 Freed, B.Z. (1995) The ecology of crowned lemurs and Sanford's lemurs in Montagne d'Ambre, Madagascar. In the Abstracts: International Conference on the Biology and Conservation of Prosimians. North of England Zoological Soc., 13-16th Sept. 1995.

L77 Freed, B.Z. (1996) Co-occurrence amongst crowned lemurs (*Eulemur coronatus*) and Sanford's lemurs (*Eulemur fulvus sanfordi*) of Madagascar. Ph.D. Thesis, Washington University, St. Louis.

L78 Ganzhorn, J.U. (1985) Utilisation of eucalyptus and pine plantations by brown lemurs in the eastern rainforests of Madagascar. *Primate Conservation* 6: 34-35.

L79 Ganzhorn, J.U. (1986) The aye-aye (*Daubentonia madagascariensis*) found in the eastern rainforest of Madagascar. *Folia Primatologica* 46: 125-126.

L80 Ganzhorn, J. U. (1988) Food partitioning amongs Malagasy primates. *Oecologia* 75: 436-450.

L81 Ganzhorn, J.U. (1989) Niche separation in seven lemur species. *Oecologia* 79: 279-286.

L82 Ganzhorn, J.U. (1993) Flexibility and constraints of *Lepilemur* ecology. In Kappeler, P.M. and Ganzhorn, J.U. (eds.) *Lemur Social Systems and their Ecological Basis*, pp. 153-165. Plenum Press, London & N.Y.

L83 Ganzhorn, J.U. (1994) Les lémuriens. In Goodman, S.M. and Langrand, O. (eds.) *Inventaire Biologique Forêt de Zombitse, Recherches pour le Developpement, Série Science Biologiques*, pp. 70-72. No. Spécial 1994. Centre d'Information et de Documentation Scientifique et Technique, Antananarivo, Madagascar.

L84 Ganzhorn, J.U. (1995) Low level forest disturbance: effects on primary production, leaf chemistry and lemur population. *Ecology* 76: 2084-2096.

L85 Ganzhorn, J.U. and Kappeler, P.M. (1996) Lemurs of the Kirindy Forest. In: Ganzhorn, J.U. and Sorg, J.-P. (eds.), Ecology and Economy of a Tropical Dry Forest in Madagascar, pp. 257-274. *Primate Report*, Special Issue, 46-1(June 1996).

L86 Ganzhorn, J.U. and Rabesoa, J. (1986) Sightings of aye-ayes in the eastern rainforests of Madagascar. *Primate Conservation* 7: 45.

L87 Ganzhorn, J.U., Abrahams, J.P. and Razanahoera-Rakotomalala, M. (1985) Some aspects of the natural history and food selection of *Avahi laniger. Primates* 26(4): 452-463.

L88 Ganzhorn, J.U., Pietsch, T., Fietz, J., Gross, S., Schmid, J. and Steiner, N. (2004) Selection of food and ranging behaviour in a sexually monomorphic folivorous lemur: *Lepilemur ruficaudatus. Journal of Zoology* (London) 263: 393-399.

L89 Garbutt, N. (2001) Brief observations of Hairy-eared Dwarf Lemur (*Allocebus trichotis*) in Analamazaotra Special Reserve, Eastern Madagascar. *Lemur News* 6: 37

L90 Garcia, G. and Goodman, S.M. (2003) Hunting of protected animals in the Parc National d'Ankarafantsika, north western Madagascar. *Oryx* 37: 115-118.

L91 Garreau, J.-M. and Manantsara, A. (2003) The Protected Area Complex of the Parc National de Marojejy and the Réserve Spéciale d'Anjanaharibe-Sud. In Goodman, S.M. and Benstead, J.P. (eds) *The Natural History of Madagascar*, pp. 1451-1458. The University of Chicago Press, Chicago, USA.

L92 Glander, K.E. and Powzyk, J.A. (1998) Morphometrics of wild *Indri indri* and *Propithecus diadema diadema. Folia Primatologica* 69 (supplement 1): 399.

L93 Glander, K.E., Wright, P.C., Seigler, D.S. and Randrianasolo, B. (1989) Consumption of cyanogenic bamboo by a newly discovered species of bamboo lemur. *American Journal of Primatology* 19: 119-124.

L94 Glander, K.E., Wright, P.C., Daniels, P.S. and Merenlender, A.M. (1992) Morphometrics and testicle size of rainforest lemur species from south eastern Madagascar. *Journal of Human Evolution* 22: 1-17.

L95 Godfrey, L.R. and Jungers, W.L. (2003) Subfossil Lemurs. In Goodman, S.M. and Benstead, J.P. (eds) *The Natural History of Madagascar*, pp. 1247-1252. The University of Chicago Press, Chicago, USA.

L96 Godfrey, L.R., Jungers, W.L., Simons, E.L., Chatrath, P.S. and Rakotosamimanana, B. (1999) Past and present distributions of lemurs in Madagascar. In Rakotosamimanana, B., Rasammimanana, Ganzhorn, J.U. and Goodman, S.M. (eds) *New Directions in Lemur Studies*, pp 19-53. Kluwer Academic Press/Plenum, New York.

L97 Godfrey, L.R., Simons, E.L., Jungers, W.L., DeBlieux, D.D. and Prithijit, S.C. (2004) New discovery of subfossil *Hapalemur simus*, the Greater Bamboo Lemur in western Madagascar. *Lemur News* 9; 9-11.

L98 Golden, C. (2005) *Eaten to Endangerment: Mammal Hunting and the Bushmeat Trade in Madagascar's Makira*

Forest. Undergraduate Thesis, University of Harvard, USA.

L99 Goodman, S.M. (2003) Predation in Lemurs. In Goodman, S.M. and Benstead, J.P. (eds) *The Natural History of Madagascar*, pp. 1221-1228. The University of Chicago Press, Chicago, USA.

L100 Goodman, S. M. and Ganzhorn J.U. (2004) Biogeography of lemurs in the humid forests of Madagascar: the role of elevational distribution and rivers. *Journal of Biogeography* 31(1): 47-55.

L101 Goodman, S.M. and Langrand, O. (1996) A high mountain population of the ring-tailed lemur, *Lemur catta* on the Andringitra Massif, Madagascar. *Oryx* 30: 259-268.

L102 Goodman, S. M. and Raselimanana, A.P. (2002) The occurrence of *Allocebus trichotis* in Parc National de Marojejy. *Lemur News* 7: 21-22.

L103 Goodman, S. M. and Raselimanana, A.P. (2003) Hunting of wild animals by Sakalava of the Menebe region: a filed report from Kirindy Mite. *Lemur News* 8: 4-6.

L104 Goodman, S. M. and Schütz, H. (2000) The lemurs of the north-eastern slopes of the Réserve Spéciale de Manongarivo. *Lemur News* 5: 30-33.

L105 Goodman, S.M. and Soarimalala, V. (2002) Les petits mammifères de la Réserve Spéciale de Manongarivo. In Gautier, L and Goodman S.M. (eds) Inventaire floristique et faunistique de la Réserve Spéciale de Manongarivo, Madagascar. *Boissiera* 59: 383-401.

L106 Goodman, S.M. and Sterling, E.J. (1996) The utilisation of *Canarium* (Burseraceae) seeds by Vertebrates in the Réserve Naturelle Intégrale d'Andringitra, Madagascar. In Goodman, S.M. (ed) A Floral and Faunal Inventory of the Eastern slopes of the Réserve Naturelle Intégrale d'Andringitra, Madagascar: with reference to elevational variation. *Fieldiana Zoology* 85: 83-89.

L107 Goodman, S.M., Langrand, O. and Raxworthy, C.J. (1993) The food habits of the Madagascar Long-eared Owl, *Asio madagascariensis*, at two habitats in southern Madagascar. *Ostrich* 64: 79-85.

L108 Goodman, S.M., Langrand, O. and Raxworthy, C.J. (1993) The food habits of the Barn Owl, *Tyto alba*, at three sites on Madagascar. *Ostrich* 64: 160-171.

L109 Goodman, S.M., O'Connor, S. and Langrand, O. (1993) A review of predation on lemurs: implications for the evolution of social behaviour in small, nocturnal primates. In Kappeler, P.M. and Ganzhorn, J.U. (eds.) *Lemur Social Systems and their Ecological Basis*, pp. 51-66. Plenum Press, London & N.Y.

L110 Goodman, S.M, Langrand, O. and Rasoloarison, R. (1997) Les lémuriens. In Langrand, O. and Goodman, S.M, (eds) *Inventaire biologique forêt de Vohibasia et d'Isoky-Vohimena.* Recherches pour le Développment, series sciences biologiques, Antananarivo 12: 156-161.

L111 Goodman, S.M, Langrand, O. and Rasolonandrasana, B.P.N. (1997) The Food Habits of *Cryptoprocta ferox* in the High Mountain Zone of the Andringita Massif, Madagascar (Carnivora, Viverridae). *Mammalia* 61: 185-192.

L112 Goodman, S. M., Razafindratsita, V. Schütz, H. and Ratsimbazafy, R. (2001) Les Lémuriens. In Goodman, S. M. and Razafindratsita, V. (eds) Inventaire biologique du Parc National de Ranomafana et du couloir forestier qui la relie au Parc National d'Andringitra. Recherches pour le Développement, série sciences biologiues, Centre d'Infromation et du Documentation Scientifique et Technique, Antananarivo. 17: 231-243.

L113 Grassi, C. (2002) Sex differences in feeding, height and space use in *Hapalemur griseus. International Journal of Primatology* 23: 677-693.

L114 Groves, C.P. (2000) The Genus *Cheirogaleus:* Unrecognised Biodiversity in Dwarf Lemurs. *International Journal of Primatology* 21: 943-962.

L115 Groves, C.P. (2001) *Primate Taxonomy.* Smithsonian Institute Press, Washington D.C.

L116 Groves, C.P. and Eaglen, R.H. (1988) Systematics of the Lemuridae (Primates, Strepsirhini). *Journal of Human Evolution* 17: 513-538.

L117 Groves, C.P. and Tattersall, I. (1991) Geographical variation in the fork-marked lemur *Phaner furcifer* (Primates, Cheirogaleidae). *Folia Primatologica* 56: 39-49.

L118 Hapke, A., Fietz, J. Nash, S.D., Rakotondravony, D., Rakotosamimanana, B., Ramanamanjato, J-B., Randria G.F.N. and Zischler, H. (2005) Biogeography of Dwarf Lemurs: Genetic Evidence for Unexpected Patterns in Southeastern Madagascar. *International Journal of Primatology* 26(4): 873-901.

L119 Harcourt, C. (1991) Diet and behaviour of a nocturnal lemur, *Avahi laniger*, in the wild. *Journal of Zoology* (London) 223: 667-674.

L120 Harcourt, C. and Thornback, J. (1990) *Lemurs of Madagascar and the Comoros.* IUCN Red Data Book. IUCN, Gland, Switzerland and Cambridge, U.K.

L121 Hawkins, A.F.A., (1999) The Primates of Isalo National Park. *Lemur News* 4: 10-14.

L122 Hawkins, A.F.A., Chapman, P., Ganzhorn, J.U., Bloxam, Q.M.C., Barlow, S.C. and Tonge, S.J. (1990) Vertebrate conservation in Ankarana Special Reserve, northern Madagascar. *Biological Conservation*, 54: 83-110.

L123 Hawkins, A.F.A., Durbin, J. and Reid, D. (1998) The primates of the Baly Bay area, north-western Madagascar. *Folia Primatologica* 69: 337-345.

L124 Hemingway, C.A. (1995) Feeding and reproductive strategies of the Milne-Edwards's Sifaka *Propithecus diadema edwardsi.* Ph.D. Thesis, Duke University, Durham, North Carolina, USA.

L125 Hemingway, C.A. (1996) Morphology and phenology of seeds and whole fruit eaten by Milne-Edwards's Sifaka *Propithecus diadema edwardsi* in Ranomafana National Park, Madagascar. *International Journal of Primatology* 17: 637-659.

L126 Hemingway, C.A. (1998) Selectivity and variability in the diet of Milne-Edwards's Sifaka *Propithecus diadema edwardsi:* Implications for folivory and seed eating. *International Journal of Primatology* 19: 355-377.

L127 Hill, W.C.O. (1953) Primates: comparative anatomy and taxonomy. I. Strepsirrhini. New York: Interscience Publishers, Inc.; Edinburgh: The University Press.

L128 Hladik, C.M., Charles-Dominique, P. and Petter, J-J. (1980) Feeding strategies of five nocturnal prosimians in the dry forest of the west coast of Madagascar. In Charles-Dominique, P., Cooper, H.M., Hladik, A., Hladik, C.M., Pagès, E., Pariente, G.F., Petter-Rousseaux, A., Petter, J-J. and Schilling, A. (eds.), *Nocturnal Malagasy Primates: Ecology, Physiology and*

Behaviour, pp. 41-73. Academic Press, N.Y.

L129 Irwin, M.T., Samonds, K.E. and Raharison, J.-L. (2001) A biological inventory of the lemur community of Réserve Spéciale de Kalambatritra, south-central Madagascar. Lemur News 6: 24-28.

L130 Irwin, M.T., Samonds, K.E., Raharison, J.-L., and Wright, P.C. (2004) Lemur Latrines: Observations of Latrine Behaviour in Wild Primates and Possible Ecological Significance. Journal of Mammology, 85 (3): 420-427

L131 Irwin, M.T., Johnson, S.E. and Wright, P.C. (2005) The state of lemur conservation in south-eastern Madagascar: population and habitat assessment for diurnal and cathemeral lemurs using surveys, satellite imagery and GIS. Oryx 39: 204-218.

L132 Ishak, B., Warter, S., Dutrillaux, B. and Rumpler, Y. (1992) Chromosomal rearrangements and speciation of sportive lemurs (Lepilemur species). Folia Primatologica 58: 121-130.

L133 Iwano, T. and Iwakawa, C. (1988) Feeding behaviour of the aye-aye (Daubentonia madagascariensis) on nuts of ramy (Canarium madagascariensis). Folia Primatologica 50: 136-142.

L134 Iwano, T., Randalana, R. and Rakotoarisoa, G. (1991) Ecology of the Aye-aye (Daubentonia madagascariensis), I. Distribution. In Ehara, A., Kimura, T., Takenaka, O. and Iwamato, M. (eds) Primatology Today, pp 41-42. Elsevier, Amsterdam.

L135 Jolly, A. (2003) Lemur catta, Ring-tailed Lemur, Maki. In Goodman, S.M. and Benstead, J.P. (eds) The Natural History of Madagascar, pp. 1329-1331. The University of Chicago Press, Chicago, USA.

L136 Jolly, A. (2004) Lords and Lemurs: Mad Scientists, Kings with Spears and the Survival of Diversity in Madagascar. Houghton Mifflin, Boston, USA.

L137 Jolly, A., Gustafson, H., Oliver, W.L.R. and O'Connor, S.M. (1982) Propithecus verreauxi population and ranging at Berenty, Madagascar, 1975-1980. Folia Primatologica 39: 124-144.

L138 Jolly, A., Rasamimanana, H.R., Kinnaird, M.F., O'Brien, T.G., Crowley, H.M., Harcourt, C.S., Gardner, S. and Davidson, J.M. (1993) Territoriality in Lemur catta groups during the birth season at Berenty, Madagascar. In Kappeler, P.M. and Ganzhorn, J.U. (eds.) Lemur Social Systems and their Ecological Basis, pp. 85-109. Plenum Press, London & N.Y.

L139 Johnson, S.E. (2002) Ecology and speciation in Brown Lemurs: White-collared Lemurs (Eulemur albocollaris) and hybrids (Eulemur albocollaris x Eulemur fulvus rufus) in southeastern Madagascar. PH.D. Thesis, University of Texas at Austin, Austin, USA.

L140 Johnson, S.E. and Wyner, Y. (2000) Notes on the biogeography of Eulemur fulvus albocolaris. Lemur News 5: 25-28.

L141 Jones, K.C. (1983) Inter-troop transfer of Lemur catta males at Berenty, Madagascar. Folia Primatologica 40: 145-160.

L142 Jungers, W.L., Godfrey, L.R., Simons, E.L. and Chatrath, P.S. (1995) Subfossil Indri from the Ankarana Massif of northern Madagascar. American Journal of Physical Anthropology 97: 357-366.

L143 Kappeler, P.M. (1997) Determinants of primate social organization: Comparitive evidence and new insights from Malagasy lemurs. Biological Reviews 72: 111-151.

L144 Kappeler, P.M. (1987) Reproduction in the Crowned Lemur Eulemur coronatus in captivity. American Journal of Primatology 12: 497-503.

L145 Kappeler, P.M. (1998) Nests, tree holes and the evolution of primate life histories. American Journal of Primatology 46: 7-33.

L146 Kappeler, P.M. (1990) The evolution of sexual dimorphism in prosimian primates. American Journal of Primatology 21: 201-214.

L147 Kappeler, P.M. (1991) Patterns of sexual dimorphism in body weight among prosimian primates. American Journal of Primatology 57: 132-146.

L148 Kappeler, P.M. (1997) Intrasexual selection in Mirza coquereli: Evidence for scramble competition polygyny in a solitary primate. Behavioural Ecology and Sociobiology 41: 115-128.

L149 Kappeler, P.M. (1998) Nests, tree holes and the evolution of primate life histories. American Journal of Primatology 46: 7-33.

L150 Kappeler, P.M. (2003) Mirza coquereli, Coquerel's Dwarf Lemur. In Goodman, S.M. and Benstead, J.P. (eds) The Natural History of Madagascar, pp. 1316-1318. The University of Chicago Press, Chicago, USA.

L151 Kappeler, P.M. and Rasoloarison, R.M. (2003) Microcebus, Mouse Lemurs, Tsidy. In Goodman, S.M. and Benstead, J.P. (eds) The Natural History of Madagascar, pp. 1310-1315. The University of Chicago Press, Chicago, USA.

L152 Kappeler, P.M., Rasoloarison, R.M., Razafimanantsoa, L. Walter, L. and Roos, C. (2005) Morphology, Behaviour and Molecular Evolution of Giant Mouse Lemurs (Mirza spp.) Gray 1870, with description of a new species. Primate Report 71: 3-26.

L153 Karpantry, S.M. and Goodman, S.M. (1999) Diet of the Madagascar Harrier-Hawk Polyboroides radiatus in south eastern Madagascar. Journal of Raptor Research 33: 313-316.

L154 Karpantry, S. M. and Wright, P. C. (2006) Predation on Lemurs in the Rainforest of Madagascar by Multiple Predator Species: Observations and Experiments. Gurskey: 21:27, pp75-97.

L155 Kelley, E. and Mayor, M.I. (2002) Preliminary study of the Silky Sifaka (Propithecus diadema candidus) in north east Madagascar. Lemur News 7: 16-18.

L156 King, S. J., Arrirgo-Nelson, S.J., Pochron, S.T., Semprebon, G.M., Godfrey, L.R., Wright, P.C. and Jernvall, J. (2005). Dental senescence in a primate links infant survival to rainfall. PNAS 102 (46): 16579-16583.

L157 Koenders, L., Rumpler, Y. and Brun, B. (1985) Notes on the recently rediscovered Sclater's lemur (Lemur macaco flavifrons). Primate Conservation 6: 35.

L158 Koenders, L., Rumpler, Y., Ratsirarson, J. and Peyrieras, A. (1985) Lemur macaco flavifrons (Gray, 1867): a rediscovered subspecies of primate. Folia Primatologica 44: 210-215.

L159 Koyama, N., Nakamichi, M., Oda, R., Miyamoto, N. and Takahata, Y. (2001) A ten-year summary of reproduction parameters for ring-tailed lemurs at Berenty, Madagascar. Primates 42: 1-14.

L160 Kress, W.J., Schatz, G.E., Adrianifihanana, M., Morland, H.S. and Love, S.H. (1994) Pollination of Ravenala madagascariensis by lemurs in Madagascar: evidence for an archaic coevolutionary system? American Journal of Botany 81: 542-551.

L161 Lehman, S.M. and Wright, P.C. (2000) Preliminary studies of the conservation status of lemur communities in the Betsakafandrika region of eastern Madagascar. *Lemur News* 5: 23-25.

L162 Lehman, S.M. and Mayor, M. (2004) Dietary patterns in Perrier's Sifakas (*Propithecus diadema perrieri*): A preliminary study. *American Journal of Primatology* 62: 115-122.

L163 Lehman, S.M., Mayor, M. and Wright, P.C. (2005) Ecogeographic size variation in sifakas: a test of the resource seasonality and resource quality hypotheses. *American Journal of Physical Anthropology* 126: 318-328.

L164 Lernould J-M. (2002). Un programme international de recherche et de conservation pour le lémur aux yeux turquoise (*Eulemur macaco flavifrons*). *Lemur News* 7:30-3.

L165 Louis, E.E., Coles, M.S., Andriantompohavana, R., Sommer, J.A., Engberg, S.E., Zaonarivelo, J.R., Mayor, M.I. and Brenneman, R.A. (2006) Revision of the Mouse Lemurs (Primates: *Microcebus*) of eastern Madagascar. *International Journal of Primatology*

L166 Louis, E. E., Engberg, S. E., Lei, R., Geng, H., Sommer, J. A., Randriamampionona, R., Randriamanana, J. C., Zaonarivelo, J. R., Andriantompohavana, R., Randria, G., Prosper, Ramamomilanto, B., Rakotoarisoa, G., Rooney, A. and Brenneman, R.A. (2006) Molecular and Morphological Analyses of the Sportive Lemurs (Family Megaladapidae: Genus *Lepilemur*) Reveals 11 Previously Unrecognised Species. *Special Publications, Museum of Texas Tech University*, No. 49: 1-47.

L167 Martin, R.D. (1973) A review of the behaviour and ecology of the lesser mouse lemur (*Microcebus murinus* J.F. Miller, 1777). In Michael, R.P. and Crook, J.H. (eds.) *Comparative Ecology and Behaviour of Primates*, pp. 1-68. Academic Press, London.

L168 Martin, R. D. (2000) Origins, Diversity and Relationships of Lemurs. *International Journal of Primatology* 21: 1021-1049.

L169 Mayor, M.I. and Lehman, S.M. (1999) Conservation of Perrier's Sifaka (*Propithecus diadema perrieri*) in Analamera Special Reserve, Madagascar. *Lemur News* 4: 21-23.

L170 Mayor, M.I., Sommer, J.A., Houck, M.L., Zaonarivelo, J.R., Wright, P.C., Ingram, C., Engel, S.R. and Louis, E.E. (2004) Specific status of *Propithecus* spp. *International Journal of Primatology* 25: 875-900.

L171 Meier, B. and Albignac, R. (1989) Hairy-eared dwarf lemur (*Allocebus trichotis*) rediscovered. *Primate Conservation* 10: 30.

L172 Meier, B. and Albignac, R. (1991) Rediscovery of *Allocebus trichotis* in north east Madagascar. *Folia Primatologica* 56: 57-63.

L173 Meier, B., Albignac, R., Peyrieras, A., Rumpler, Y. and Wright, P.C. (1987) A new species of *Hapalemur* (Primates) from south east Madagascar. *Folia Primatologica* 48: 211-215.

L174 Meyers, D.M. (1993) The effects of resource seasonality on behaviour and reproduction in the golden-crowned sifaka (*Propithecus tattersalli*, Simons 1988) in three Malagasy Forests. Ph.D. Thesis, Duke University, Durham, North Carolina, USA.

L175 Meyers, D.M. (1993) Conservation status of the golden-crowned sifaka, *Propithecus tattersalli*. *Lemur News* 1(1): 6-8.

L176 Meyers, D.M. (1996) Update on the endangered sifaka of the north. *Lemur News* 2:13-14.

L177 Meyers, D.M. and Ratsirarson, J. (1989) Distribution and conservation of two endangered sifakas in northern Madagascar. *Primate Conservation* 10: 81-86.

L178 Meyers, D.M. and Wright, P.C. (1993) Resource tracking: food availability and *Propithecus* seasonal reproduction. In Kappeler, P.M. and Ganzhorn, J.U. (eds.) *Lemur Social Systems and their Ecological Basis*, pp. 179-192. Plenum Press, London & N.Y.

L179 Meyers, D., Rabarivola, C. and Rumpler, Y. (1989) Distribution and conservation of Sclater's lemur: implications of a morphological cline. *Primate Conservation* 10: 78-82.

L180 Mittermeier, R.A., Valladares-Pádua, C. Rylands, A.B., Eudey, A.A., Butynski, T.M., Ganzhorn, J.U., Kormos, R. and Walker, S. (2005) Primates in Peril: The World's 25 Most Endangered Primates 2004-2006. Conservation International / IUCN/SSC Primate Specialist Group.

L181 Mittermeier, R.A., Konstant, W., Hawkins, A.F.A., Louis, E.E., Langrand, O., Ratsimbazafy, J., Ganzhorn, J.U., Rajaobelina, S., Tattersall, I. and Meyers, D.M. (2006) *Lemurs of Madagascar*. Conservation International Tropical Field Guide, second edition. Conservation International, Washington, D.C.

L182 Morland, H.S. (1989) Infant survival and parental care in ruffed lemurs (*Varecia variegata*) in the wild. *American Journal of Primatology* 18: 157.

L183 Morland, H.S. (1990) Parental behaviour and infant development in ruffed lemurs (*Varecia variegata*) in a northeast Madagascar rain forest. *American Journal of Primatology* 20: 253-265.

L184 Morland, H.S. (1991) Social organisation and ecology of Black and White Ruffed Lemurs (*Varecia variegata variegata*) in lowland rainforest, Nosy Mangabe, Madagascar. Ph.D. Thesis, Yale University, New Haven.

L185 Morland, H.S. (1991) Preliminary report on the social organisation of ruffed lemurs (*Varecia variegata variegata*) in a northeast Madagascar rain forest. *Folia Primatologica* 56: 157-161.

L186 Morland, H.S. (1993) Seasonal behavioural variation and its relation to thermoregulation in ruffed lemurs. In Kappeler, P.M. and Ganzhorn, J.U. (eds.) *Lemur Social Systems and their Ecological Basis*, pp. 193-203. Plenum Press, London & N.Y.

L187 Morland, H.S. (1993) Reproductive activity of ruffed lemurs (*Varecia variegata variegata*) in a Madagascar rain forest. *American Journal of Physical Anthropology* 91: 71-82.

L188 Müller, A.E. and Thalmann, U. (2000) Origin and evolution of primate social organization: a reconstruction. *Biological Reviews* 75: 405-435.

L189 Mutschler, T. (1999) Folivory in a small-bodied lemur: the nutrition of the Aloatran Gentle Lemur (*Hapalemur griseus alaotrensis*). In New Directions in Lemur Studies pp 221-239.

L190 Mutschler, T. (1999) The Aloatran Gentle Lemur (*Hapalemur griseus alaotrensis*): a study in behavioural ecology. Ph.D. Thesis, University of Zurich.

L191 Mutschler, T. (2000) Taxonomic distinctiveness of *Hapalemur* and phylogenetic relationships within the genus: evidence from vocal communication. St Louis: Washington University.

L192 Mutschler, T. and Feistner, A.T.C. (1995) Conservation status and distribution of the Alaotran gentle lemur *Hapalemur griseus alaotrensis*. *Oryx* 29: 267-274.

L193 Mutschler, T. and Tan, C. L. (2003) *Hapalemur*, Bamboo or Gentle Lemurs. In Goodman, S.M. and Benstead, J.P. (eds) *The Natural History of Madagascar*, pp. 1324-1329. The University of Chicago Press, Chicago, USA.

L194 Mutschler, T. and Thalmann, U. (1994) Sightings of *Avahi* (woolly lemur) in western Madagascar. *Primate Conservation* 11: 15-17.

L195 Mutschler, T., Feistner, A.T.C. and Nievergelt, C.M. (1998) Preliminary field data on group size, diet and activity in the Aloatran Gentle Lemur (*Hapalemur griseus alaotrensis*). *Folia Primatologica* 69: 325-330.

L196 Mutschler, T., Nievergelt, C.M. and Feistner, A.T.C. (2000) Social organisation of the Aloatran Gentle Lemur (*Hapalemur griseus alaotrensis*). *American Journal of Primatology* 50: 9-24.

L197 Mutschler, T., Randrianarisoa, A.J. and Feistner, A.T.C. (2001) Population status of the Aloatran Gentle Lemur (*Hapalemur griseus alaotrensis*). *Oryx* 35: 152-157.

L198 Müller, A.E. (1999) Social organisation of the fat-tailed dwarf lemur (*Cheirogaleus medius*) in northwest Madagascar. In Rakotosamimanana, B., Rasammimanana, Ganzhorn, J.U. and Goodman, S.M. (eds) *New Directions in Lemur Studies*, pp 139-157. Kluwer Academic Press/Plenum, New York.

L199 Müller, A.E. (1999) Aspects of social life in the fat-tailed dwarf lemur (*Cheirogaleus medius*): Inferences from body weights and trapping data. *American Journal of Primatology* 49: 265-280.

L200 Müller, A.E. and Thalmann, U. (2002) Biology of the fat-tailed dwarf lemur (*Cheirogaleus medius* E. Geoffroy 1812): New results from the field. *Evolutionary Anthropology* (Supplement 1): 79-82.

L201 Müller, P. (1997) The behaviour and ecology of the Crowned Sifaka (*Propithecus verreauxi coronatus*) in north west Madagascar. University of Zürich (unpublished Ph.D. research).

L202 Müller, P., Velo, A. Rahelarisoa, E.-O., Zaramody, A. and Curtis, D.J. (2000) Surveys of five sympatric lemurs at Anjamena, northwest Madagascar. *African Journal of Ecology* 38: 248-257.

L203 Nash, L.T. (1998) Vertical clingers and sleepers: Seasonal influences on the activity and substrate use of *Lepilemur leucopus* at Beza Mahafaly Special Reserve, Madagascar. In Harcourt, C., Crompton, R. H. and Feistner, A.T.C. (eds.) *Biology and Conservation of Prosimians. Folia Primatologica* 69 (supplement): 204-217.

L204 Nicoll, M.E. and O. Langrand (1989) *Madagascar: Revue de la Conservation et des Aires Protégées*. WWF, Gland, Switzerland.

L205 Nievergelt, C.M., Mutschler, T. and Feistner, A.T.C. (1998) Group encounters and territoriality in Aloatran Gentle Lemur (*Hapalemur griseus alaotrensis*). *American Journal of Primatology* 46: 251-258.

L206 Nilsson, L.A., Rabakonandrianina, E., Petterson, B. and Grunmeier, R. (1993) Lemur pollination in the Malagasy rainforest: Liana *Strongylodon craveniae* (Leguminosae). *Evolutionary Trends in Plants* 7: 49-56.

L207 O'Connor, S.M. (1987) The effect of human impact on vegetation and the consequences to primates in two riverine forests, southern Madagascar. Ph.D. Thesis, University of Cambridge, UK.

L208 Oda, R. (1996) Predation on a chameleon by a ring-tailed lemur in the Berenty Reserve, Madagascar. *Folia Primatologica* 67: 40-43.

L208a Olivieri, G., Zimmermann, E., Randrianambinina, B., Rasoloharijaona, S., Rakotondravony, D., Guschanski, K. and Radespiel, U. (in press). The Ever-increasing Diversity of Mouse Lemurs: Three new Species in north and northwestern Madagascar. *Molecular Phylogenetics and Evolution* (2006), doi:10.1016/j.ympev.2006.10.026

L209 Ortmann, S., Heldmaier, G. Schmid, J., and Ganzhorn, J.U. (1997) Spontaneous daily torpor in Malagasy mouse lemurs. *Naturwissenschaften* 84: 28-32.

L210 Overdorff, D.J. (1992) Territoriality and home range use by *Eulemur rubriventer* in Madagascar. *American Journal of Physical Anthropology* 14: 219.

L211 Overdorff, D.J. (1992) Differential patterns in flower feeding by *Eulemur fulvus rufus* and *Eulemur rubriventer* in Madagascar. *American Journal of Primatology* 28: 191-196.

L212 Overdorff, D.J. (1993) Ecological and reproductive correlates to range use in Red-Bellied Lemurs (*Eulemur rubriventer*) and Rufous Lemurs (*Eulemur fulvus rufus*). In Kappeler, P.M. and Ganzhorn, J.U. (eds.) *Lemur Social Systems and their Ecological Basis*, pp. 167-178. Plenum Press, London & N.Y.

L213 Overdorff, D.J. (1993) Similarities, differences and seasonal patterns in the diets of *Eulemur rubriventer* and *Eulemur fulvus rufus* in the Ranomafana National Park, Madagascar. *International Journal of Primatology* 14: 721-753.

L214 Overdorff, D.J. (1996) Ecological correlates to activity and habitat use of two prosimian primates: *Eulemur rubriventer* and *Eulemur fulvus rufus*. *American Journal of Primatology* 40: 327-342.

L215 Overdorff, D.J. (1996) Ecological correlates to social structure in two prosimian primates in Madagascar. *American Journal of Physical Anthropology* 100: 487-506.

L216 Overdorff, D.J. and Johnson, S. (2003) *Eulemur*, True Lemurs. In Goodman, S.M. and Benstead, J.P. (eds) *The Natural History of Madagascar*, pp. 1320-1324. The University of Chicago Press, Chicago, USA.

L217 Overdorff, D.J. and Rasmussen, M.A. (1995) Determinants of night-time activity in 'diurnal' lemur primates. In Alterman, L. Doyle, G.A. and Izard, K. (eds.) *Creatures of the Dark: the Nocturnal Prosimians*, pp. 61-74. Plenum Press, London & N.Y.

L218 Overdorff, D.J., Strait, S.G. and Telo, A. (1997) Seasonal variation in activity and diet in a small-bodied folivorous primate, *Hapalemur griseus*, in southeastern Madagascar. *American Journal of Primatology* 43: 211-223.

L219 Pagès, E. (1980) Ethoecology of *Microcebus coquereli* during the dry season. In Charles-Dominique, P., Cooper, H.M., Hladik, A., Hladik, C.M., Pagès, E., Pariente, G.F., Petter-Rousseaux, A., Petter, J.-J. and Schilling, A. (eds.), *Nocturnal Malagasy Primates: Ecology, Physiology and Behaviour*, pp. 97-116. Academic Press, N.Y.

L220 Pastorini, J., Zaramody, A., Scheffrahn, W., Clark, M., Waters, M. and Curtis, D. J.

(1998) Body measurements from wild Mongoose Lemurs at Anjamena. XVIIth Congress of the International Primatological Society, poster abstracts, Antananarivo, Madagascar.

L221 Pastorini, J., Forstner, M.R.J. and Martin, R. D. (2001) Phylogenetic history of sifakas. (*Propithecus*: Lemuriformes) derived from mtDNA sequences. *American Journal of Primatology* 53: 1-17.

L222 Pastorini, J., Forstner, M.R.J. and Martin, R. D. (2002) Phylogenetic relationships of gentle lemurs (*Hapalemur*). *Evolutionary Anthropology* Suppl. 1: 150-154.

L223 Pastorini, J., Thalmann, U. and Martin, R. (2003) A molecular approach to comparative phylo-geography of extant Malagasy lemurs. *Proceedings of the National Academy of Science* 100: 5879-5884.

L224 Patel, E.R. (2003). Behavioural Ecology, Communication and Conservation of Silky Sifakas. Exit Report submitted to MICET.

L225 Patel, E.R. (2005). Silky Sifaka Predation (*Propithecus candidus*) by a Fossa (*Cryptoprocta ferox*). *Lemur News* 10: 25-27.

L226 Patel, E. R. (2006) Activity Budget, Ranging and Group Size in Silky Sifakas (*Propithecus candidus*). *Lemur News*, 11: 42-45.

L227 Patel, E.R. (2006). Scent marking in wild silky sifakas: Sex differences and seasonal effects in usage and response across multiple scent-mark types. *International Primatological Society* conference presentation.

L228 Patel, E.R., Coke, C.S., Richie, A. and Santorelli, C. (2003) Assessing production specificity of free-ranging Silky Sifaka (*Propithecus diadema candidus*) 'anti-predator' vocalisations: weak evidence for 'aerial predator' but not 'terrestrial predator' calls. *American Journal of Primatology* 60 (Supplement 1): 71-72.

L229 Patel, E.R., Coke, C.S., Richie, A. and Santorelli, C. (2003) Alloparental care (including allon-ursing) in free-ranging Silky Sifakas (*Propithecus diadema candidus*) in a primary northeastern montane rainforest in Madagascar. *American Journal of Primatology* 60 (Supplement 1): 71-72.

L230 Patel, E.R., Anderson, J.D., Irwin, M.T. and Owren, M.J. (2005) Quantifying the vocal repertoire of wild adult Diademed Sifakas

(*Propithecus diadema diadema*) in Madagascar. *American Journal of Primatology* 66 (suppl 1): 48.

L231 Patel, E.R., Anderson, J.D., and Owren, M.J. (2005) Sex differences in the acoustic structure in a monomorphic primate: wild Silky Sifakas (*Propithecus diadema candidus*) of northeastern Madagascar. *American Journal of Primatology* 66 (suppl 1): 46-47.

L232 Patel, E.R., Marshall, J. J. and Parathian. (2005) Silky Sifaka (*Propithecus diadema candidus*) conservation: Village presenta-tions in northeastern Madagascar. *Laboratory Primate Newsletter* 44(3): 8-11.

L233 Patel, E.R., Anderson, J.D., and Owren, M.J. (2006). Exploring the function of 'Zzuss' alarm vocalizations in wild Silky Sifakas: Moderate evidence for individual distinctiveness. *International Journal of Primatology* conference presentation.

L234 Pereira, M.E. and Weiss, M.L. (1991) Female mate choice, male migration, and the threat of infanticide in ring-tailed lemurs. *Behavioural Ecology and Sociobiology* 28: 141-152.

L235 Pereira, M.E., Klepper, A. and Simons, E.L. (1987) Tactics of care for young infants by forest living ruffed lemurs (*Varecia variegata variegata*): ground nests, parking and biparental care. *Amererican Journal of Primatology* 13: 129-144.

L236 Pereira, M.E. Seeligson, M.L. and Macedonia, J.M. (1988) The behav-ioural repertoire of the black and white ruffed lemur, *Varecia variegata variegata* (Primates: Lemuridae). *Folia Primatologica* 51: 1-32.

L237 Petter, J.-J., Albignac, R. and Rumpler, Y. (1977) Mammifères Lémuriens (Primates Prosimians). Vol 44 of *Faune de Madagascar*. ORSTOM/CNRS, Paris.

L238 Petter-Rousseaux, A. (1964) Reproductive physiology and behaviour of Lemuroidae. In Buettner-Janusch, J. (ed) *Evolutionary and Genetic Biology of Primates*, pp 91-132. Academic Press, New York.

L239 Petter-Rousseaux, A. (1980) Seasonal activity rhythms, repro-duction and body weight variations in five sympatric nocturnal prosim-ians, in simulated light and climatic conditions. In Charles-Dominique, P., Cooper, H.M., Hladik, A., Hladik, C.M., Pagès, E., Pariente, G.F., Petter- Rousseaux, A., Petter, J.-J.

and Schilling, A. (eds.), *Nocturnal Malagasy Primates: Ecology, Physiology and Behaviour*, pp. 137-152. Academic Press, N.Y.

L240 Pietsch, T. (1998) Geschlechtsabhängige Strategien im Ernährungsverhalten und der Habitatnutzung bei Braunen Wieselmakis (*Lepilemur rudicau-datus*). Diplomerbeit, Universität Hamburg.

L241 Pitts, A. (1995) Predation by *Eulemur fulvus rufus* on an infant *Lemur catta* at Berenty, Madagascar. *Folia Primatologica* 65: 169-171.

L242 Pochron S.T., and Wright P.C. (2003). Variability in adult group compositions of a prosimian primate. *Behavioral Ecology and Sociobiology* 54: 285-293.

L243 Pochron, S.T., Fitzgerald, J., Gilbert, C.C., Lawrence, L., Grgas, M., Rakotonirina, G., Ratsimbazafy, R., Rakotosoa, R., and Wright P.C. (2003). Patterns of female dominance in *Propithecus diadema edwardsi* of Ranomafana National Park, Madagascar. *American Journal of Primatology* 61(4): 173-185.

L244 Pochron, S.T., Tucker, W.T., and Wright, P.C. (2004). Demography, life history and social structure in *Propithecus diadema edwardsi* from 1986-2000 in Ranomafana National Park, Madagascar. *American Journal of Physical Anthropology* 125: 61-72.

L245 Pochron, S.T., Morelli, T.L., Terranova, P., Scirbona, J., Cohen, J., Rakotonirina, G., Ratsimbazafy, R., Rakotosoa, R., and Wright, P.C. (2005). Patterns of male scent marking in *Propithecus edwardsi* of Ranomafana National Park, Madagascar. *American Journal of Primatology* 65: 103-115.

L246 Pochron, S.T., Morelli, T.L., P., Scirbona, J. and Wright, P.C. (2005). Sex differences in scent marking in *Propithecus edwardsi* of Ranomafana National Park, Madagascar. *American Journal of Primatology* 66: 97-110.

L247 Pollock, J.I. (1975) Field observations on *Indri indri*: A preliminary report. In Tattersall, I. And Sussman, R.W. (eds) *Lemurs Biology*, pp. 287-311. Plenum, New York.

L248 Pollock, J.I. (1975) Social behaviour and ecology of *Indri indri*. Ph.D. Thesis, University of London, UK.

L249 Pollock, J.I. (1977) The ecology and sociology of feeding in *Indri*

indri. In Clutton-Brock, T.H. (ed.) *Primate Ecology: Studies of Feeding and Ranging Behaviour in Lemurs, Monkeys and Apes*, pp. 37-69. Academic Press, London.

L250 Pollock, J.I. (1979) Spatial distribution and ranging behaviour in lemurs. In Doyle, G.A. and Martin, R.D. (eds) *The Study of Prosimian Behaviour*, pp 359-409. Academic Press, New York

L251 Pollock, J.I. (1979) Female dominance in *Indri indri. Folia Primatologica* 31: 143-164.

L252 Pollock, J.I. (1986) The song of the indris (*Indri indri*, Primates, Lemuroidea): natural history form and function. *International Journal of Primatology* 7: 225-267.

L253 Pollock, J.I. (1986) A note on the ecology and behaviour of *Hapalemur griseus. Primate Conservation* 7: 97-100.

L254 Pollock, J.I., Constable, I.D., Mittermeier, R.A., Ratsirason, J. and Simons, H. (1985) A note on the diet and feeding behaviour of the aye-aye, *Daubentonia madagascariensis. International Journal of Primatology* 6: 435-447.

L255 Porter, L. M. (1998) Influences on the distribution of *Lepilemur microdon* in the Ranomafana National Park, Madagascar. *Folia Primatologica* 69: 172-176.

L256 Powzyk, J.A (1997) The socioecology of two sympatric Indriids, *Propithecus diadema diadema* and *Indri indri*: a comparison of feeding strategies and their possible repercussions on species-specific behaviours. Ph.D. Thesis, Duke University, Durham, North Carolina.

L257 Powzyk, J.A. and Mowry, C.B. (2003) Dietry and feeding differences between sympatric *Propithecus diadema diadema* and *Indri indri. International Journal of Primatology* 24: 1143-1162.

L258 Powzyk, J.A. and Thalmann, U. (2003) *Indri indri*, Indri. In Goodman, S.M. and Benstead, J.P. (eds) *The Natural History of Madagascar*, pp. 1342-1345. The University of Chicago Press, Chicago, USA.

L259 Rabarivola, C., Meyers, D. and Rumpler, Y. (1991) Distribution and morphological characteristics of intermediate forms between the black lemur (*Eulemur macaco macaco*) and Sclater's lemur (*E. m. flavifrons*). *Primates* 32: 269-273.

L259a Rabarivola, C., Zaramody, A., Fausser, J.-L., Andriaholinirina, N., Roos, C., Zinner, D., Marcel, H.

and Rumpler, Y. (2006) Cytogenic and molecular characteristics of a new species of Sportive Lemur from Northern Madagascar. *Lemur News* 11: 45-49.

L260 Radespiel, U. (2000) Sociality in the grey mouse lemur (*Microcebus murinus*) in northwestern Madagascar. *American Journal of Primatology* 51: 21-40.

L261 Radespiel, U., Ehresmann, P. and Zimmerman, E. (2003) Speciesspecific usage of sleeping sites in two sympatric mouse lemur species (*Microcebus murinus* and *M. ravelobensis*) in north west Madagascar. *American Journal of Primatology* 59: 139 – 151.

L262 Rahajanirina, L.P. and Dollar, L. (2004) Confirmation of the Ayeaye (*Daubentonia madagascariensis*) in Tsingy de Bemaraha National Park. *Lemur News* 9: 11-12.

L263 Rakotoarison, N. (1995) First sighting and capture of the Hairy-eared dwarf lemur (*Allocebus trichotis*) in the Strict Nature Reserve of Zahamena. Unpublished report to Conservation International.

L264 Rakotoarison, N., Mutschler, T. and Thalmann, U. (1993) Lemurs in Bemaraha (World Heritage Landscape, Western Madagascar). *Oryx* 27: 35-40.

L265 Rakotoarison, N., Zimmermann, H. and Zimmermann, E. (1996) Hairy-eared dwarf lemur (*Allocebus trichotis*) discovered in a highland rain forest of eastern Madagascar. In Lourenco, W.R. (ed.) *Biogéographie de Madagascar*, pp. 275-282. Editions de l'ORSTOM, Paris.

L266 Rakotondratsima, M and Kremen, C (2001) Suivi écologique de deux espèces de lémuriens diurnes *Varecia variegate rubra* et *Eulemur fulvus albifrons* dans la presqu'île de Masoala (1993-1998). *Lemur News* 6: 31-35.

L267 Rakotondravony, D. and Razafindramahatra, L.V. (2004) Contribution à l'étude des populations de *Hapalemur aureus* dans le couloir foriestier RanomafanaAndringitra. *Lemur News* 9: 28-32.

L268 Ralainasolo, F.B. (2004) Influence des effects anthropiques sur la dynamique de population de *Hapalemur griseus alaotrensis* ou 'Bandro' dans son habitat naturel. *Lemur News* 9: 32-35.

L269 Ralison, J. M. (2006) A Lemur Survey of the Réserve Spéciale de Marotandrano, Madagascar. *Lemur*

News, 11: 35-37.

L270 Ranaivoarisoa, J. F., Ramanamahefa, R., Louis, E. E. and Brenneman, R.A. (2006) Range Extension of Perrier's Sifaka, *Propithecus perrieri*, in the Andrafiamena Classified Forest. *Lemur News*: 11: 17-21.

L271 Randriatahina, G.H. and Rabarivola, J.C. (2004) Inventaire des Lémuriens dans la partie nord-ouest de Madagascar et Distribution d'*Eulemur macaco flavifrons. Lemur News* 9: 7-9.

L272 Rasmussen, D.T. (1985) A comparative study of breeding seasonality and litter size in eleven taxa of captive lemurs (*Lemur* and *Varecia*). *International Journal of Primatology* 6: 501-517.

L273 Rasoazanabary, E. (2004) A preliminary study of mouse lemurs in Beza Mahafaly Special Reserve, southwest Madagascar. *Lemur News* 9: 4-7.

L274 Rasoloarison, R.M., Goodman, S.M. and J.U. Ganzhorn (2000) Taxonomic Revisions of Mouse Lemurs (*Microcebus*) in the Western Portions of Madagascar. *International Journal of Primatology* 21: 963-1019.

L275 Rasoloarison, R.M., Rasolonandrasana, B.P.N., Ganzhorn, J.U. and Goodman, S.M. (1995) Predation on vertebrates in the Kirindy Forest, western Madagascar. *Ecotropica* 1: 59-65.

L276 Ratsimbazafy, J. (2002) Responses of Black and White Ruffed Lemurs (*Varecia variegata variegata*) to disturbance in Manombo Forest, Madagascar. Ph.D. Thesis, State University of New York at Stony Brook, USA.

L277 Ratsirarson, J. and Rumpler, Y (1988) Contribution à l'étude compare de l'éco-éthologie de deax espèces de lémuriens, *Lepilemur mustelinus* (I. Geoffroy 1850) et *Lepilemur septentrionalis* (Rumpler and Albignac 1975). In Rakotovao, L., Barre, V. and Sayer, J., *L'Equilibre des Ecosystèmes Forestiers à Madagascar, Actes d'un Séminaire International*, pp. 100-102. IUCN Gland, Switzerland and Cambridge, UK.

L278 Raxworthy, C.J. and Rakotondraparany, F. (1988) Mammals Report. In Quansah, N. (ed.) *Manongarivo Special Reserve (Madagascar), 1987/88 Expedition Report*. Madagascar Environmental Research Group, London, U.K.

L279 Rigamonti, M.M. (1993) Home range and diet in red ruffed lemurs

(*Varecia variegata rubra*) on the
Masoala Peninsula, Madagascar. In
Kappeler, P.M. and Ganzhorn, J.U.
(eds.) *Lemur Social Systems and
their Ecological Basis*, pp. 25-39.
Plenum Press, London & N.Y.

L280 Rigamonti, M.M. (1996) Red
Ruffed Lemur (*Varecia variegata
rubra*): A rare species from the
Masoala rain forests. *Lemur News*
2:9-11.

L281 Richard, A.F. (1974) Patterns of
mating in *Propithecus verreauxi
verreauxi*. In Martin, R.D., Doyle,
G.A. and Walker, A.C. (eds.)
Prosimian Biology, pp. 49-74.
Duckworth, London.

L282 Richard, A.F. (1974) Intra-specific
variation in the social organisation and ecology of *Propithecus
verreauxi*. *Folia Primatologica* 22:
178-207.

L283 Richard, A.F. (1976) Preliminary
observations on the birth and
development of *Propithecus
verreauxi* to the age of six months.
Primates 17: 357-366.

L284 Richard, A.F. (1977) The feeding
behaviour of *Propithecus verreauxi*.
In Clutton-Brock, T. (ed.) *Primate
Ecology: Studies of Feeding and
Ranging Behaviour in Lemurs,
Monkeys and Apes*, pp. 71-96.
Academic Press, London.

L285 Richard, A.F. (1978) Variability
in the feeding behaviour of a
Malagasy prosimian, *Propithecus
verreauxi*: Lemuriformes. In
Montgomery, G.G. (ed.) *The
Ecology of Arboreal Folivores*, pp.
519-533. Smithsonian Inst. Press,
Washington, D.C.

L286 Richard, A.F. (1985) Social boundaries in a Malagasy prosimian,
the sifaka (*Propithecus verreauxi*).
International Journal of Primatology
6: 553-568.

L287 Richard, A.F. (1992) Aggressive
competition between males,
female controlled polygyny and
sexual monomorphism in a
Malagasy primate, *Propithecus
verreauxi*. *Journal of Human
Evolution* 22: 395-406.

L288 Richard, A.F. (1993) Dispersal
by *Propithecus verreauxi* at Beza
Mahafaly, Madagascar. *American
Journal of Primatology* 30: 1-20.

L289 Richard, A. (2003) *Propithecus,
Sifakas*. In Goodman, S.M. and
Benstead, J.P. (eds) *The Natural
History of Madagascar*, pp. 1345-
1348. The University of Chicago
Press, Chicago, USA.

L290 Richard, A.F. and Nicoll, M.E.
(1987) Female social domi-

nance and basal metabolism in
a Malagasy primate, *Propithecus
verreauxi*. *American Journal of
Primatology* 12: 309-314.

L291 Richard, A.F., Rakotomanga, P. and
Schwartz, M. (1991) Demography
of *Propithecus verreauxi* at Beza
Mahafaly: sex ratio, survival
and fertility, 1984-88. *American
Journal of Physical Anthropology* 84:
307-322.

L292 Richard, A.F., Dewer, R.E.,
Schwartz, M. and Ratsirarson,
J. (2002) Life in the slow lane?
Demography and life histories of
male and female sifaka (*Propithecus
verreauxi verreauxi*). *Journal of
Zoology, London* 256: 421-436.

L293 Roth, O. (1996) Ecology and
Social Behaviour of the Woolly
Lemur (*Avahi laniger*) a nocturnal
Malagasy prosimian. Masters
Thesis, University of Basel,
Switzerland.

L294 Rumpler, Y. (2004)
Complementary approaches
of cytogenetics and molecular
biology to taxonomy and the
study of speciation process in
lemurs. *Evolutionary Anthropology*
13: 67-78.

L295 Rumpler, Y., Andriaholinirina,
N., Warter, S., Hauwy, M. and
Rabarivola (2004) Phylogenetic
history of the Sifakas (*Propithecus*:
Lemuriformes) derived from
cytogenetic studies. *Chromosome
Research* 12: 1-12.

L296 Russell, R.J. (1980) The environmental physiology and ecology
of *Lepilemur ruficaudatus* (=*L.
leucopus*) in arid southern
Madagascar. *American Journal
of Physical Anthropololology* 52:
273-274.

L297 Santorelli, C., Parathian, H. and
Patel, E.R. (2006). Silky sifaka
demography, ranging, and activity
budget. *International Journal of
Primatology* poster presentation.

L298 Sarikaya, Z. and Kappeler, P.
(1997) Nest Building Behaviour of
Coquerel's Dwarf Lemur (*Mirza
coquereli*). *Primate Report* 47: 3-9.

L299 Sauther, M.L. (1991) Reproductive
behaviour of free-ranging *Lemur
catta* at Beza-Mahafaly Special
Reserve, Madagascar. *American
Journal of Physical Anthropololology* 84:
463-478.

L300 Sauther, M.L. (1993) Resource
competition in wild populations of
Ring-tailed Lemur (*Lemur catta*):
Implications for female dominance.
In Kappeler, P.M. and Ganzhorn,
J.U. (eds.) *Lemur Social Systems and

their Ecological Basis*, pp. 135-152.
Plenum Press, London & N.Y.

L301 Sauther, M.L. and Sussman, R.W.
(1993) A new interpretation of
the social organisation and mating
system of the Ring-tailed Lemur
(*Lemur catta*). In Kappeler, P.M.
and Ganzhorn, J.U. (eds.) *Lemur
Social Systems and their Ecological
Basis*, pp. 111-122. Plenum Press,
London & N.Y.

L302 Sauther, M.L., Sussman, R.W. and
Gould, L. (1999) The socioecology
of the Ring-tailed Lemur: Thirty
five years of research. *Evolutionary
Anthropology* 8: 120-132.

L303 Scharfe, F. and Schlund, W. (1996)
Seed removal by lemurs in a
dry deciduous forest of western
Madagascar. In Ganzhorn, J.U.
and Sorg, J.-P. (eds.) Ecology and
Economy of a Tropical Dry Forest
in Madagascar, pp. 295-304.
Primate Report, Special Issue, 46-
1(June 1996).

L304 Schmid, J. (1999) Sex-specific
differences in the activity patterns
and fattening in the grey mouse
lemur (*Microcebus murinus*) in
Madagascar. *Journal of Mammology*
80: 749-757.

L305 Schmid, J. (2001) Daily torpor
in free-ranging grey mouse
lemurs (*Microcebus murinus*) in
Madagascar. *International Journal of
Primatology* 22: 1021-1031.

L306 Schmid, J. and Ganzhorn, J.U.
(1996) Resting metabolic rates of
Lepilemur ruficaudatus. *American
Journal of Primatology* 38: 169-174.

L307 Schmid, J. and Kappeler, P.M.
(1994) Sympatric mouse lemurs
(*Microcebus* spp.) in western
Madagascar. *Folia Primatologica* 63:
162-170.

L308 Schmid, J. and Kappeler, P.M.
(1998) Fluctuating sexual
dimorphism and differential
hibernation by sex in a primate,
the grey mouse lemur (*Microcebus
murinus*). *Behavioural Ecology and
Sociobiology* 43: 125-132.

L309 Schmid, J. Ruf, T. and Heldmaier,
G. (2000) Metabolism and
temperature regulation during
daily torpor in the smallest
primate, the pygmy mouse
lemur (*Microcebus myoxinus*) in
Madagascar. *Journal of Comparitive
Physiology* B 170: 59-68,

L310 Schmid, J. and Smolker, R. (1998)
Lemurs of the Réserve Spécial
d'Anjanaharibe-Sud, Madagascar.
In Goodman, S.M. (ed) A Floral
and Faunal Inventory of the
Réserve Spéciale d'Anjanaharibe-

Sud, Madagascar: with reference to elevational variation. *Fieldiana Zoology* 90: 227-238.

L311 Schülke, O. (2003) *Phaner furcifer*, Fork-marked Lemur, *Vakihandry, Tanta*. In Goodman, S.M. and Benstead, J.P. (eds) *The Natural History of Madagascar*, pp. 1318-1320. The University of Chicago Press, Chicago, USA.

L312 Schütz, H and Goodman, S.M. (1998) Photographic evidence of *Allocebus trichotis* in the Réserve Spécial d'Anjanaharibe-Sud. *Lemur News* 21-22.

L313 Schwab, D. (2000) A preliminary study of spatial distribution and mating system of the pygmy mouse lemur (*Microcebus* cf. *myoxinus*). *American Journal of Primatology* 51: 41-60.

L314 Schwab, D. and Ganzhorn J.U. (2004) Distribution, population structure and habitat use of *Microcebus berthae* compared to those of other sympatric cheirogaleids. *International Journal of Primatology* 15: 307-330.

L315 Schwitzer, C. (2004) Sahamalaza Field Trip 28/09 to 19/11 2003. Report to the Board of AEECL. Köln: Zoologischer Garten Köln. 10 p.

L316 Schwitzer, C. and Kaumanns, W. (2005) Blue-eyed black lemur (*Eulemur macaco flavifrons* GRAY, 1867): Perspectives for *in situ*- and *ex situ*-research and conservation activities. Proceedings of the 2004 EAZA Conference. Amsterdam: EAZA Executive Office.

L317 Schwitzer, C. and Lork, A. (2004) 'Projet Sahamalaza – Iles Radama': Ein internationales Schutzprojekt für den Sclater's Maki (*Eulemur macaco flavifrons* GRAY, 1867). *Zeitschrift des Kölner Zoo* 47(2):75-84.

L318 Simons, E.L. (1988) A new species of *Propithecus* (Primates) from north east Madagascar. *Folia Primatologica* 50: 143-151.

L319 Simons, E.L. (1993) Discovery of the western aye-aye. *Lemur News* 1(1): 6.

L320 Simons, E.L. (1994) The giant aye-aye, *Daubentonia robusta*. *Folia Primatologica* 62: 14-2.

L321 Simons, E.L. (1995) History, anatomy, subfossil record and management of *Daubentonia madagascariensis*. In Alterman, L. Doyle, G.A. and Izard, K. (eds.) *Creatures of the Dark: the Nocturnal Prosimians*, pp.133-140. Plenum Press, London & N.Y.

L322 Simons, E.L. and Meyers, D.M.

(2001) Folklore and Beliefs about the Aye-aye (*Daubentonia madagascariensis*). *Lemur News* 6: 11-16.

L323 Simons, E.L. and Rumpler, Y. (1988) *Eulemur*: new generic name for species of *Lemur* other than *Lemur catta*. *C.R. Academy of Science*, Paris, Series 3 307: 547-551.

L324 Stanger, K., Coffman, B. and Izard, M. (1995) Reproduction in Coquerel's dwarf lemur (*Mirza coquereli*). *American Journal of Primatology* 36: 223-237.

L325 Stephenson, P.J., Rakotoarison, N. and Randriamahazo, H. (1994) Conservation of lemurs in Ambohitantely Special Reserve, Madagascar. *Primate Conservation* 14-15: 22-24.

L326 Sterling, E.J. (1992) Timing of reproduction in aye-ayes (*Daubentonia madagascariensis*) in Madagascar. *American Journal of Primatology* 27: 59-60.

L327 Sterling, E.J. (1993) Behavioural ecology of the aye-aye (*Daubentonia madagascariensis*) on Nosy Mangabe. Ph.D. thesis, Yale University, New Haven, Connecticut, U.S.A.

L328 Sterling, E.J. (1993) Patterns of range use and social organisation in aye-ayes (*Daubentonia madagascariensis*) on Nosy Mangabe. In Kappeler, P.M. and Ganz-horn, J.U. (eds.) *Lemur Social Systems and their Ecological Basis*, pp. 1-10. Plenum Press, London & N.Y.

L329 Sterling, E.J. (1994) Taxonomy and distribution of *Daubentonia*: a historical perspective. *Folia Primatologica* 62: 8-13.

L330 Sterling, E.J. (1994) Evidence for non-seasonal reproduction in Aye-ayes (*Daubentonia madagascariensis*) in the wild. *Folia Primatologica* 62: 46-53.

L331 Sterling, E.J. (1994) Aye-ayes: specialists on structurally defended resources. *Folia Primatologica* 62: 142-154.

L332 Sterling, E.J. (1998) Preliminary report on a survey for *Daubentonia madagascariensis* and other primate species in the west of Madagascar, June-August 1994. *Lemur News* 3: 7-8.

L333 Sterling, E. J. (2003) *Daubentonia madagascariensis*, Aye-aye, *Aye-aye*. In Goodman, S.M. and Benstead, J.P. (eds) *The Natural History of Madagascar*, pp. 1348-1351. The University of Chicago Press, Chicago, USA.

L334 Sterling, E.J. and Feistner, A.T.C.

(2000) Aye-aye (*Daubentonia madagascariensis*). In Reading, R. and Miller, B. (eds) *Endangered Animals: A Reference Guide to Conflicting Issues*, pp 45-48. Westport, Greenwood.

L335 Sterling, E.J. and McFadden, K. (2000) Rapid census of lemur populations in the Parc National de Marojejy, Madagascar. In Goodman, S.M. (ed) A Floral and Faunal Inventory of the Parc National de Marojejy, Madagascar: with reference to elevational variation. *Fieldiana Zoology* 97: 265-274.

L336 Sterling, E.J. and Ramaroson, M.G. (1996) Rapid assessment of the primate fauna of the eastern slopes of the Réserve Naturelle Intégrale d'Andringitra, Madagascar. In Goodman, S.M. (ed) A Floral and Faunal Inventory of the Eastern slopes of the Réserve Naturelle Intégrale d'Andringitra, Madagascar: with reference to elevational variation. *Fieldiana Zoology* 85: 293-305.

L337 Sterling, E.J and Rakotoarison, N. (1998) Rapid assessment of the richness and density of primate species on the Masoala Peninsula, eastern Madagascar. In Harcourt, C., Crompton, R. H. and Feistner, A.T.C. (eds.) *Biology and Conservation of Prosimians. Folia Primatologica* 69(1): 109-116.

L338 Sterling, E.J. and Richard, A.F. (1995) Social organisation in the aye-aye (*Daubentonia madagascariensis*) and the perceived distinctiveness of nocturnal primates. In Alterman, L. Doyle, G.A. and Izard, K. (eds.) *Creatures of the Dark: the Nocturnal Prosimians*, pp. 439-451. Plenum Press, London & N.Y.

L339 Sterling, E.J., Dierenfeld, E.S., Ashbourne, C.J. and Feistner, A.T.C. (1994) Dietary intake, food consumption and nutrient intake in wild and captive populations of *Daubentonia madagascariensis*. *Folia Primatologica* 62: 115-124.

L340 Sussman, R.W. (1974) Ecological distinctions in sympatric species of *Lemur*. In Martin, R.D., Doyle, G.A. and Walker, A.C. (eds) *Prosimian Biology*, pp 75-108. Duckworth, London.

L341 Sussman, R.W. (1975) A preliminary study of the behaviour and ecology of *Lemur fulvus rufus* Audebert 1800. In Tattersall, I. And Sussman, R.W. (eds) *Lemur Biology*, pp 237-258. Plenum Press, New York.

L342 Sussman, R.W. (1989) Demography of *Lemur catta* in southern Madagascar. *American Journal of Physical Anthropology* 78: 312.

L343 Sussman, R.W. (1991) Demography and social organisation of free-ranging *Lemur catta* in Beza Mahafaly Special Reserve. *American Journal of Physical Anthropology.*, 84: 43-58.

L344 Sussman, R.W. (1992) Male life history and intergroup mobility among Ring-tailed Lemurs (*Lemur catta*). *International Journal of Primatology* 13: 395-410.

L345 Tan, C. L. (1999) Group composition, home range size and diet in three sympatric bamboo lemur species (genus *Hapalemur*) in Ranomafana National Park, Madagascar. *International Journal of Primatology* 20: 547-566.

L346 Tan, C. L. (2000) Behaviour and ecology of three sympatric bamboo lemur species (genus *Hapalemur*) in Ranomafana National Park, Madagascar. Ph.D. Thesis, State University of New York, Stony Brook.

L347 Tattersall, I (1977) Distribution of Lemurs. Part I: The Lemurs of northern Madagascar. *Annals of the New York Academy of Sciences* 293: 160-169.

L348 Tattersall, I. (1982) *The Primates of Madagascar*. Columbia Unioversity Press, New York.

L349 Tattersall, I. (1987) Cathemeral activity in primates: a definition. *Folia Primatologica* 49: 200.

L350 Tattersall, I. (1998) Lemurs of the Comoro Archipelago: Status of *Eulemur mongoz* on Mohéli and Anjouan and of *Eulemur fulvus* on Mayotte. *Lemur News* 3: 15-17.

L351 Tattersall, I. and Schwartz (1991) Phylogeny and nomenclature in the *Lemur* group of Malagasy Strepsirhine primates. *Anthropological Papers of the Amererican Museum of. Natural History* 69: 1-18.

L352 Tattersall, I and Sussman, R.W. (1998) 'Little Brown Lemurs' of Northern Madagascar: Phylogeny and Ecological Role in Resource Partitioning. In Harcourt, C., Crompton, R. H. and Feistner, A.T.C. (eds.) *Biology and Conservation of Prosimians. Folia Primatologica* 69 (supplement): 379-388.

L353 Terranova, C.J. and Coffman, B.S. (1997) Body weights of wild and captive lemurs. *Zoo Biology* 16: 17-30.

L354 Thalmann, U. (2000) Greater Dwarf Lemurs from the Bongolava (Central Western Madagascar). *Lemur News* 5: 33-35.

L355 Thalmann, U., (2001) Food resource characteristics in two nocturnal lemurs with different social behaviour: *Avahi occidentalis* and *Lepilemur edwardsi*. *International Journal of Primatology* 22: 287-324.

L356 Thalmann, U. (2002) Contrasts between two nocturnal leaf-eating lemurs. *Evolutionary Anthropology* (Supplement 1): 105-107.

L357 Thalmann, U. (2003) *Avahi, Woolly Lemur, Avahy, Fotsefe, Ampongy, Tsarafangitra, Dadintsifaky*. In Goodman, S.M. and Benstead, J.P. (eds) *The Natural History of Madagascar*, pp. 1340-1342. The University of Chicago Press, Chicago, USA.

L358 Thalmann, U. and Ganzhom, J.U. (2003) *Lepilemur, Sportive Lemur*. In Goodman, S.M. and Benstead, J.P. (eds) *The Natural History of Madagascar*, pp. 1336-1340. The University of Chicago Press, Chicago, USA.

L359 Thalmann, U. and Geissmann, T. (2000) Distribution and Geographic Variation in the Western Woolly Lemur (*Avahi occidentalis*) with Description of a New Species (*A. unicolor*). *International Journal of Primatology*, 21: 915-941.

L360 Thalmann, U. and Geissmann, T. (2005) A New Species of Woolly Lemur *Avahi* (Primates: Lemuriformes) in Bemaraha (Central Western Madagascar). *American Journal of Primatology*, 67: 371-376.

L361 Thalmann, U. and Geissmann, T. (submitted) Conservation assessment of the recently described Cleese's Woolly Lemur *Avahi cleesei* (Lemuriformes, Indridae). *Primate Conservation*.

L362 Thalmann, U. and Rakotoarison, N. (1994) Distribution of lemurs in central western Madagascar, with a regional distribution hypothesis. *Folia Primatologica* 63: 156-161.

L363 Thalmann, U., Geissmann, T., Simona, A. and Mutschler, T. (1993) The Indris of Anjanaharibe-Sud, north east Madagascar. *International Journal of Primatology* 14: 357-381.

L364 Thalmann, U., Kümmerli, R. and Zaramody, A. (2002) Why *Propithecus verreauxi deckeni* and *P.v. coronatus* are valid taxa

– quantitative and qualitative arguments. *Lemur News* 7: 11-16.

L365 Thalmann, U., Müller, A.E., Kerloc'h, P. and Zaramody, A. (1999) A Visit to the Strict Nature Reserve Tsingy de Namoroka (NW Madagascar). *Lemur News* 4: 16-19.

L366 Tilden, C.D. and Oftedal, O. (1997) Milk composition reflects pattern of maternal care in prosimian primates. *American Journal of Primatology* 41: 195-212.

L367 van Schaik, C.P. and Kappeler, P.M. (1993) Life history, activity period and lemur social systems. In Kappeler, P.M. and Ganzhom, J.U. (eds.) *Lemur Social Systems and their Ecological Basis*, pp. 241-260. Plenum Press, London & N.Y.

L368 Vargas, A., Jiménez, I., Palomares, F. and Palacios, M.J. (2002) Distribution, Status and Conservation needs of the Golden-crowned Sifaka (*Propithecus tattersalli*). *Biological Conservation* 108(3): 325-334.

L369 Vasey, N. (1995) Human resource use and habitat availability for red ruffed lemurs (*Varecia variegata rubra*) in the Anaovandrano river watershed, Masoala Peninsula, Madagascar. In Patterson, B.D., Goodman, S.M. and Sedlock, J.L. (eds.) *Environmental Change in Madagascar*, pp. 37-38. Field Museum of Natural History, Chicago.

L370 Vasey, N. (1996) Clinging to life: *Varecia variegata rubra* and the Masoala coastal forests. *Lemur News*, 2: 7-9.

L371 Vasey, N. (1997) How many Ruffed Lemurs are left?. *International Journal of Primatology* 18: 207-216.

L372 Vasey, N. (1997) The cooperative breeding system of *Varecia variegata*. *American Journal of Physical Anthropology* 24 (supplement): 232.

L373 Vasey, N. (1999) Positional behaviour of *Varecia variegata rubra* and *Eulemur fulvus albifrons*. *American Journal of Physical Anthropology* 28 (supplement): 270.

L374 Vasey, N. (2000) Niche separation in *Varecia variegata rubra* and *Eulemur fulvus albifrons*: I Interspecific patterns. *American Journal of Physical Anthropology* 112: 411-431.

L375 Vasey, N. (2000) Plant species composition of diet in two sympatric lemurs: *Varecia variegata rubra* and *Eulemur fulvus albifrons*: I Interspecific patterns. *American Journal of Physical Anthropology* 30 (supplement): 309-310.

L376 Vasey, N. (2002) Niche separation in *Varecia variegata rubra* and *Eulemur fulvus albifrons*: II Intraspecific patterns. *American Journal of Physical Anthropology* 118: 169-183.

L377 Vasey, N. (2003) *Varecia*, Ruffed Lemurs. In Goodman, S.M. and Benstead, J.P. (eds) *The Natural History of Madagascar*, pp. 1332-1336. The University of Chicago Press, Chicago, USA.

L378 Vasey, N. (in press) Impact of seasonality and reproduction on social structure, ranging patterns, and fission-fusion social organisation in red ruffed lemurs. In Gould, L. and Sauther, M. (eds) *Lemurs: Ecology and Adaptation*. New York: Springer/Kluwer.

L379 Vasey, N. and Tattersall, I. (2002) Do ruffed lemurs form a hybrid zone? Distribution and discovery of *Varecia*, with systematic and conservation implications. *American Museum Novitates* 3376: 1-26.

L380 Vuillaume-Randriamanantena, M., Godfrey, L. and Sutherland, M. (1985) Revision of *Hapalemur (Prohapalemur) gallieni* (Standing, 1905). *Folia Primatologica* 45: 89-116.

L381 Warren, R.D. (1994) Lazy Leapers: A Study of the Locomotor Ecology of Two Species of Saltatory Nocturnal Lemur in Sympatry at Ampijoroa, Madagascar. Ph.D. Thesis, University of Liverpool, UK.

L382 Warren, R.D. (1997) Habitat use and support preference of two free-ranging saltatory lemurs, *Lepilemur edwardsi* and *Avahi occidentalis*. *Journal of Zoology* (London), 241: 325-341.

L383 Warren, R.D. and Crompton, R.H. (1997) A comparative study of the ranging behaviour, activity rhythms and sociality of *Lepilemur edwardsi* (Primates, Lepilemurinae) and *Avahi occidentalis* (Primates, Indriidae) at Ampijoroa, Madagascar. *Journal of Zoology* (London) 243: 397-415.

L384 Warren, R.D. and Crompton, R.H. (1998) Diet, body size and the energy costs of locomotion in saltatory primates. . In Harcourt, C., Crompton, R. H. and Feistner, A.T.C. (eds.) *Biology and Conservation of Prosimians. Folia Primatologica* 69 (supplement): 86-100.

L385 Warren, R.D. and Crompton, R.H. (1998) Lazy Leapers: Locomotor behaviour and ecology of *Lepilemur*

edwardsi and *Avahi occidentalis*. *American Journal of Physical Anthropology* 104: 471-486.

L386 Warter, S. and Tattersall, I. (1994) Update to the article 'Cytogenetic study of a new subspecies of *Hapalemur griseus'*. *Folia Primatologica* 63: 170.

L387 Warter, S. Randrianasolo, G. Dutrillaux, B. and Rumpler, Y. (1987) Cytogenetic study of a new subspecies of *Hapalemur griseus*. *Folia Primatologica* 48: 50-55.

L388 Wilson, J.M., Stewart, P.D., Ramangason, G.-S., Denning, A.M. and Hutchings, M.S. (1989) Ecology and conservation of the crowned lemur, *Lemur coronatus*, at Ankarana, northern Madagascar, with notes on Sanford's lemur, other sympatric and sub-fossil lemurs. *Folia Primatologica* 52: 1-26.

L389 Wimmer, B., Tautz, D. and Kappeler, P.M. (2002) The genetic population structure of the grey mouse lemur, *Microcebus murinus*, a basal primate from Madagascar. *Behavioural Ecology and Sociobiology* 52: 166-175.

L390 Wright, P.C. (1986) Diet, ranging behaviour and activity pattern of the gentle lemur (*Hapalemur griseus*) in Madagascar. *American Journal of Physical Anthropology* 69: 283.

L391 Wright, P.C. (1987) Diet and ranging patterns of *Propithecus diadema edwardsi* in Madagascar. *American Journal of Physical Anthropology* 72: 218.

L392 Wright, P.C. (1988) Social behaviour of *Propithecus diadema edwardsi* in Madagascar. *American Journal of Physical Anthropology* 75: 289.

L393 Wright, P.C. (1989) Comparative ecology of three sympatric bamboo lemurs in Madagascar. *American Journal of Physical Anthropology* 78: 327.

L394 Wright, P.C. (1995) Demography and life history of free-ranging *Propithecus diadema edwardsi* in Ranomafana National Park, Madagascar. *International Journal of Primatology* 16: 835-854.

L395 Wright, P.C. (1998) Impact of predation risk on the behaviour of *Propithecus diadema edwardsi* in the rainforests of Madagascar. *Behaviour* 135: 483-512.

L396 Wright, P.C. and Martin, L.B. (1995) Predation, pollination and torpor in two nocturnal prosimians, *Cheirogaleus major* and *Microcebus rufus*, in the rainforests of Madagascar. In Alterman,

L., Doyle, G.A. and Izard, K. (eds.), *Creatures of the Dark: the Nocturnal Prosimians*, pp. 45-60. Plenum Press, London & N.Y.

L397 Wright, P.C. and Randriamanantena, M (1989) Behavioural ecology of three sympatric bamboo lemurs in Madagascar. *American Journal of Physical Anthropology* 78 (supplement): 327.

L398 Wright, P.C., Heckscher, S.K. and Dunham, A.E. (1997) Predation on Milne-Edward's Sifaka *Propithecus diadema edwardsi* by the Fossa *Cryptoprocta ferox* in the rain forest of south east, Madagascar. *Folia Primatologica* 68: 34-43.

L399 Wright, P. C., Razafindratsita, V. R., Pochron, S. T. and Jernvall, J. (2005) The Key to Madagascar Frugivores. In Dew, J. L. and Boubli, J. P. (eds) *Tropical Fruits and Frugivores: The Search for Strong Interactions*. Springer, pp 121-138.

L400 Yoder, A. D. (1996) Pilot study to determine the status of *Allocebus trichotis* in Madagascar. *Lemur News* 2: 14-15.

L401 Yoder, A. D (2003) Phylogeny of the Lemurs. In Goodman, S.M. and Benstead, J.P. (eds) *The Natural History of Madagascar*, pp. 1242 – 1247. The University of Chicago Press, Chicago, USA.

L402 Yoder, A.D., Rakotosamimanana, B. and Parsons, T. (1999) Ancient DNA in subfossil lemurs: Methodological challenges and their solutions. In Rakotosamimanana, B., Rasammimanana, Ganzhorn, J.U. and Goodman, S.M. (eds) *New Directions in Lemur Studies*, pp 1-17. Kluwer Academic Press/Plenum, New York.

L403 Yoder, A. D, Rasoloarison, R.M., Goodman, S.M., Irwin, J.A., Atsalis, S., Ravosa, M.J. and Ganzhorn, J.U. (2000) Remarkable species diversity in Malagasy mouse lemurs (primates, *Microcebus*). Proceedings of the National Academy of Sciences, USA 97: 11325-11330.

L404 Zaramody, A. and Pastorini, J. (2001) Indications for hybridisation between Red-fronted Lemurs (*Eulemur fulvus rufus*) and Mongoose Lemurs (*Eulemur mongoz*) in northwest Madagascar. *Lemur News* 6: 28-31.

L405 Zimmermann, E. (1995) Acoustic communication in nocturnal prosimians. In Alterman, L., Doyle, G.A. and Izard, K. (eds.) *Creatures* of the Dark: the Nocturnal Prosimians, pp. 311-330. Plenum Press, London & N.Y.

L406 Zimmermann, E., Cepok, S., Rakotoarison, N., Zietemann, V. and Radespiel, U. (1998) Sympatric mouse lemurs in north west Madagascar: a new rufous mouse lemur species (*Microcebus ravelobensis*). *Folia Primatologica* 69: 106-114.

L407 Zinner, D., Ostner, J., Dill, A., Razafimanantsoa, L., and Rasoloarison (2001) Results of a reconnaissance expedition in the western dry forests between Morondava and Morombe. *Lemur News* 6: 16-18.

L408 Zinner, D., Hilgartner, R.D., Kappeler, P.M., Pietsch, T. and Ganzhorn, J.U. (2003) Social organization of *Lepilemur ruficaudatus*. *International Journal of Primatology* 24: 869-888.

Cited Literature: Order Carnivora

C1 Albignac, R. (1972) The Carnivora of Madagascar. In Battistini, R and Richard-Vindard, G. (eds.) *Biogeography and Ecology of Madagascar*, pp. 667-682. Dr W. Junk, The Hague.

C2 Albignac, R. (1973) *Faune de Madagascar* vol. 36 Mammifères. Paris, O.R.S.T.O.M.C.N.R.S.

C3 Albignac, R. (1974). Observations eco-éthologiques sur le genre *Eupleres*, viverride de Madagascar. *Terre Vie*, 28: 321-351.

C4 Albignac, R. (1976). L'ecologie de *Mungotictis decemlineata* dans les forêt decidues de L'ouest de Madagascar. *Terre Vie*, 30: 347-376.

C5 Albignac, R. (1984) the carnivores. In Jolly, A., Oberle, P. and Albignac, R. (eds.). *Key Environments – Madagascar*, pp. 167-181. Pergamon Press, Oxford.

C6 Barden, T.L., Evans, M.I., Raxworthy, C.J., Razafimahimodison, J.C. and Wilson, A. (1991) The mammals of Ambatovaky Special Reserve. In Thompson, P.M. and Evans, M.I. (eds.) *A Survey of Ambatovaky Special Reserve, Madagascar*, pp. 19-20. Madagascar Environmental Research Group.

C7 Bininda-Edmonds, O.R.P., Gittleman, J.L. and Purvis, A. (1999) Building large trees by combining phylogenetic information: A complete phylogeny of the extant Carnivora (Mammalia). *Biological Reviews of the Cambridge Philosophical Society* 74: 143-175.

C8 Britt A. (1999) Observations of two sympatric diurnal herpstids in Betampona Nature Reserve, eastern Madagascar. *Small Carnivore Conservation* 20: 14.

C9 Britt A. and V. Virkaitis (2003) Brown-tailed Mongoose *Salanoia concolor* in Betampona Reserve, eastern Madagascar: Photographs and ecological comparison with the Ring-tailed Mongoose *Galidia elegans*. *Small Carnivore Conservation* 28: 1-3.

C10 Britt, A., Welch, C. and Katz, A.

(2001) The impact of *Cryptoprocta ferox* on the *Varecia variegata* reinforcement project at Betampona. *Lemur News* 6: 35-37.

C11 Dollar, L. (1999) Preliminary report on the status, activity cycle and ranging of *Cryptoprocta ferox* in the Malagasy rain forest, with implications for conservation. *Small Carnivore Conservation* 20: 7-10.

C12 Dollar, L. (1999) Notice of *Eupleres goudotii* in the rain forest of south eastern Madagascar. *Small Carnivore Conservation* 20: 30-31.

C13 Dollar, L.J., Forward, Z.A. and Wright, P.C. (1997) First study of *Cryptoprocta ferox* in the rainforest of Madagascar. *American Journal of Physical Anthropology* 24 (supplement); 103-104.

C14 Duckworth, J.W. and Rakotondraparany, F. (1990) The mammals of Marojejy. In Safford, R. J. and Duckworth, J.W. (eds.) *A Wildlife Survey of Marojejy Nature Reserve, Madagascar*, pp.54-60. *Int. Council Bird Preserv. Study Report No. 40*.

C15 Dunham, A. E. (1998) Notes on the Behaviour of the Ring-tailed Mongoose, *Galidia elegans* at Ranomafana National Park, Madagascar. *Small Carnivore Conservation* 19: 21-24.

C16 Flynn, J.J., Finarelli, J.A., Zehr, S., Hsu, J., Nedbal, M.A. (2005) Molecular Phylogeny of the Carnivora (Mammalia): Assessing the Impact of Increased Sampling on Resolving Enigmatic Relationships. *Syst. Biol.* 54(2): 317-337.

C17 Garbutt, N. (1994) Two together: Fossas look a lot more special. *BBC Wildlife* 12(5): 11.

C18 Golden, C. (2005) *Eaten to Endangerment: Mammal Hunting and the Bushmeat Trade in Madagascar's Makira Forest*. Undergraduate Thesis, University of Harvard, USA.

C19 Goodman, S.M. (1996) A subfossil record of *Galidictis grandidieri* (Herpestidae: Galidiinae) from

southwest Madagascar. *Mammalia* 60(1): 150-151.

C20 Goodman, S.M. (1996) The Carnivores of the Réserve Naturelle Intégrale d'Andringitra, Madagascar. In Goodman, S.M. (ed) *A Floral and Faunal Inventory of the Eastern slopes of the Réserve Naturelle Intégrale d'Andringitra, Madagascar*: with reference to elevational variation. *Fieldiana Zoology* 85: 289-292.

C21 Goodman, S.M. (2003) Predation on Lemurs. In Goodman, S.M. and Benstead, J.P. (eds), *The Natural History of Madagascar*, pp. 1221 – 1225. The University of Chicago Press, Chicago, USA.

C22 Goodman, S.M. (2003) Carnivora: *Galidia elegans*, Ring-tailed Mongoose, *Vontsira Mena*. In Goodman, S.M. and Benstead, J.P. (eds), *The Natural History of Madagascar*, pp. 1351 – 1354. The University of Chicago Press, Chicago, USA.

C23 Goodman, S.M. (2003) *Galidictis*, Broad-striped Mongoose, *Vontsira Fotsy*. In Goodman, S.M. and Benstead, J.P. (eds), *The Natural History of Madagascar*, pp. 1354 – 1357. The University of Chicago Press, Chicago, USA.

C24 Goodman, S.M. and Pidgeon, M. (1999) Carnivora of the Réserve Naturelle Intégrale d'Andohahela, Madagascar. In Goodman, S.M. (ed) *A Floral and Faunal Inventory of the Eastern slopes of the Réserve Naturelle Intégrale d'Andohahela, Madagascar*: with reference to elevational variation. *Fieldiana Zoology* 94: 256-268.

C25 Goodman, S.M., O'Connor, S. and Lngrand, O. (1993) A review of the predation on lemurs: Implications for the evolution of social behaviour in small nocturnal primates. In Kappeler, P.M. and Ganzhorn, J.U. (eds), *Lemur Social Systems and their Ecological Basis*, pp 51-66. New York, Plenum.

C26 Goodman, S.M, Langrand, O. and Rasolonandrasana, B.P.N. (1997) The Food Habits of

Cryptoprocta ferox in the High Mountain Zone of the Andringita Massif, Madagascar (Carnivora, Viverridae). *Mammalia* 61: 185-192.

C27 Goodman, S.M., Ganzhorn, J.U. and Rakotndravony (2003) Introduction to the Mammals. In Goodman, S.M. and Benstead, J.P. (eds) *The Natural History of Madagascar*, pp. 1159 – 1186. The University of Chicago Press, Chicago, USA.

C28 Goodman, S.M, Kerridge, F.J. and Ralisoamalala, R.C. (2003) A note on the diet of *Fossa fossana* (Carnivora) in the central eastern humid forests of Madagascar. *Mammalia* 67: 595-598.

C29 Hawkins, A.F.A. (1994) *Eupleres goudotii* in western Malagasy deciduous forest. *Small Carnivore Conservation* 11: 20.

C30 Hawkins, A.F.A., Hawkins, C. E. and Jenkins, P.D. (2000) *Mungotictis decemlineata lineata* (Carnivora: Herpestidae), a mysterious Malagasy mongoose. *Journal of Natural History* 34: 305-310.

C31 Hawkins, C.E. (1998) The behaviour and ecology of the Fossa, *Cryptoprocta ferox* (Carnivora: Viverridae) in a dry deciduous forest in western Madagascar. PhD thesis, University of Aberdeen.

C32 Hawkins, C.E. (2003) *Cryptoprocta ferox*, Fossa, *Fosa*. In Goodman, S.M. and Benstead, J.P. (eds) *The Natural History of Madagascar*, pp. 1360 – 1363. The University of Chicago Press, Chicago, USA.

C33 Hawkins, C.E. and Racey, P.A. (2005) Low population density of a tropical forest carnivore, *Cryptoprocta ferox*: implications for protected areas management. *Oryx* 39(1): 35-43.

C34 Kerridge, F.J., Ralisoamalala, R.C., Goodman, S.M. and Pasnick, S.D. (2003) *Fossa fossana*, Malagasy Striped Civet, *Fanaloka*. In Goodman, S.M. and Benstead, J.P. (eds) *The Natural History of Madagascar*, pp. 1363 – 1365. The University of Chicago Press, Chicago, USA.

C35 Kohncke, M. and Leonhardt, K. (1986) *Cryptoprocta ferox*. *Mammalian Species* 254.

C36 Laborde, C. (1986) Caractères d'adaptation des members au mode de vie arboricole chez *Cryptoprocta ferox* par comparaison avec d'autres Carnivores Viverridés. *Annales des Sciences Naturelles, Zoologie*, Paris

13:25-39.

C37 Laborde, C. (1986) Description de la locomotion arboricole de *Cryptoprocta ferox* (Carnivores Viverridés, Malgache). *Mammalia* 50:369-378.

C38 Lekagul, B and McNeely, J.A. (1977) *Mammals of Thailand*. Sahakarnbhat, Bangkok.

C39 Mahazotahy, S., Goodman S.M. and Andriamanalina, A. (in press). Notes on the distribution and habitat preference of *Galidictis grandidieri* Wozencraft, 1986 (Carnivora: Eupleridae), a poorly known endemic species of southwestern Madagascar. *Mammalia*

C40 Nowak, R.M. (1991) *Walker's Mammals of the World* (5th ed.). John Hopkins University Press, USA.

C41 Rabeantoandro, Z.S. (1997) Contribution à l'étude du *Mungotictis decemlineata* (Grandidier 1867) de la forêt de Kirindy, Morondava. Mémoire D.E.A., Université d'Antananarivo.

C42 Rasoloarison, R.M., Rasolonandrasana, B.P.N., Ganzhorn, J.U. and Goodman, S.M. (1995). Predation on vertebrates in the Kirindy Forest, western Madagascar. *Ecotropica* 1: 59-65.

C43 Raxworthy, C.J. and Rakotondraparany, F. (1988) Mammals Report. In Quansah, N. (ed.) *Manongarivo Special Reserve, Madagascar 1987/88 Expedition Report*, pp. 121-131. Madagascar Environmental Research Group.

C44 Razafimanantsoa, L. (2003) *Mungotictis decemlineata*, Narrow-striped Mongoose, *Boky-boky*. In Goodman, S.M. and Benstead, J.P. (eds), *The Natural History of Madagascar*, pp. 1357 – 1360. The University of Chicago Press, Chicago, USA.

C45 Roberts, T.J. (1977) *The Mammals of Pakistan*. Ernest Benn, London.

C46 Ryan, J.M. (2003) *Nesomys*, Red Forest Rat, *Voalavo Mena*. In Goodman, S.M. and Benstead, J.P. (eds) *The Natural History of Madagascar*, pp. 1388 – 1389. The University of Chicago Press, Chicago, USA.

C47 Schreiber, A., Wirth, R., Riffel, M. and van Rompaey, H. (1989) *Weasels, Civets, Mongooses and their Relatives. An Action Plan for the Conservation of Mustelids and Viverrids*. IUCN, Gland, Switzerland.

C48 Veron, G. (1995) La position

systématique de *Cryptoprocta ferox* (Carnivora). Analyse cladistique des caractères morphologiques de carnivores Aeluroidea actuels et fossiles. *Mammalia* 59(4): 551-582.

C49 Woolaver, L., Nichols, R., Rakotombololona, W.F., Volahy, A.T. and Durbin, J. (2006) Population Status, Distribution and Conservation Needs of the Narrow-striped Mongoose *Mungotictis decemlineata* of Madagascar. *Oryx* 40 (1): 67-75.

C50 Wozencraft, W.C. (1986) A new species of striped mongoose from Madagascar. *Journal of Mammalogy*. 67: 561-571.

C51 Wozencraft, W.C. (1989) The classification of recent Carnivora. In Gittleman, J.L. (ed.) *Carnivore Behaviour, Ecology and Evolution*, pp. 569-593. Chapman and Hall, London.

C52 Wozencraft, W.C. (1990) Alive and well in Tsimanampetsotsa. *Natural History Magazine* 12 (90): 28-30.

C53 Wozencraft, W.C. (1993) Order Carnivora. In Wilson, D.E. and Reeder, D.H. (eds.) *Mammal Species of the World: a taxonomic and geographic reference* (2nd ed.), pp. 279-348. Smithsonian Inst. Press. Washington, D.C.

C54 Wright, P.C., Heckscher, S.K. and Durham, A.E. (1997) Predation on Milne-Edwards's Sifaka (*Propithecus diadema edwardsi*) by the Fossa (*Cryptoprocta ferox*) in the rain forest of south eastern Madagascar. *Folia Primatologica* 68: 34-43.

C55 Yoder, A. D. and Flynn, J.J. (2003) Origin of Malagasy Carnivora. In Goodman, S.M. and Benstead, J.P. (Eds) *The Natural History of Madagascar*, pp. 1253 – 1256. The University of Chicago Press, Chicago, USA.

C56 Yoder, A. D., Burns, M.M., Zehr, S., Delefosse, T. Véron, G., Goodman, S.M. and Flynn, J.J. (2003) Single Origin of Malagasy Carnivora from an African Ancestor. *Nature* 421: 734-737.

C57 Zahmel, N. (2002) First experience with keeping and breeding Narrow-striped Mongoose *Mungotictis decemlineata* in Berlin Zoo, Germany. *Small Carnivore Conservation* 26: 4-6.

Cited Literature: Order Rodentia

R1 Carleton, M.D. (1994) Systematic studies of Madagascar's endemic rodents (Muroidea: Nesomyinae): revision of the genus *Eliurus*. *Amer. Mus. Novitates* 3087.

R2 Carleton, M.D. (2003) *Eliurus*, Tuft-tailed Rats. In Goodman, S.M. and Benstead, J.P. (eds) *The Natural History of Madagascar*, pp. 1373 – 1380. The University of Chicago Press, Chicago, USA.

R3 Carleton, M.D. and Goodman, S.M. (1996) Systematic studies of Madagascar's endemic rodents (Muroidea: Nesomyinae): a new genus and species from the Central Highlands. In Goodman, S.M. (ed) A Floral and Faunal Inventory of the Eastern slopes of the Réserve Naturelle Intégrale d'Andringitra, Madagascar: with reference to elevational variation. *Fieldiana Zoology* 85: 231-256.

R4 Carleton, M.D. and Goodman, S.M. (1998) New Taxa of Nesomyine Rodents (Muroidea: Muridae) from Madagascar's northern highlands, with taxonomic comments on previously described forms. In Goodman, S.M. (ed) A Floral and Faunal Inventory of the Réserve Spéciale d'Anjanaharibe-Sud, Madagascar: with reference to elevational variation. *Fieldiana Zoology* 90: 163-200.

R5 Carleton, M.D. and Goodman, S.M. (2000) Rodents of the Parc National de Marojejy, Madagascar. In Goodman, S.M. (ed) A Floral and Faunal Inventory of the Parc National de Marojejy, Madagascar: with reference to elevational variation. *Fieldiana Zoology* 97: 231-263.

R6 Carleton, M.D. and Goodman, S.M. (2003) Rodentia: *Brachytarsomys*, White-tailed Tree Rat, *Antsangy*. In Goodman, S.M. and Benstead, J.P. (eds) *The Natural History of Madagascar*, pp. 1368 – 1370. The University of Chicago Press, Chicago, USA.

R7 Carleton, M.D. and Goodman, S.M. (2003) *Gymnuromys*. In Goodman, S.M. and Benstead, J.P. (eds) *The Natural History of Madagascar*, pp. 1381 – 1383. The University of Chicago Press, Chicago, USA.

R8 Carleton, M.D. and Goodman, S.M. (2003) *Macrotarsomys*, Big-footed Mice. In Goodman, S.M. and Benstead, J.P. (eds) *The Natural History of Madagascar*, pp. 1386 – 1388. The University of

R9 Carleton, M.D. and Musser, G.G. (1994) Muroid Rodents. In Anderson, S. and Jones, J.K. (eds) *Orders and Families of Recent Mammals of the World*, pp. 289-379. John Wiley & Sons, N.Y.

R10 Carleton, M.D. and Schmidt, D.F. (1990) Systematic studies of Madagascar's endemic rodents (Muroidea: Nesomyinae): an annotated gazetteer of collecting localities of known forms. *Amer. Mus. Novitates* 2987.

R11 Carleton, M.D., Goodman, S.M. and Rakotondravony (2001) A new species of tufted-tailed rat, genus *Eliurus* (Muridae: Nesomyinae), from western Madagascar, with notes on the distribution of *E. myoxinus*. *Proceedings of the Biological Society of Washington* 114: 972-987.

R12 Cook, J.M., Trevelyan, R., Walls, S.S., Hatcher, M. and Rakotondraparany, F. (1991) The ecology of *Hypogeomys antimena*, an endemic Madagascan rodent. *J. Zool.* (London) 224: 191-200.

R13 Duplantier, J.-M. and Duchemin, J.-B. (2003) Introduced Small Mammals and their Ectoparasites: A Description of their Colonisation and its Consequences. In Goodman, S.M. and Benstead, J.P. (eds) *The Natural History of Madagascar*, pp. 1191 – 1194. The University of Chicago Press, Chicago, USA.

R14 Ganzhorn, J.U., Lowry II, P.P., Schatz, G.E. and Sommer, S. (2001) Madagascar: One of the World's hottest biodiversity hotspots on its way out. *Oryx* 35: 346-348.

R15 Ganzhorn, J.U., Goodman, S.M. and Dehgan, A. (2003) Effects of Forest Fragmentation on Small Mammals and Lemurs. In Goodman, S.M. and Benstead, J.P. (eds) *The Natural History of Madagascar*, pp. 1228 – 1234. The University of Chicago Press, Chicago, USA.

R16 Goodman, S.M. (1994) A description of the ground burrow of *Eliurus webbi* (Nesomyinae) and case of cohabitation with an endemic bird (Brachypteraciidae, *Brachypteracias*). *Mammalia* 58(4): 670-672.

R17 Goodman, S.M. (1995) *Rattus* on Madagascar and the dilemma of protecting the endemic rodent

fauna. *Conservation Biology*, 9(2): 450-453.

R18 Goodman, S.M. and Carleton, M.D. (1996) The Rodents of the Réserve Naturelle Intégrale d'Andringitra, Madagascar. In Goodman, S.M. (ed) A Floral and Faunal Inventory of the Eastern slopes of the Réserve Naturelle Intégrale d'Andringitra, Madagascar: with reference to elevational variation. *Fieldiana Zoology* 85: 257-283.

R19 Goodman, S.M. and Carleton, M.D. (1998) The Rodents of the Réserve Spéciale d'Anjanaharibe-Sud, Madagascar. In Goodman, S.M. (ed) A Floral and Faunal Inventory of the Réserve Spéciale d'Anjanaharibe-Sud, Madagascar: with reference to elevational variation. *Fieldiana Zoology* 90: 201-221.

R20 Goodman, S.M. and Ganzhorn, J.U. (1994) Les petits mammifères. In Goodman, S.M. and Langrand, O. (eds.) *Inventaire Biologique Forêt de Zombitse, Recherches pour le Developpement, Série Science Biologiques*, pp. 58-63. No. Spécial 1994. Centre d'Information et de Documentation Scientifique et Technique, Antananarivo, Madagascar.

R21 Goodman, S.M. and Rakotondravony, D. (1996) The Holocene distribution of *Hypogeomys* (Rodentia: Muridae: Nesomyinae) on Madagascar. In Lourenco, W.R. (ed.) *Biogéographie de Madagascar*, pp. 283-293. Editions de l'ORSTOM, Paris.

R22 Goodman, S.M. and Soarimalala, V. (2002) Les petit mammifères de la Réserve Spéciale de Manongarivo. In Gautier, L and Goodman S.M. (eds) *Inventaire floristique et faunistique de la Réserve Spéciale de Manongarivo, Madagascar. Boissiera* 59: 383-401.

R23 Goodman, S.M. and Soarimalala, V. (2005) A new species of *Macrotarsomys* (Muridae: Nesomyinae) from the Forêt des Mikea of southwestern Madagascar. *Proceedings of the Biological Society of Washington* 118(2): 450-464.

R24 Goodman, S.M. and Sterling, E.J. (1996) The utilisation of *Canarium* (Burseraceae) seeds by vertebrates in the Réserve Naturelle Intégrale d'Andringitra, Madagascar. In Goodman, S.M. (ed) A Floral and Faunal Inventory of the Eastern slopes of the Réserve Naturelle Intégrale d'Andringitra, Madagascar: with reference to elevational variation. *Fieldiana Zoology* 85: 83-89.

R25 Goodman, S.M. and Schütz (2003) Specimen evidence of the continued existence of the Malagasy rodent *Nesomys lambertoni* (Muridae: Nesomyinae). *Mammalia* 67: 445-449.

R26 Goodman, S.M. and Thorstrom, R. (1998) The diet of the Madagascar Red Owl (*Tyto soumagnei*) on the Masoala Peninsula, Madagascar. *Wilson Bulletin* 110: 417-421.

R27 Goodman, S.M. and Rasolonandrasana, B.P.N. (2001) Elevational zonation of birds, insectivores, rodents and primates on the slopes of the Andringitra Massif, Madagascar. Journal of Natural History 35: 285-305.

R28 Goodman, S.M., Langrand, O. and Raxworthy, C. J. (1993) The food habits of the Madagascar Long-eared Owl *Asio madagascariensis* in two habitats in southern Madagascar. *Ostrich* 64: 79-85.

R29 Goodman, S.M, Andrianarimisa, A., Olson, L.E. and Soarimalala, V. (1996) Patterns of elevational distribution of birds and small mammals in the humid forests of Montagne d'Ambre, Madagascar. *Ecotropica* 2: 87-98.

R30 Goodman, S.M, Langrand, O. and Rasolonandrasana, B.P.N. (1997) The Food Habits of *Cryptoprocta ferox* in the High Mountain Zone of the Andringita Massif, Madagascar (Carnivora, Viverridae). *Mammalia* 61: 185-192.

R31 Goodman, S.M. Carleton, M.D. and Pidgeon, M. (1999) Rodents of the Réserve Naturelle Intégrale d'Andohahela, Madagascar. In Goodman, S.M. (ed) A Floral and Faunal Inventory of the Eastern slopes of the Réserve Naturelle Intégrale d'Andohahela, Madagascar: with reference to elevational variation. *Fieldiana Zoology* 94: 217-249.

R32 Goodman, S.M, Soarimalala, V. and Rakotondravony (2001) The rediscovery of *Brachytarsomys villosa* F. Petter, 1962 (Rodentia, Nesomyinae), in the northern highlands of Madagascar. *Mammalia* 65: 83-86.

R33 Goodman, S.M., Ganzhorn, J.U. and Rakotndravony (2003) Introduction to the Mammals. In Goodman, S.M. and Benstead,

J.P. (eds) *The Natural History of Madagascar*, pp. 1159 – 1186. The University of Chicago Press, Chicago, USA.

R34 Hawkins, C.E. (2003) *Cryptoprocta ferox*, Fossa, Fosa. In Goodman, S.M. and Benstead, J.P. (eds) *The Natural History of Madagascar*, pp. 1360 – 1363. The University of Chicago Press, Chicago, USA.

R35 Hutterer, R. and Tranier, M. (1990) The immigration of the Asian House Shrew (*Suncus murinus*) into Africa and Madagascar. In Peters, G. and Hutterer, R. (eds) *Vertebrates in the Tropics*, pp 309-319. Bonn: Museum Alexander Koenig.

R36 Jansa, S.A. and Carleton, M.D. (2003) Systematics and Phylogenetics of Madagascar's Native Rodents. In Goodman, S.M. and Benstead, J.P. (eds) *The Natural History of Madagascar*, pp. 1257 – 1265. The University of Chicago Press, Chicago, USA.

R37 Jansa, S.A. and Carleton, M.D. (2003) *Brachyuromys*, Short-tailed Rats or Malagasy Voles. In Goodman, S.M. and Benstead, J.P. (eds) *The Natural History of Madagascar*, pp. 1370 – 1373. The University of Chicago Press, Chicago, USA.

R38 Jansa, S.A., Goodman, S.M. and Tucker, P.K. (1999) Molcular phylogeny and biogeography of the native rodents of Madagascar (Muridae: Nesomyinae): A test of the single-origin hypothesis. *Cladistics* 15: 253-270.

R39 Landrand, O. and Goodman, S.M. (1997) Inventaire biologique des oiseaux et des micromammifères des zones sommitales de la Réserve Naturelle Intégrale d'Andringitra. *Anok'ny ala* 20: 39-54.

R40 Letellier, F. and Petter, F. (1962) Reproduction en captivité d'un rongeur de Madagascar – *Macrotarsomys bastardi. Mammalia* 26: 132-133.

R41 Musser, G.G. and Carleton, M.D. (1993) Family Muridae. In Wilson, D.E. and Reeder, D.H. (eds.) *Mammal Species of the World: a taxonomic and geographic reference* (2nd ed.). Smithsonian Inst. Press. Washington, D.C.

R42 Nowak, R.M. (1991). *Walker's Mammals of the World* (5th edition). Johns Hopkins Uni. Press.

R43 Petter, F. (1959) Un nouveau rongeur de Madagascar (Nesomyinae): *Macrotarsomys*

ingens nov. sp. *Mammalia* 23: 139-148.

R44 Petter, F. (1972) The Rodents of Madagascar: the seven genera of Malagasy rodents. In Battistini and Richard-Vindard (eds.) *Biogeography and Ecology of Madagascar*. Dr W. Junk, The Hague, 1972, pp. 661-665.

R45 Pidgeon, M. (1996) An ecological survey of Lac Alaotra and selected wetlands of central and western Madagascar in analysing the demise of the Madagascar *Pochard Aythya innotata*. Antananarivo: WWF and Missouri Botanical Garden.

R46 Rakotondravony, D.A. (1987) Les rongeurs à Madagascar. In *Priorités en Matière de Conservation des espèces à Madagascar*. pp. 93-94. Occasional papers IUCN SSC No. 2.

R47 Rakotondravony, D.A. (1996) Biogéographie des rongeurs. In Lourenco, W.R. (ed.) *Biogéographie de Madagascar*, pp. 303-306. Editions de l'ORSTOM, Paris.

R48 Rakotozafy, L.M.A. (1996) Etude de la constitution du régime alimentaire des habitants du site de Mahilaka du Xiè au XIVè siècle à partir des produits de fouilles archéologiques. Doctorat de Troisième Cycle. Université d'Antananarivo.

R49 Rand, A.L. (1935) On the habits of some Madagascar mammals. *Journal of Mammology* 16: 89-104.

R50 Randrianjafy, V. (1993) Contribution à l'étude bio-écologique du peuplement de micromammifères dans la forêt de l'Ankarafantsika. Mémoire D.E.A., Université de Antananarivo.

R51 Rasoloarison, R.M., Rasolonandrasana, B.P.N., Ganzhorn, J.U. and Goodman, S.M. (1995). Predation on vertebrates in the Kirindy Forest, western Madagascar. *Ecotropica* 1: 59-65.

R52 Raxworthy, C.J. and Nussbaum, R.N. (1994) A rainforest survey of amphibians, reptiles and small mammals at Montagne d'Ambre, Madagascar. *Biol. Conserv.* 69: 65-73.

R53 Ryan, J.M., Creighton, G.K. and Emmons, L.H. (1993) Activity patterns of two species of *Nesomys* (Muridae: Nesomyinae) in a Madagascar rainforest. *J. Tropical Ecol.* 9: 101-107.

R54 Ryan, J.M. (2003) *Nesomys*, Red

Forest Rat, *Voalavo Mena*. In Goodman, S.M. and Benstead, J.P. (eds) *The Natural History of Madagascar*, pp. 1388 – 1389. The University of Chicago Press, Chicago, USA.

R55 Seddon, N., Tobias, J., Yount, J.W., Ramananpamonjy, J.R., Butchart, S. and Randrianizahana, H. (2000) Conservation Issues and Priorities in the Mikea Forest of south-west Madagascar. *Oryx*, 34(4): 287-304.

R56 Singleton, G., Dickman, C.R. and Delany, M.J. (2001) Old World Rats and Mice. In MacDonald, D. W (ed) *The New Encyclopedia of Mammals*, pp 636-643. Oxford University Press, UK.

R57 Sommer, S. (1996) Ecology and social structure of *Hypogeomys*

antimena, an endemic rodent of the dry deciduous forest in western Madagascar. In Lourenco, W.R. (ed.) *Biogéographie de Madagascar*, pp. 295-302. Editions de l'ORSTOM, Paris.

R58 Sommer, S. (1997) Monogamy in *Hypogeomys antimena*, an endemic rodent of the deciduous dry forest in western Madagascar. *J. Zool.* (London) 241: 301-314.

R59 Sommer, S. (2000) Sex specific predation rates on a monogamous rat (*Hypogeomys antimena*, Nesomyinae) by top predators in the tropical dry forests of Madagascar. *Animal Behaviour* 56: 1087-1094.

R60 Sommer, S. (2001) Reproductive ecology of the endangered

monogamous Malagasy Giant Jumping Rat, *Hypogeomys antimena*. *Mammalian Biology* 66: 111-115.

R61 Sommer, S (2003) *Hypogeomys antimena*, Malagasy Giant Jumping Rat, *Vositse, Votsotsa*. In Goodman, S.M. and Benstead, J.P. (eds) *The Natural History of Madagascar*, pp. 1383 – 1385. The University of Chicago Press, Chicago, USA.

R62 Stephenson, P.J. (1993) The small mammal fauna of *Réserve Spéciale d'Analamazaotra*, Madagascar: the effects of human disturbance on endemic species diversity. *Biodiversity and Conservation* 2: 603-615.

Cited Literature: Non-endemic Mammals

NE1 Andrianjakarivelo, V. (2003) Artiodactyla: *Potamochoerus larvatus*, Bush Pig, *Lambo, Lambodia, Lamboala, Antsanga*. In Goodman, S.M. and Benstead, J.P. (eds) *The Natural History of Madagascar*, pp. 1365 – 1367. The University of Chicago Press, Chicago, USA.

NE2 Goodman, S.M., Ganzhorn, J.U. and Rakotndravony (2003) Introduction to the Mammals. In Goodman, S.M. and Benstead, J.P. (eds) *The Natural History of Madagascar*, pp. 1159 – 1186. The University of Chicago Press, Chicago, USA.

NE3 Goutard, F. (1999) Investigations épidémiologiques sur le potamo-chère et son role dans le maintient de la PPA à l'état enzootique à Madagascar. Montpellier: CEAV Pathologie Tropicale.

NE4 Grubb, P. (1993) Taxonomy and description of the Afrotropical suids, *Phacochoerus, Hylochoerus* and *Potamochoerus*. In Oliver, W.L.R. (ed.) *Pigs, Peccaries*

and Hippos: Status Survey and Conservation Action Plan, section 4.1, pp. 66-75. IUCN/SSC Action Plan. IUCN, Cambridge, U.K. and Gland, Switzerland.

NE5 Lever, C. (1985) *Naturalised Mammals of the World*. Longman, London.

NE6 Kerr, R. (1792) *The Animal Kingdom, or Zoological System of the Celebrated Sir Charles Linnaeus*. John Murray, London.

NE7 Paulian, R. (1984) Introduction to the mammals. In Jolly, A., Oberle, P. and Albignac, R. (eds.) *Key Environments – Madagascar*, pp. 151-154. Pergamon Press, Oxford, U.K.

NE8 Pedrono, M. and Smith, L.L. (2003) Testudinae, Land Tortoises. In Goodman, S.M. and Benstead, J.P. (eds) *The Natural History of Madagascar*, pp. 951 – 956. The University of Chicago Press, Chicago, USA.

NE9 Rakotozafy, L.M.A. (1996) Etude de la constitution du régime alimentaire des habitants du site

de Mahilaka du Xiè au XIVè siècle à partir des produits de fouilles archéologiques. Doctorat de Troisième Cycle. Université d'Antananarivo.

NE10 Rasoloarison, R.M., Rasolonandrasana, B.P.N., Ganzhorn, J.U. and Goodman, S.M. (1995). Predation on vertebrates in the Kirindy Forest, western Madagascar. *Ecotropica* 1: 59-65.

NE11 Souvenir Zafindrajaona, P. and Lauvergne, J.J. (1993) Comparison de populations de zebu Malgache à l'aide des distances génétiques. *Genetics, Selection* and *Evolution*, Paris 25: 373-395.

NE12 Vercammen, P., Seydack, A.H.W. and Oliver, W.L.R. (1993) Bush pigs (*Potamochoerus porcus* and *P. larvatus*). In Oliver, W.L.R. (ed.) *Pigs, Peccaries and Hippos: Status Survey and Conservation Action Plan*, section 4.4, pp. 93-101. IUCN/SSC Action Plan. IUCN, Cambridge, U.K. and Gland, Switzerland.

INDEX